Dedicated to my wife, Jane

The one message: You can achieve the full benefits of the quality movement by learning to use the tool of customer value analysis to choose the right markets and win the competitive game with dramatically superior profits in them.

Contents

Preface

On December 11, 1987, I found myself something of a lonely voice among a group of thirty U.S. quality experts, gathered at the sprawling campus of the National Bureau of Standards in Gaithersburg, Maryland, to review the examination process and criteria for the newly created Malcolm Baldrige National Quality Award.

I had long believed that quality was something ultimately defined by customers. I believed customers' opinions of products (both goods and services) could be measured with rigor, and that those opinions could be used to drive a business. Many member companies of the Profit Impact of Market Strategy (PIMS) program had already learned to do this.

But at the Gaithersburg meeting I found that most U.S. quality experts did not think customer opinions could be measured with the same rigor as the conformance of products to specifications. They thought any such data would be "subjective," and they doubted it should play a key role in the judging for a national quality award.

At the time, quality experts and managers tended to focus on the widely publicized story of how the Japanese had learned from U.S. quality specialists such as W. Edwards Deming and J. M. Juran in the 1950s. U.S. businesspeople had then ignored quality experts' teachings and the Japanese, with superior quality, overwhelmed them in the 1970s.

When Americans discovered their mistake, a natural reaction ensued: Deming, Juran, and their followers were suddenly prophets with great honor in their own country. Every Fortune 500 company wanted to hear their wisdom. Slowly, in the 1980s, U.S. quality began to improve.

But a lot had happened in Japan between the 1950s and the 1980s. The Japanese had not only listened to Deming (a statistician) and Juran (a manufacturing expert with degrees in engineering and law); the Japanese had also learned to listen to customers. And they had learned to give customers what they wanted.

Meanwhile Deming and Juran were forced—by top management's lack of interest in their teachings—to spend three decades earning their livings as manufacturing specialists. It wasn't exactly that they didn't recognize the importance of listening to customers. But their techniques and their measures of success were primarily factory tools. And most Americans who called themselves quality experts were Deming and Juran disciples.

Thus it is not surprising that, when the U.S. Congress authorized the Baldrige award, the National Bureau of Standards turned primarily to such experts for help: brilliant people like Blanton Godfrey of the Juran Institute, statistics professor George Box, James Bakken of Ford, and Mary Anne Rasmussen of American Express. Their advice, moreover, was basically excellent: They talked about ensuring that top executives take the lead in a quality effort, that companies provide statistical evidence of quality success, and that companies train the entire workforce in separating the "vital few" quality problems from the "trivial many."

But something was missing. I was one of a handful of people outside the traditional quality profession who had been invited to the initial Baldrige meeting in Gaithersburg. My expertise was in tracking the results of various corporate strategies.

Among quality professionals, I was known for my participation in the discovery—based on work with the 3,000-business-unit database compiled by the Profit Impact of Market Strategy program—that quality as perceived by the customer is the most important single long-run determinant of market share and profitability.

The hero behind this and many other discoveries was a former professor of mine named Sidney Schoeffler, who had been hired by the corporate strategy operation of General Electric in the 1970s to study what really determines corporate success. Schoeffler's work had made measurable what had previously been a matter of blind faith. He created a database of detailed, strictly comparable information on General Electric business units, so researchers could accurately calculate to what extent high-market-share businesses outperformed low-market-share businesses, or heavy advertisers outperformed low advertisers. This database was the original source of the famous finding that high-market-share businesses consistently achieve better performance than low-market-share businesses (a finding to which we will return in Chapters 4 and 6).

Then later, Schoeffler persuaded hundreds of businesses to make proprietary business-unit-level data available for the creation of the Profit Impact of Market Strategy database. This larger database not only allowed us to demonstrate the close correlation between quality and business success, but also provided numerous other findings we will have occasion to mention throughout this book. Schoeffler is surely one of the most underappreciated contributors to contemporary economics. He should be given credit for making testable the predictions at the heart of economics and business strategy. I had the opportunity to follow him to GE and the PIMS program, and later I was managing director of the Strategic Planning Institute, which runs the PIMS project.[1]

Thus, my background differed sharply from that of the other experts, most of whom had spent the bulk of their careers studying manufacturing.

At Gaithersburg, we outsiders soon noticed a strange thing. When the word "customer" came up, most of the quality experts were curiously inarticulate. They were eager to advocate that the award committee require mathematical tests to measure whether manufacturing processes were "in control." But as for measuring customer satisfaction relative to competitors, they were either uninformed or downright skeptical of the idea that anyone could provide statistical evidence to identify which companies were truly creating happy customers.

In that belief, I was sure they were wrong. And gradually most quality professionals and managers have come to agree with me.

Six years later, almost everyone agrees in principle that quality must be defined by the customer. Executives preach about "100 percent customer satisfaction," "customer delight," and "providing value to customers."

Yet to this day most companies have not yet installed or become proficient in any metrics or other tools enabling them to dependably defeat their competitors in providing value to the customer. The purpose of this book is to change that impasse, and thereby help create better businesspeople.

Two terms are essential to the discussion. *Market-perceived quality* is the customer's opinion of your products (or services) compared to those of your competitors'. *Customer value* is market-perceived quality adjusted for the relative price of your product.

This book will show that both of these measures are every bit as objectively measurable as market share. Indeed, sometimes market-perceived quality and customer value are actually more objective measurements than the statistical tests that tell whether a factory process is "in control." Factory experts have to check the reliability of a process by measuring a few dimensions of the results or of the process itself. But they can't measure all the dimensions that might ultimately have importance to the customer, and they usually have few completely objective methods for deciding which measures are most important.

But when we measure market-perceived quality, we can ask customers and potential customers to list which attributes are important to them. A valid sample of customers in a target market will list attributes that describe the same needs for *any* researcher. Then, valid statistical analyses of actual purchase decisions can accurately determine which of those attributes play the biggest role in customers' choices. They can also show how much changes in price affect those choices.

Naturally, researchers can make mistakes in carrying out this analysis. They can fail to get customers to list all the key product attributes. Or they can take shortcuts in analyzing purchase decisions so that they get an inaccurate picture of the relative importance of the attributes.

But as we'll show in Chapter 2, if the customer research is conducted rightly, any two researchers should get the same results.

Market-perceived quality and customer value aren't in any way less "objective" than engineers' measures of quality. And their "bottom line" importance to a business—not to mention to the customer—is far greater.

Happily, from the meeting in Gaithersburg came agreement that *customers'* view of quality, not factory statisticians', should be the focus of any national quality award. This book is in some senses an extension of the debate between the traditional quality people and us outsiders at that meeting. It provides an inside perspective on the Baldrige award and its judging criteria, which have become the United States' consensus answer to the question, "What is total quality management?"

But more important, the real focus of this book is on how to measure relative quality and value as perceived by customers, and—most of all—on how to drive every part of your business from the knowledge those measurements create. When you do that, you'll achieve quality your customers will recognize with clarity. They'll pay extra for it. They'll give you market leadership. And you'll be making a superior contribution to society.

Acknowledgments

This book owes debts to hundreds of people. Over the past thirty years I've spent time with several organizations that have shaped my thinking about strategic management, marketing strategy, and total quality.

The General Electric Corporate Planning Operation

During the mid 1960s I worked as an employee and consultant for General Electric's Corporate Planning Operation under the guidance of Jack McKitterick and Sidney Schoeffler. General Electric was a pioneer in:

1. Establishing an executive school for general managers
2. Translating relevant parts of industrial organization economics into a business strategy, rather than a public policy, context
3. Defining "business units" and their "served markets"
4. Developing metrics to characterize the competitive position (market share, customer perceived quality), operating effectiveness (capital intensity and productivity), market attractiveness (growth, differentiation, and price insensitivity),

and business results (residual income) of its business/market segments

5. Creating the evolving disciplines of competitive strategy analysis, strategic thinking, and strategic management.

Working with Sid Schoeffler's Business-Unit Strategy team within McKitterick's Corporate Planning Operation during their heydays in the late 1960s and early 1970s was a stimulating experience that I will always cherish. Once the competitive strategy framework, concepts, and metrics were transferred to GE's operating units, business-unit general managers and their teams carried out strategy and strategic thinking far more effectively.

Without the powerful, generally accepted metrics, concepts, and language of the GE competitive strategy paradigm put in place during the 1960s and 1970s by Jack McKitterick's group under CEO Fred Borch, Jack Welch could not have held the spirited strategy review sessions between operating managers and the Office of the Chairman that have characterized his tenure as GE's CEO in the 1980s and 1990s.[1] And this book on how to achieve competitiveness by providing superior market-perceived quality and customer value could never have been written. I owe a major debt to Fred Borch, Jack McKitterick, Sid Schoeffler and GE's academic consultants, Ed Mansfield (University of Pennsylvania, industrial organization economics and technological innovation and diffusion), and Martin Shubik (Princeton, practical applications of oligopoly theory) for putting the competitive strategy framework in place.

PIMS, the Marketing Science Institute, and the Strategic Planning Institute

During the early 1970s Sid and I teamed up with Harvard Business School professors Robert D. Buzzell and Ralph G. M. Sultan at the Marketing Science Institute (MSI) to establish the PIMS® (Profit Impact of Market Strategy) Program and the PIMS competitive strategy database of business-unit experiences. In 1975, as the needs of PIMS member companies expanded beyond the mission of the Marketing Science Institute, we established the Strategic Planning Institute® to carry out the evolving activities of the PIMS Program. At first the database leaned heavily on GE's experience, but it quickly grew because of the participation of a broad cross-section of consumer and industrial companies in North America and later expanded to include service businesses and businesses from most Western European countries and other parts of the world. I'm grateful to every company that contributed.

Former colleagues and researchers at PIMS have shaped my thinking about competitive strategy. I would like to acknowledge, in particular, my debts to Sid Schoeffler and Bob Buzzell, my academic colleagues Dick Caves (Economics, Harvard, and currently Director of the Joint Program of Business and Economics at the Harvard Business School), Harvard Business School professors Steve Bradley and Michael Porter, Professors David Reibstein and Jerry Wind of the Wharton School Marketing Department, and Ben Branch (Finance, University of Massachusetts). My MSI colleagues George Day (now at Wharton) and Paul Root (MSI President), and last, but not least, my PIMS colleagues in North America and Europe, Joel Rosenfeld, Don Swire, Phill Thompson, Mark Chussil, Dev Dion, Julie Takahashi, Keith Roberts, John Guiniven, and Bob Luchs all taught me an enormous amount. (After a dozen years as research director and five years as managing director, in 1989 I left the Strategic Planning Institute and PIMS team to establish Market Driven Quality, Inc., an executive education and market strategy consulting firm.)

The Baldrige National Quality Award

In 1988 I was asked to join the original Board of Overseers that would help launch the just-created Malcolm Baldrige National Quality Award and report on its start-up progress to William Verity, who succeeded Malcolm Baldrige as Ronald Reagan's Secretary of Commerce. Serving with the Baldrige overseers and interacting with the Baldrige team at the National Institute of Standards and Technology shifted my thinking closer to the intersection of strategic management, marketing strategy, and total quality. I would like to acknowledge, in particular, my debt to quality consultants J. M. Juran and Val Feigenbaum, quality practitioners Tom Murrin (Westinghouse, now Dean of the Business School at Duquesne) and Bob Galvin (Motorola), Professor David Garvin of the Harvard Business School, and especially Dr. Curt Reimann and his Baldrige team at the National Institute of Standards and Technology (NIST).

By happenstance, during my first year as a Baldrige Overseer Tom Peters was taking a six-month tour of China and asked me to write a guest article for his syndicated weekly news column. At the time I was attempting to bridge the gap between the traditional, internal operations view of quality and the outside customer view. So I wrote a column that identified (1) conformance quality, (2) customer satisfaction, and (3) market-perceived quality as three stages of the total quality movement. This helped me to zero in on the third stage as the topic for this book. Tom subsequently asked me to write a piece on quality measurement for his newsletter *On Excellence.* I wrote a piece that covered some of the ideas that have since evolved into the metrics of customer value analysis presented in this book. Thanks, Tom, for encouraging more work on market-perceived quality and the customer value approach to management. Organizations do need to focus on "things gone right" and revenue generation as well as "things gone wrong" and cost cutting.

The Conference Board's Total Quality Management Center

Since 1990 I have served on the Planning Committee and now the Steering Committee for the Conference Board's Total Quality Management Center. As we worked to get the center up and running I had the opportunity to exchange ideas with many quality executives from companies that are leading the quality movement. Special thanks to Frank Pipp and Norm Ricard (Xerox), Doug Anderson (3M), Dave Auld (Baxter International), Jim Bakken (Ford), Jerry Cianfrocca (Johnson & Johnson), Bill Hensler (Florida Power and Light), Ed Kane (Dun & Bradstreet), Les Papay (IBM), Paul Staley (the PQ Corporation), Kent Sterett (Southern Pacific), David Luther (Corning), Professor Jack Evans (University of North Carolina), and Larry Schein (The Conference Board).

Thanks to Jack Weiss (IBM super salesman, retired) for the phrase "Customer sat. is where it's at!" I used a competitive strategy version, "Customer sat.—*relative to competitors*—is where it's at!" as the title for my keynote presentation at the Conference Board's annual Quality Conference in 1993. This material became the first part of Chapter 12.

The Planning Forum and the Strategic Management Society

For some twenty years I have participated in conferences sponsored by the Planning Forum and the Strategic Management Society. Every year or so I touch base with Liam Fahey and Sam Felton (who line up the intellectual content of the Planning Forum conference), Robert Randall (who edits the *Planning Review*) and Dan Schendel (who runs the Strategic Management Society) to learn about the latest thinking in competitive strategy. My thanks to these gentlemen for their enduring efforts to identify and disseminate the best and latest thinking in competitive strategy, and to the many practitioners, academics, and consultants whose ideas have come to me through them.

The Practitioner Network on Customer Value, Retention, and Satisfaction

While writing this book in 1993, I organized a start-up group of practitioners from companies interested in moving customer satisfaction from a slogan to a science. Together we are finding better ways to measure and improve the market perceived quality, customer satisfaction, and competitiveness of our organizations. Interacting with Donnee Ramelli (Allied Signal), Ray Kordupleski (AT&T), Clifford Simpson (DuPont), Ken Driver, Steve Petitt and Ivan Raupp (Johnson & Johnson, Ethicon), and Herb Schneider (Pitney Bowes) has helped me to clarify and refine the tools and metrics of customer value management.

Fine Tuning the Contents

I am especially grateful to the many people who carefully reviewed and commented on one or more chapters of the book. Thanks go to Dr. Thomas Malone (President of Milliken & Company) for reviewing Chapter 3; Ray Kordupleski (Director Customer Satisfaction) and Phil Scanlan, (VP Quality), AT&T, for reviewing Chapter 4; Joe Smith

(President) and John Montgomery (VP Cardiovascular Marketing), Parke-Davis, and Dr. Bruce Mirbach (internist at the Leahy Clinic) for comments on Chapter 5; Robert Hughes (Manager of Quality, AT&T Universal Card Services), Robert J. Baer (President), Mike Dace (Director of Organization Development), and Cliff Saxton, Jr. (Director of Corporate Communications) United Van Lines for reviewing and refining Chapter 6.

Thanks to Larry Light (the brand strategist at Arcature) and Larry Huston (Director, R&D Total Quality, Procter & Gamble) for comments on Chapter 7, Dr. Donald W. Collier (Senior VP Corporate Strategy, Borg-Warner, retired), Dr. David Cave (St. Elizabeth's Hospital of Boston), Robert Croce (President, Ethicon Endo-Surgery worldwide), and F. Bennett Williams (Sonoco Products, retired) for comments on Chapter 8; Ken Driver (Director Quality Administration, Ethicon, Inc.) and John Guiniven (Professor at the Ashridge Management School) for comments on Chapter 10.

Thanks to Jack Frey (John B. Frey, Associates, formerly with DuPont Corporate Marketing) for comments on Chapters 9–11; Keith Roberts (Managing Director, PIMS Europe) for supervising the research for Chapters 7 and 12; Dr. Curt Reimann (Baldrige Award Program, National Institute of Standards and Technology) for reviewing Chapter 13; and Dr. Guiniven for reviewing Chapter 14.

Thanks go to my daughter, Deborah Gale (Boston University law student), for reviewing, editing, and commenting on the entire manuscript and laying out many of the exhibits.

My colleague, Robert Chapman Wood (Modern Economics at Boston University) was a pleasure to work with. He provided penetrating questions, structure, and sound editorial guidance at each stage of the book writing process. José Salibi Neto (HSM Cultura & Desenvolvimento, São Paulo) provided useful insights on the design and positioning of the book. Discussions of early versions of the manuscript with Dr. Larry Light helped me to clarify the message, focus, and thrust of the book.

And thanks to Bob Wallace, Loretta Denner, and Elena Vega for fine editorial guidance from The Free Press. Any errors or omissions are the sole responsibility of the author.

Special thanks to my wife Jane for her endless patience and support.

The path to competitiveness

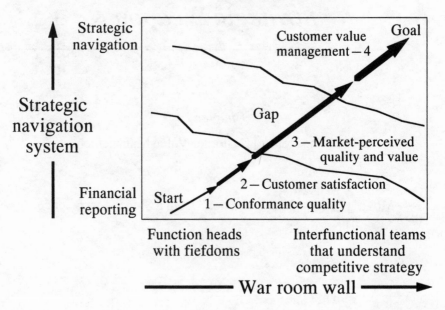

CHAPTER 1

The Four Steps to Customer Value Management

Curt Reimann is the most unlikely national leader imaginable—a mild-mannered chemist who has spent virtually his entire career in Gaithersburg, Maryland, at the National Bureau of Standards and its successor, the National Institute of Standards and Technology.

He hasn't had much business experience. But he clearly has not lacked vision. No one in the decades since World War II has done more to advance U.S. management thinking.

Reimann deserves primary credit for the success of the Malcolm Baldrige National Quality Award. In the mid-1980s, when Reimann was the unknown deputy director of the Bureau of Standards' National Measurement Laboratory, he was chosen to head the bureau's Quality Council.

Then things began to happen fast. Malcolm Baldrige, Ronald Reagan's secretary of commerce and an advocate of a national quality award, died suddenly in a fall from a horse. Backers of the award suggested it be named after Baldrige. The Bureau of Standards promised to give the first award in Baldrige's memory before the Reagan administration left office. As a result, the administration threw its whole support behind the idea, and Congress approved it in the summer of 1987.

Thus, Reimann had to develop ways to define quality, to select companies that really achieved it, and to present the first awards, all within seventeen months. It was an almost unimaginably difficult task.

Most difficult of all, he had to do everything without alienating the thousands of advocates of "quality"—who defined that term in hundreds of different, often contradictory ways.

In 1987, quality advocates were divided into factions supporting competing gurus—W. Edwards Deming, J. M. Juran, Philip Crosby, and others. And unfortunately, companies could achieve quality as any of the gurus defined it, yet still fail to produce a product that would win and keep customers.

So Reimann's job was hard. "Trying to create a state religion might have been easier," Reimann says.

Yet Reimann succeeded to a far greater extent than anyone had a right to expect. From the time President Reagan gave out the first award in December 1988, the Malcolm Baldrige National Quality Award has been a key standard of excellence throughout the United States and, indeed, much of the world. Thousands of executives testify that studying the Baldrige award criteria has helped them make dramatic improvements in their organizations.

How did Reimann do it? The most important fact was that he thought carefully about the basic question: "What is quality?"

As a result, he and his committee defined quality in a more complete way than anyone had up to that time. And in doing so, Reimann not only made his award highly sought-after; he also made it easier for U.S. companies to deliver quality and value their customers would recognize and delight in.

The quality movement in the United States has developed in four stages, driven largely by the learning that Reimann set in motion. Many organizations today are just entering the third stage; only a handful are ready to enter the fourth.

The entire period prior to the introduction of the Baldrige award can be called the *conformance quality* stage. The introduction of the award, with its customer-oriented judging criteria, quickly moved the movement to a second stage focused on *customer satisfaction.* The Baldrige award criteria laid the groundwork for a third, more sophisticated stage, focusing on the achievement of superior *market-perceived quality and value versus competitors.* Finally, the Baldrige award and its judging criteria pointed toward a fourth stage, *customer value man-*

agement, that will build on the learning of the first three and enable organizations to understand and think about their strategies and their roles in society better than they ever have in the past. That stage is just now on the horizon.

The purpose of this book is to help you and your organization achieve the full benefits of the third and fourth stages of the quality movement by learning to use a set of tools called *customer value analysis.* The development of these tools began before the Baldrige award was even conceived of. The experience that went into them helped Reimann and his staff develop the original Baldrige criteria.

Today, these tools have been greatly refined. With them, you can now reliably track how customers in your marketplace judge your product or service in comparison to the competition's. Then you can use that knowledge to delight customers and to choose profitable markets and technologies, thus creating a truly prosperous organization.

This book will offer a tested set of metrics that will tell you how well you're doing and where to focus your efforts so you'll satisfy more customers more profitably. It will present a clearly defined set of methods that will help you learn from those metrics and communicate the learning to the key people who must understand it. It will tell detailed stories of numerous companies that have used these tools successfully. And finally, it will provide clear evidence, from new studies using the world's only complete database of corporate competitive information, that achieving superior quality and customer value as we are defining those terms in this book really leads to superior profits.

In other words, this book will introduce a complete customer value management methodology, based on ideas that helped Reimann and his associates create the Baldrige Award. It will provide clear evidence that the methodology works. And it will demonstrate that this is an approach to strategic management that will dependably produce superior profits through happy customers.

When a Company Does It Right

American Telephone & Telegraph is one company that has learned to track and provide customer value well. Over the past six years it has developed some of the methods of customer value analysis we will discuss in this book, and its commitment to customer value management makes it one of the leaders in moving into Stage Four of the quality movement.

Consider how customer value analysis methods have benefited AT&T in just one business, long-distance network services. They showed the company how to turn around a potential disaster.

AT&T spent the years after its breakup in 1983 losing market share. As we'll describe in Chapter 4, the losses were particularly painful to quality advocates, because AT&T's old-fashioned "customer satisfaction" surveys showed the company was scoring well even in the businesses that were losing share most dramatically.

In long-distance, the company's core business, the share losses were running at six points a year—equivalent to more than a billion dollars a year in sales. Many executives despaired of maintaining AT&T's premium-priced position. They advocated wholesale cost-cutting and a price war with MCI and Sprint.

But two AT&T associates, Ray Kordupleski and Paul Dernier, began to use customer value analysis techniques to analyze the problem. We'll discuss the techniques in detail in later chapters, but here it's enough to say that Kordupleski and Dernier showed that customers *were* willing to pay for quality in long-distance and that customers *could* recognize superior quality. Moreover, even as AT&T lost market share, customers *still* perceived AT&T's technical quality to be better than that of competitors.

Kordupleski and Dernier showed the key problem was that AT&T's overall lead in perceived quality just wasn't enough to justify its perceived higher price: First, customers perceived AT&T's price premium to be higher than it really was. And second, AT&T's lead in perceived quality was narrowing. MCI and Sprint had newer networks, with more modern fiber optic cable and thus less noise. The competitors were also challenging AT&T in billing and installation quality.

If AT&T continued with its existing programs, it would continue to provide excellent technical quality—but it wouldn't be the *best relative quality* any more. And Kordupleski and Dernier's analysis showed that AT&T needed superior relative quality to justify its market leadership.

What happened? Influential young executives convinced AT&T's

top leadership to make changes. One decision: AT&T would write off fully $6 billion of obsolete plant and equipment years ahead of schedule and add $2 billion a year to capital spending.

As a result, in 1988 AT&T reported the first loss in its one-hundred-year history.

But spending began to boost AT&T's technical quality. And not a moment too soon. Surveys showed that AT&T's perceived technical quality continued to decline during 1988. It hit a low in October 1988—when customers found AT&T's performance was just at parity with competitors'. But then it bounced back. Meanwhile, AT&T set up teams to improve the billing and installation processes. And the company used its new understanding of perceived prices to design a series of "I came back" ads, in which customers declared that the savings they expected in switching from AT&T proved illusory. Surveys showed the company's perceived price disadvantage reached its maximum in May 1988, and then declined through August 1989—though *actual* relative prices were stable.

Follow-up research showed AT&T had nearly lost its leadership in long-distance. Its overall worth-what-paid-for score actually fell behind competitors in May 1988, and the company didn't return to parity until March 1989. But then after remaining even with MCI for two months, it began to pull ahead in mid-1989.

The ultimate result: AT&T's market share losses were virtually halted and its dominant position in the marketplace maintained. The company, which as we'll show in Chapter 4 has begun to use customer value techniques throughout its operations, has become a model of excellent American management as well as a paradigm of profitable growth. According to AT&T's 1992 Annual Report, it earned $6.27 billion of operating income in 1992.

Why Customer Value Analysis?
The Legacy of Stage One

In this chapter, we'll look at the evolution of the "quality movement" and show why it must move toward "customer value management." To understand what needs to be changed in your own organization, it's vital to comprehend what America has already accomplished.

Today, the performance of a handful of companies like AT&T, who understand market-perceived quality versus competitors and customer value management, differs vastly from the business world of 1987, when the Baldrige award was introduced. At that time, most managers and consultants were still at Stage One in the management of quality: they focused on *quality as conformance.*

They'd been inspired by the NBC "White Paper" television documentary "If Japan Can—Why Can't We?" which introduced W. Edwards Deming in 1980. Or they had read Philip Crosby's 1980 book *Quality Is Free.* Deming and Crosby both emphasized getting control of processes so that production would conform to specifications. They helped companies realize that "doing things right the first time" would lead to better products at lower costs. As a result, companies introduced statistical quality control and sought every opportunity to reduce errors, scrap, and rework. By 1987, American products had begun to improve because of these efforts.

This work was vitally important. It had been neglected for decades. Disputes among the gurus dealt with important matters of both style and substance.

Unfortunately, however, the conformance quality that companies were seeking in Stage One wouldn't, by itself, lead to business success. A product with "zero defects" won't necessarily make customers happy. What if the specifications that a company is trying to conform to are wrong—that is, what if they don't represent what the customer actually wants to buy?

Stage Two: Customer Satisfaction

Inevitably, companies had to move beyond Stage One. Exhibit 1–1 shows the path that companies have typically taken.[1] By 1987 a few, led by Xerox and its president David Kearns, had moved into Stage Two, *customer satisfaction.* They realized that the purpose of quality programs was to create happy customers. So they began talking to customers more and asking them if they were satisfied on a range of issues.

When Reimann started work on the Baldrige award, not many companies focused on customer satisfaction. But Reimann decided from the beginning that the Baldrige would view quality from the customer's point of view. That's why he invited not just traditional

EXHIBIT 1–1

Making quality a strategic weapon – the four stages

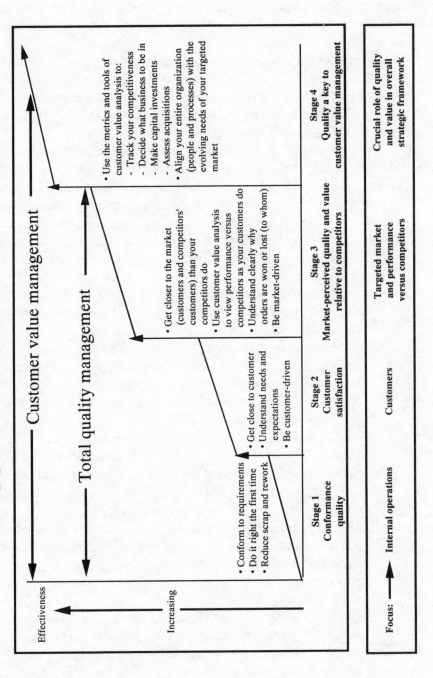

quality specialists to review the Baldrige award criteria, but also people like me who studied how customers' desires could be understood and fulfilled.

Against a tight deadline, Reimann managed to persuade the overwhelming majority of quality specialists that the customer's perspective was the right way to measure quality. Improving conformance to technical standards was essential, but only as part of the larger process of making customers happy.

Reimann's Baldrige review panel set out to define the management elements any company needs to deliver quality as perceived by customers. We all finally agreed that if an organization could achieve excellence on such criteria, it could deliver quality its customers would recognize. Today, Baldrige examiners measure excellence by analyzing an organization's performance in the following seven areas, which form a very good—though not perfect—set of standards:

1. *Leadership (95 points)*. Senior executives' personal leadership and involvement in creating and sustaining a customer focus and clear and visible quality values.
2. *Information and Analysis (75 points)*. The scope, validity, analysis, management, and use of data to drive quality excellence and improve competitive performance.
3. *Strategic Quality Planning (60 points)*. The company's planning process and how the company integrates all key quality requirements into overall business planning.
4. *Human Resource Development and Management (150 points)*. How the company develops its workforce and realizes the workforce's full potential so it can pursue the company's quality and performance objectives.
5. *Management of Process Quality (140 points)*. The systematic processes the company uses to pursue ever-higher quality, including design, quality assessment, systematic quality improvement, and the management of process quality in all work units and suppliers.
6. *Quality and Operational Results (180 points)*. The company's actual measured quality levels and improvement trends, company operational performance, and supplier quality. Also, current quality and performance levels relative to competition.

7. *Customer Focus and Satisfaction (300 points)*. The company's relationship with customers and its knowledge of customer requirements and of the key quality factors that determine marketplace competitiveness. Also, the company's methods of determining customer satisfaction, current trends and levels of satisfaction, and these results relative to competitors.

Total points: 1,000

The complete Baldrige award criteria appear in Appendix A.

By causing companies to focus on customer satisfaction, the Baldrige criteria put American business firmly into Stage Two of the quality movement. Soon hardly anyone would launch a "quality program" without claiming that customer satisfaction was its central goal.

The categories relate closely to each other, and can be thought of as a customer satisfaction system. At the first meeting of quality "experts" called to discuss a draft of the criteria, I sketched out a flowchart linking the categories. It's been revised several times since 1987, and in its present form it appears in Exhibit 1–2a. Thanks to Reimann's leadership, the criteria made clear that quality was more than a technical specialty—that pursuit of quality should drive an entire business. As a result, companies throughout the United States, and indeed all over the world, found the Baldrige criteria formed a definition of quality superior to those used in the past—more complete, easier to act on, and more closely linked to business results. The criteria were not without faults, but a company that achieved excellence on these dimensions would indeed have delivered quality that the customer could see, and unless it faced unusually brilliant competitors it would reap the fruits of that excellence on the bottom line. That's why the Baldrige criteria became the consensus definition of total quality management throughout the United States.

Stage Three: Market-Perceived Quality Versus Competitors

But "customer satisfaction"—at least as it was traditionally measured by research firms—didn't fully summarize what the Baldrige criteria sought to promote. The Baldrige award criteria asked about customer

EXHIBIT 1–2a

Baldrige award criteria framework:
Dynamic relationships

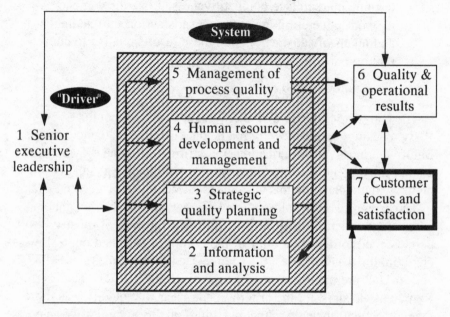

Source: *1994 Baldrige Award Criteria*, National Institute of Standards and Technology, Gaithersburg, Maryland.

EXHIBIT 1–2b

Baldrige award criteria:
Goals and measures of progress

Measures of progress

- Product/service quality
- Productivity improvement
- Waste reduction/ elimination
- Supplier quality

Goals

- Customer satisfaction
- Customer satisfaction relative to competitors*
- Customer retention
- Market-share gain

* *Market-perceived quality*

Adapted from *1994 Baldrige Award Criteria.*

satisfaction differently from traditional survey approaches. And so they did a good deal to push companies toward Stage Three, the focus on *market-perceived quality and value versus competitors.*

Most companies today spend a good deal of money on research about their customers and their markets. But mostly this research still fails to tell them why they win or lose customers.

Consider what some of the better "customer satisfaction measurement" programs do. They ask customers questions like:

- What are the attributes that count in your purchase decision?
- What is the relative importance of each attribute?
- How would you rank our performance score on each attribute—poor, fair, good, or excellent?

Unfortunately, it isn't unusual for customers to say performance is "good"—occasionally even "excellent"—and nonetheless stop buying a product.

Two key issues are missing from these surveys. First, they fail to obtain data from noncustomers who are buying the competition's product. Thus, they don't track the opinions of the market as a whole.

Second, customer satisfaction surveys usually don't measure the product's performance *relative to competitors' products.* If your performance is improving, your customers will probably say they are satisfied. But if your competitors are improving faster, customers will soon realize they could be even more satisfied if they bought from your rival.

For instance, Cadillac's customer-satisfaction score remained high with an aging, loyal customer base during the 1980s. But in the marketplace as a whole, Mercedes, BMW, Acura, and Lexus were eroding Cadillac's relative perceived quality. Thus Cadillac lost a great deal of market share despite high "customer satisfaction" scores. (Recently Cadillac has awakened, and models introduced in the 1990s are designed to counter this trend.)

The Baldrige criteria asked companies to provide data on customer satisfaction as it was traditionally measured. But they also asked companies to provide data on their quality performance *relative to competitors.* For hundreds of companies, reading the Baldrige criteria provided the first impetus to develop rigorous ways of comparing their own performance to their competitors'.

Today, most companies are just now understanding the defects in their customer-satisfaction tracking processes, and thus they're just starting to enter Stage Three. Where companies have truly entered Stage Three, they've adopted a new, more careful approach to measuring their performance in the marketplace:

- First, they set out to learn how the whole of the market they seek to serve feels about their products. Cadillac, for example, asks not just its customers, but all luxury car buyers, what they want in a luxury car and how they perceive Cadillac cars perform on those attributes of quality. (That's why we talk about *market*-perceived quality rather than *customer*-perceived quality.)
- Second, companies ask not just what people think of *their* products, but how their products compare with the competition on each of the quality attributes. Then, with this data, they construct a clear, reliable picture of just what causes customers to make their decisions.

In this book, we'll show that the few companies who do this well obtain a clear picture of what they must change to induce more customers to buy from them.

A few companies, mainly members of the Profit Impact of Market Strategy (PIMS) program of the Strategic Planning Institute, had entered Stage Three long before the Baldrige award was born (see box). Milliken & Co., for instance, whose story we will tell in Chapter 3, was a pioneer in entering the "customer satisfaction" stage in the early 1980s and had achieved a fully developed understanding of market-perceived quality versus competitors by 1985. But most are just beginning to understand market-perceived quality versus competitors today.

This kind of understanding finally makes "quality" a clearly understood strategic weapon. In Stage Three, an organization armed with the tools in this book can thoroughly analyze how the buyer makes the purchase decision. The business team can accurately understand why orders are won or lost. It can clarify which competitors are winning or losing orders in which market segments and why. And it can determine what strategic moves might change the situation. In short:

Focusing on market-perceived quality versus competitors is essential to make true strategic thinking possible.

The advance from Stage Two to Stage Three, when companies have managed to achieve it, has involved a dramatic shift in focus—from satisfying current customers to *beating competitors* by attracting both customers and noncustomers in the targeted market.

And providing superior quality pays off on the bottom line. Using the market-perceived quality metric that we will describe in Chapter 2 and the Profit Impact of Market Strategy (PIMS) database, we can demonstrate that companies who move into a superior quality position with a market-perceived quality ratio that is at least 24 percent better than their competitors earn a return-on-sales of more than 12 percent (Exhibit 1–3). (See the Preface and the description of the PIMS database in Chapter 3 for details.) Businesses that get pushed into an

---

ABOUT THE STRATEGIC PLANNING INSTITUTE

The Strategic Planning Institute (SPI®) is a not-for-profit research and service organization dedicated to helping its members develop and implement successful market strategies. The focus is on helping strategists learn from the experience of others.

SPI manages the PIMS® (Profit Impact of Market Strategy) program, maintaining a database of the detailed market-strategy experiences of 3,000 businesses. SPI, member company, and university researchers use these data to identify and quantify relationships between market strategies and business results.[2]

SPI sponsors councils that are working groups of managers responsible for a particular area of business practice. In regular meetings, council members seek to understand and advance the state of the art in their area of interest.

The SPI staff uses the findings from the PIMS database and the SPI Councils to help managers develop and implement market strategies in specific situations. [The Strategic Planning Institute, 1030 Massachusetts Avenue, Cambridge, MA 02138.]

EXHIBIT 1–3

Superior quality boosts margins

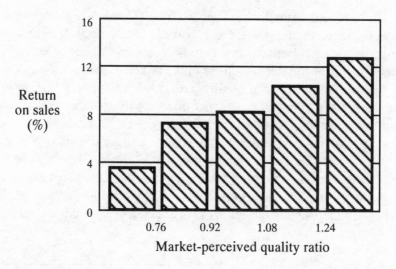

Information: PIMS database.

inferior quality position with a market-perceived quality ratio that is 24 percent or more worse than the competition earn a profit that is less than 4 percent of sales.

In other words, businesses that deliver superior quality are three times more profitable than businesses that find themselves offering quality that customers consider inferior.

"Quality" means little in business unless customers perceive your quality as superior to your competitor's. Knowing how to achieve this kind of quality is all that matters. So true total quality management, as articulated in the Baldrige award criteria and also in some approaches that attempt to go beyond those criteria, must combine the insights companies have achieved in Stages One, Two, and Three.

Stage Four: Customer Value Management

Today the Baldrige criteria, administered by the National Institute of Standards and Technology, influence how most large businesses are managed. The goal of a business, however, should not be to win awards but to serve customers and, by doing so, earn superior profits and make a contribution to society. Businesses reach Stage Four, true customer value management, when they integrate total quality management developed in the first three stages with the company's classic management systems (strategic planning, budgeting and control, capital investment, competitive analysis, performance measurement and reward).

The Baldrige criteria are excellent measures of whether a company is set up to serve customers. But they are not, and were not meant to be, a complete guide to management. They do not focus on such classic questions as:

- What business should we be in?
- How should we measure financial results (accounting versus cash flow measures)?
- How should we allocate capital across businesses?
- Are there good linkages among our company's budgeting, strategic planning, capital investment, and performance and reward systems?
- Is there a good linkage between our incentive compensation system and our measures of business results?
- Should we be a one-nation or a global business?

In addition, the Baldrige criteria don't cover all aspects of the innovation process. A company that achieves excellence on the Baldrige criteria will be in a good position to manage its innovation processes well. The whole organization will be attuned to customers and committed to continuous, rapid improvement. But the Baldrige criteria by themselves don't guarantee a complete innovation process appropriate to businesses in fast-moving fields such as computer software or pharmaceuticals.

And they won't prevent companies from failing because they neglect or mismanage big strategic decisions. Several excellent organizations have pursued total quality in their core businesses but also made strategic decisions to expand into other fields where they did not know how to become market-perceived quality leaders. Xerox created a Baldrige award-winning total quality process that converted its copier business from a dying old manufacturer to a profitable world leader. But its expansion into financial services led to disaster. Westinghouse Electric made many of the same mistakes.

A complete customer value management system must build on total quality management as described in the Baldrige criteria. But true customer value management adds a sophisticated understanding of these other issues. It uses the knowledge developed in the first three stages to understand whole businesses better. Then it applies management discipline to ensure that this knowledge is used, so companies enter and invest only in businesses where they can be quality and value leaders.

Customer value management is what discussions of "strategic management" should have sought from the beginning. In the 1970s and '80s, "strategists" often failed to consider the management of processes within the organization or the processes by which customers made their decisions to buy. Without analyzing these important issues, strategic discussions often produced "plans" without any clear explanation of how the plans should be executed.

Such attempts at strategic management were wasted—and indeed often led to multibillion-dollar fiascoes.

Today, companies that have learned the lessons of the three stages of total quality management have their processes under control and understand how to analyze customer decisions. Thus, they can really manage strategically in ways that companies of the 1970s and '80s could not.

In Stage Four, corporate strategists fully understand quality efforts, and they know how changes in market-perceived quality drive other aspects of competitive position. They use this information to make decisions that will enable the company to produce the most value and will thus have maximum benefit in the long run for shareholders, customers, and society (Exhibit 1–4).

A Methodology to Create Quality That Customers Can See

In the language of the Baldrige criteria, this book is about "customer focus and satisfaction"—the central element of "quality" for which the Baldrige criteria wisely give 300 of the 1,000 total points. This book will show how companies have identified the attributes that are important to customers, how to understand the importance customers

EXHIBIT 1–4

Creating value that customers can see

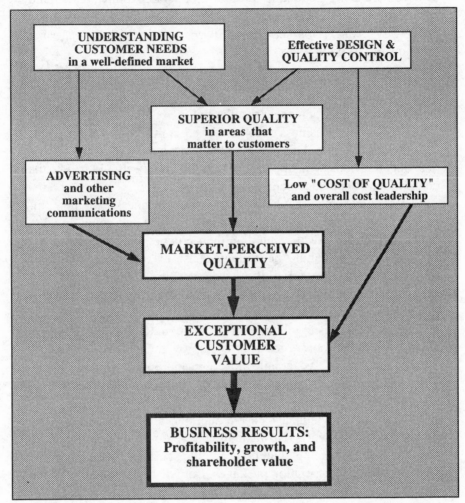

give those attributes, and how to analyze performance relative to competitors on each attribute.

Then, it will show how to drive your business from this understanding of what quality means to your customers.

The measurement systems discussed here complement traditional quality-control technology, but are ultimately of more fundamental strategic importance.

If you are starting a quality program for scratch today, you should begin with what has been Stage Three for most companies—aiming to create *better market-perceived quality than your competitors,* using the tools in this book to do so.

A Focused Company

Although total quality management as outlined in the Baldrige criteria isn't the whole of business excellence, and in this book we are pointing out the need for a stage that goes beyond what the Baldrige criteria describe, this book will emphasize that total quality should still be the central focus of management.

When today's successful managers discuss business with their employees, they talk unceasingly about total quality and about creating better market-perceived value than their competitors. Top managers by themselves can handle the strategic questions outside the realms of total quality and innovation. But wise managers know they can only achieve excellent quality and value with constant support from everyone in the organization.

The wrong way is to talk to employees about total quality and *also* about "cost reduction," "productivity improvement," and "enhancing shareholder value," as though those are additional, separate goals. This usually produces confusion, alienation, and minimal progress toward any goals.

Most employees equate "cost reduction" and "productivity improvement" with layoffs. How can they develop deep commitment to such goals? "Enhancing shareholder value" certainly excites people who have large stock-option packages. But what about the rest of the organization? Top management's favorite programs are "turnoffs" to the majority!

You need everyone in your organization involved and empowered. Quality is the theme that can get *everyone committed* because they know this means:

- Secure, satisfying, enjoyable jobs
- A chance to learn and grow
- Opportunity for increased responsibility and advancement

Moreover, once your employees have developed commitment to providing the highest market-perceived quality and customer value, it's relatively easy to show that achieving those goals *demands* that the company cut costs, increase productivity, and increase shareholder value better than anyone else in your industry.

Thus, the executive whose company will achieve true customer value management and truly maximize shareholder value is the executive who focuses on total quality without neglecting other strategic variables.

An Overview of This Book

This book is designed to show in detail how to achieve success. We'll describe how to create market-perceived quality and value superior to your competitors'. And we'll tell how to integrate the building blocks of a total quality management system (conformance quality, customer satisfaction, and market-perceived quality) with the other strategic management systems of your company (including financial budgeting and control, strategic thinking and planning, and capital investment systems).

In the chapter that follows this one, Chapter 2, we'll present a basic model of how the customer makes the purchase decision and we'll summarize the tools of customer value analysis ensuring that the customer has good reason to choose *your* product or service. We use the classic Perdue chicken story to illustrate the customer's supplier-selection process and to show how to calculate and improve your business's market-perceived quality. Frank Perdue converted an ordinary farm, producing a quintessential commodity product (chickens), into a large business with a dominant power brand in his targeted market (the eastern United States). He did it by decoding the signals that the market was willing to give to any chicken producer who would listen, and subsequently achieving superior market-perceived quality.

Then in Part Two (Chapters 3 through 6), we'll look at companies that are truly achieving total quality management and leadership in market-perceived quality through the use of the techniques we're describing. Chapter 3 describes how Milliken used these tools to transform its business. Chapter 4 shows how AT&T is achieving unprecedented success by using these tools to ensure that the company is the customer value leader in all its markets.

Chapter 5 examines Warner-Lambert's Parke-Davis unit and tells how it repositioned itself in the enormous market for cholesterol-regulating drugs by using the tools of customer value analysis. Parke-Davis used a customer value profile to understand what the customer was failing to comprehend about its drug Lopid. Then it developed education programs to ensure that customer understanding improved in the areas where the profile showed it was weak.

In Chapter 6 we focus on service businesses, using AT&T's Universal Card and United Van Lines' moving business as examples. And we look at the role of customer-service quality in all kinds of businesses. The market-perceived quality approach helps United Van Lines serve customers in both the moving of goods (the "core service" of the company) and in providing "customer service" attributes such as friendly, knowledgeable people answering the phone both in the city where the move begins and in the city where it ends.

These chapters are focused on the basics: providing superior customer value in your existing businesses. But there's more to customer value management than that. Part Three (Chapters 7 and 8) looks at some issues that involve more comprehensive customer value management: the creating and maintaining of "power brands," and the achievement of excellence in technology management.

Chapter 7 asks the question, "What is a power brand?" It provides a balanced understanding of branded products, using the tools of customer value analysis and data from the PIMS database. We seek to replace the hype that has surrounded brand issues with a reasoned approach based on the principles of customer value management.

Chapter 8 then tells the stories of several companies that have used customer value analysis and similar approaches to understand technological opportunities and transitions—and to profit thereby.

By the end of Part Three we will have demonstrated conclusively that real companies are using customer value analysis and are profiting. In Part Four (Chapters 9 through 11), we describe the specific techniques in more detail and show how to integrate them with other management systems to achieve true strategic management. Chapter 9 describes each of the seven tools of customer value analysis comprehensively. Chapter 10 tells how to bring all the knowledge of your organization to bear on your problems through the "war-room" method of conducting meetings and through the development of a powerful strategic navigation system to guide your business. Chapter 11 then tells how to integrate your existing management tools with the market-driven quality philosophy.

Finally, in Part Five (Chapters 12 through 14), we go beyond what scholars sometimes dismiss as "anecdotal evidence" to look at evidence from the "big picture" and show how to avoid problems that have caused potentially successful total quality management efforts to fail. In Chapter 12 we provide hard, statistical evidence, based on the PIMS database, of just how quality drives business results. The strategic management of market-perceived quality pays off, as Exhibit 1–3 showed. The experience of three thousand businesses in the PIMS competitive strategy database overwhelmingly indicates that businesses with superior quality create shareholder value by earning larger market shares and premium prices.[3]

In Chapter 13 we look closely at the Baldrige award and alternative schemes for judging "total quality." We show why, despite the flaws of some Baldrige winners, the Baldrige criteria and the lessons companies have learned in trying to meet those criteria deserve to be seen as the central guiding force in the renovation of management today.

Last, Chapter 14 focuses on making comprehensive alignment of a business actually occur—starting with the business unit general manager and his or her cross-functional team. An excellent methodology doesn't guarantee success, and even when you know the power of customer value analysis, you can still fail. Chapter 14 shows how to avoid the traps, and win.

Customer value is the most important concept and the most important target in business management. I think this book provides a reliable way to achieve it.

Customer value map: Chicken business

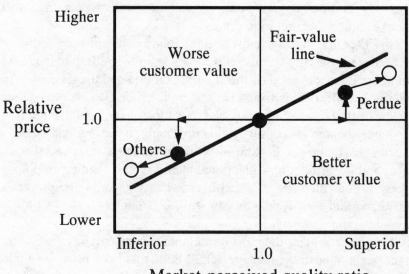

CHAPTER 2

Moving "Customer Satisfaction" from a Slogan to a Science

Why do customers choose one product or service over another? The reason is simple: They believe that they'll get better value than they could expect from the alternative.

Unfortunately, most efforts to plan business strategy neglect this simple truth. They do not ensure that organizations will be value leaders. Thus they set themselves up for failure.

Businesses follow "generally accepted accounting principles" (GAAP) in financial management. As a result, everyone can agree on financial goals, understand how they'll be measured, and work together to achieve them.

But companies have lacked *generally accepted strategic principles* (GASP) that would define the customer value metrics at the heart of a company's strategic navigation system. There has been little agreement on how the components of competitive advantage should be pursued or how to measure progress. This has made it hard for the people in organizations to work together to achieve competitive success.

The last two decades have taught Western businesses some difficult lessons. The oil crisis of the 1970s ended an era of almost effortless prosperity. Before the quality movement began, companies were tempted by an orgy of schemes to "restructure," "find synergy," "feed the stars," and otherwise deal strategically with a new epoch in which markets experienced little or no real growth. But few of these popular nostrums worked. If you pursued them and you faced competition from the Japanese, your firm is probably out of business today. Even if you survived, you've realized that the few companies that did well were those who avoided the most "sophisticated" strategies. In other words, most of the best-publicized strategic principles of the past two decades failed to achieve general acceptance for a simple reason: they did not work.

Successful companies, on the other hand, have tended to employ simple strategies. They identified real customers and gave those customers what they wanted to buy. If you're a survivor, therefore, you've probably come to recognize that the basis of generally accepted strategic principles (GASP) should be a simple idea:

Companies succeed by providing superior customer value.

And value is simply quality, however *the customer* defines it, offered at the right price.

While this strategic principle is simple, it's also very powerful. As a survivor, you've probably realized that committing yourself to superior quality and customer value is far more important than committing yourself to attaining financial goals as measured by GAAP. Superior customer value is the best leading indicator of market share and competitiveness. And market share and competitiveness in turn drive the achievement of long-term financial goals such as profitability, growth, and shareholder value.

These facts are not only supported by common sense; they're also supported by rigorous research. AT&T, as we'll show in Chapter 4, has found that changes in the real, technically measured quality of its products are followed only about three months later by changes in the customer's perception of the quality of those products. And, AT&T data show, changes in perceived quality are in turn followed a mere two months afterward by changes in market share.[1]

In the early 1980s, most U.S. organizations needed Stage One of the quality movement—the stage that focused on conformance quality. Why? Because most did not know how to control their business processes well enough to guarantee they would achieve what they set out to achieve for the customer. Teachings that emphasized "doing things right the first time" helped companies create that ability.

Stage Two of the quality movement, which adopted the slogan "customer satisfaction," helped companies move toward an understanding of customer value. But no one could define "customer satisfaction" clearly. There's been no well-defined *science* of customer satisfaction.

The purpose of this chapter is to show how to move customer satisfaction from slogan to science. As organizations recognize the defects of their traditional measurements of customer satisfaction, they're forced to think more clearly about customer value. This, as we discussed in the last chapter, puts them into Stage Three of the quality movement.

In this chapter, we will outline how to achieve the goals of Stage Three: superior market-perceived quality and value versus competitors. To do this, we'll show step-by-step how to conduct a simple *customer value analysis*. That is, we'll show how to measure the components of customer value (market-perceived quality and market-perceived price) and plot a map that shows how the quality offered by each competitor in any given marketplace compares to the price it charges and the quality/price position of the other competitors.

This analysis gives you a crystal clear, simple, and deadly accurate picture of your marketplace. You'll almost always find that companies with a strong position on the customer value map are earning superior returns and gaining market share, while companies with a weak position are withering and dying. Moreover, this analysis will point to the most effective strategic moves you need to make to improve your own position.

Thus, this chapter will provide the basic elements for achieving leadership in market-perceived quality and value. It will show you the basic steps you need to achieve a strong, premium position on the value map. When you've done that with your existing businesses, you will have accomplished the tasks of Stage Three.

Finally, this chapter will introduce basic principles of strategic management that *deserve* general acceptance and that are essential to attaining value leadership. The rest of the book will tell the stories of how real organizations have followed these principles and achieved a powerful market advantage, and will provide details showing how you can do the same.

This chapter and the four chapters that follow it (Chapters 3–6) will concentrate on the problems of Stage Three of the path to customer value management—that is, the problems of consistently achieving superior market-perceived quality versus competitors and superior customer value in your existing businesses. We will look at examples from textiles, telecommunications, pharmaceuticals, financial services, and transportation. At least two of the companies we'll discuss—Milliken & Co. and American Telephone and Telegraph—deserve to be called Stage Four companies. They're pioneering the use of true customer value management to run their entire businesses. But the focus in these chapters will be on the essentials.

You need to know how to achieve market-perceived quality and value leadership in a single business before you can meaningfully attack Stage Four. Stage Four involves using the tools of customer value analysis not only to run businesses but also to make crucial long-term strategic decisions that may involve more than one business. We will discuss the company-wide systems of Milliken and AT&T in Part Two, but we'll deal with details of how you manage specific kinds of large strategic issues in Part Three (Chapters 7–8), using examples from fast-moving consumer goods, tires, medical supplies, and packaging. Then in Part Four we will provide a more detailed look at customer value analysis tools useful in both Stages Three and Four. Finally, we'll summarize and provide comprehensive data to demonstrate the payoff from customer value management in Part Five.

But before we can do all that, we must first introduce the basics of customer value analysis.

How Do You Track Whether You're Providing Superior Customer Value?

The first step in achieving leadership in market-perceived quality and value is to understand what causes customers in your targeted market to make their decisions—to decide that one product offers better value than another. Understanding that is the most central objective of a customer value analysis.

Exhibit 2–1 summarizes how customers make purchase decisions. The factors that contribute to quality in the customer's mind need not be mysterious. Customers will gladly tell you what they are. A customer value analysis uses information from customers to show how customers make decisions in your marketplace. And in giving you that information, it suggests what you need to change to ensure that more of them will buy from you.

EXHIBIT 2–1

**How customers select
among competing suppliers**

- Customer buys on value
- Value equals quality relative to price
- Quality includes all nonprice attributes
  - Product   – Customer service
- Quality, price, and value are relative

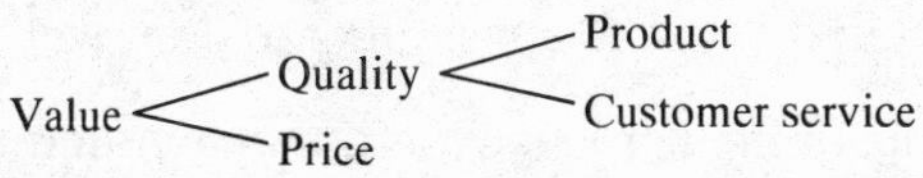

$$\text{Value} \diagdown \begin{array}{l} \diagup \text{Quality} \diagdown \begin{array}{l} \diagup \text{Product} \\ \diagdown \text{Customer service} \end{array} \\ \diagdown \text{Price} \end{array}$$

The simplest customer value analysis consists of two parts: First, you create a customer value profile that compares your organization's performance with that of one or more competitors. This customer value profile itself usually has two elements:

- A market-perceived quality profile
- A market-perceived price profile

Second, once you have created the customer value profile, you draw a customer value map.

In this chapter we will demonstrate how to use these tools to win in the marketplace. Then we'll introduce additional tools in later chapters before summarizing a wider array in Part Four.

The Basics of a Market-Perceived Quality Profile

Of the elements of a customer value analysis, the single most important is the market-perceived quality profile. This is a chart that does three things:

1. It identifies what quality really is to customers in your marketplace.
2. It tells you which competitors are performing best on each aspect of quality.

3. It gives you overall quality performance measures based on the definition of quality that customers actually use in making their purchase decisions.

The market-perceived quality profile is the most important part of the customer value analysis because it summarizes the aspects of the marketplace that are usually easiest to change to improve your business. In many markets, price is an even greater driver of customer decisions than market-perceived quality. But cutting prices won't usually improve your bottom line.

The process of creating a market-perceived quality profile is relatively simple, though it's time consuming to do it well:

1. Ask people in the market served—both your customers and competitors' customers—to list the factors that are important in their purchase decisions. You can ask them in forums such as focus groups.
2. Establish how the various quality attributes are weighted in the customer's decision. One way to do this is through sophisticated statistical analysis of customers' statements about their overall satisfaction and actual purchase decisions. AT&T's General Business Systems group has pioneered such analysis, as we'll show in Chapter 4. But in most cases it's almost as good—and much easier and cheaper— simply to ask customers how they weight the various factors. Ask them to distribute 100 points of "decision weight" among all the high-level factors they listed in the previous round of research.
3. Ask customers to rate, on a scale of, say, 1 to 10, the performance of each business on each competing factor. Then multiply each business's score on each factor by the weight of that factor, and add the results to get an overall customer satisfaction score.

Customer Value Analysis: The Chicken Business

To understand customer value analysis, let's look at the case of Perdue Farms, which has in the last twenty years become the dominant brand of uncooked chicken on the eastern seaboard of the United States.

In the early 1980s I had a chance to speak before the members of the Southeast Egg and Poultry Association, a group of Perdue's competitors. I asked them how consumers compared Perdue's chicken with their own. I've often used the results to demonstrate how to create a market-perceived quality profile—and to illustrate its power by showing how and why Frank Perdue changed the chicken market and became a very rich man.

Many of the members of the association remembered the days before Perdue inherited his chicken business from his father Arthur. In that era, chickens were a commodity—as they had been for generations. The customer generally ignored the brand names that some companies put on their chickens, and bought principally on price.

Exhibit 2–2 shows a simple market-perceived quality profile describing the chicken business in Perdue's father's day—*before the consumer perceived any significant differences among chicken producers.* This profile and the one that follows were created by a panel of Southeast Egg and Poultry Association members under my guidance. First, I asked the panel to list the key characteristics (other than price) that affected buying decisions. They are shown in the first column of Exhibit 2–2. Second, I asked them the relative weight of these

EXHIBIT 2–2

Quality profile: Chicken business– the old days –
NO REAL DIFFERENCES AMONG PRODUCERS

Quality attributes:	Importance weights:	Performance scores: Perdue	Others	Ratio
Yellow bird	5	7	7	1.0
Meat-to-bone	10	6	6	1.0
No pinfeathers	15	5	5	1.0
Fresh	15	7	7	1.0
Availability	55	8	8	1.0
Brand image	0	6	6	1.0
	100			
Customer satisfaction score:		7.15	7.15	
Market-perceived quality ratio:				1.0

issues in Perdue's father's day. These appear in the second column. In those days, "availability" represented an overwhelming share of the nonprice factors in chicken purchases—people usually bought whatever was on the shelves. Third, the panel estimated customers' opinions of Perdue's father's performance and the performance of the rest of the industry for each criterion, on a scale of 1 to 10. Not surprisingly, there were no differences. In the old days, the ratings of Arthur Perdue's chickens and those of the rest of the industry were identical. The last column of Exhibit 2–2 is the ratio of Perdue's performance to his competitors'. Naturally, because the Perdue performance and the performance of the industry were the same, all of the ratios are 1.0. The overall market-perceived quality ratio is also 1.0—indicating (of course) no significant difference.

That was in the old days. Next, we analyzed the market situation under Frank Perdue. This provides a good example of how a market-perceived quality profile helps explain a typical market.

Frank started his work by learning what customers wanted in their chickens, and then learning how to deliver it. That changed the chicken market forever.

The market-perceived quality profile based on the Southeast Egg and Poultry Association panel's report on the chicken market under Frank Perdue appears in Exhibit 2–3.

We used the same quality attributes for the analysis of today's markets as we used for the analysis of the market in Perdue's father's day. I started by asking the panel to estimate the weighting of the different nonprice purchase criteria in customer decisions today. As the second column of Exhibit 2–3 shows, Perdue's better chickens had caused customers to change their decision making dramatically. The weight on "availability" fell from 55 percent to 10 percent as consumers began to place more weight on attributes where Perdue had pulled ahead ("meat-to-bone," "no pinfeathers," and "brand image").

Next, I asked the panel to estimate, on a scale of 1 to 10, customers' ratings of the quality of Perdue chickens on those quality attributes versus customers' ratings of average chickens (i.e., the chickens sold by other members of the association). These figures appear in the next two columns.

From this information, we can calculate customer satisfaction scores for both Perdue chicken and the rest of the industry. These

EXHIBIT 2–3

Quality profile: Chicken business, after Frank Perdue

Performance scores

Quality attributes 1	Weight 2	Perdue 3	Avg. comp. 4	Ratio 5=3/4	Weight times ratio 6=2×5
Yellow bird	10	8.1	7.2	1.13	11.3
Meat-to-bone	20	9.0	7.3	1.23	24.6
No pinfeathers	20	9.2	6.5	1.42	28.4
Fresh	15	8.0	8.0	1.00	15.0
Availability	10	8.0	8.0	1.00	10.0
Brand image	25	9.4	6.4	1.47	36.8
	100				126.1

Customer satisfaction: 8.8   7.1

Market-perceived quality ratio:

Adapted from *The PIMS Principles*, by Robert D. Buzzell & Bradey T. Gale; copyright © 1978 by The Free Press.

scores, created by multiplying the performance ratings for each purchase criterion by the estimated relative weighting of that criterion, appear in the "customer satisfaction" row under the ratings of Perdue chicken and the ratings of the average competitor's chicken.

By themselves, the individual customer satisfaction ratings are not very meaningful. Any researcher who tells you, "You should be really excited because you scored an 8.8 in customer satisfaction" is misleading you. The 8.8 is meaningful only relative to how other people score.

Thus, what is truly meaningful in this chart are the *ratios* of the ratings customers give the different competitors. The "ratio" column of the chart shows ratios between ratings given Perdue for each quality attribute and the ratings given his competitors.

Moreover, we can also calculate an overall market-perceived quality score for Perdue chicken versus the rest of the industry. Assigning a weight from Column 2 to each number in the "Ratio" column, we get the numbers in the "Weight times ratio" column. Adding these together, we get a market-perceived quality score of 126.1.

If you want to produce a weighted ratio of Perdue's scores to his competitors' scores, you can simply divide this market-perceived quality score by 100. The result is the market-perceived quality ratio. It is a strongly favorable 1.26.[2] Either way, Frank Perdue had produced a market-perceived quality rating 26 percent higher than his father's.

Comparing column 6 with column 2 also allows you to pinpoint *why* Perdue is so far ahead. Of Perdue's 26.1 point lead, 1.3 comes from "yellower bird," 4.6 comes from "meatier chicken," 8.4 comes from "fewer bruises or pinfeathers," and 11.8 come from superior "brand image."

Creating a Value Map

In the chicken business, retailers buy from chicken producers and then list the retail price per pound in their advertisements. Customers, therefore, can make a simple decision, and there is no need for a complex analysis of how consumers understand the price of the product. We don't have to create a market-perceived price profile. If Perdue chickens cost 69 cents a pound this week and Brand X costs 59 cents a pound, we can produce a customer value map like that shown in Exhibit 2–4.

EXHIBIT 2–4

Customer value map: Chicken business

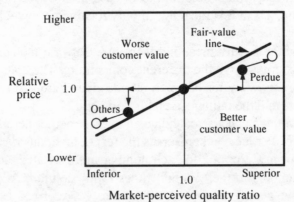

Running from the upper right of the customer value map to the lower left is the "fair-value line," which indicates where quality is balanced against price. The fair-value line should be the line of points at which a competitor would neither gain nor lose market share. That is usually difficult to calculate with precision, but ordinarily we can approximate it simply by asking customers how much weight they put on quality and how much weight they put on price, and plotting a line with a slope equal to the percentage of the decision the average customer says is based on quality divided by the percentage of the decision the average customer says is based on price.

Anyone below and to the right of the line is in a strong, share-gaining position. Anyone above and to the left of the line is in a share-losing position.

Before Frank Perdue took over the business and began to make pull-ahead moves on different quality attributes, all competitors plotted more or less at the center of the value map with the same perceived quality and price. As Frank made his moves, Perdue Farms moved to the right into the "grow and prosper zone" and competitors were pushed to the left. Unable to quickly match or offset Perdue's quality improvements, competitors then cut prices, which increased Perdue's price relative to theirs. A succession of customer value maps over time would allow one to track these changes in relative perceived price and quality. Here, the same progress over time is indicated by two different sets of points. The dark point indicates where Perdue was when he first started to advertise his chickens; the lighter point above and to the right indicates the position he achieved after his brand name was more established.

We have drawn this map on the assumption that chicken buyers place two thirds of the weight of their buying decisions on price and one third on quality. (Despite the Perdue revolution in the chicken market, chicken buyers remain highly price sensitive.) Nonetheless, Frank Perdue remained on the share-gaining side of the line for an extended time period. And he earned better margins than the producers of lower-priced chickens, too. Frank Perdue was in the best position on the value map: below the fair-value line, but in the upper right corner. His organization was producing a higher-priced, premium product and yet still offering better value than his competitors.

How Did Frank Do It?

As this analysis shows, Frank Perdue's competitors recognized that his product was superior to ordinary chickens on almost every non-price criterion.

This success wasn't surprising: Perdue had started his efforts to create his brand with research to learn just what customers wanted in their chickens. He began from a position where consumers perceived all chickens to be more or less equal, as we showed in Exhibit 2–2. But he invested in careful breeding and improved feed to give customers what his surveys showed they wanted: meatier, yellower chickens. He even purchased a turbine engine to blow-dry his chickens thoroughly, just before they reached the torching station where their pinfeathers were supposed to be burned off. Though a few pinfeathers still slip through, they're less common on Perdue chickens than on his competitors'. Finally, Perdue invested heavily in advertising and promotion to tell customers what he had done. In recent years, under Frank Perdue's son Jim, the company has even begun improving its once-uneven labor relations.[3] The result: a product that dominates its competitors in what was previously a "commodity" market.

You Can Do It Too

If Frank Perdue's competitors really want to challenge him, Exhibit 2–3 provides the right place for them to start. The competitors should, of course, check the impressions of the experts by surveying real consumers to learn if this is an accurate picture of how they make their decisions. When they do that, they'll encounter at least a few minor complexities. Customers probably won't all agree on a neat list of quality attributes such as we've shown in Exhibits 2–2 and 2–3. Some will refer to "yellow bird," others will refer to "good color," still others to "a fresh-looking bird." Researchers must work out a short, "clean" list of non-overlapping attributes that accurately represents what the customers are saying.

If customers list numerous attributes (as they probably will), it's good to summarize them in a list of a few "high-level" attributes—major issues which in this case might be items such as "appearance," "brand image," and perhaps "the eating experience." The rating on the "high-level" attribute "appearance" would be a summary of performance on subattributes such as "yellowness," "no pinfeathers," and whatever other appearance issues the customer says are important.

In other businesses, as we'll see in later chapters, the high-level attributes might be issues such as "customer service," "quality of sales staff," and "product quality." For each, you'd produce a list of subattributes—attributes that contribute to whether the organization has achieved quality on the main attributes. For example, for the quality attribute "customer service," subattributes might include "friendly personnel," "knowledgeable personnel," and "promptness." This produces a hierarchy of attributes. We'll look at some real examples of such hierarchies in Chapters 4 and 6.

Once Perdue's competitors had generated a list of attributes and subattributes from customers, they could ask customers how they weighted them. Then they could ask how the customers rated each competitor. A properly researched market-perceived quality profile from real customers would give them the data they needed to decide how to meet Perdue's challenge by matching his strong points and developing their own strong points.

You can conduct a customer value analysis of any products in any market. Indeed, if you can't afford expensive scientific research, you can still gain some insights by informally surveying customers you'd talk to anyway. Start by writing down how you and your fellow managers *think* customers make decisions. Then ask them.

To do a customer value analysis right, be sure to include all the most important competitors—which means the two or three largest competitors, the fastest-growing competitor, and any competitor with new or unusual technology. (Be sure you don't leave out any new competitors from the rapidly growing ranks in Asian countries.)

Customer value analysis is especially powerful if you conduct separate customer value analyses for various segments of your market and for different customers in your distribution chain.

If you discover that poor relative performance on one or more criteria is hurting you, you should probably try to design a *leapfrogging* move. (Japanese automakers did that when they went from producing cars known as "tinny rustbuckets" in the 1960s to cars that provided the kind of transportation customers wanted—and couldn't get from U.S. manufacturers—in the 1970s.)

Try experimenting with a market-perceived quality profile right now, using the customer value profile form shown in Exhibit 2–5. Better yet, make copies of the form and have several people in your organization complete it. Then compare how you each understand customer decision making today.

This is a "Hard" Analysis

Note that there is nothing "subjective" about a customer value analysis, when it is properly conducted. Any market research firm should be able to determine, objectively, whether or not the opinions of the panel of Southeast Egg and Poultry Association members were correct. If market researchers do their jobs well and the definition of the market served is held constant, then a market-perceived quality profile and a customer value map produced by one research firm will be essentially the same as a market-perceived quality profile and customer value map produced by another.

Thus, a properly calculated market-perceived quality profile pro-

EXHIBIT 2–5

Customer value profile: Our business vs. competitors

Served market:	Importance weights		Competitors:		
		Our business	1 ___ 2 ___	3 ___ 4 ___	5 ___
Selection criteria [Quality (nonprice) attributes]	↓	Performance scores: 1–10, 10 is best			
1. _____	—	— —	— —	— —	— —
2. _____	—	— —	— —	— —	— —
3. _____	—	— —	— —	— —	— —
4. _____	—	— —	— —	— —	— —
5. _____	—	— —	— —	— —	— —
6. _____	—	— —	— —	— —	— —
7. _____	—	— —	— —	— —	— —
8. _____	—	— —	— —	— —	— —
9. _____	—	— —	— —	— —	— —
10. _____	—	— —	— —	— —	— —
Sum of importance weights	100	(Companies may have the same score on an attribute)			

Price (perceived transactions price) ☐ ☐ ☐ ☐ ☐

Weight on quality (non price) attributes ☐ + weight on price ☐ = [1][0][0]

Price competitiveness (1–10) ___ ___ ___ ___ ___

vides an objective, impersonal measure of how the customers in any given marketplace really judge products. It is an impartial description of which products are preferred, why, and to what extent. Because it is based on customer opinions—the very opinions that are involved in real purchase decisions—it reveals a product's real strengths and weaknesses. And thus it provides a firm foundation for improvement.

Of course, we could imagine minor changes in methodology that might have led to minor changes in results. We could have used different rating scales, for instance, and that might have affected the size of Perdue's favorable ratios. If we had asked for customers' ratings on a scale of 1 to 7 instead of 1 to 10, for instance, the final ratios might have come out slightly differently.

But that's just like saying you can measure the distance between New York and Washington in either miles or kilometers, and you'll get different numbers. The distance between New York and Washington is real and unchanging. Who does the measuring and what scale is used are ultimately unimportant, as long as he or she is objective.

So if two different market research firms measure the U.S. new car market's perception of the relative quality of the Honda Accord versus the Ford Taurus, the two should come up with essentially the same results. The same is true about market research firms measuring the U.S. equity mutual fund market's perceptions of the relative quality of Fidelity Group versus Vanguard Group. And the same is true about firms measuring the Fortune 500 corporate treasurers market's perceptions of the relative quality of Bankers Trust corporate cash management service versus First Chicago's corporate cash management service.

TRY ACTION LEARNING TO BRING THE CUSTOMER VALUE PHILOSOPHY TO LIFE FOR YOUR BUSINESS

At a workshop at a major U.S. company, I recently presented the tools and metrics of customer value analysis to managers from marketing, quality, and market research. One marketing executive asked "Isn't this Marketing 101?" "Yes," I answered, "in a sense it is." At that point he seemed to feel that he was wasting his time.

Then we split the group into two teams and asked them to produce a one-page quality profile for their *own* business, using a form like the one in Exhibit 2–5. Each team struggled and was unable to complete the profile in the allotted time. The members scanned recent market research reports, but they seemed to provide little help. Each team requested more time. Finally each team produced a quality profile that represented a compromise among widely differing opinions.

The startling revelation was that each person had a story to tell about how the customer selected among competing suppliers—but the stories were all different, even though members of each team were serving the *same* customers every day.

To dramatize this point, I decided to role-play, pretending I was a new vice president for sales. I asked one of the marketing directors to send experienced lecturers to describe how the customer selects among competing suppliers at our upcoming sales training courses.

The group then realized that the salespeople, who would hear a variety of well-expressed but different points of view, would be confused. So would any executive who asked several different team members about the likely usefulness of any move designed to defeat competitors.

The result of the team efforts was that the discussion shifted from "Isn't this Marketing 101?" to "How can we get real data, by customer and market segment, in a format that we can easily understand, have confidence in, and act on to improve our customer value and competitiveness?"

This kind of "action learning"—quickly applying a new idea to your own situation—helps people grasp, adapt, and apply the concepts of customer value analysis much more effectively than mere participation in presentations of cases dealing with somebody else's business.

Why Customer Value Analysis Beats "Customer Satisfaction" Surveys

You can easily see why this analysis is more useful than traditional customer satisfaction measurement. An old-line chicken producer's customers may give their chicken a rating of 8 out of a possible 10, and that may translate to "highly satisfied." But they'll nonetheless switch to Perdue if Perdue's innovations make them even more satisfied. A customer value analysis, on the other hand, can provide early warning of what is happening and give the competitor insights into how to prevent it.

Market-perceived quality profiles also highlight other key issues that simple customer satisfaction studies obscure. Take the case of AT&T's General Business Systems division, the U.S. market leader in small-business telephone switching systems. The strength of telephone-switching-system manufacturers varies from region to region because customer service plays an even bigger role in customer satisfaction than hardware quality. And service varies depending on the performance of each region's managers. Moreover, different promotional strategies work differently in different regions.

AT&T General Business Systems (GBS) had always been strong in New York. And that seemed strange to headquarters executives because customer-satisfaction data showed AT&T customers were more dissatisfied in New York than elsewhere. Could it be that customer satisfaction wasn't so important?

When General Business Systems began conducting market-perceived quality analyses in each region, executives came to understand their markets in a new and profound way. In New York, they learned what studies had hidden: New York is a difficult place to do business and the customers of *almost all* brands of switching equipment were more dissatisfied in New York than in other parts of the country.

So even though AT&T's New York customers showed more dissatisfaction than customers elsewhere, satisfaction *relative to competition* in New York significantly exceeded customer satisfaction relative to competition in other regions. A plot of two of GBS's twenty-six regional operating units ranked by customer satisfaction and relative perceived quality reveals how the New York City unit differs from a region where customers are easier to satisfy (Exhibit 2–6). Prior to the new approach, many managers were more focused on competition with other

CUSTOMER VALUE ANALYSIS VERSUS TRADITIONAL VALUE ANALYSIS TECHNIQUES

Customer value analysis differs from traditional "value analysis," a technique developed at General Electric just after World War II to help engineers meet customer needs at the lowest possible cost. Traditional value analysis methodology involves defining the function of a product or component, usually in two words, one verb and one noun. (The function of a table leg might be "support weight.") Then, design teams seek alternative ways of performing that function more efficiently. In conducting a good value analysis, engineers both brainstorm to come up with new ways of solving problems and use standard reference sources that describe how other engineers have solved similar problems.

Value analysis has played a key role in economic progress in both the U.S. and Japan, especially in improvement of complicated products like electronics and automobiles. In Japan it inspired the development of quality-function deployment, a methodology which includes the "house of quality" method of product design. (See Chapter 11.)

But neither value analysis, nor most of the variations developed by the Japanese, provide methods for driving the whole business, including customer service, from a careful study of the customer's real desires. Moreover, most traditional value methodologies haven't been driven by a mechanism to learn customer needs directly from the customer.

Customer value analysis, in contrast, is a technique to drive whole organizations from a sophisticated understanding of customers' real needs—obtained from interviews with the customers themselves. When customer value analysis is employed, the improved understanding of customers' needs greatly expands the usefulness of other value methodologies, which can be used to solve the key customer issues that the market-perceived quality profile and other tools uncover. Customer value analysis will multiply geometrically the opportunities to use traditional value analysis and "house of quality" methodologies throughout the organization.

EXHIBIT 2–6

Two geographic regions ranked by absolute quality vs. relative quality

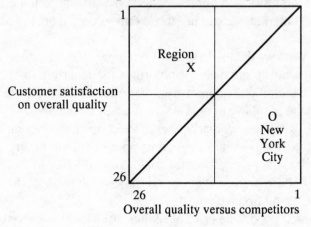

Information: AT&T General Business Systems.

regions than on beating real live competitors in their own regions. At GBS, the focus on *relative* market-perceived quality shifted managers to competing knowledgeably in the real world.

Using a Market-Perceived Price Profile: Luxury Cars

Price plays a powerful role in most buying decisions, but usually it cannot be mapped as simply as in the chicken business. The customer's perception of how much a product costs is often a composite of several different factors.

One simple way to study price is to ask customers how satisfied they are with the price of the product, on the same scale you ask them their satisfaction with the quality attributes. The ratio of customers' satisfaction with prices of the average competitor to customers' satisfaction with prices of the firm being analyzed can then be used on the price side of the value map.

But that doesn't give you a deep understanding of the price side of the equation. A better approach for many businesses is to create a market-perceived price profile, analogous to the market-perceived quality profile.

Exhibit 2–7 shows *Consumer Reports'* comments on some mid-sized luxury cars. *Consumer Reports* also gives cars a percentage rating from 0 to 100 percent, which summarizes its "assessment of performance, comfort, and convenience."[4] If we want to understand the automobile market, we can use those ratings on the quality axis of the value map.

But how do we deal with price? *Consumer Reports* prints list prices for the cars, but automakers are notorious for departing from list price. And some automakers depart from list price much more than others. Others make more use of aggressive financing packages.

Exhibit 2–8 shows a market-perceived price profile comparing the price of the Honda Acura Legend to prices of other luxury cars. For automobiles, the price attributes customers consider include the perceived purchase price, the expected trade-in allowance, the probable resale price, and finance rates.

For capital goods, the price attributes often include not only the initial purchase price, but also maintenance costs, energy costs, the costs of spare parts, and the salvage value. Marketers advertising in maga-

EXHIBIT 2–7

Consumer Reports comments on selected midsized car models over $25,000

Model	Price ($000)	Comment
Lexus LS 400	47	Competes successfully with the world's top luxury cars.
BMW 5-Series	37 to 44	Can't be surpassed for driving fun with its responsive handling and supple suspension. V8 due in spring.
Lincoln Continental	33 to 35	Big and roomy, with all the amenities Detroit can muster.
Acura Legend	29 to 38	Smooth and refined. A roomy and comfortable sedan.
Cadillac Seville	37 to 42	STS version with Northstar V8 aimed at world's best.
Mercedes Benz 300	44 to 77	Getting old, but still very competent.

Adapted from *Consumer Reports*, April 1993.

EXHIBIT 2–8

Market-perceived price profile: Luxury cars

Price attributes:	Importance weights:	Satisfaction scores:		
1	2	Acura 3	Others 4	Ratio 5=4/3*
Purchase price	*60*	*9*	*7*	*0.78*
Trade-in allowance	20	6	6	1.00
Resale price	10	9	8	0.89
Finance rates	10	7	7	1.00
	100			
Price satisfaction score:		8.3	7.0	
Relative price ratio*				0.86

*If customers score you better on "price satisfaction," they score you lower on "relative price" vs. competition.

zines consider the price per page, the price per thousand circulation, and the probable number of readers, which depends on the readers per copy.

Knowing your market-perceived price profile can help you to decide how best to improve your price competitiveness score without just cutting the purchase price across the board. For example, one AT&T equipment business found that its price competitiveness was perceived to be worse than competitors'. AT&T's analysis showed that labor rates for installation services had been set nationally and thus upset customers in low-labor-cost regions. Rather than cutting equipment prices, AT&T gave regional managers the flexibility to set installation rates at levels that customers perceived to be more reasonable.

Using the *Consumer Reports* data and relative price ratios calculated as in Exhibit 2–8, we can create a customer value map, Exhibit 2–9.

The "fair-value line," which indicates where quality is balanced against price, is more steeply sloped in the luxury-car market, especially at the upper end, than in the chicken market. It takes a small difference in quality to compensate for a large difference in price in luxury cars.

EXHIBIT 2–9

Luxury cars: Customer value map

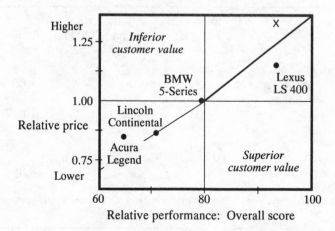

Information for relative performance based on *Consumer Reports* ratings, April 1993.

Overall Lexus has achieved the position furthest below the fair-value line. It offers quality perceived superior to any competitor, with a market-perceived price that is only slightly above the other cars. It's not surprising that Lexus has been running away with this segment of the luxury car market. Although Mercedes performance score was not graphed in the April 1993 issue of *Consumer Reports,* its quality ratings have been high in the past, but its price is perceived to be the highest of any of these six luxury car models. Perhaps it is positioned somewhere near the "X" in Exhibit 2–9. During the summer of 1993 Mercedes experienced a drop-off in sales as consumers became more price sensitive in the depressed European car market.

To conduct a competitive strategy analysis of the luxury car market, one wouldn't take the data from *Consumer Reports* but would gather perceptions from a large number of real customers (both customers of the sponsoring company and of its rivals) to obtain accurate estimates about market perceived quality and relative price for the overall luxury-car market and for customer and market segments. A complete study would reveal how quality profiles based on Cadillac customers differ from the quality profiles based on BMW or Lexus customers. These data from customers could then be compared to objective data on relative quality and price, to reveal where the sponsoring company had most opportunity to improve its market position.

How To Use Market-Perceived Quality and Customer Value Data

As we'll see in future chapters, a well-run organization uses the market-perceived-quality profile and the customer-value map, or similar tools, in several ways:

- To understand how customers score its performance versus competitors on the most important quality attributes.
- To explain that information throughout the organization, using it to focus everyone on improving customer satisfaction versus competitors for the most crucial selection criteria.
- To develop strategies for improving on the quality attributes and to help everyone understand why those strategies are important.
- To identify and manage key business processes that must work well for the most important customer needs to be met.
- To think about entirely new products that can remake the way customers think about a product category, as Frank Perdue remade the chicken business.

By doing these things, the organization achieves cost-effective improvement in market-perceived quality and competitiveness.

The market-perceived quality profile and the customer-value map tell as much about a business as a one-page financial statement and balance sheet.

Strategic Principles That Deserve "General Acceptance"

The Baldrige award criteria provide the best framework for determining whether a company is organized to achieve dominance in market-perceived quality. The criteria also provide an essential checklist, helping organizations ensure that they are attacking all the key issues they must address to become world-class.

But the Baldrige criteria do not provide the best guide to day-to-day management or strategic decision making. Executives can get so wrapped up in fixing shortcomings found in a Baldrige self-examination that they miss key market signals and fail to take the "vital few" actions that would achieve leadership in market-perceived quality. Thus, they miss their opportunities to achieve dominant market share.

The goal is to manage an organization that constantly makes the right moves to deliver what the customer will want *tomorrow*. The question is: How can the organization be run so that every manager—indeed every employee—consistently makes wise strategic moves?

To drive a company wisely, we need a few clear, widely accepted principles—the "generally accepted strategic principles" (GASP) mentioned at the beginning of the chapter. I'd like to propose four such principles. The first two we've discussed already:

1. Companies succeed by providing superior customer value.
2. Companies should track the customer value they provide through a method like customer value analysis.

In this book we'll also deal with the following additional strategic principles that deserve general acceptance:

3. Companies should use a method of business planning that allows for *action learning,* such as the *war-room* method of conducting business meetings.
4. Companies need a comprehensive *strategic navigation system* to provide data on *both* financial performance and customer value performance.

This list is certainly not complete; the whole idea of developing "generally accepted strategic principles" and generally accepted metrics for customer value analysis implies the need for extensive discussion. Other thinkers will certainly propose additional strategic principles and competitive strategy metrics that call for general acceptance.

But let me take a few paragraphs to explain why I advocate "action learning" systems and a comprehensive strategic navigation system. We'll deal with them in detail in Chapter 10, where we'll show they are an essential complement to customer value analysis. Here, let's just take a brief look at these principles so you can understand clearly what is meant by comprehensive customer value management.

Action Learning Systems

The big problem in ensuring that everyone consistently makes wise strategic moves resembles the problem that generals have faced in wars throughout history: People have too much of the wrong kind of data. Most organizations give their managers mainly financial and sales data. With such data, it is almost impossible to address customer needs. Even adding the market-perceived quality profile and the customer value map to the data, it's not easy to deliver excellence to the customer.

It turns out that good generals have already solved exactly this kind of problem. To deal with too much confusing data, they create a *war room,* and on the wall of the war room they display all of the important information necessary to understand their current position and their targeted future position, and thus plot a strategy for victory.

Generals and everyone who gets access to the war room experience *action learning.* They don't have to wait for someone to tell them what to think; they can look at a rich selection of data and learn by thinking about it on their own. If someone wants to influence the general, the best way is not to ask for an hour to make a presentation, it is to put data on the war-room wall that supports a new idea. And displaying data on the war-room wall is a highly efficient means of communication and group thinking.

Businesses must do the same. A war-room wall will include the most crucial information for analysis of customer satisfaction and competitive position. The seven tools of customer value analysis, which we will introduce over the next six chapters and describe in detail in Chapter 9, can be placed at the center of your war-room wall:

1. The *market-perceived quality profile* of the company's position relative to competitors in each key business segment, showing the key quality attributes, relative importance weights, and performance scores
2. The *market-perceived price profile* plus data on both perceived and actual relative transactions price
3. *Customer value maps,* showing the market-perceived quality score of each key competitor versus price, for each market segment
4. An *orders won/lost analysis,* showing recent sales efforts

won or lost versus the competition, with an explanation of why each was won or lost

5. A *head-to-head area chart* that graphs the components of customer value relative to your best competitor(s)

6. A *key events time line* that traces how the actions that you take to improve competitiveness affect your customer value position versus competitors

7. A *what/who matrix* that links key quality attributes to the business processes that drive performance on those attributes and shows who is the "process owner."

Other important exhibits for the war room wall include:

- A Pareto chart of recent complaints, showing the major categories
- A list of latent and emerging attributes that will drive the market in the future
- The targeted position versus competitors on the customer value map
- A list of planned action steps to improve relative performance or shift importance weights

If an assessment of the organization's performance on the Baldrige criteria has recently been conducted, a summary also belongs on the war-room wall. Ideally the wall should include assessments of how competitors perform on the Baldrige criteria, too. Chapter 10 describes additional war-room-wall data in detail.

The Strategic Navigation System

The data for the war-room wall comes from the strategic navigation system. This tracks all the key information for competitive analysis and makes it available in easily usable form.

Today, most organizations already track financial information this way. But most of the key competitiveness information is nonfinancial—the result of market research and competitive benchmarking. Sadly, most Western companies do not systematically assemble and track key nonfinancial data in any one place. The top management team can't even get this data easily, much less use it effectively.

The strategic navigation system should use a customer-value analysis as its centerpiece. It should also include the following statistics and graphs:

- Failure rates, productivity, capital intensity, and cost, each compared with competitors
- Innovation, responsiveness, cycle time, lead time, and on-time performance versus competitors
- Customer service, customer satisfaction, customer complaints, and customer loyalty
- How customers think—including the latest information on their desires and needs
- Market-perceived quality, price, and customer value relative to competitors
- Market share, profitability, growth, and shareholder value

A strategic navigation system should focus on customers, on best-in-the-world performance versus competitors, and on best performance of key processes in other industries. This kind of system cuts across functional fiefdoms in an organization and is crucial to business success. Pulling this information together and making it available is not easy.

But some companies do it. In the 1980s, a General Electric task force studying GE business units found that winners in market-perceived quality use (1) a cross-functional process; and (2) well-chosen customer-based measures throughout their management system.

Losers in market-perceived quality do not. An excellent strategic navigation system is essential to the unified pursuit of competitiveness.

Can Companies Act on the Voice
of the Market Without These Tools?

Very few companies have market-perceived quality profiles and fewer still have customer value maps, war-room walls, and comprehensive strategic navigation systems. But executives often argue that most operating managers have an "implicit model" in their heads. Managers have a "feel" for who their competitors are, for what is important to purchasers, and for how their company performs versus competitors.

Sometimes, in organizations with exceptionally good leadership, these "implicit models" work well and are truly aligned to the real needs of customers. But you can easily check whether that's true in your organization. Simply ask each top-ranking member of the business-unit team to produce, individually, his or her picture of the customer value profile for the business and its key competitors. Use a one-page quality profile template, like the one shown in Exhibit 2–5, so that you can easily summarize and contrast their opinions about customers' perceptions.

If, when you do this, you find that all top managers have similar opinions, there's a reasonable chance that the implicit models in their heads are accurate. This is particularly true if several members of the top management team spend most of their time with customers.

But check managers' perceptions carefully. Are all of their purchase-selection criteria, weights, and relative performance scores beautifully aligned within the management group—and with customers in the targeted market?

Most organizations find when they make this "implicit model" check that the alignment within the organization is much worse than the management team imagined. And if managers can't even agree among *themselves* about the customers' desires, it's unlikely they can achieve rapid progress toward fulfilling those desires without explicitly creating at least a market-perceived quality profile and a customer value map and then contrasting their diverse opinions with the perceptions of customers in their targeted market.

How Do Customer Value Analysis Tools Relate to the Income Statement?

An income statement is a financial table that shows sales, costs, and profit. It tells you what happened in the past. It tells you the components of sales and costs, and tells the amount of the resulting profit. But it does not tell you much about *why* your sales are growing or shrinking.

By contrast, the customer value map shows you whether you are competitive in the marketplace. And the market-perceived quality profile shows you *why* customers rank you higher or lower than your competitor. The customer value map and market-perceived quality profile are forward-looking.

The Work of Good Companies Today

The work of a company that has largely achieved conformance quality—that is, has mostly completed Stage One in the progress toward customer value management as described in Chapter 1—is shown in Exhibit 2–10. Today many companies are stuck in the lower left corner. They suffer from two profound problems:

- First, the major tool used to run the business is the income statement, which tells nothing about why orders and customers are won or lost.
- Second, companies are organized functionally. The heads of functions like marketing, sales, finance, research, design, and manufacturing run their own fiefdoms without understanding either the other functions necessary to make the business succeed or any overall competitive strategy.

EXHIBIT 2–10

The path to competitiveness

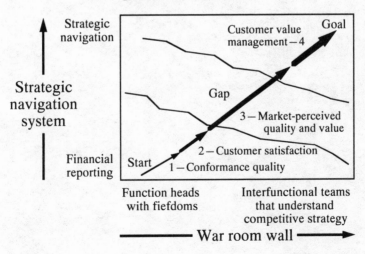

These problems powerfully impair competitiveness and indeed an organization's ability to make truly major improvements of any kind.

By developing customer value analysis, a strategic navigation system, and a war-room wall that tracks how the whole organization is performing, interfunctional business unit teams can truly manage themselves strategically. Thus, they can move rapidly toward competitiveness.

The rest of this book will show you how to make any kind of business prosper by delivering quality and value that your customers, your competitors' customers, and perhaps people who never even thought of buying your product will recognize.

PART TWO

Role Models: Companies That Delivered Market-Perceived Quality and Value

The competitiveness matrix
**Achieving competitiveness by
creating quality that customers can see**

Views of quality

	Internal operations	External customers
Measuring and improving	Statistical process control ('50s–'80s)	Customer value management ('90s–)
Roles of outsiders Motivating	Zero defects ('70s–'80s)	Excellence ('80s–'90s)

CHAPTER 3

How Milliken & Co.
Built a Competitive Powerhouse

Milliken & Co. has led in virtually all the major improvements in American management over the past two decades. It excelled in *productivity* in the 1970s. It achieved some of America's best *conformance quality* in the years after NBC launched the U.S. quality movement with the documentary "If Japan Can—Why Can't We?" in 1980. It was a star pupil of Tom Peters when he urged *listening to the customer* in his book *In Search of Excellence* in 1981.

Milliken has always understood that companies succeed by providing superior customer value. The company's Japanese customers, who buy fabrics for use in Japanese auto seats, carpeting, and other products, find they have nothing to teach Milliken. However, the Milliken team would never agree that they can't learn from other leading companies.

So it is natural that Milliken has led in understanding relative-perceived quality and using it as the foundation of corporate strategy. This chapter shows how Milliken sponsored a pioneering study on measuring market-perceived quality and then used those measurements to improve its business dramatically. By 1985, Milliken had deployed systematic measurement of customer satisfaction and customer-perceived quality relative to competitors for all of its fifty-plus business units—a key reason Milliken achieves quality leadership and premium prices in an amazingly wide array of niches.

Milliken's experience shows how organizations can transform their competitive position through customer value analysis and customer value management.

Milliken & Co.'s Start in the Quality Movement

I first met key Milliken executives through the Institute for Textile Technology (ITT) in Charlottesville, Virginia, a membership organization strongly supported by Milliken.

Threatened by cheaper imports during the 1970s, U.S. textile executives desperately pursued "productivity improvement." In 1978, Institute for Textile Technology officers projected foreign competitors would drive many of their members out of business in five years. So they came to the Strategic Planning Institute in Cambridge, Massachusetts, where I was director of research at the time. They wanted to learn about our research on productivity, and ultimately they invited us to speak to their members.

Traditionally, economists had tended to assume capital investment caused productivity. If you wanted productivity, they said, buy more machines. But we had shown, using the PIMS database of confidential business information, that capital-intensive companies often earned poorer returns than their less capital-intensive counterparts. (See "The PIMS Database" on page 60 for a description of the database and an explanation of why it is uniquely suitable for this kind of research.)

We argued that the data showed productivity investments only benefited companies when a clear corporate strategy drove the investments and gave customers a strong reason to support the business's existence. While many proposed investments in mediocre businesses appear, on paper, to offer high potential returns, our data showed that such investments rarely delivered the promised profits. Businesses that lacked a strong market position or a market-winning strategy before the investments frequently couldn't produce profitable sales after the investments had been made.[1]

ITT invited me to Charlotte in the fall of 1978 to speak on "A Strategic View of Productivity Management." Most listeners were steeped in a textile-engineering mentality, and they found my arguments strange.

But Roger Milliken, president and CEO of Milliken & Co., cared deeply about competitiveness. He had deployed tens of millions of dollars worth of technology. He easily understood me.

Milliken asked John Rampey, who was in charge of Milliken management training, to disseminate our data. Milliken's top executives soon declared that Milliken should make heavy investments only in businesses that had a strong position in delivering benefits to customers or in businesses that had a clear strategy to create such a position.

Already, Milliken was not just a textile industry leader but also a leader in recognizing how radically American business would have to change. In the late 1970s, Milliken had begun an intensive series of management study-trips to Japan. After Roger Milliken read Phil Crosby's book *Quality is Free* in 1980, Milliken had become one of the first clients of Crosby's Quality College in Winter Park, Florida, and begun to systematically reduce failure rates everywhere in the company.

In 1981, Milliken began company-wide management meetings on quality at Pine Isle, Georgia. Crosby spoke at "Pine Isle I" in 1981 and "Pine Isle II" in 1982. Tom Peters, co-author of *In Search of Excellence,* participated in Pine Isle III in 1983 by telephone. In 1984 Peters opened the four-day Pine Isle IV conference. I had had a chance to speak to Milliken's top managers in October 1983 on "How Quality Drives Profitability and Growth," and at Pine Isle IV I followed Peters with a talk on "Quality as a Strategic Weapon."

From Strategic Vision to Implementation

Strategic concepts mean little until businesses implement them and implement them well. Milliken knew how to implement.

After I spoke to Milliken's top management in October 1983, Milliken and Rampey asked me to speak to Tom Malone, president of the Home Furnishings division in La Grange, Georgia. Malone would succeed Roger Milliken as president of Milliken & Co. the next year when Roger Milliken took the title of chairman. Malone introduced me to Wayne Hunter, who was to run the Interior Furnishings division after Malone's promotion, and Rusty Willimon, head of Milliken's carpet tile business.

Carpet tiles are eighteen-inch square pieces of carpeting typically

---

THE PIMS DATABASE

The Profit Impact of Market Strategy (PIMS) database, from which much of the evidence in this book comes, was created in 1972 at the Marketing Sciences Institute in Cambridge, Massachusetts. Companies who participate in the PIMS program—some 450 to date—contribute confidential financial, market, customer, and quality information on their lines of business. The database stores information on each of more than 3,000 strategic business units of these companies without identifying them by name. Thus, researchers can study correlations and trends without violating the confidentiality of the participating organizations.

The PIMS database is widely recognized to be the only complete database of strategic information on a wide variety of industries. A number of other databases can be used to study the effects on *sales* of changes in such strategic variables as advertising expenditures, automation, or manufacturing costs, for instance. Sales estimates are readily available for a wide variety of companies from a wide variety of sources. But the PIMS database is the only source that enables the analysis of the relationships between key strategic variables and the *profits and estimated cash flows* of individual strategic business units.

Since 1975 the PIMS database has been maintained by the Strategic Planning Institute, an independent Cambridge-based membership organization of which the author was formerly managing director.

---

used in commercial and institutional settings. Malone, Hunter, and Willimon chose the carpet tile business for Milliken's first study of customer-perceived relative quality. It was, in fact, the first project in any organization to use the methodology in this book as a strategic tool for improving a business. And it promptly led to the use of the same methodology company-wide.

Milliken's Customer-Perceived Quality Study in Carpet Tile

Carpet tile was still an emerging business in the United States. Tiles from both Milliken and its competition were taking market share from traditional twelve-foot-wide broadloom carpeting, because they were easier to install and because they made it easier for maintenance people to access the floor underneath when necessary.

Milliken's carpet tile business was growing rapidly. So if company executives had relied mainly on financial statements, they might have remained content.

But Milliken had always paid profound attention to other key variables like market share. Executives knew their share of the carpet tile business was in danger of eroding.

We cannot reveal Milliken's proprietary data. But what we can report of the carpet-tile case is worth recounting. Milliken was the first organization to cover all the key steps of the relative-perceived quality profiling process, and it reaped big gains as a result.

Quality Profiling with Milliken Executives

Since we developed relative-perceived quality profiles, we've found that many organizations bypass key steps in the quality profiling process or do a hurried, superficial job. Managers who advocate "do it right the first time" on the factory floor often think they're "too busy" to create a quality profile the right way. Milliken carpet tile executives, confronting a rapidly changing, high-pressure challenge to their business, took time to go through each step. Their work shows how a first-rate organization operates and how a quality profile *should* be created.

We at the Strategic Planning Institute started by reviewing key product, marketing, and sales literature for Milliken and its competition. We toured the La Grange plant and learned about Milliken's design capabilities. Then we assembled the carpet tile management team—eight key managers, including the chief executive of the business unit and also a sales manager, a marketing manager, an expert on dealer finances, a manufacturing person, and a research-and-development person. We wanted each key manager's opinion on how customers make decisions.

Gathering executive opinions is a crucial first step for several reasons. First, just bringing managers together to struggle with how customers make decisions strengthens their customer focus. Managers usually differ dramatically in opinions about customer decision making, and when managers list their opinions and talk about them the whole group usually comes to understand customer needs better and works together better to meet them.

Second, managers' ideas are essential to the research process. Their theories about who actually makes purchase decisions should play a key role in determining whom researchers will interview. Savvy managers have a better idea than anyone else about what factors may be important. And frequently customers themselves can't articulate what is important. Learning executives' ideas and then testing them on customers allows researchers to discover how decisions are really made.

Finally, everyone has a natural human tendency to overestimate the extent to which he or she "already knew" the results of a research project on human behavior.[2] When managers write down their opinions in advance, they're much less likely to fool themselves when the research is completed. It becomes much harder for them to say, "I already knew that."

Suppose a group of managers starts with vague opinions on how customers make decisions, for instance. Next, suppose that research shows customers put tremendous weight on how long it takes for their orders to be filled. It's easy for managers reading the report to say, "Oh, I already knew that lead times were important." And then the research may generate only a few half-hearted efforts to reduce lead times. It may not change the organization's strategy at all, because the managers believe the research has produced nothing new.

However, when managers write down their opinions at the beginning, it's easy to show that the way customers *really* make decisions differs from the way managers *thought* they make decisions. When you can show that difference, it's much easier to help managers develop action plans.

So we wanted the managers of the carpet tile group to write down:

- who they thought were the key people in customer organizations who made the decision on which brand of carpet tile to buy
- what were the important factors in customer decision making

- how customers weighted those factors
- how customers would rate Milliken and its competitors on each of those factors

Phil Thompson, a Strategic Planning Institute colleague, and I served as facilitators, using the nominal group technique (a structured form of brainstorming) to generate a master list of attributes that the management team thought contributed to customer decisions. We asked each participant to list on a blank sheet of paper the factors, other than price, that count when customers decide to buy from Milliken or a competitor. Then we went around the room taking one attribute at a time from each team member to add to the master list. No one was allowed to challenge a teammate as we added new attributes. When the list was complete, it contained about three dozen attributes on four flip-chart pages.[3]

The team then reviewed the list to eliminate redundancy, rephrase the attributes using words that customers actually use, and distinguish between attributes and subattributes.

At this point it became difficult to remember which team member had nominated which attribute. Individuals began to work as a team to get the attribute list correct, rather than defending the phrasing of attributes that they had originally put on the list. Ultimately we drafted a sentence or two to clarify exactly what each attribute did and did not mean.

Next, we asked each participant to select the six most important quality attributes from the remaining list, giving six votes to the most important, five to the next, and so on. Tallying votes, we found a large gap between the twelfth and thirteenth attributes. So we took the top twelve attributes to be management's opinion of the attributes customers consider most important.

After a break, each participant received a worksheet with a list of these attributes—issues like freedom from defects, lead time to fulfillment of an order, on-time delivery, and so on. We asked them to indicate the relative importance to customers of each attribute by distributing 100 points among the twelve.

Next, we asked them to assign performance scores (on a scale of one to ten, where ten is best) to each attribute. The performance scores were supposed to reflect the customer's opinion of the carpet tile products and services of Milliken and each of Milliken's main competitors.

It had been three hours of hard work. Now the fun began. We were ready to display a spreadsheet showing how each team member weighted the attributes.

As we'd agreed at the outset, we identified participants' opinions by name. A lively discussion followed as participants realized how much their opinions differed. One manager gave "delivery of samples" 40 percent of the weight in the customer's decision, while another gave it no weight at all. The discussion revealed that the differences depended in part on who each manager thought was the key decision maker at the customer.

So now we were ready to focus intensively on: Who *really is* the customer? Who makes the purchase decision? Is it (1) the building owner, (2) the dealer/installer, or (3) the designer/architect? How much weight does each carry? How does this weighting differ from customer to customer? By market segment? Which attributes are weighted most heavily by which customer type and which segment? Another lively discussion took place, showing that managers also didn't agree on *who* Milliken was selling to.

Next we displayed a spreadsheet showing how each manager had rated Milliken's performance relative to its competitors. Do you really think that we are behind on delivery of samples? Do you think that the customer really perceives us to be behind? What exactly does "service after the sale" mean? Have we defined it clearly enough?

Researching With the Customer

We used the information from the managers to design the market research process. First, we showed the managers' list of quality attributes to building owners, dealers, and designers who were customers. We asked them whether they understood the wording. We asked them to list additional important attributes. Through this process we created a clearer, more complete list.

Next, we interviewed more building owners, dealers, and designers in person and by telephone. We asked these new interviewees to indicate the relative importance of the factors on the new list, then asked them to indicate how they believed Milliken and key competitors scored on each attribute. We also asked who played the key roles in their buying decisions. Conducting some of the interviews in person, we could persuade many of the customers to offer helpful suggestions on how Milliken could improve its performance.

When the research was done, we held review sessions with the managers so they could compare their initial opinions to customers' real perceptions. Milliken was only slightly ahead of its competitors on some key attributes—it didn't have a lead sufficient to support a leading market position.

The team began to see more clearly who really made the purchase decision and how it was made. And they learned their customers' needs and how well Milliken was really perceived to be performing. For instance, the team found to its surprise that in many cases designers had a greater influence on purchase decisions than the building owners or contractors. They discovered numerous opportunities for Milliken to serve designers better.

This resulted in Milliken placing more focus on designers, and designers responded by specifying more Milliken carpet tiles.

Another key finding was the importance of service rather than product attributes. Designers were especially sensitive to service. The team made many process changes to improve performance on service quality attributes such as lead time for delivery, on-time delivery, and order-fill rate.

Managing the Relative-Perceived Quality of Every Milliken Business

In 1984 Milliken concluded that the company as a whole needed to go beyond the conformance quality emphasis it had begun in the late 1970s. It decided to apply a market-driven quality philosophy and to track perceived quality relative to competitors in all its businesses.

Early studies showed that most Milliken customers shared similar customer service desires. This made it easier to roll out a standard research methodology across the company. Today, Milliken uses a standard set of attributes to track relative-perceived quality in all its businesses. Many (lead time, on-time delivery, order-fill rate, etc.) are the same as those attributes that managers listed in our original quality profiling sessions on carpet tile in La Grange. Milliken started tracking customer satisfaction and relative-perceived quality for each of its businesses in 1985.

Milliken executives were soon using the information in two ways—to create pressure to improve and to provide insights on how to do so. Each business unit team worked to convert small performance advantages to larger advantages as each year's round of research tracked its progress.

Milliken achieved enormous improvements. Its success culminated in winning the Malcolm Baldrige National Quality Award in 1989, during the award's second year of existence. Dr. Malone noted at the Quest for Excellence II Malcolm Baldrige Conference in 1990 that Milliken receives "price premiums" in some market segments because of its quality improvements and value-added services.

Today, managers of all Milliken business units get the relative-perceived quality measures for their own businesses each year, and corporate executives get the data for all Milliken's businesses. Business-unit managers review their scores in meetings with top management.

One of the great strengths of relative-perceived quality measures is that they allow managers to make comparisons across different businesses. A fabric manufacturing business will probably have different lead times, defect rates, and service problems from a carpet-tile business. These differences mean that in most multidivision companies, top executives can't easily compare the performance of two divisions on any trustworthy broad criteria except financial performance.

But relative-perceived quality profiles helped bridge this gap at Milliken. If one division's customers report that it performs better relative to competitors on lead time, for instance, than a second division's customers report that it performs relative to *its* competitors on lead time, top managers can readily understand what questions to ask that second division.

Business-unit managers use their data to align Milliken's products, services, and processes ever more closely to the voice of the marketplace.

Some competitors offset Milliken's relative-perceived quality improvements, somewhat, by cutting prices. Many, however, won't be able to fund the future investments required to make them long-term survivors. Milliken has achieved a dominant market position and high profitability in an industry that, just as the Institute for Textile Technology forecast in 1978, has to a large extent been in decline.

Getting Still Better

Milliken's research has evolved and improved. Today, each customer is asked not just to rank Milliken's and competitor's quality performance on each key quality attribute, but also whether he or she feels Milliken is providing "good value." Milliken is the undisputed quality leader in many segments, but it must also track its "value" leadership.

Individual Milliken businesses have begun to survey customers more than once a year when the competitive environment is shifting rapidly. Milliken has also attempted to better understand the attributes of product quality and how they differ from one Milliken textile business to the next. For most businesses, the standard corporate list of service attributes works well. But "product quality" is obviously a key factor in many customers' decisions, and the subattributes of "product quality" differ among yarn, fabric, and carpet businesses. Each business needs to take the same careful look at its customers as the carpet tile managers did.

A Winner

Comparing Milliken to other companies I've worked with, I conclude that Milliken achieves rapid deployment of key competitive strategy ideas for several reasons:

- First, top management is not afraid of—and in fact thrives on—cerebral concepts and systems as the way to attain competitive leadership. Milliken managers are very smart, and are not afraid to show it.
- Second, Milliken & Co. not only hires good people, but pays well and promotes from within, rewarding actions that will lead to long-term success. The average plant manager at Milliken can earn 30 percent more than plant managers at other firms.
- Third, the passion and drive of Roger Milliken and Tom Malone are unsurpassed.
- Fourth, Milliken and Malone expect their managers to work every bit as hard as they do.
- Finally, Milliken & Co. trains its people thoroughly and teaches everyone to think and innovate for the customer.

In 1989 *Forbes* called Milliken & Co. "by far the textile industry's leader in research, technology, quality and services." And it described Roger Milliken as "one of the era's great businessmen."[4]

Milliken's journey will never be completed. Its relative-perceived quality analyses could still be improved. Since 1985 we've realized that, to truly understand relative-perceived quality in the market in which you serve, you need to interview not only your own customers, but also your competitors' customers. Milliken's studies generally in-

EXHIBIT 3–1
President Bush Congratulates Baldrige
Award Winners Milliken & Co. and Xerox in 1989

From the left: Roger Milliken, Chairman and CEO of Milliken & Co., President George Bush, and David Kearns, Chairman and CEO of Xerox, at the Baldrige Award ceremony in Washington.

volve only its own customers (though of course many of these also buy from competitors).

And rather than asking customers to indicate the relative importance of each quality attribute by distributing 100 points among the attributes, Milliken simply asks them to rank the importance of these attributes on a scale of 1 to 10. Often this makes it impossible to judge how customers really weight various factors, because many customers will give most of the attributes a high importance rating.

But still Milliken is a leader, and a leader of a very unusual kind. Milliken & Co. and Xerox won Baldrige awards in 1989. In his remarks at the "Quest for Excellence Conference" Roger Milliken told the audience that his company had applied, but not won, in 1988. In their feedback report on the 1988 application, the Baldrige judges had indicated that his "company and key executives needed to improve their knowledge and practice of statistical process control."

When I heard Roger say this, my thoughts went back to the early Pine Isle quality meetings. After the Pine Isle meeting in 1984, I thought about the difficulty that most practitioners were having as they tried to understand the full spectrum of total quality management. This led me to sketch out an exhibit I call the "competitiveness matrix." It is designed to clarify the two major views of quality and the two key roles that outsiders play in helping companies to achieve continuous quality improvement (Exhibit 3–2).

The left column represents the internal operations view of quality: what goes on inside the office, factory, or plant. The right column represents the external, customer-oriented view of quality.

The bottom row focuses on motivation. The top row focuses on scientific measurement and continuous improvement. While no individual truly fits into one corner of the matrix, many managers have found that this matrix helps them to position different quality experts and to integrate the different concepts.

I realized just how exceptional Milliken was in its deployment of total quality management concepts. Among early Baldrige applicants, Milliken was almost alone in how well it had covered the four corners of the matrix. Most of the Baldrige award applicants in the first year of the award had begun their quality programs with statistical process control and were just starting to develop processes and measures to understand and improve customer satisfaction.

EXHIBIT 3–2

The competitiveness matrix
Achieving competitiveness by
creating quality that customers can see

Views of quality

	Internal operations	External customers
Measuring and improving	Statistical process control ('50s–'80s)	Customer value management ('90s–)
Roles of outsiders Motivating	Zero defects ('70s–'80s)	Excellence ('80s–'90s)

Milliken, by contrast, had its customer satisfaction and relative-perceived quality tracking system in place several years before the Baldrige award process was even started. Milliken had covered the zero-defects corner in 1981. Then it covered the right half of the competitiveness matrix (excellence and market-driven quality) at Pine Isle IV in 1984. Even then, Milliken was learning to clearly understand its customers and markets better than its competitors.

The only part of the matrix Milliken didn't fully cover during the early 1980s was statistical process control. So after the feedback portion of the 1988 Baldrige award cycle told Roger Milliken and his associates that they needed to do more thorough statistical process control, they took quick, thorough steps that led to a Baldrige award in 1989.

All along, Milliken businesses focused on what the customer wanted and where Milliken wanted to take the customer and market. They avoided the mistake of conforming closer and closer to specifications that might be wrong or obsolete. After Milliken won the U.S. quality award as a company-wide applicant in 1989, its carpet tile business went on to win the U.K. quality award in 1990 and the Canadian quality award in 1991. In 1992 a Milliken division was among the first five winners of the European Quality Award.

Each year the European Quality Foundation names several winners of the "European Quality Prize" and then chooses exactly one of them as "the most successful exponent of Total Quality Management in Western Europe." Rank Xerox won the top award in 1992, the first year of the European award. Milliken & Co. won this distinction in 1993.

Historically, most companies have started, and continue to start, their quality improvement efforts with conformance quality. They often make enormous investments in statistical quality control to achieve specifications before they even think about whether specifications are correct. Milliken shows it's possible to move quickly into a full understanding of market-perceived quality and value versus competitors—Stage Three of the quality movement for most organizations. To win in the marketplace, and also to win awards, business teams need a comprehensive understanding of total quality that is genuinely market-driven.

Mapping AT&T surveys
to
customer value analysis concepts

PIMS database metrics	AT&T survey
Value Index	Worth what paid for
Relative perceived quality	Overall quality vs. competitors' quality
Relative price	Price satisfaction vs. competitors' price

CHAPTER 4

"Customer Value Added" at AT&T: A Competitive Strategy Milestone

Even more than Milliken, AT&T is today leading a revolution in corporate strategy. The changes AT&T is making today are comparable to—and perhaps ultimately far more important than—the revolution Jack Welch launched at General Electric in the early 1980s.

Soon after he became GE's chief executive, you may recall, Welch made a profoundly important strategic statement: *GE will be Number 1 or Number 2 in the markets that we choose to serve, or we will get out.*

Welch's declaration was a culmination of the business strategy research of the 1970s. As discussed in the preface, GE had invented serious strategy research in the late 1960s when it worked with the brilliant University of Massachusetts professor Sidney Schoeffler. Schoeffler demonstrated the strong correlation between market share and profitability—and disproved the claimed correlations between profitability and a host of other factors—by creating a database of GE businesses. Later, Sid and I, together with Harvard Business School professors Bob Buzzell and Ralph Sultan, expanded that database into the PIMS database (see page 60) by adding data from hundreds of other companies and refining the research methodology. (I was a young economics professor working with Schoeffler when he started his work.)

The research demonstrated that high-market-share businesses outperformed lower-market-share businesses regardless of their position on the "learning curve," the growth of the served market, or other factors strategy gurus then touted. When Welch made his declaration, he was trusting good research and shifting dramatically away from the use of exclusively financial measures to assess a business.

No other strategic policy has had the impact of Welch's statement. As noted in the *Wall Street Journal,* "For GE as a whole, Mr. Welch's strategies have been paying off. Ever since he was named chairman a dozen years ago, the company has reported higher annual profits (excluding accounting changes). Last year [1992], GE earned a record $4.7 billion on sales of $57 billion. And this year [1993], analysts say, the company is headed for another record."[1]

Today, however, an equally important strategic change is developing at AT&T. The emerging strategic principle there is: *Be better than your best competitors in providing customer value.*

AT&T is developing a measurement system that has the potential to drive the whole organization from that goal. It has already seen dramatic successes as it has applied the new approach in businesses ranging from long-distance telephone calls to the company's Universal Card. When fully implemented, AT&T's efforts will represent an important milestone in competitive strategy—perhaps the archetype of Stage Four of the quality movement.

In June 1993, AT&T began to report customer value metrics from its operating business units to its board of directors. The metrics the board now receives include:

- Customer value
- Overall quality
- Price competitiveness (quality and price are the two basic components of customer value)

Each of these is measured relative to each business's top competitors.

By deciding that each AT&T business should achieve a customer value score superior to any competitor, AT&T is shifting management attention from profit-and-loss statements (which as we've shown are short-run, backward-looking tools) toward tools like the market-perceived quality profile and the customer value map. It is committing itself to clear, simple methods for navigating and building each business's future competitive position. Even if a business isn't number one in market share today, it nonetheless has an awesome market position if it is better than competitors in customer value and market-perceived quality.

In the last few years it's fair to say that AT&T has done more than any other company to turn customer value analysis into a new business science. This chapter (and part of Chapter 6 dealing with AT&T's Universal Card) will show how the change happened and why great results have already been achieved.

At GE, as we'll discuss in Chapter 9, chief executives Fred Borch, Reginald Jones, and Jack Welch pioneered the shift away from trying to do "long-range planning" using backward-looking financial-reporting tools. They began tracking competitive metrics and using tools such as market share measures to do true strategic navigation.

AT&T chairman Bob Allen and the rest of his team have chosen to go one step deeper in the causal chain. Changes in customer value and market-perceived quality drive changes in market share, profitability, and shareholder value. By adapting the tools and metrics of customer value analysis, Allen will increase the precision of AT&T's strategic navigation systems enormously. He will lengthen the lead time of the warnings those systems give, and improve all AT&T's managers' understanding of their jobs.

The AT&T Story: From Successful Monopoly to Struggling Competitor

Prior to its breakup in 1983, parts of AT&T exhibited all the evils of a protected monopoly. You could find inefficient practices no one bothered to improve, measurement systems designed to satisfy regulators rather than to serve customers, and thousands of employees doing jobs that didn't really need to be done.

But AT&T may have been the best of all the protected monopolies in the world. Citizens of France, Germany, and even some "independent telephone company" regions of the United States could only dream of telephone service like AT&T's. Management experts from AT&T played key roles in training the leaders of the Japanese electronics industry after World War II, and even today they get considerable credit for Japanese management successes.

Early in the twentieth century, AT&T had pioneered customer-satisfaction measurement by survey. Originating in the monopoly era, however, AT&T's survey naturally couldn't focus on how well customers thought AT&T performed versus competitors. As we discussed in Chapter 1, AT&T found after its breakup that even business units scoring well on measures intended to track "customer satisfaction" were suffering significant market-share losses. Worse, there seemed to be no correlation at all between good performance on what was called "customer satisfaction" within AT&T and the success or failure of AT&T businesses in the marketplace. The company's customer-satisfaction measurement system was not used as a competitive tool; in fact the information it provided was useless for understanding an organization's competitive position.

Measuring Customer Satisfaction
the Old-Fashioned—and Wrong—Way

AT&T's measurements relied on monthly telephone surveys. For example, the General Business Systems unit (GBS), which made and installed small-business telephone switching systems, asked customers to rate its performance as either excellent, good, fair, or poor on the following quality attributes:

Equipment	Repair
Marketing and Sales	Training
Installation	Billing

The survey also asked about AT&T's performance on numerous subattributes and on overall "satisfaction."

Within AT&T, "customer satisfaction" was defined as the percentage of "good" and "excellent" responses. Executives' target was to maximize the sum of "good" plus "excellent." Exhibit 4–1 shows the three-month moving average of the trend in overall customer satisfaction, defined in this manner, for one AT&T business unit.

Executives usually came close to 90 percent customer satisfaction and often exceeded it. The company used these good-plus-excellent measures as the basis for recognition programs, presenting awards to the regions with the highest scores. Regional managers competed with each other, and often focused more on beating their internal competi-

EXHIBIT 4–1

Trend in customer satisfaction: "Overall quality"

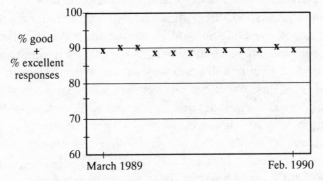

Source: Raymond E. Kordupleski and West C. Vogel, "The Right Choice — What Does It Mean?" AT&T, 1988.

tor for the awards than on beating external competitors. In many businesses, customers continued to abandon AT&T's premium-priced products.

"Good" Isn't Good Enough

AT&T made numerous efforts to change. The first effort that improved understanding of customer value occurred in 1987, when executives organized a team to address problems in AT&T customer equipment businesses—which make everything installed in end users' homes and offices, from twenty-dollar telephones to enormous switching systems. These businesses were facing vicious competition. They achieved only marginal profitability despite good "customer satisfaction" numbers.

One part of the team worked on cutting costs. But two team members, Ray Kordupleski and West Vogel, started to study customer satisfaction systematically.

This seemed a frustrating topic. Since AT&T was already reporting satisfaction levels of 90 percent and more, yet was still losing customers, many executives believed that there was no reason to invest more resources in customer satisfaction. And the lack of any sta-

tistical relationship between customer satisfaction (as AT&T then defined it) and market share growth made it hard to argue otherwise.
"With customer satisfaction as you'd traditionally measured it, there
was no correlation with market share," Kordupleski recalls.

But Kordupleski and Vogel immediately began to make discoveries
that challenged the conventional wisdom within AT&T. Their first
was that the percentage of customers "very willing to repurchase" an
AT&T product declined dramatically as one moved from the group
that rated AT&T as "excellent" in overall quality to a group who rated
AT&T as "good." As indicated in Exhibit 4–2, the percentage of
customers willing to "shop around" was 40 percent among customers
who rated AT&T as only "good." But it was just 10 percent among
customers who rated AT&T as "excellent." The data in Exhibit 4–2 is
from General Business Systems, but the data took the same shape for
AT&T's other businesses too.

This may sound like common sense. However, both the "excellent"
and the "good" groups were lumped in the "satisfied" category in
most of AT&T's internal reporting. Therefore, AT&T customer-
satisfaction reports did nothing to encourage managers to turn
customers who rated quality as "good" into customers who would rate

EXHIBIT 4–2

"Good" isn't good enough

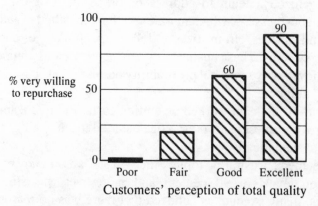

Customers' perception of total quality

Source: Raymond E. Kordupleski and West C. Vogel, "The Right Choice – What Does It
Mean?" AT&T, 1988.

it as "excellent." AT&T was finding no correlation between the "percent satisfied" and customer loyalty. But if it had looked exclusively at the percentages of customers who rated AT&T as "excellent," it would have found an imperfect but useful indicator of how well its businesses were doing.

AT&T's long tradition of surveying customers had created a superb database to study. AT&T had not only collected raw data on the satisfaction of its own customers in numerous businesses; it also collected data on the satisfaction of its competitors' customers. From these data, it was shown that competitors' customers behaved the same way as AT&T's:

- Customers who rated their supplier "excellent" were very loyal
- Customers who merely rated their supplier "good" could often be persuaded to switch.

Kordupleski and Vogel concluded that "good" was just not good enough. They wrote:

"Good" and "excellent" are clearly different satisfaction values, implying significantly different levels of satisfaction. By combining these very different levels into a customer satisfaction index approaching 100 percent, an illusion is inevitably created that AT&T customer satisfaction is approaching the penultimate. . . . It is not surprising, therefore, that disappointment sets in as AT&T's market share erodes.[2]

When they brought these facts to the attention of other AT&T managers, Kordupleski and Vogel made an important step in the right direction.

AT&T Moves Toward the Customer-Value Philosophy

There still was a good deal more work to do so that the pursuit of value for customers could drive the whole business. Late in 1987, Ray Kordupleski visited Federal Express in Memphis to study its quality improvement processes. When I met Ray three years later I was excited to hear that an important turning point for him occurred when he found a book I'd written with Robert D. Buzzell, *The PIMS Principles,*

widely used at Federal Express. "The books weren't in bookcases—
they were out on people's desks," he recalled.

Learning from the book, Kordupleski and Vogel began a fascinat-
ing series of research projects applying market-driven quality concepts to AT&T operating units.[3]

The book's biggest contribution, Ray Kordupleski says, was "the
simple fact that quality was a relative thing"—the recognition that
what ultimately matters is not the percentage of customers *satisfied,*
but the extent to which customers are *more satisfied* by your product
than by the competition's product. Ray began to shift his focus from
customer satisfaction (Stage Two), to market-perceived quality and
value (Stage Three).

Many companies had for years measured whether their own
customers were satisfied; some had measured whether their
competitors' customers were satisfied. But until the past few years,
virtually none had carefully tracked *changes in the relative satisfaction* of their customers and their competitors' customers. AT&T's
enormous database allowed the company to confirm the conclusions
of the *PIMS Principles* study independently just by analyzing existing
data. This helped large parts of AT&T quickly to adopt the new approach.

AT&T surveys had long asked one highly significant question that
received relatively little attention when the survey results were reported within the company:

> "Considering the products and services that your vendor offers, are
> they worth what you paid for them?"

Kordupleski noticed that, with AT&T's premium prices, businesses reporting 95 percent "customer satisfaction" often achieved
scores on "worth what paid-for" in the low 80s or worse. He looked at
how worth-what-paid-for scores related to market share changes and
immediately discovered that, with a few months' lag, the correlation
was strong.

Moreover, when the researchers started to look at *relative* worth-
what-paid-for—AT&T's worth-what-paid-for score divided by its
competitors' scores—the correlation was even stronger. These relative worth-what-paid-for scores were, of course, essentially an indication of whether companies were above or below what we called in

Chapter 2 the "fair-value line." They were also essentially identical to the relative customer value scores we had calculated in creating the PIMS database. In fact, Kordupleski was able to find functional equivalents in AT&T's existing market research data for most key customer value concepts from PIMS. (See Exhibit 4–3.)

With the support of researchers from AT&T Bell Laboratories, Kordupleski and his team went on to demonstrate empirically, first using monthly data from General Business Systems and later using data from the long-distance telephone network and other businesses, the linkages among relative-perceived quality and price premiums, customer value, and market share change.

In one business they found, not surprisingly, that while customers perceived AT&T's overall quality to be higher than that of competitors, customers perceived AT&T's price to be higher as well (Exhibit 4–4). Statistical research also showed that 75 percent of customers' evaluations of GBS's value came from quality, and only 25 percent was based on price.

The most important discovery was the dramatic relationship between relative worth-what-paid-for today and market share four months from now (Exhibit 4–5). General Business Systems' monthly data dramatically demonstrated that customer value was a leading in-

EXHIBIT 4–3

**Mapping AT&T surveys
to
customer value analysis concepts**

PIMS database metrics	AT&T survey
Value Index	Worth what paid for
Relative perceived quality	Overall quality vs. competitors' quality
Relative price	Price satisfaction vs. competitors' price

EXHIBIT 4–4

An AT&T business relative to competitors: Perceived price and quality

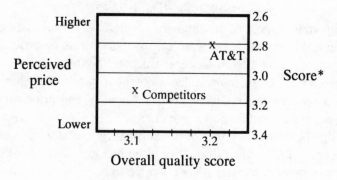

* Score on "competitively priced."
Information: AT&T General Business Systems.

dicator of short-term market share. In other words, changes in customer value predicted market share changes in the short run in AT&T's data just as they had predicted market share changes in the long term in the PIMS data. (PIMS data is annual, while AT&T data is monthly.)

At this point, Kordupleski and Vogel summarized their studies in a

EXHIBIT 4–5

Customer value is a leading indicator of market share

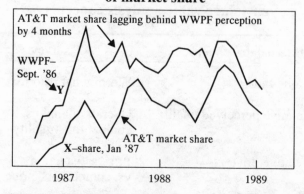

Adapted from speech given by Raymond E. Kordupleski at the American Marketing Association's Customer Satisfaction Congress, 1991.

white paper, "The Right Choice—What Does it Mean?"[4] Senior executives responded immediately. AT&T Vice Chairman Randy Tobias wrote a cover memo and distributed the paper within the company on November 2, 1988. In his memo to operating executives of the End User Organization, the vast portion of AT&T that deals with all end-user customers, Tobias declared he "completely endorsed" the work and its conclusions.

Going to School on Customer Value as the Key to Market Share

The power of the research became even more apparent once people began putting its findings to work within the company.

AT&T created a customer value map for customer-premises telephone switching equipment. It showed a wide variety of competitive positions. (See Exhibit 4–6—note that we have deleted the names of the competing suppliers from this map and we have not shown AT&T's position.)

Some suppliers had a superior value position, while others were clearly inferior. Businesses in the "worse value" zone would be ex-

EXHIBIT 4–6

Customer value map: Phone equipment

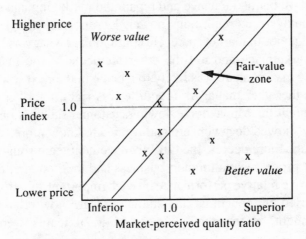

Information: AT&T General Business Systems.

pected to go out of business if they did not change (and several of them subsequently did go out of business). GBS's job was to achieve a position that resulted in clearly superior value and high profitability.

Managers went to work to clarify the attributes that counted when customers made purchase decisions, to learn the importance of each quality and price attribute, and to determine how AT&T performed versus key competitors on the key attributes.

A tree diagram shows some of their findings on the relative importance of quality attributes and how attributes can be broken into sub-attributes (Exhibit 4–7). Equipment quality, which is essentially what other businesses call "product quality," counted for 31 percent of overall quality, according to customers.

The remaining quality attributes could be considered "customer service." In descending order of importance, the quality attributes of customer service were:

Marketing and Sales	30 percent
Bills and Billing	15 percent
Repair	15 percent
Installation	10 percent

The importance weights listed here are for the market as a whole, including both AT&T customers and competitors' customers. The GBS team found that AT&T customers placed more weight on equipment quality and billing services. Competitors' customers placed more weight on maintenance and repair and marketing and sales.

This analysis had enormous power. Kordupleski now knew what caused changes in market share. He could look at what was happening in the marketplace and tell the other members of the management team how market share was likely to change in the next few months!

When the other managers found he was right, they began to pay serious attention. Managers reviewing customer satisfaction numbers suddenly showed deep concern and wanted to know more.

To probe more deeply, the GBS management team sought to identify what processes within their business and their competitors' businesses drove relative performance on each important subattribute. The team carried out benchmarking studies to learn how relative performance might be improved. Cross-functional teams were created

EXHIBIT 4–7
Tree Diagram of Quality Attributes, Importance Weights,
Subattributes and Internal Metrics

Main Attributes & Weight		Key Subattribute & Weight		Internal Metrics
Equipment	30	Reliability	40	% Repair call
		Easy to use	20	% Calls for help
		Features/Functions	40	Function performance test
Sales	30	Knowledge	30	Supervisor observations
		Response	25	% Proposals made on time
		Follow-up	10	% Follow-up made
Installation	10	Delivery interval	30	Average order interval
		Does not break	25	% Repair reports
		Installed when promised	10	% Installed on due date
Repair	15	No repeat trouble	30	% Repeat reports
		Fixed fast	25	Average speed of repair
		Kept informed	10	% Customers informed
Billing	15	Accuracy, no surprises	45	% Billing inquiries
		Resolve on first call	35	% Resolved of first call
		Easy to understand	10	% Billing inquiries
	100			

Source: Raymond E. Kordupleski, Roland T. Rust, and Anthony J. Zahorik, "Marketing: The Missing Dimension in Quality Management," *California Management Review*, Spring 1993.

within GBS to improve performance on subattributes that no single part of the organization could address. The company improved its billing system, added salespeople, and improved the upgradeability of its products. The data suggested that customers were perceiving a bigger price difference between AT&T and its competitors than really existed; GBS both reduced its own prices and gave the marketing department the flexibility to structure pricing deals to meet individual customers' needs—emphasizing a lower installation price or a longer warranty where those were the customers' concerns.

Success in the Marketplace

Initially, the research knowledge mainly helped GBS hold its own against continuing aggressive attacks from lower-priced competitors. GBS market share fell in 1987, recovered a couple of percentage points in 1988, then remained stable in 1989 and 1990.

It was in 1990 and 1991 that the entire senior leadership team of GBS committed itself to making "worth what paid-for" a top priority and to delivering the highest perceived value in the marketplace. They "cascaded" that commitment to everyone in the organization—teaching each person his or her role in creating the best perceived value. Every manager was required to determine an appropriate role and teach it to each person under him or her. If you worked in billing, you'd know how important billing was to value, and you'd know the customer's level of billing satisfaction relative to competitors. You could relate your function or task to that attribute and know what you had to do to improve AT&T's performance.

Also in 1991 and 1992, new AT&T products based on the company's improved understanding of the customer reached the marketplace. Meanwhile, some of the competitors in untenable, share-losing positions on the value map dropped out of the business.

AT&T gained significant market share in 1992. In this huge market one point of market share is worth as much as $40 million in annual revenues. AT&T is now earning strong profits selling telephone switching equipment. Its margins are an order of magnitude higher than they had been in the past.

The competition remains tough. But AT&T now knows it must

improve quality as perceived by customers faster than the competition if it is to remain a winner. There's an excellent chance it will succeed.

Victory from the Jaws of Defeat in Long-Distance

Even as AT&T was starting to rejuvenate the equipment business, it began turning incipient failure into success in long-distance, in a story we briefly described in Chapter 1.

As we pointed out there, AT&T had lost billions of dollars worth of market share in long-distance in the 1980s to MCI and Sprint.[5] In 1988, the losses were running at about 6 points per year—in an industry where one point of share was worth around $300 million a year in revenues. Something had to be done.

As the usefulness of customer value analysis became apparent in the business telephone switching-equipment market, Ray Kordupleski began to work with Paul Dernier, one of AT&T's best market researchers, who analyzed data from the customer satisfaction surveys of AT&T's Network Services businesses.

Kordupleski and Dernier's analysis pointed out enormous danger for AT&T.

The analysis showed that customers perceived AT&T's technical quality to be better than that of competitors. AT&T's advantage, however had started to narrow in March of 1988. AT&T installation service and sales quality were also losing their leads. Bills and billing services were inferior to competitors'. And, the analysis indicated, customers perceived the price difference between AT&T and its competitors to be larger than it really was.

There was good reason for the narrowing gap in perceived technical quality: The MCI and Sprint networks were more modern than AT&T's. In 1988 AT&T's own technical measurements showed that all the long-distance carriers were achieving excellent technical performance. But MCI and Sprint surpassed AT&T on such attributes as noise level. Although AT&T was replacing old copper wires and analog switches with fiber optics and electronics, it had planned much of the program during the monopoly era, when government commissions set its prices. The commissions, trying to "protect" rate-payers, had required telephone companies to depreciate their networks over decades. AT&T had matched its replacement program to its depreciation schedules.

Dernier completed his initial study in the fall of 1988. A report by Dernier concluded that AT&T's own data demonstrated that customers recognized real quality with a lag of only a few months after it was made available. Thus, he said, it was only a matter of a short time until perceptions of the difference in technical quality between AT&T and its competitors caught up with the actual technical difference—in other words, until customers realized that MCI and Sprint's technical quality were at least as good as AT&T's. When that happened, AT&T would lose share precipitously.

Dernier and an influential young executive, Joe Nacchio, convinced AT&T's leadership that if the customer perception of AT&T's network quality reached parity with the competition's, disaster would occur. The data helped persuade senior executives to write off $6 billion of obsolete plant and equipment years ahead of schedule. It encouraged them to add $2 billion a year to the network's capital improvement program.

The initial result was that in 1988 AT&T reported a huge loss (the first in its hundred-year history). But increased spending and capital improvements began improving AT&T's quality.

Surveys showed the improvements came just in time. AT&T's perceived technical quality continued to decline during 1988. It hit a low in October 1988—when customers found AT&T's performance was just at parity with competitors'.

Then, AT&T's relative score began to improve slightly. And after March 1989, when AT&T felt the real benefits of increased commitment, it started to increase substantially. (The specific data are proprietary to AT&T, so we have not reproduced a chart here.)

AT&T's difficulties weren't just due to older plants and equipment, either. To deal with challenges on other fronts, AT&T launched several more quality improvement efforts.

Dan Carroll, another young executive, was assigned to head a new group to improve the billing process. AT&T improved its sales force's responsiveness by adding five thousand people, most from staff positions and some from units that the company was reducing in size.

Numerous quality teams were formed to improve installation quality. Where it once took up to two weeks to get a WATS line connected, a process-improvement team found ways to reduce the time to hours. AT&T introduced and advertising "Ready Line" service, which could start operating the day you ordered it. AT&T also developed new maintenance programs that allowed it to guarantee two-hour restoration time for interrupted 800 services, as well.

Market surveys showed that customers recognized these changes.

Of course, you could say such programs were just common sense. But perhaps the most important function of data from customers is to make sure that common sense is used where it can improve the customer's life. The combination of the product and service quality improvements gave AT&T back its lead on overall quality, as measured by overall relative customer satisfaction with its network products and services.

Meanwhile, AT&T pursued another customer-data-driven "common sense" strategy in its price advertising. Data had shown that customers believed competitors' prices were some 20 percent below AT&T's. The real price differential varied depending on what the customer was buying, but 5 percent was typical.

So AT&T launched its "I came back" ads, in which customers declared that the savings they expected in switching from AT&T proved illusory. Surveys showed the company's perceived price disadvantage versus competitors reached its maximum in May of 1988. From that point the perceived price disadvantage declined almost steadily through August of 1989.

Follow-up research showed just how close AT&T had come to losing its leadership in the long distance market. AT&T's worth-what-paid-for rating fell behind competitors in May of 1988. Although its quality improvement efforts and new, price-oriented advertising strategy began to produce improvements in AT&T's relative worth-what-paid-for score, the company didn't reach a point where it equaled its competitors in the long-distance business until March of 1989. It remained even with MCI for two months, and then began to pull ahead in mid-1989.

Improving customer value paid off on the bottom line. As early as July 21, 1989, the *Wall Street Journal* reported:

American Telephone & Telegraph Co. said second-quarter net income rose 18 percent to record levels, as it continued to cut costs

TESTING THE CUSTOMER VALUE
PHILOSOPHY AT TELECOM OF NEW ZEALAND

Telephone companies all over the world look at AT&T as the leader in the industry. Ray Kordupleski has taught customer value philosophy and techniques in Western Europe, Eastern Europe, and New Zealand.

Telecom of New Zealand, a strategic partner of AT&T for long-distance calls, asked AT&T for help in 1990 after MCI announced it would enter the market. Kordupleski worked with Rodger Gallagher, manager of Telecom's national quality center.

Relying on AT&T's help, Telecom of New Zealand was able to change itself much more quickly than AT&T had. It began research in 1990 and began using the data for action and improvement in 1991. Overall ratings for Telecom South show substantial improvement in "percent excellent" from January through December 1991.

Gallagher noted:

The same market-share linkages that AT&T found have been built at Telcom based on the same statistical analyses. Telecom of New Zealand executives use the customer value map as a tool to plan pricing and service-quality improvement strategies. They have found it to be a very effective tool. . . .

The Policy Deployment approach of Assess/Plan/Do/Check has been adopted as the way of managing and operating Telecom of New Zealand. This allows us to (1) feed the results of the customer satisfaction value research directly into business decision making during the formulation of tactical plans at the Assess stage and (2) progressively check the achievement of plans using the ongoing relative value results on our War Room Wall.

and showed strength in the cutthroat long-distance market. . . . Analysts were encouraged by the 7 percent rise in long-distance usage, given that AT&T had been losing market share to competitors. The business market, where competition has been most intense, was especially strong for AT&T.[6]

AT&T has continued to gain. In 1993 *Forbes* noted that its profits were running at a rate higher than MCI's, IBM's, and Microsoft's combined.

Customer Value and Shareholder Value Drive AT&T

Today, AT&T is well on its way to systematically managing the creation of shareholder value through the creation of value for customers.

During 1991, several AT&T executives visited Westinghouse. The visit played a key role in AT&T's advance toward Stage Four, the creation of true strategic customer value management.

The team brought back three key messages.

First, the team reported that Westinghouse followed a market-driven quality philosophy throughout its manufacturing businesses. Westinghouse calls its management approach the "Value Edge Process." Though losses in its financial services business (where the Value Edge Process was not used) have cost Westinghouse deeply, some parts of the company remain leaders in profitability and growth.

Second, the team learned that Westinghouse uses "cost-time line" analysis to reduce cycle time and working-capital costs.

Third, Westinghouse's executive compensation system, called the Value-based Strategic Management System (VABASTRAM), backs up the Value Edge emphasis on long-term competitiveness and the cost-time line emphasis on the time-value of money. It rewards operating executives based on long-run, cash-flow-based shareholder value measures of performance instead of current-year profit measures.

The Westinghouse visit reinforced several initiatives at AT&T. In 1991, the company had acquired NCR, which already had a compensation system based on shareholder value.

Formerly, AT&T had gauged operating managers' success against targets for measured operating income (MOI)—essentially short-term profit as it appears on the profit-and-loss statement. For 1993 AT&T

changed the measure of financial success to "economic value added"—a measure of profitability that adjusts for taxes and the cost of capital. An AT&T spokesman told the *Wall Street Journal:*

> The basic reason that we adopted this new pay program is that our chairman is committed to long-term growth for the corporation. We have passed the time of shrinking our way to profitability.[7]

The emphasis on economic value-added naturally supports the commitment to customer value, and vice versa.

Early in 1992, moreover, AT&T Chairman Robert Allen asked the corporation's operations committee to make sure customer data was used in operating reviews and in the planning process in each AT&T business unit. That June, the operations committee prepared a statement for comment by every business unit president. It said that as a matter of corporate policy, AT&T businesses should have "customer-value-added" scores higher than those of their best competitors. By the end of 1992, every business unit president had responded favorably.

The chairman also requested that all applicants for AT&T's Chairman's Quality Award submit business unit customer-value data and plans. Some AT&T businesses applying for that award have even estimated their "Baldrige score" *relative to their best competitor* (see Chapter 13 for a discussion of using both absolute and relative Baldrige scores to assess the position of a business). As noted at the beginning of this chapter, in June 1993, AT&T began to report customer value metrics from its operating business units to its board of directors. The metrics the board receives include:

- customer value
- overall quality
- price competitiveness

Each of these is measured relative to each business' top competitors.

A Triple Winner

In 1992 (between the first and second drafts of this chapter) AT&T won what Phil Scanlan calls the "triple crown of quality"—two Baldrige awards and the Shingo prize.

The Shingo Prize for Excellence in American Manufacturing,

given by Utah State University and named after Japanese manufacturing expert Shigeo Shingo, was launched in 1988 and captured in 1992 by AT&T's Microelectronics Power Systems business in Dallas, Texas.

AT&T's Universal Card business, which we'll discuss in Chapter 6, won the Baldrige award in the service category.

And AT&T's Transmission Systems business unit, a part of AT&T's Network Systems group that makes telephone equipment such as multiplexing, digital loop carrier, cross-connect, and network control systems, won the Baldrige award in manufacturing.

Transmission Systems had always been a good manufacturer. But around 1989, the business began examining the quality and reliability of its products and its customer satisfaction. Transmission Systems employees conducted a self-assessment based on the Baldrige award criteria that looked at how the strong individual "islands of quality" within the organization related to the rest of the unit.

The team's findings were painful for top management. At a contentious meeting, executives insisted the unit was better than the assessment suggested. They suggested that perhaps "the wrong people were writing the application."

The team struggled to remain calm, and answered, "No, this is really the way we are and we'd better work on some of this stuff."

Ultimately, the executives decided to do so. They launched efforts such as the "one-in-ten-thousand project," which aims to reduce the number of product returns to one in every ten thousand shipped units in the first year of a new product. Bell Laboratories is designing products to make them less susceptible to failure; the engineering group is testing products more vigorously, and field managers are more closely monitoring installed systems to reach the one-in-ten-thousand goal.

Positioned for Competitive Success

In summary, AT&T now has:

1. An internal Baldrige-style Chairman's Quality Award helping AT&T business units to improve their performances.
2. A new executive compensation system, approved by the board, that emphasizes not only profitability but also custo-

mer value, growth, shareholder value, and the value of
AT&T employees.

3. Clearly articulated policies, developed by the operating
committee, that tell business units how to achieve shareholder value through superior customer value.

4. A system for reporting customer value metrics to the operating committee and board of directors.

With all this, many AT&T businesses seem destined to win more
than just awards. They seem destined to win in the marketplace.

Plot your LDL and HDL cholesterol levels and ratio as a step to assess your heart attack risk

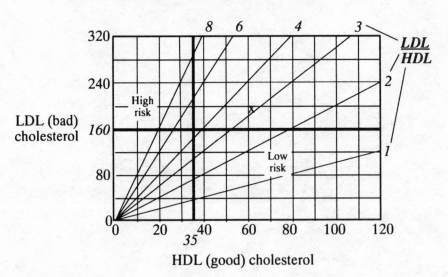

CHAPTER 5

Communicating the Complex Truth About Cholesterol

Stew Leonard, Sr., the Norwalk, Connecticut dairy-store owner, achieved fame in the 1980s for satisfying customers and infamy in the 1990s for alleged financial peccadillos. His store achieved more sales per square foot than anyone else in the grocery business, and he was known for the two rules that he had carved in stone in front of his store:

Rule 1: THE CUSTOMER IS ALWAYS RIGHT!
*Rule 2: IF THE CUSTOMER IS EVER WRONG,
       REREAD RULE 1!*

Those rules meant success for Stew Leonard. But don't take them too literally. Sometimes customers' perceptions really do differ from reality.

What do you do when you think that's happening? What, in fact, if you have hard scientific evidence that the drug selection criteria doctors are using and the weights they are giving those criteria are obsolete and contradict the latest evidence in medical journals?

Suppose people—including even readers of this book—may die because the customer's decision-making criteria are out-of-date? And yet even after customers hear your explanations, the customers go back to making the same mistakes?

How do you persuade the customer that he really *should* change?

Parke-Davis faced exactly this situation in the late 1980s. The market share of its cholesterol-regulating drug Lopid began to erode dramatically in 1987 when Merck, a Parke-Davis competitor, introduced a drug called Mevacor. Lopid executives watched these losses believing deeply that misunderstanding was not only causing them to lose sales, but also causing thousands of patients to miss treatment that might save their lives.

Customers (heart physicians and internists) were using outdated criteria to decide whether patients needed more exercise, changes in diet, or drugs. The wrong criteria caused people to miss lifesaving treatments. They also caused doctors to prescribe some treatments people didn't need. Moreover, when the doctors did prescribe medicine for people who needed it, the same wrong criteria often caused them to prescribe the competition's product instead of Lopid.

Yet, as in most cases where a good product does poorly, the truth was maddeningly difficult to communicate. Parke-Davis's experts disagreed on just what it was that the doctors didn't understand. And the truth Parke-Davis had to communicate seemed to contradict the "Cut your cholesterol" messages that follow us all through modern life.

In the end, market-perceived quality profiles enabled Parke-Davis management to navigate a strong recovery.

Their experience is not only a good example of how marketers can save lives—maybe even yours. It also shows how a clear, simple understanding of customer value and how customers perceive it—obtained from the tools of customer value analysis—can lead to success in the marketing of any hard-to-explain product or service. A product must be good, but it's equally important that its excellence be understood by the customer.

Understanding Cholesterol-Regulating Drugs

Customer value management means tracking both customer perceptions and hard realities. It means you take on the hard work of changing how you and your product perform when the data show you're not providing excellent value for the customer.

But sometimes changing the realities isn't what's necessary. Sometimes educating customers is most important. That's what Parke-Davis faced.

In the United States, as in many countries, coronary heart disease kills more people than any other cause. My own father suffered his first heart attack in 1960, at age fifty. He lived ten more years, in poor health, and died of another heart attack at sixty.

The role of the different types of cholesterol in heart attacks wasn't understood in time to do him any good. Early research published in the 1970s demonstrated that high total cholesterol levels were correlated with heart disease. By the early 1980s, when Lopid was introduced, this was an agreed-upon scientific consensus. In 1988 the National Cholesterol Education Program (NCEP) ratified this consensus by issuing guidelines that advised people to watch their total cholesterol levels and keep them down.[1]

Unfortunately, as often happens in medicine, new knowledge advanced so fast that it was difficult for the medical profession as a whole—let alone the general public—to keep up. State-of-the-art medical researchers knew the formal national guidelines were obsolete even when they were issued (although the guidelines did contain important information that was new to some physicians and to most of the general public).

Today, knowledge of the relationships between components of total cholesterol and heart attacks is much improved from even a few years ago. Millions of patients' future heart attacks *can* be prevented. Yet many are not getting the treatment that would prevent heart attacks, while others get treatment that's unnecessary.

Parke-Davis's job is simple but difficult: to manage its business so it delivers lifesaving prevention.

Cholesterol-regulating drugs reduce "bad" cholesterol and increase "good" cholesterol in the bloodstream. Parke-Davis's Lopid, introduced in 1982, was the first major cholesterol-regulating drug. Although several competing products now exist, Lopid remains the only drug with an "indication" from the U.S. Food and Drug Administration that the drug really prevents heart attacks. That means the FDA's staff has concluded, based on a careful review of scientific evidence, that the drug not only increases good and decreases bad cholesterol levels, but actually prevents the attacks.

At routine physicals, doctors test older patients' cholesterol levels. When the doctors judge a patient is at risk of a heart attack, they prescribe diet and exercise first. If cholesterol levels do not improve, they can either prescribe a drug or refer the patient to a heart specialist who will prescribe a drug.

From the perspective of pharmaceutical companies, the customer is the physician. He or she decides whether drug therapy is warranted and which drug to prescribe. The patient, called the "consumer," almost always follows doctors' orders—at least initially.

Naturally, since heart attacks are so common (1.5 million per year) and deadly, the market is enormous. Not only are cholesterol-regulating drugs unusually important, but to reduce risk and keep it reduced patients must take the drugs for a long time. Lopid is Parke-Davis's most important brand. In 1992 its sales were over $500 million.

Lopid, Mevacor, and the Three Kinds of Cholesterol

Merck introduced Mevacor in 1987. Everyone agrees that Mevacor powerfully reduces the total amount of cholesterol in humans. And National Cholesterol Education Program guidelines told patients and doctors to control total cholesterol.

Mevacor sales took off like a rocket. It soon outsold Lopid by a wide margin. A victory for technological progress? Sadly, no.

By the late 1980s, when Mevacor was introduced, leading heart experts knew that total cholesterol was far from the best indicator of heart attack risk. There are three kinds of cholesterol, or "lipoproteins," in human blood:

- Very low density lipoproteins, also called "triglycerides" or "VLDL cholesterol"
- Low density lipoproteins, also called "LDL cholesterol"
- High density lipoproteins, or "HDL cholesterol"

The total cholesterol score is the sum of the amount of all three. Typically blood laboratories conducting a complete set of tests measure total cholesterol, HDL cholesterol, and triglyceride, and calculate LDL cholesterol as: LDL = TC − HDL − VLDL. (If you're trying to understand a lab report and it doesn't list VLDL, look for a report on "triglycerides." Your VLDL level is your triglyceride level divided by 5.)

By the late 1980s, researchers knew that the three had very different effects. LDL (certainly) and VLDL (with a slightly lower degree of certainty) lead to the build-up of fatty deposits in blood vessels. They increase the risk of heart attack.

But HDL cholesterol's effect is the opposite. It *decreases* heart attack risk because it *prevents* the build-up of fatty deposits.

The effects of "total cholesterol" are thus the sum of three different effects:

LDL cholesterol	*Bad*
VLDL cholesterol	*Bad*
HDL cholesterol	*Good*

In other words, your total cholesterol score is the sum of the amounts of two *bad* substances and one *good* substance.

The test to measure total cholesterol is simple and widely available. Some physicians use it to indicate whether a patient should receive further tests. But even that use is problematic, because passing the screen with low total cholesterol is no guarantee that you are not at risk. If your level of good cholesterol is very low, you can be at risk even with low total cholesterol.

Researchers working on the Framingham (Massachusetts) Heart Study, the Helsinki Heart Study, The Physicians Health Study, and on the Münster, Germany PROCAM study have shown that a high *ratio* of total cholesterol to HDL cholesterol is a better predictor of heart attacks than a high total cholesterol score.[2] In their January 1991 American Heart Association Science Advisory, the Framingham research team stated,

> Measurement of the ratio of total cholesterol to HDL cholesterol has been found to be superior to measurement of serum (total) cholesterol as a predictor of CHD (coronary heart disease).[3]

For several reasons, however, new National Cholesterol Education Program guidelines were not issued until June 1993.

This helped the sales of Mevacor, which was positioned as a "cholesterol-lowering drug." Mevacor is more effective than Lopid at reducing LDL cholesterol and, since LDL cholesterol is by far the largest component of total cholesterol levels, Mevacor reduces total cholesterol levels more effectively than Lopid.

But scientific evidence shows just as clearly that Lopid is more effective at reducing VLDL cholesterol (triglycerides) and increasing

HDL (good) cholesterol. To the extent that physicians based risk assessment and drug selection choices heavily on total cholesterol, Lopid's great strength in increasing HDL cholesterol counted *against* it.

The media continue to drum the message "Cut your cholesterol!" into everyone's mind. Just before the 1992 presidential elections, a *Wall Street Journal* cartoon (Exhibit 5–1) even depicted a politician bragging, " . . . and, furthermore, my cholesterol level is lower than my opponent's."

One result seems to be that the idea that a drug should "reduce cholesterol" lingers as a key criterion for the choice of drugs not only in the minds of the public at large, but also in the minds of practicing physicians. Overcoming this was the key challenge for Lopid's marketers—and ultimately a challenge for anyone who wants to limit heart attacks.

The real human tragedy, however, is profound and complex. Patients facing high heart attack risk can probably benefit from treatment

EXHIBIT 5–1

" . . . and, furthermore, my cholesterol level
is lower than my opponent's."

From the *Wall Street Journal*—permission, Cartoon Features Syndicate.

with either Lopid, Mevacor, or the newer competitors Pravachol and Zocor, which are also positioned as cholesterol-lowering drugs. A patient's full lipid profile should determine which drug physicians prefer.

But often the *wrong* patients are getting drugs because doctors still use "total cholesterol" as a key element in diagnosis. Exhibit 5–2 looks at recent recommendations for male patients from the Framingham Heart Study and compares it with the diagnoses that take place when doctors use the "total cholesterol" standard.

Exhibit 5–2a graphs Framingham Heart Study conclusions. The higher the *ratio* of total cholesterol to HDL cholesterol in your bloodstream, the higher your risk of heart attack. The average ratio for the over-forty male population is about 4.8 to 1. The average heart attack victim has a ratio of about 6.2 to 1. If your ratio is 3.4 to 1 or less, you're in the low-risk group.

Your risk of coronary heart disease declines as you move from the upper left to the lower right of Exhibit 5–2a, in any of the directions indicated by the arrows. If you're a man and your own doctor has ordered cholesterol tests for you, you can locate where you fall in the risk spectrum by plotting your position and tracking it over time. A man with a total cholesterol level of 270 and a HDL cholesterol level of 62 would be positioned at point "X"—with a slightly lower risk than average. He is in the (relatively) safe half of the population.

But look at Exhibit 5–2b. It shows how the older "total cholesterol" standard diagnoses people. In general, everyone with a total cholesterol level of more than 210 is judged to be "at risk"; everyone with less than 210 is judged to be (relatively) safe.

Note the upper right corner of the graph in Exhibit 5–2b. Everyone in this section is in a relatively low-risk category according to the most recent research. But doctors who use the total cholesterol standard will still prescribe drugs for these people.

Now note the lower left corner of the graph. People in this section are in a relatively high-risk category, according to the most recent research. *But if doctors use the total cholesterol standard, people in this group are not treated with exercise, diet, or drugs.*

Recent PROCAM findings from Germany provide more detailed light on how risk diagnosis should change. Exhibit 5–3 displays PROCAM findings.[4]

EXHIBIT 5–2a

Plot your total and HDL cholesterol levels as the first step to assess your heart attack risk

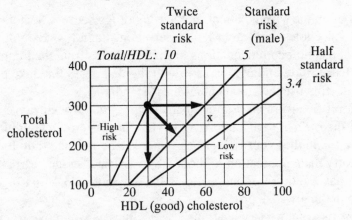

Diagonal risk contour lines based on data from Framingham Heart Study; shown on Lahey Clinic lab reports.

EXHIBIT 5–2b

Who is really at risk?

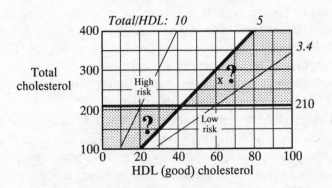

Framingham Heart Study data for men aged 30-74:
  –Median total cholesterol = 210
  –Median ratio of TC/HDL = 4.8

EXHIBIT 5–3a

Contrasting recent research insights with the older total cholesterol guidelines

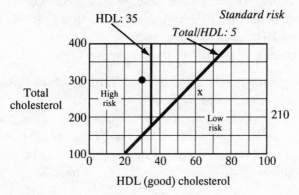

Data for cut points: PROCAM.

EXHIBIT 5–3b

Who really is at risk?

1. What percent of the population are in the high-risk zone?
2. What percent of all coronary heart disease incidents occur in the high-risk group?
3. How much greater is their risk?

Zone	Population (%)	CHD incidence (per 1000)	Percent of CHD incidents	Risk vs. average	Risk vs. low risk
High risk	*19*	*91*	65	*3.42*	*10.1*
Middle	34	15	19	0.56	1.7
Low risk	47	9	16	0.34	1.0

Information: PROCAM study.

The PROCAM doctors agree with the Framingham doctors that people with a ratio of total cholesterol to HDL cholesterol of less than 5.0 are in a relatively low-risk category. People in this group make up 47 percent of the population and had only 16 percent of the coronary heart disease incidents. But among patients with a total-to-HDL ratio greater than 5.0, they recommend looking at whether the *absolute level* of HDL cholesterol is greater than 35. People with a TC-to-HDL ratio greater than 5, but with an HDL level greater than 35, make up 34 percent of the population but have only 19 percent of the coronary heart disease incidents. Their risk is about 1.7 times the risk of people with a TC-to-HDL ratio of less than 5.

The remaining 19 percent of the population is in a high-risk zone.

Although people in the high-risk zone, with a TC-to-HDL ratio greater than 5 and HDL level less than 35, make up only 19 percent of the population, they have 65 percent of the coronary heart disease incidents. The likelihood of heart disease for a person in the high-risk zone is 10.1 times as great as the likelihood for someone with a TC-to-HDL ratio of less than 5.

PROCAM data also show triglycerides can play an important additional role in pinpointing who is most at risk. Within the high-risk zone of Exhibit 5–3, coronary heart disease is 7.1 times as frequent as for the low-risk group for patients whose triglycerides (VLDL cholesterol) are less than 150. The incidence increases to 9.3 times that of the low-risk group for patients whose triglycerides are between 150 and 200. It's 12.8 times that of the low-risk group for patients whose triglycerides are greater than 200.

Research scientists have written papers, had them published in leading journals, discussed them at conferences, and even talked to journalists about the superior predictive ability of HDL compared to "total cholesterol." Most research scientists believed by the early 1990s that all doctors understood that the new data had made the old total cholesterol standard obsolete. "Doesn't everyone know it's HDL cholesterol that's the key?" asked one Boston University scientist we interviewed.

But not everybody does. As one internist puts it, "The average patient *only* understands total cholesterol." For some overworked physicians it may be easier to respond to clear patient understanding than it is to sort through the confusion of scientific evidence.

As Parke-Davis executives watched the growth of Mevacor sales during the late 1980s and tried to explain why Mevacor wasn't necessarily a better drug than Lopid, they realized that the majority of doctors weren't hearing them.

CEOs LEARN ABOUT
CHOLESTEROL THE HARD WAY

A strange survey by *Forbes* magazine shows how confused the situation was even when the scientific evidence on the key issue was clear. A few years ago a *Forbes* journalist who obviously didn't understand the latest research launched a survey to find out if corporate CEOs knew their "total cholesterol scores."

CEOs, a high-risk group for coronary heart disease, had apparently developed a much clearer understanding of the cholesterol issue than *Forbes*. First, United Telecom's William Esrey dutifully sent *Forbes* his total cholesterol level as they had asked, but, the magazine reported,

> [Esrey] took us [*Forbes*] to the woodshed for using a faulty criterion. "The total cholesterol level," he complained, "is not nearly as useful an index as the ratio of total to HDL cholesterol."

When the magazine reported Esrey's comments, they triggered a "flood" of businessmen writing to attack *Forbes* for inquiring about an obsolete metric when better risk indicators were readily available. "Every fairly educated person knows that the plain cholesterol level is unimportant," fumed one. But these knowledgeable businessmen actually represent a small minority of the general population. As one physician commented, "Only a small percent of patients know (or care) about the details."

The letters themselves showed that some doctors weren't communicating the full story about cholesterol. One executive reported he had received a "sudden education"—when his heart without warning sent him into emergency surgery. The total cholesterol screen had missed the fact that he was at high risk.

Bewildered, the *Forbes* journalist dutifully called some of the nation's top experts on cholesterol—and came away even more bewildered. Some leading experts defended the continuing use of total cholesterol levels as a "screening mechanism" to decide who should receive further tests. More important, none of the

experts provided a quick, clear explanation of the evidence and
relationships between the different kinds of cholesterol and coronary heart disease risk. So after thoroughly interviewing the experts, *Forbes* responded with an article that gave the impression
that total cholesterol was still a perfectly appropriate measure.[5]

The company could tell that doctors weren't quite in tune with the
latest findings of medical researchers. But they had no easy way of
quantifying how doctors made their decisions. And without a clear
picture of decision making, they had no way of changing the decision
making. That was where customer value analysis helped out.

The Market-Perceived Quality Profile

In 1990, Parke-Davis began to use customer value analysis. The result
was a clear picture of how doctors actually made their decisions—a
picture that the company could then work on changing.

The first step was to gather the opinions of key people in Parke-
Davis and put them into profiles that indicated how the organization
thought decisions were being made. First, of course, we gathered the
key people at the company's headquarters for an interfunctional quality profiling session. President Joe Smith, marketing vice president
Harry Oberkfell, and top people from medical affairs, manufacturing,
the Lopid brand management team, and Lopid's advertising agency
attended. We also gathered opinions from members of the Parke-
Davis sales force by meeting with them at a medical convention, and
conducted another quality profiling session with experts from the
Parke-Davis pharmaceutical research laboratories in Ann Arbor,
Michigan.

The quality profiling process helped Parke-Davis executives realize that they themselves had failed to make their message clear. Even
some of Parke-Davis' own communications were continuing to reinforce the message "Cut your total cholesterol!" after scientific evidence had shown it to be an oversimplification. Why was the drug
called "Lopid"—a name derived from the word "low"—when its

strongest selling point was probably not its ability to *lower* bad cholesterol but its ability to *raise* good cholesterol? The answer was that the drug had been named when Parke-Davis pioneered the market, and at that time the drug's strong point had been thought to be its ability to lower total cholesterol and triglycerides.

The next step was to understand how real customers made their decisions. Oberkfell and Mike Hoffman, director of marketing for cardiovascular drugs, asked me to facilitate three focus groups to gather market-perceived quality perceptions from general practitioners, internists, and cardiologists.

Next, we reviewed 1989 data that a market research team had gathered from a large sample of doctors who prescribed cholesterol-regulating drugs and put it into the quality profile format. (It had been selected so that about half the doctors were Lopid customers and half were competitors' customers—mostly Mevacor prescribers. This probably caused Lopid to score slightly better than it would have in a random sample of all physicians.) We show excerpts from the resulting relative-perceived quality profile in Exhibit 5–4. The original profile has been modified to conceal proprietary details.

The profile showed, not surprisingly, that the largest share of the drug selection criteria related to efficacy. The first factor on the list in Exhibit 5–4, "Reduce CHD risk," is the portion of doctors' judgment that is based on the FDA-approved "indication to reduce the risk of coronary heart disease (CHD)." Lopid had the indication and Mevacor did not. Many of the doctors apparently knew this, because they made Lopid the clear winner on this measure, giving it a performance score advantage of 2.0 versus Mevacor. But apparently the doctors didn't have much faith that this meant Lopid was really more likely to reduce heart disease. The importance column shows this factor received only 8 percent of the weight.

The remainder of efficacy factors shown in Exhibit 5–4 are the rival drugs' perceived relative performance on specific, measurable criteria. Reducing LDL, reducing triglycerides, and increasing HDL all receive some weight.

Lopid's perceived performance score versus Mevacor on "lower LDL" (–0.9), shows that many doctors accurately understood that Mevacor lowered LDL cholesterol better than Lopid. (At Parke-Davis we had measured performance as the *difference* between Lopid and

EXHIBIT 5–4
Quality Profile: Lopid vs. Mevacor, 1989

Selection Criteria	Importance Weights	Performance Score Differences (Lopid minus Mevacor)
Efficacy		
Reduce CHD risk	8	2.0
Raise HDL	3	0.4
Lower LDL	8	−0.9
Lower triglycerides	6	1.5
Lower TC	16	−1.4
Nonefficacy		
Safety		
Dosage convenience		
Monitoring ease		
Compliance		
GI side effects		
Sum of weights	100	
Cost per day		1.9

Source: Arbor, Inc. report, fall 1991

Mevacor scores rather than the *ratio* between the scores as shown in the market-perceived quality discussions in previous chapters.) Lopid's score versus Mevacor on triglycerides (+ 1.5) shows that doctors clearly understood that Lopid lowered triglycerides much more than Mevacor. The small positive score of Lopid versus Mevacor for HDL (+ 0.4) shows, however, that doctors had much less understanding of Lopid's strength on this issue than the scientific evidence would warrant.

The biggest shock, however, was the weight that doctors put on "total cholesterol." Total cholesterol, the research showed, carried more weight in the drug selection decision than any other efficacy issue.

Remember, by 1990 scientific data clearly showed that "total choles-terol" was a mix of bad and good elements and that a total cholesterol criterion often resulted in treatment for the wrong people. Yet "lower total cholesterol" carried twice the weight of either "reduce CHD risk" or "lower LDL." It carried five times the weight of "raise HDL."

Clearly, doctors' decisions were still being driven largely by the old, obsolete total-cholesterol guideline. That was why Mevacor was doing so well.

The Confusion of Some Well-Educated, Trusted Customers

Prescribing heart drugs is not necessarily as simple as Exhibits 5–2 and 5–3 made it look, of course, Different well-educated doctors can interpret the evidence in different ways.

A few scientific facts are clear, however, and they clearly show that using the level of total cholesterol is obsolete. The *mix* of good and bad cholesterol (i.e., the ratio of total cholesterol to good cholesterol) is a much better indicator of risk than the *sum* of good cholesterol and bad cholesterol.

Indeed, when stated this way it seems obvious. Why focus on the sum of two numbers when you know that one of them is good and the other is bad? If my father or mother or brother or wife were being diagnosed for coronary heart disease risk, I'd want the doctor to use the indicator supported by the best current research. But that wasn't what the doctors were doing.

Taking Action

Once Parke-Davis understood the results of its quality profiling ses-sions, its market research, and its survey of the medical research, it could act decisively. Lopid needed a carefully coordinated new cam-paign to communicate a thorough understanding of the misunderstood facts. The Lopid brand team had to reposition Lopid as the lipid-regulating drug, not a "cholesterol-lowering" drug. The idea was to strengthen Lopid's perceived usefulness for people who have low lev-els of good cholesterol, which, as we saw in Exhibit 5–3b, is the seg-ment of the population most at risk.

Hoffman and his successor, John Montgomery, arranged to sponsor physician education programs at key medical conventions. At the annual meetings of the American Heart Association, for instance, Parke-Davis supported special symposia where the world's leading heart experts spoke specifically about how to train doctors in assessing CHD risk and the choice of lipid-regulating drugs.

A drug company doesn't control the *content* of presentations at a scientific society like the American Heart Association. But it can support the association's research and education programs. By working to attract the leading experts—people like Dr. Anthony Gotto of Baylor College of Medicine in Texas—to the education effort, the company could ensure the sessions would be state-of-the-art, well-attended and influential.

Parke-Davis also created carefully designed communications programs for patients and for pharmacists. In addition, the company worked with blood-testing laboratories to make the forms that they used to report a person's blood lipid profiles clearer and easier to interpret. It produced a "Cholesterol Watch" newsletter for patients taking Lopid, and launched programs to train the medical school professors who would train the next generation of cardiologists.

Success in Perceived Quality

Within eighteen months, Parke-Davis noted significant success. There was evidence that prescribing physicians had made significant (though still limited) progress in better understanding current scientific thinking.

The 1991 relative-perceived quality profile showed how Parke-Davis' efforts were changing the perceptions of practicing physicians—but it also indicated the work Parke-Davis had yet to do (Exhibit 5–5).

By 1991, physicians had significantly increased the weight they placed on the FDA indication that Lopid actually has demonstrated ability to prevent coronary heart disease—from 8 percent to 12 percent of the total decision. The relative performance data shows that Lopid's relative quality score on this issue was even better than before—indicating that even more physicians accurately understood that only Lopid had this FDA approval.

Physicians had also dramatically increased the weight they placed on raising HDL, and for the first time accurately understood that

EXHIBIT 5–5
Change in Quality Profile and Score 1989 to 1991: Lopid vs. Mevacor

Selection Criteria	Importance Weights		Performance Score Differences (Lopid – Mevacor)		Weighted Difference	
Efficacy	'89	'91	'89	'91	'89	'91
Reduce CHD risk	8	12	2.0	2.8	0.16	0.34
Raise HDL	3	13	0.4	1.4	0.01	0.18
Lower LDL	8	9	−0.9	−1.9	−0.07	−0.17
Lower trig.	6	2	1.5	3.5	0.09	0.07
Lower TC	16	14	−1.4	−2.6	−0.22	−0.36
Net effect of efficacy criteria on MPQ score	41	50			−0.03	+0.06
Nonefficacy						
Safety						
Dosage convenience						
Monitoring ease						
Compliance						
GI side effects						
Sum of weights	100	100				
Cost per day			1.9	0.9		

Source: Arbor, Inc., report, fall 1991

Lopid was better at this than Mevacor. Lopid's relative quality score on this issue rose from +0.4 to +1.4.

On the other hand, physicians also better understood that Mevacor did a better job of reducing LDL cholesterol. Lopid's relative quality score on this attribute fell from −0.9 to −1.9. What did the 1991 scores suggest about the tragically behind-the-times emphasis on total cholesterol that had been seen in the study eighteen months before? They showed progress. But total cholesterol still got far too much emphasis.

The data show a decline in the amount of weight physicians put on "lower total cholesterol"—but only from 16 percent to 14 percent. This somewhat understates how much doctors had turned away from total cholesterol as a criterion, because the percentage weight doctors gave overall to efficacy attributes had increased from 41 to 50 between 1989 and 1991 as doctors, apparently more confident of the reliability of these drugs, were putting less weight on safety.

Within the efficacy category, the share of the weight given to total cholesterol has declined from 39 percent to 28 percent. Thus, some doctors are much more aware of the limitations of total cholesterol as an indicator—and they're correspondingly less likely to rely on it in deciding who needs to be treated.

But though reduced in importance, total cholesterol was still *the largest single factor* other than safety in physician drug choices. The American Heart Association and Parke-Davis still need to close the gap between the latest scientific knowledge from medical researchers and how practicing physicians think.

Overall, however, Parke-Davis had achieved a small but significant change in market-perceived quality versus Mevacor—enough to dramatically strengthen its market position. In 1991, Lopid's market-share loss ended and sales of Lopid rose significantly, with the market still expanding. In 1992, when Bristol Myers Squibb introduced Pravachol and Merck introduced Zocor, two new cholesterol-lowering drugs, the new drugs took market share from Mevacor only. Lopid held its share against the new assault, and its sales continued to rise.

The Lopid team had faced the complexity issue head-on and positioned Lopid as the lipid-regulating brand, as distinct from the cholesterol-lowering brands. This repositioning worked because it was based on a genuine improvement in physicians' and even patients' understanding of lipid risk indicators and differences in the performance of the two drugs. Lopid's progress is therefore likely to be sustainable.

Conclusion: How to Align Customer Perceptions with Reality

Few marketers have the opportunity to improve life-and-death decisions as Parke-Davis's do.

But hundreds of organizations are struggling with products that are performing poorly—even failing—though they have the potential to meet powerful customer needs.

Parke-Davis's work not only dramatized how marketers can improve customers' lives. It also shows how any organization, by understanding the components of market-perceived quality, can help customers comprehend their real interests and act on them. To sustain success, your quality advantages must be real—and they must *also* be perceived by customers. Used carefully, a market-perceived quality profile can help you do that.

Addendum: A New Set of Guidelines

In June 1993 a new set of guidelines became available from the National Cholesterol Education Program (NCEP), a coalition of forty private and governmental groups coordinated by the National Heart, Lung and Blood Institute.[6] With luck, the new guidelines will result in better diagnosis and therapy. But everyone will have to work hard to understand them.

LDL, or "bad cholesterol," is now clearly the NCEP panel's main target for cholesterol-lowering therapy. But the new guidelines are complex.

In people with no symptoms of heart disease, the guidelines state that LDL should be measured if total cholesterol is borderline high (200 to 239 mg/dl) *and* HDL is below 35 *or* at least two other risk factors (such as diabetes or high blood pressure) are present. (LDL is more difficult to test for than total cholesterol or HDL because to achieve accuracy the patient must fast before taking the test.) If doctors and patients react rightly to the 1993 guidelines, they should place even more weight on LDL and HDL and much less weight on total cholesterol.

You can begin to assess and track the lipid portion of your coronary heart disease risk by plotting your LDL and HDL levels in a graph like the one in Exhibit 5–6.

The NCEP panel supports the findings that an HDL level below 35 mg/dl increases the risk of coronary disease. An LDL level of 160 or more is considered high. These levels are shown in italics in Exhibit 5–6. Risk increases as one moves from the lower right to the upper left. To complete the lipid risk analysis you should also track your level of triglycerides, especially if your HDL is low.

EXHIBIT 5–6

Plot your LDL and HDL cholesterol levels and ratio as a step to assess your heart attack risk

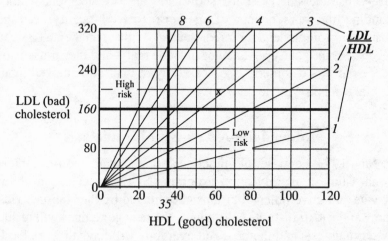

HDL (good) cholesterol

A New Cholesterol Quiz

The first guidelines the National Cholesterol Education Program issued in 1988 made the public at large aware of the link between cholesterol levels and coronary disease. People were asked, "What's your (total cholesterol) number?"

By 1992, researchers at the Münster, Germany PROCAM study had come to the conclusion that:

> For practical purposes it appears advisable to base risk prediction for atherosclerotic CHD and treatment decision on a full lipid profile (cholesterol, triglycerides, LDL cholesterol, HDL cholesterol) rather than cholesterol or LDL cholesterol determinations alone.[7]

The second-round NCEP guidelines issued in 1993 should spawn a new series of questions. The focus has shifted from creating awareness about cholesterol to helping the public develop a more thorough understanding of the different types of cholesterol. So perhaps it is

EXHIBIT 5–7

The new cholesterol quiz

The *old* cholesterol quiz (the NCEP *asked you*):

- What's your (total cholesterol) number?

A *new* cholesterol quiz (*You ask* your doctor):

- What is my full cholesterol profile?
    HDL?   LDL?   Triglycerides (VLDL)?

- What is my LDL to HDL ratio?
    How many times standard risk does it represent?

- For a person at very high risk (LDL/HDL ratio = 8):
    How many mg/dl must LDL be lowered to achieve
    the same risk reduction as a 5 mg/dl increase in HDL?
                [See Appendix B for some clues to the answer.]

- How long does it take drug therapy to reduce CHD risk?
    How long does the average patient stay on a drug?
    What happens to my lipid profile if I stop drug therapy?

---

time for a new, more complex cholesterol quiz that you can take to your physician. Exhibit 5–7 offers some questions that patients can ask their doctors.

If enough patients ask these types of questions, risk diagnosis and therapy will become substantially more effective.

Customer satisfiers

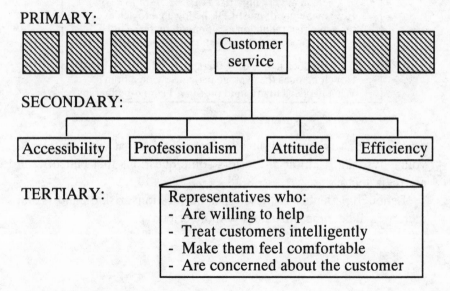

Source: AT&T Universal Card Services.

CHAPTER 6

How to Achieve Quality Service

> AT&T Universal Card Services Corp. did not adopt the Malcolm Baldrige National Quality Award standards—it was built on them.
>
> *Electronic Business*
> October 1992

High-quality customer service means profits. Look at Exhibit 6–1. It shows that customers of Profit Impact of Market Strategy (PIMS) database companies place enormous weight on customer service in making their purchase decisions. Customer service represented more than 40 percent of the importance weight of quality in customer decisions in over half of a cross-sectional sample of the PIMS businesses. Customers put less than 20 percent of purchasing importance weight on customer service in only 15 percent of businesses.[1]

Moreover, the businesses where customers put high weight on service are more profitable than those where the weight on customer-service is low (Exhibit 6–2).

Thus, it's not surprising that businesses that achieve better quality customer service earn more than businesses that do not. Look at Exhibit 6–3. It compares quality of customer service to profitability—not only for businesses in industries where service quality is very important in the purchase decision, but also for industries where service

EXHIBIT 6–1

Customer services play a key role in many markets

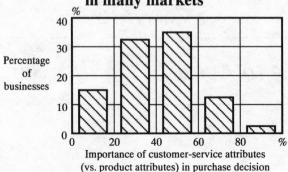

Importance of customer-service attributes
(vs. product attributes) in purchase decision

Copyright © Quality Progress.

EXHIBIT 6–2

Profits are high in markets where customer service is important

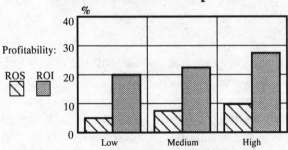

Importance of customer service
(vs. product) in purchase decision

Copyright © Quality Progress.

quality is less important. As you can see, companies whose service is rated better than competitors' earn more than double the return on investment of companies whose service is worse.

Yet until recently manufacturing companies, who were spending millions of dollars to achieve excellence in their factories, rarely used the same techniques to manage the customer service they provided.

EXHIBIT 6–3

Superior customer service pays off

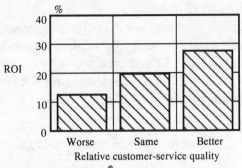

Relative customer-service quality

Service businesses doubted that "quality techniques" mattered to them at all.

Banks, supermarkets, and hotel companies thought their businesses were somehow different from manufacturing businesses like Toyota and Milliken where total quality management first proved its value.

Of course AT&T, which pioneered many quality techniques and taught them to the Japanese after World War II, is primarily a service business. It gets the vast majority of its revenue and profits from the sale of telephone services. But many service businesses didn't think of AT&T as a "normal" service company, and even AT&T often failed to use the same care in quality control of ancillary customer-service that it applied in its core network and manufacturing operations.

Failing to manage service strategically doesn't make sense, however, and leading companies are realizing that it not only leaves their customers angry, but also costs them profits. Today the benefit of strategically managing service quality is being proven by dramatic successes in important businesses that can't be called "atypical." Manufacturing companies like Xerox are strategically managing the quality of the customer service they provide to support their products. Likewise, service businesses are proving that, while managing service quality may sometimes be more difficult than managing factory quality, the tools that produce quality in a factory will also produce quality in services. The management of service is central to the management of customer value.

In this chapter we'll look at two service businesses that are showing how the quality and customer value of service can be managed and consistently achieved. They are AT&T's phenomenally successful Universal Card Services credit and calling card business, and the moving business of United Van Lines, which has just seized the Number 1 position in its industry. Each demonstrates different aspects of how to manage for superior quality service.

The Awesome Rise of the Universal Card

So many people use AT&T's Universal Card today that it's hard to remember that the business didn't even exist at the beginning of 1990. At that time AT&T management, noting the millions of AT&T telephone credit cards in customers' pockets and the mediocre service of many highly profitable general-purpose credit-card issuers, decided to enter a business that seemed far from its core business of communications.

AT&T wanted the Universal Card business as a way of keeping in touch with its customers. After the breakup of AT&T as a nationwide all-purpose telephone company, the regional Bell operating companies supplied operators and sent out phone bills. If "AT&T" was nothing but a line on the local phone company's bill, customers might inevitably think of long-distance service as a commodity—even if AT&T's long-distance service really excelled in comparison with its competitors'. AT&T Chairman Bob Allen wanted to make AT&T's quality visible—to enhance AT&T's image rather than living off it.

AT&T had an unbeatable advantage in addition to its existing contacts with telephone credit card holders: It recognized from the beginning that it had to be a quality and value leader, and built the entire business on that principle. "We really tried to have quality built into the fiber of the unit," recalled Rob Davis, Universal Card quality vice president. AT&T hired Paul Kahn to run the business. He was a brilliant manager who had already completed quality-oriented turnarounds of the credit-card businesses at Mellon Bank and First Chicago Corporation.

The most publicized aspect of the Universal Card's success was the creative way it built on AT&T's existing position in the calling-card marketplace and consumer services generally. AT&T offered a "no-fee for life" Universal Card to all its calling-card users and millions of others. In addition to the regular benefits of a credit card, you could use the AT&T Universal Card as a calling card to make long-distance telephone calls at a 10 percent discount from AT&T's regular calling-card rates.

But that wasn't all the Universal Card offered. As you can tell by checking your mailbox, the credit-card business is full of competitors offering special prices. Unlike most others, however, the managers of AT&T Universal Card Services (UCS) used the Malcolm Baldrige National Quality Award criteria as a template for their total quality management structure as they built a new business from the ground up. In hiring, for instance, they used the human resources section of the Baldrige criteria as a guide.[2]

Similarly, UCS built a customer-satisfaction system from the beginning. Learning from Ray Kordupleski's research at AT&T's communications businesses (see Chapter 4), it practiced customer value analysis from the beginning. It started in 1990 with customer focus groups to identify the key "satisfiers" of credit-card users—the quality attributes. It determined the phrases customers use for these attributes and then, beginning January 1991, surveyed users monthly to determine the weighting customers put on them and to learn how they rated AT&T and its competitors. AT&T currently surveys two hundred UCS customers and four hundred competitors' customers each month.

The Universal Card Services business unit is driven by the need to excel on the eight "primary attributes" or "customer satisfiers" its research has identified as most important. It considers the names of those attributes themselves to be proprietary; they were the product of intense research and are among the "crown jewels" of the UCS business. But executives do say that the primary attributes are subdivided into twenty-six "specific attributes" and there are a total of one hundred attributes measured including both the specific attributes and subattributes of those specific attributes. Exhibit 6–4 is an adaptation of a chart UCS management presented at the 1993 "Quest for Excellence" conference sponsored by the National Institute of Standards and Technology.

EXHIBIT 6–4

Customer satisfiers

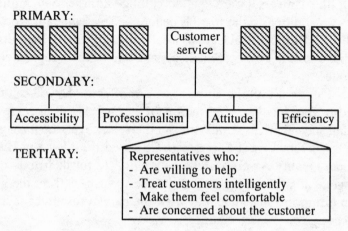

Source: AT&T Universal Card Services.

"Customer service" is one of the eight primary attributes. "Attitude," which is one of the four secondary attributes of customer service, is further broken into four tertiary attributes. The tertiary attributes tend to be the "actionable" items. Telephone associates can relate to being "willing to help" the customer, "treating the customer intelligently," "making the customer feel comfortable," and letting the customer sense that they "are concerned about the customer's question or problem."

Just nine days before learning that UCS had won the Baldrige award, president Paul Kahn noted at the second Service Quality Summit at the Commerce Department on October 5, 1992, that in UCS's typical monthly surveys it leads all competitors on six or seven of the primary attributes. "In many months we win on all eight," he noted.

Superior quality and lower price positioned AT&T's Universal Card well into the "grow and prosper zone" on the customer value map.

Such a move typically forces at least one competitor into the "wither and die zone." Often the business being displaced feels no fear because it doesn't have a customer value map or any other comparable tool. Indeed, as we'll see, financial analysts frequently miss the change, as well.

Although I had not seen Universal Card's market research data, I anticipated a major disruption of the credit-card market as soon as Phil Scanlan, AT&T's vice president for quality, explained the Universal Card's positioning to me in May of 1990 (no annual fee, low interest rate differential that floated up *and down* with the prime rate, 10 percent discount on AT&T long-distance calls, one universal card for calling and credit in your wallet instead of two separate cards, all the benefits of a VISA or MasterCard card, and customer service designed to enhance the AT&T corporate brand image—it clearly added up to superior value positioning). By the time Lakewood Publications, which focuses on service quality, held its October 1990 conference, I'd become an AT&T Universal Card user, and I could predict the Universal Card's dramatic success.

Converting Charges to the Universal Card

My own experience with the card helps to illustrate how superior customer value positioning affects a marketplace. I have been an American Express cardmember since 1969. I also had an AT&T calling card that allowed me to place calls just by punching in my business telephone number plus a four-digit personal identification number (PIN), which I had, after years of use, finally memorized. When a telemarketer called me in mid-1990 to offer me an AT&T Universal Card, I learned that to use it I would have to punch in a new ten-digit UCS number plus a new four-digit PIN just to save 10 percent on long-distance calls. If I hadn't heard about the key attributes from Phil Scanlan, I probably would have rejected the offer. This is typical of what happens even to organizations like UCS that achieve a strong position on the value map. It's difficult for customers to change from suppliers like American Express. The new organization that has moved into the strong position usually has to invest large amounts of resources in well-designed marketing. But more people will change to the new organization than to its competitor.

I grumbled, but told the telemarketer that I would accept a Universal Card.

As of September 1990, my Universal Card was still a virgin. I was still using my AT&T *calling* card to make calls. I hadn't started making "universals" because I could never remember my new PIN number.

Realizing that I had to use the card at least once before year end to qualify for continuance of the card with no annual fee, I first charged a hotel bill to the Universal Card instead of American Express in late September. The clerk didn't seem to mind—so I started to use the Universal Card in hotels. Second, I located my new PIN number and started to save the 10 percent on my AT&T phone calls.

Then came the Boston restaurant owners' rebellion against American Express in the spring of 1991. Boston restaurants that catered to business people were suffering in a weak New England economy. For years American Express, noting that its "charge" card members were typically richer than people who used other "credit" cards, had charged a higher fee to establishments and repaid them more slowly than other card issuers. The difference could be as much as double—a 4 percent charge for American Express versus a 2 percent charge for MasterCard and VISA.

Recalling the Boston Tea Party two centuries earlier, upscale restaurants like Davio's and Grill 23 rebelled. They concluded American Express wasn't doing enough for them. So they began urging diners to put their charges on other cards.

Furious, American Express told the restaurants that if they showed preference for other cards, they couldn't continue to accept American Express at all. The restaurant owners stopped overtly encouraging customers to use other cards. But the news media got wind of the tiff, and as a result American Express had to cope with nasty newspaper articles that produced similar rebellions in other cities. In one report American Express was meeting with the restaurant owners, offering them rate reductions reported to be in the 0.45 percent range.[3]

Naturally, AT&T Universal Card's unique feature of a 10 percent discount on long-distance phone calls not only positioned it to offer superior value against other cards, but also positioned it to appeal to business travelers who had traditionally used American Express. Business travelers are always calling their offices and families.

The restaurant owners' rebellion taught me about American Express's higher premiums for the first time. So about that time I started using my Universal Card in restaurants—especially if I liked the service. Why stiff a nice restaurant owner with an extra cost in the middle of a recession? Over eighteen months, I had progressively switched most of the expense categories where I use a charge card from American Express to AT&T UCS.

My travel agent would ask, "Charge it to your American Express?" and I would say yes (she told me her commission is not affected by vendor service charges). But during winter 1991–92 I didn't do much traveling. My AmEx charges fell to nearly zero.

This triggered a nice February 18, 1992, letter from Abby F. Kohnstamm, AmEx's senior vice president, Personal Card Marketing.

Dear Mr. Gale:

We noticed that you have not been using the American Express Card as frequently as you had in the past and we would like to know if there is something we can do to better serve you. . . .

Using a Customer Value Profile
to Analyze Head-to-Head Competitors

To link the conversion behavior just described to the model of how a customer selects among competing service providers, I've prepared a customer value profile of how I personally viewed AT&T's Universal Card competing head-to-head with American Express's charge card during 1990–91 (Exhibit 6–5).

For a service business, I separate the quality attributes into those that represent the "core" service (the product offered) and those that can be viewed as "customer service." To me, vendor acceptance of the card was the single most important quality attribute. What's the purpose in having a card if it is not accepted when you want to use it? AmEx gets a 6 on "phone calls" because sometime after the Universal Card came out, AmEx arranged a deal with MCI which allows their card holders to charge phone calls on the MCI network.

Since Exhibit 6–5 is a complete customer-value profile, it includes a price profile as well as a quality profile. I have listed three price attributes:

- the *annual fee* (for keeping your card-use privileges active)
- the *interest rate* (charged on unpaid balances)
- the *vendor service fee* (that card companies charge vendors like restaurants, stores, and airlines that accept the card).

EXHIBIT 6–5

Simplified customer value analysis
AT&T UCS vs. AMEX*

	Importance weights**	Performance scores (1–10) UCS	AMEX	Ratio	x	Weight ratio
Quality attributes:						
Core service:						
- Vendor acceptance	.30	9	8	1.13		0.38
- Phone calls	.20	10	6	1.67		0.33
- Protect purchases	.10	7	9	0.78		0.08
Customer service:						
- Company logo	.20	10	8	1.25		0.25
- Professional	.20	9	8	1.13		0.23
Sum of quality weights	1.00				MPQ ratio:	1.27
Customer satisfaction scores:		9.2	7.7			
Price attributes:						
- Annual fee	.80	10	5	2.00		1.60
- Interest rate	.00	9	NA	NA		0.00
- Vendor service fee	.20	9	6	1.50		0.30
	1.00		Price satisfaction ratio:			1.90

Weight on quality (0.9) + weight on price (0.1) = 1.0
Customer value ratio, UCS versus AMEX = (0.9)1.27 + (0.1)1.9 = 1.33

*   Brad Gale's transactor perception
** Importance weights have been divided by 100

I don't leave balances unpaid, so I place zero weight on the interest rate. My empathy with restaurant owners caused me to place 20 percent of the overall price weight on "vendor service fee" and 80 percent on "annual fee." My Universal card is a VISA card and VISA charges vendors a lower service fee than AmEx, so UCS gets a higher price satisfaction rating than AmEx (9 versus 6).

At the bottom of Exhibit 6–5 I show that quality gets 90 percent of the weight and price only 10 percent in my decisions about which cards to renew and which to use for charging. These weights are used to calculate the customer-value ratio. In my 1990–91 example, AT&T UCS's performance versus AmEx is 27 percent better on quality and 90 percent better on price. Overall, that made it 33 percent better on customer value.

To perform a careful analysis of a market as complex as the charge card market, we should break it into two or more segments. For simplicity, we'll consider just two. People like me use a card to charge items when traveling because we don't want to carry cash. We don't need credit, and we pay our entire balance each month. We are known as "transactors."

The people in another segment use a card primarily in their home towns, often when they are short on cash. They may not be able to pay the balance each month. These people are known as "revolvers." They often leave an unpaid balance and pay finance charges. This is not a segment eagerly waiting for the calling card feature of a "Universal Card," because its members place little weight on being able to charge phone calls.

My daughter, Debbie, is a "revolver." In contrast to my profile shown in Exhibit 6–5, she tells me she places 50 percent of the weight on price and 50 percent on quality. She likes AT&T UCS because the interest rate is low and there is no annual fee. Among the quality attributes, she places a great deal of weight on professional, courteous service. As she commented, "After several dissatisfying conversations with AmEx phone reps and a six-month ordeal to get my address changed, I canceled my AmEx card." We could construct a customer value analysis for "revolvers" that would differ dramatically from Exhibit 6–5. But AT&T would still beat American Express. As Debbie comments, "We both moved from AmEx to AT&T UCS, but for different reasons."

When a start-up enters a market with better product quality, superior customer service, and a lower price as perceived by the two major market segments, it has the kind of dramatic impact that UCS has had.

Exhibit 6–6 plots the data from the customer value profile in a "head-to-head area map of customer value" as perceived by Brad Gale during 1990–91. The length of each bar reflects my perception of AT&T's performance relative to AmEx. When the bar extends to the right of 1.0, that indicates that I perceive UCS to be superior. When it extends to the left, I perceive AmEx to be better. The height of each bar reflects the relative importance of each quality attribute.

(Doing this kind of quick customer value analysis based on your own perceptions can often be extremely useful. If you're a supplier, it may show you why you're not doing as well as you had thought you should. And it can provide a clear summary of your own perceptions which can be a vitally important baseline for analyzing feedback from customers and others. If you are a customer, on the other hand, a quick

EXHIBIT 6–6

Head-to-head area map* of customer value

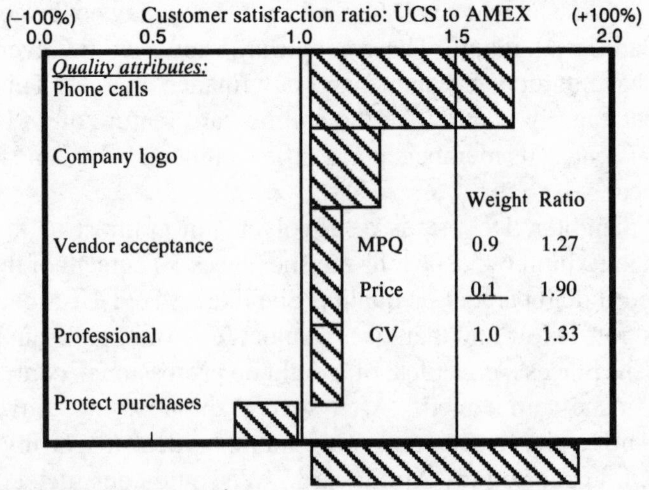

```
(–100%)        Customer satisfaction ratio: UCS to AMEX      (+100%)
   0.0         0.5           1.0              1.5              2.0
```

Quality attributes:		Weight	Ratio
Phone calls			
Company logo			
Vendor acceptance	MPQ	0.9	1.27
	Price	0.1	1.90
Professional	CV	1.0	1.33
Protect purchases			

* Brad Gale's transactor perception.
Vertical distance in proportion to importance.

customer value analysis may show you that it's time to switch suppliers.)

Since AT&T was ahead on almost every attribute, most of the shaded area winds up on the right, the AT&T side of the chart. Most of my charges during this time period wound up on the Universal Card. AT&T was the "right choice" for me, but, as I mentioned above, I renewed my AmEx card in the spring of 1991 thinking AmEx might come back with some counter moves that dramatically alter Exhibits 6–5 and 6–6.

Converting Charges Back to AmEx

Sure enough AmEx came out with a "member miles" attribute in June of 1991. By November, my wife, Jane, had signed us up for the air miles program and was encouraging me to charge big-ticket items on my American Express card. Every dollar charged to AmEx earns one membership mile. Citibank had had great success with an air miles program with American Airlines. AmEx responded with a mileage program that now includes five airlines (Delta, Continental, Northwest, Southwest, and USAir).

The air miles benefit is the major reason why I'm still a member of the American Express Card club. For a transactor like myself who travels frequently, the prospects of earning free tickets quickly are very real and worth a considerable amount. For me, AmEx has leapfrogged UCS in price satisfaction and the worth of airline tickets has dramatically increased the weight that I place on price versus quality in deciding which card to use. The price competitiveness bar now falls on the AmEx side of the head-to-head area map and is so wide and deep that it dominates my charge card use.

By contrast, my daughter Debbie, the revolver, doesn't "care very much for the airmiles deal. At a cost of twenty-five dollars a year with my low charges, it is unlikely that I will get a free ticket any time soon." The member miles attribute positions AmEx to attract the frequently travelling, and thus heavier spending, more profitable subsegment of the transactor segment.

The Universal Card's Success

Whatever happens to *my* American Express charges, however, the AT&T Universal Card is a success. In July 1992, Universal Card Services hit profitability well ahead of plan. The unit celebrated with a black-tie dinner attended by two thousand UCS associates and their guests. Recently the organization had 10 million charge accounts, and a total of 15 million VISA and MasterCards issued. In three years it had become the second largest bank-card issuer in the United States, behind Citibank.

On October 14, 1992, the Commerce Department announced AT&T Universal Card Services had won the Baldrige National Quality Award. At AT&T's annual Quality Conference seven days later, Kahn was already scheduled to receive a *bronze* award on behalf of Universal Card Services—an award two steps below the top AT&T category. (AT&T had not yet given a "gold" or "silver" award to any of its businesses. The AT&T evaluation system has produced lower scores on the Baldrige scale). In his acceptance speech, UCS's Paul Kahn had the pleasure of looking back over his shoulder at AT&T

chairman Bob Allen and commenting that it was interesting that UCS had won a national Baldrige award and a "bronze" AT&T award.

Dale H. Meyers, the quality planning manager who oversees the AT&T Chairman's Quality Award, prepares a "Pockets of Excellence" report that names all business units in AT&T that score 60 percent or more of the maximum points on each of the items (twenty-nine in 1992) that make up the criteria for both the Baldrige and the AT&T Chairman's Quality awards. This internal benchmarking mechanism tells AT&T business units which of their sister businesses can serve as a role model to help them improve. In 1992, UCS was the only AT&T business that won a "pocket of excellence" citation for Baldrige item 7.5—*Customer satisfaction comparison versus competitors.*

Kahn resigned as president of UCS in 1993. He had wanted to expand rapidly into other financial products, such as certificates of deposit and mutual funds. AT&T executives, remembering that the reason they'd entered the credit-card business was to strengthen ties with long-distance customers, wanted to move more slowly. Analysts praised both Kahn *and* AT&T. Kahn had led the highly successful start-up. And Sanford C. Bernstein & Co. analyst Gregory Sawyers noted that AT&T had "resisted the temptation to diversify away from its core communications business, which is terrific."

Kahn said: "After completing two turnarounds at other companies in the past ten years, not to mention leading this startup at AT&T, it's time to do this again for my own portfolio." Later, he added: "I wouldn't mind being the first executive to win the Baldrige award twice for two different businesses."

Can Companies Help Stock Market Analysts to Understand Strategy?

At AT&T's 1992 Quality Conference, employees were sky high about the successes of AT&T's Universal Card, its Transmission Systems business, and its Microelectronics Power Systems unit in national award competitions. Meanwhile, executives at American Express's card and travel division were putting finishing touches on a major restructuring. To make room for AT&T UCS to grow, someone had to get hurt. The *New York Times* headline read: AMERICAN EXPRESS'S BIG LOSS—$205 MILLION DEFICIT SURPRISES ANALYSTS.[4]

The poor value the American Express card provided in many segments of the market had been clear for years. One wonders how the analysts missed this. Perhaps CEOs and CFOs can brief analysts on changes in competitive position as well as changes in financial results and prospects. Someday companies may issue quarterly customer value maps as well as quarterly earnings reports.

The Attribute Life Cycle

It's worthwhile to use the credit card business to make one more point before moving on to a very different kind of service business. The competitive dynamics of the calling/credit/charge card market are also a good illustration of how attributes can pass through a life cycle. When first introduced, AT&T's Universal Card had a "unique" attribute—unlike other credit cards, it was named "Universal" because people could use it to *make and charge telephone calls* in addition to paying for other goods and services.

For about eighteen months, the Universal Card was the only card with this feature. When the Universal Card hit the market, a new attribute which we can call "phone calls chargeable" was added to the list of quality attributes for many card users. For some card users, the "phone calls" attribute had been on their list of "wants." But no one had offered phone calls except on special phone cards. So this desired attribute received zero weight in selection of charge cards.

Some time after the Universal Card was introduced, AmEx struck a deal with MCI so AmEx card users could charge phone calls on the MCI network. The phone calls feature is no longer unique, but it is still a *key* attribute. In my personal customer value analysis, AT&T's Universal Card scores higher in performance on this attribute because the AT&T network still dominates the long-distance market.

When I facilitate a quality profiling session I usually ask the participants to place each attribute into one of seven stages that make up the attribute life cycle (Exhibit 6–7).

A *latent* attribute is not visible or apparent. These attributes lie hidden in the minds of customers and designers. Companies use probing questions and float ideas to customers in an attempt to uncover what customers will desire.

A *desired* attribute is known but not currently supplied by any com-

EXHIBIT 6–7

Stages of the attribute life cycle

1	Latent:	Not yet visible or apparent
2	Desired:	Known but not currently supplied — no weight
3	Unique:	Only the pioneer scores well — some weight
4	Pacing:	One supplier is already ahead and weight is shifting onto this attribute
5	Key:	Differences in performance determine competitiveness "Niche" attribute — important in one segment. "Power" attribute — important in all segments
6	Fading:	"Catch-up" moves and/or declining weight begin to take away the top performer's competitive edge
7	Basic:	All suppliers perform well — no competitive edge — required, expected; no weight unless you mess up

petitor. It will become a unique attribute when some supplier fulfills the need. As people experience the benefits of this attribute without fully anticipating them, it will provide unexpected quality.

For a *unique* attribute only one supplier, the pioneer, scores well. Therefore, the pioneer commands a big advantage with the customer segment that weights this attribute heavily. If the benefits of this attribute are unexpected or only partially expected, as customers buy from this product supplier for the first time or switch to this service provider, they will react with delight.

An attribute is in the *pacing* stage when one supplier is ahead and weight is shifting to this attribute. If it attracts enough weight, it will become a key attribute.

Differences in performance on *key* attributes determine competitiveness. An attribute that is "key" to only one segment is a "niche" attribute. A key attribute that is important in all segments of the targeted market is a "power" attribute.

As catch-up moves and/or declining weight take away the top

performer's competitive edge, a key attribute becomes a *fading* attribute.

An attribute reaches the *basic* stage when all suppliers in the buyers' consideration set perform well. No supplier has a competitive edge. The attribute is required, and typically receives little weight in the supplier selection decision. But buyers will react to a decline in performance on these attributes and remove that supplier's business from consideration.

When a supplier pulls ahead of the pack on an emerging attribute at the beginning of the life cycle, customers tend to react very positively. When an attribute is in stages 3 through 5, buyers make a more deliberate assessment of performance. When a supplier slips in performance on a basic attribute, buyers tend to react negatively.

Some Japanese manufacturers see quality as existing on three levels: "expected" quality, "performance" quality, and "unexpected" quality. Exhibit 6–8 shows how these three levels of quality can be linked to an attribute's stage in its life cycle.

To stay at the cutting edge of quality leadership, a company needs to innovate continuously or achieve top performance on key attri-

EXHIBIT 6–8

Aligning a simplified Kano model
with the attribute *life-cycle stages*

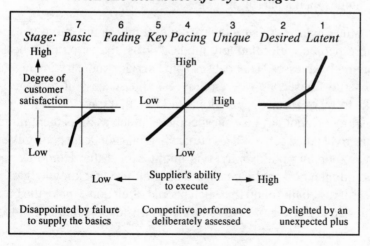

QUALITY IN RETAILING

Creating a New Customer-Service
Attribute: Home Depot

In 1989 my stepmother noticed an interesting development in the
home-center business near her home in Deerfield Beach, Florida.
A new chain, Home Depot, gave her service that its competitors
did not. Home Depot offered more items, had friendlier employees, and *transferred more how-to-do-it "know-how"* to customers. As Home Depot stores opened, competitors closed. My
stepmother hurried to buy stock in the chain.

That decision has considerably eased my stepmother's retire-
ment. For Home Depot is another service industry success story.

Probably the biggest strength of Home Depot is its founding
philosophy:

> Home Depot's two guiding lights, Bernard Marcus and Arthur
> Blank, who founded the company in Atlanta with one store in
> 1979, preached that in a do-it-yourself time, it was as impor-
> tant to teach people *how* to do it themselves as it was to pro-
> vide the materials. And so to a greater extent than any other
> home-improvement retailer, Mr. Marcus, as chairman and
> chief executive, and Mr. Blank, president and chief operating
> officer, have trained their salespeople to train the customers in
> home repair and refurbishing.

Since many service industries are highly competitive yet require people with relatively modest skills, they aren't the best-
paying businesses. That causes some service-industry managers
to settle for second-rate employees. But successful managers,
like those of Home Depot, don't fall into that trap.

Home Depot pays its salespeople as much as 25 percent more
than rival home centers. This attracts a strong applicant pool. Given
their founding philosophy, one might expect that Home Depot
would then hire applicants based on their product knowledge.

But the chain found that such people often don't make the best
sales and customer service employees. Instead, Home Depot fo-

cuses on hiring people "for their ability to raise the customer's enthusiasm about a product or project." Then they train them to train the customers. Taking this approach, Home Depot added "*shows me how* to do it myself" to the list of selection criteria in its targeted D-I-Y home-improvement market. In geographic markets like Atlanta, Florida, and California where Home Depot has clustered its stores around big cities, "shows me how to do it myself" has already passed through the unique and pacing stages to become a key attribute in determining competitiveness.

> Featuring customer training, low prices and more than 34,000 items, Home Depot has leapfrogged over its rivals over the last five years and is currently more than twice the size of its nearest competitor, a feat considering that the Atlanta-based retailer is only 13 years old.

When Home Depot enters a new geographic area, customer training becomes a unique attribute, a pacing attribute, and then a key attribute as Home Depot knocks out competitors.

Of course, other factors play a role in Home Depot's success. Warehouse-sized stores clustered in big cities give Home Depot buying clout, operating economies, and marketing economies. But it is interesting to note the depth of Home Depot's commitment to customer training.

This dedication to customer training is epitomized by "Depot Don" how-to displays throughout Home Depot stores. But, as Home Depot's record-setting store in Elmont, Long Island, *clinics,* as many as four a day, are the store's main customer aid.

> Trained staff or supplier representatives teach customers how to install dry wall, put up a fence or plan a new kitchen, among other projects. A year ago, the store hired three interior decorators to assist the customers in color matching and other design considerations. . . . [5]

Special guidance on energy-saving products is among the newest customer-training services being introduced as Home Depot continues to shine in an otherwise troubled industry.

butes. As we'll see in the next chapter, seventy-year-old Gillette, the quality and category leader in male grooming products, derives 35 percent of its sales from products it has introduced in the past five years.

United Van Lines: Quality as "Differentiator" in a Traditional Service

United Van Lines differs from ventures such as AT&T's Universal Card Services and Home Depot in several significant ways:

- While AT&T UCS and Home Depot are relatively new service entities, United Van Lines is an association of moving companies, some of which were founded as long ago as the late 1800s.
- AT&T succeeds partially by centralizing much of its service work in one facility and relying on technology to track and communicate with its customers. United must rely on hundreds of independently owned agent companies around the world to deliver its service.
- In the United system, three or more geographically disparate agents must often be involved in a move: one company writes the order; another picks up the goods; a third provides the transportation; and a fourth may unpack the shipment at destination.
- United's business is highly labor-intensive, with physical strength required for the most essential tasks—packing, loading, hauling, and unloading families' treasured possessions. Normally, one might not associate physical strength with customer focus.

But United Van Lines is not a "normal" company.

Founded in 1947, United has always been owned by its affiliated agents, some of which have passed through two or three generations under the United banner. At the van line's world headquarters outside St. Louis, all 950 employees, including President Bob Baer, are on a first-name basis; a participatory management process involves all supervisory personnel in the annual crafting of a comprehensive business plan to implement the company's activities; and commitment to the organization is such that, during the company's infrequent "lean" years, employees voluntarily took time off without pay to preclude the possibility of layoffs.

For over a decade, United has been implementing the same kinds of quality methods as Milliken, the many businesses of AT&T, and the most successful manufacturing companies. And it seems to be achieving the goal of "dependable excellence for customers" every bit as effectively. United's dramatic increase in market share—from 10 percent in 1970 to more than 20 percent today—reflects its success and makes it a good model for service businesses of all kinds—and for anyone's customer-service operations.

Rising to the Deregulation Challenge—
with Service Excellence

Because of the complexity of long-distance relocation, large moving companies tend to suffer from service inconsistency. Maurice Greenblatt, United's board chairman, is the owner of United affiliate Ware's Van & Storage in Vineland, New Jersey. In a recent speech to United agents he noted that "a customer relocating twice in relatively quick succession with the very same van line can have a great move the first time followed by a major disappointment the next."

To cope with this problem, United has been working hard to achieve what Greenblatt terms "seamless service" throughout its 1,100-agent network.

Prior to 1980, interstate movers functioned under strict government regulations which controlled pricing and operations. When the regulatory framework was removed, one widely anticipated result—a sudden influx of new coast-to-coast movers—failed to materialize. But movers' new-found freedom caused them to plunge into a vicious price war, characterized by one industry observer as "sheer madness." Although marketing techniques have since stabilized to some degree, competition remains intense and margins thin.

When deregulation hit, United president Bob Baer recognized something that most of the other major carriers did not—that the only way to survive and prosper was to win business not by arbitrarily cutting costs but by differentiating United from other movers in nonprice areas. How? Through a "Commitment to Excellence" designed to enable every employee to do his or her job in the most effective manner possible.

Baer's concept, fleshed out by the company's management team, was enthusiastically received by the board of directors, and board and management have since coordinated closely on every step of the quality process. United's Organization Development Department plays a key role in managing the change.

Gerald P. Stadler, a United Van Lines agent, board vice-chairman, and chairman of the board's marketing committee, has strongly advocated the "differentiator" effort since its inception. "As individual agents," he noted early in the process, "our ability to do something about service quality is limited. Leadership must come from the van line, because it sees the big picture and can zero in on problematic areas."

The First Steps

President Baer summarized the concept in a 1986 position paper:

'Excellence' at United is a practical, down-to-earth application of common-sense techniques for distilling the best elements of what we're already doing well . . . and for identifying ways to expand this success formula into a process shared by everyone.

Improvement efforts initially focused on internal operations and on giving customers what *the company* thought they wanted. During the early 1980s, United launched some sixty internal improvement programs under a "Commitment to Excellence" umbrella; many programs remain in place today.

In 1979 United's 15.6 percent market share placed it third among major carriers. In the 1980s it demonstrated its seriousness about quality by even more carefully monitoring the performance of its affiliated agents. Approximately 120 United agents from all regions of the United States own the company, and eighteen shareholder agents make up United's board of directors. These leading representatives themselves recognized that the greatest barrier to improvement was the agent unable to provide consistently good service.

Through the "Commitment to Excellence," agents performing below van line standards either were required to submit "performance improvement plans" or had to forfeit their van line affiliation altogether. United considers agency cancellation a last resort to be pursued only after its headquarters staff have done everything possible to help an agent remedy deficiencies. But it has sometimes been used.

As a result of quality efforts and the inability of some agents to cope in a more competitive market, United's U.S. agency network dropped from 690 representatives in 1982 to 500 in 1992 while, at the same time, United's business volume was growing five times faster than any other major carrier's. Obviously, fewer but higher-quality agents were making this growth possible. By 1989, the van line's market share had risen to 19.2 percent, and it was ranked second in the industry.

But United's board and management still were not satisfied. United had not yet achieved a quality difference significant enough to prompt the general public to turn routinely to United expecting superior service. President Baer remained convinced that future success would require even higher levels of quality performance and consistency.

National surveys by major periodicals indicated United Van Lines enjoyed higher performance ratings than its major competitors. But survey results also revealed a persisting degree of customer dissatisfaction. Thus, United faced both a major problem and a substantial business opportunity—how to find out what was bothering the customer, how to fix the problem, and how to show the customer that United service was truly superior.

A Comprehensive Approach to Service Quality

In 1990, under Baer's leadership, United embarked on the next step—a comprehensive plan based on five elements:

- A *customer service pledge* summarizing United's approach to moving and its commitment to quality service
- *Standards of performance* which specify what is expected in service delivery from every United team member
- *Quality measurements* which quantify how well the organization and its components are living up to the standards of performance
- *Training and development* to enable team members to develop

or enhance skills and knowledge to meet and exceed customer expectations
- *Recognition* to acknowledge the "best of the best" and further increase motivation.

While still evolving, United's quality service process can already be considered a prototype that could be applied to a wide range of hard-to-manage, decentralized services.

United's Customer Service Pledge

In refocusing its quality efforts, United did not begin with a customer value analysis. Its own survey data indicated reasonably high levels of customer satisfaction already existed. Instead, United built its process around a succinctly worded "customer service pledge" which had been formulated in 1988:

> Our goal is to develop and maintain permanent relationships with our customers by providing outstanding service, move after move, with no exceptions. We pledge to find a way to get the job done to the customer's satisfaction, no matter how great the challenge; to stand behind every service commitment; and to employ friendly, skilled, knowledgeable people who, in the event of a problem, will do whatever is necessary to make things right . . . right away. In short, we are dedicated to proving, through our performance, that United is the very best professional mover in the world, in the eyes of our most demanding critics—our customers.

United also prepared a clear "vision" of itself for the coming decade. It targeted ambitious increases in market share predicated largely on the expected marketing differentiation benefits of recognized service-quality superiority.

Standards of Performance

It's easy to make promises and create visions; the difficulty lies in fulfilling them. And service businesses like United Van Lines face special challenges.

In manufacturing, an engineer usually defines in detail how the product should work, and another engineer lays out the manufacturing process. They may neglect key aspects of customer needs, but at least basic standards exist which, if met, ensure reasonably predictable performance.

In service businesses, performance standards traditionally either don't exist or are rudimentary. The moving business was no exception. That's why United believed that setting and achieving service standards would differentiate it from competitors.

But United had experimented with standards of performance in the 1980s. And it had soon discovered that subjective measures were fraught with peril. Agents supported the concept of standards. But they insisted the measures be objective, that they be monitored systematically, and that they involve comparisons against "norms" rather than just against other agents. The agents also wanted to receive regular, specific feedback about their strengths and weaknesses.

In the early 1990s, five attributes of appropriate standards were identified. United determined that the standards should be:

1. Measurable
2. Realistic
3. Customer-focused
4. Flexible to adapt to changing customer expectations
5. Developed in a manner which would lend meaning ("teeth") to the company's customer service pledge.

A series of employee teams at United headquarters had primary responsibility for developing the standards. They sought help from agents across the nation, and both United management and a cross section of agents reviewed the draft standards extensively once they'd been prepared.

United began the process of creating workable, realistic performance standards by identifying clear lines of responsibility and standards of performance. Several agents may be involved in one move, and failure can occur at any of a variety of points, which United termed "moments of truth." Such miscues often result from blurred interpretations of responsibilities and accountability, by both the customer and the participating agents.

A key to United's Quality Service Process is recognition by everyone in the system that a service failure anywhere reflects badly on everyone. If the customer notes in a follow-up survey that he wouldn't be "likely to recommend" United Van Lines to friends, it's a black mark on the booking agent's record, regardless of where the service problem occurred in the service delivery chain.

But recognizing that everyone shares responsibility isn't enough. Roles have to be clearly defined. The company recognized the magnitude of the challenge it faced. An internal document noted: "Clearly defined roles and the related accountability . . . represent a major paradigm shift for the entire system."

United needed standards. If the customer was mad because a shipment showed up two hours late, was it the fault of the agent responsible for the delivery? Or was it the fault of the booking agent for promising more than any moving organization could reasonably be expected to deliver?

The ten basic standards, which were introduced to the United agency family in 1992, cover every fundamental step of the moving process:

1. Responsibilities of the booking agent
2. Effective inter-agent coordination
3. Sales ethics
4. Appearance and competence of service delivery personnel
5. Estimating
6. On-time provision of services
7. Operational safety requirements
8. Claims-handling
9. Household goods packing and transportation liability
10. Utilization of the van line's automated pricing system and timely processing of paperwork

The first link in the chain is the "booking agent"—the United representative who sells the order, registers it with United World Headquarters, and relays pertinent information to all other agents involved. The booking agent may or may not handle all aspects of the actual move. Regardless, at United that agent's responsibility does not end with the signing of the "order for service."

United's first Standard of Performance addresses the issue directly and concisely:

As a United booking agent, you will be expected to accept respon-sibility for determining the customer's expectations; arranging the agreed-upon services; and resolving issues arising between the customer and origin agent, hauling agent, destination agent, or van line.

Measurement

The standards, themselves, make good reading. More complex than drafting them, however, was the task of developing the means to mea-sure compliance. To that end, United, together with an outside re-search company, created a fifteen-page (since reduced to an eight-page), 120-question customer survey. The researchers had expected some customer resistance to filling out such an extensive form, so they were pleasantly surprised by a return rate of over 40 percent without reminder phone calls—nearly three times the anticipated response. The emotion of moving, it seems, makes customers willing to relive the experience by filling out the forms.

United gradually phased in its measurement process. In the summer of 1991, a pilot group of 31 agents volunteered to have the service quality of their shipments monitored, using the survey form; in 1992, agent participation grew to 154; during 1993, 265 agents took part, still on a voluntary basis. In 1994, the measurements program be-comes mandatory for all 500 United agents across the United States.

On the survey, customers rate the carrier's performance on an abso-lute scale of 0 to 10 with respect to each of more than a hundred move-related attributes. They also answer some "yes/no" questions, such as, "Were you given adequate time to complete the inventory check-off at destination?"

The customer returns completed forms to a central information pro-cessing center. There, survey data is assembled into a number of re-ports, which are shared with both the individual agent and the van line. The surveys are so comprehensive that they enable United and its agents to chart the performance of individual service providers—salespeople, packers, van operators, and the like. They thus become an ideal means of pinpointing individuals who may be causing recurring problems, and they also permit the identification of "superstars."

Naturally, such feedback forms cannot measure United's performance relative to the competition. (The van line regularly employs outside survey firms to collect such data.) But that's not the objective of this element of the Quality Service Process. It is more important to indicate to team members whether their performance is really good enough to earn a "premium grade" from customers who, the next time, will choose between again retaining United and calling on another (possibly lower-cost) mover.

United tracks each agent's performance by comparing the agent's scores to the *differentiation score* for each attribute of the move. The differentiation score is the average rating given United on that attribute by those customers who say they "definitely would recommend" United to their friends. In other words, the differentiation score is the satisfaction level required to convince a customer to use United next time.

In addition to giving each agency feedback on its performance in moves in which it was involved, United provides agent-to-agent surveys that measure how agents support one another. Because successful moves depend on smooth coordination among multiple agents, this survey provides highly "actionable" data that tells United and its representatives where they must work toward improvement.

Training and Development

For many years, United Van Lines has maintained what may be the most comprehensive internal training program in the moving industry. Each year, the company publishes a 160-plus-page "Training & Resource Catalogue) which lists hundreds of courses (both internal and external), books, and audio and video tapes. All these are readily available to the agent, some at no charge.

But in implementing the Quality Service Process, United recognized that a new level of training and development would be necessary. How could an agent be sure of, in the terminology of United's Standards of Performance, providing "professional, knowledgeable, ethical, and courteous customer sales representatives?" How could the agent be certain he or she is using "van line–recognized techniques, materials, and equipment?" Existing training programs didn't provide adequate guidance. But consistent, van-line-administered training obviously was the key.

United focused first on its front-line service delivery personnel, who help pack and load shipments. The objective: to create a pool of "certified" labor in an area of the moving industry traditionally more prone than most to service inconsistency. (By contrast, the van operator, who serves as the "crew chief" for the move, generally receives higher customer satisfaction marks. Thus, van operator training received a lower priority.)

What should the "quality labor" training teach? One effective means of preparing the curriculum was to identify van operators with the highest customer satisfaction scores and benchmark the practices they required of their crews to see what set them apart. By studying twenty-five exceptional van operators United learned, for example, that top performers would wrap furniture in pads while still in the customer's home, rather than taking the item outside before wrapping it. Exceptional van operators also stressed the importance of a detailed, accurate inventory as a positive communications link between mover and customer. Claims often occur when the customer becomes aware, after the move, of a furniture condition which may have gone unnoticed for years in the previous home. A chair which has been in the same spot for twenty years may have been faded on one side by sunlight; by making the customer aware of this as the shipment is loaded, the mover can head off problems at delivery.

What is the "front" of a round table? The question sounds bizarre, particularly if there is no drawer or other obvious indication. But United found that misunderstandings often arose when movers made imprecise references to the location of preexisting damage on round tables. The solution? Consider the "front" to be the point at which an inventory sticker is applied on the underside of the table. These and other "good ideas" to impart to packers and helpers were accumulated in part through an exhaustive, three-hundred-page questionnaire completed by seventy United agents, taking the packing and loading process step-by-step from beginning to end.

United adopted a four-step approach to its quality training for packers and movers.

- A three-day "Train-The-Trainer Certification Workshop," facilitated by United headquarters personnel, prepares agency employees to become "certified agency trainers" who can administer training within their own organizations to front-line service personnel.

- Once an agency acquires a "certified" trainer, the next phase is to identify and train "coaches" (lead people or senior packers and helpers). The coaches are responsible in the field for reinforcing classroom training, coaching labor trainees on performance improvement, and determining when trainees have achieved certain proficiency levels.
- Packer and helper classroom training, conducted by the certified agency trainer, imparts specific instructions in such areas as packing materials; labeling; the handling of fragile items; and safe lifting and carrying techniques.
- After the fifty hours of classroom instruction, trainees develop further proficiency during actual household goods moves under the direct supervision of a coach. Final certification is awarded after the trainee's successful completion of classroom training, 400 hours of on-the-job field experience, demonstrated proficiency in 160 separate skills, and final review.

United plans to soon unveil a similar certification program for agency sales representatives. Ultimately the training will come full circle, with van operators undergoing advanced certification instruction enabling them to be more effective "crew chiefs" in the field.

"When I look back at how we used to teach people, it's really kind of scary," says Joe Conley, owner of Cook Moving System in Buffalo, New York, and three other United agencies. "You'd take a new man out in the warehouse, and you'd show them what kind of boxes there are, and you'd show them how to pack dishes, but almost everything was learned on-the-job. The result of that was they were being taught different ways by different drivers. And when you're dealing with shipments going all over the country, you're building in differences. Now it's to the point where when you mark a carton, everyone in the whole country is marking the same corner in the same way."

Recognition

United regards "recognition" as an important motivational tool, especially in the quality service area. For many years United has selected "Agents of the Month" and "Van Operators of the Month" on the basis of performance. Their honors are publicized both within the organization and externally via regional and national news media. To provide added impetus to its quality service process, in 1992 United unveiled the first in a series of special awards conferred at the carrier's annual convention.

- "Customer Choice Awards" are conferred upon a certain top percentage of agents, based on performance data tabulated from customer surveys and focusing on the areas of sales, packing, van operator performance, shipment loading, and shipment delivery.
- As the process evolves, "Agent Choice Awards" will be presented to a top percentage of agents, based on the surveys in which agents evaluate services provided by their fellow agents.
- When the process is fully in place, a single "Quality Agent of the Year" will be selected from the top performers in the other two award categories. This agent will be recognized as United's "super quality mover."

Dependably Satisfying Customers with Superior Service

The extraordinary growth of AT&T's Universal Card Services and its receipt of the Baldrige award are well-known. United Van Lines' success is equally impressive. One testimony to the effectiveness of its approach is that United is a leader in signing contracts with major corporations that give the van line the opportunity to earn better compensation for exceptional performance—performance which United expects to make the "norm" in coming years.

At an early-1993 meeting of agency sales representatives, United president Baer, architect of the firm's quality service process, summarized the company's total commitment to differentiating its services from those of any other mover:

For ten years, through our excellence initiatives, we have been working hard to find ways of doing our jobs better in recognition of a rapidly changing operating environment. Through our quality process, we've been zeroing in on customer expectations and develop-

THE BODY SHOP: PRICE PREMIUMS
IN A RETAIL BUSINESS

The Body Shop, a United Kingdom-based cosmetics and toiletries chain, has proven that a great business can be created—yielding price premiums—even in retailing and even during a recession. By fully understanding the quality attributes that would attract young women to a cosmetic business, it has grown at an enormous rate.

The Body Shop emphasizes that it is run by a woman managing director, Anita Roddick. It preserves the earth and appeals to environmentally conscious young women by refilling empty containers at the store. It is kind to animals, using labels that claim "Against animal testing."

The Body Shop always positions its products as a "treat" rather than as a commodity. Because it understands its customers and listens to them, the chain is positioned as a lovable do-gooder that provides differentiated products, battling with less-lovable giants like Procter & Gamble and Unilever. The Body Shop delights its customers and relies heavily on word of mouth to promote its products and stores.

ing monitoring/support systems to help us all improve, regardless of what role we play. Quality, without question, is a requirement for business survival and success in the 1990s. And at United, we view it as something more . . . as the means to making "United" the household name in moving, not just in the U.S. but worldwide, as well.

United, like AT&T, has a clear, simple methodology for providing quality—and value—to its customers.

PART THREE

Managing Some Big Issues with Customer Value Management

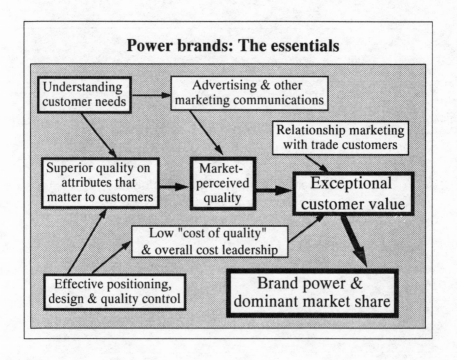

CHAPTER 7

Creating Power Brands

Nothing produces more wealth more quickly than the creation of a power brand—a name people respond to in their shopping decisions like "Tide," "Tylenol," "Nintendo," or "Gillette Sensor." A few letters like C-o-c-a C-o-l-a can coin money for generations.

Companies like Gillette, Procter & Gamble, Mars, and AT&T realize that what makes a brand name worth billions of dollars is essentially simple:

A power brand is a name that means satisfaction, quality, and value to the customer.

If customers associate your brand name with satisfaction, quality, and value, you'll win customer loyalty, price premiums, repeat purchases, word-of-mouth advertising, and a continuous stream of high profits. If your brand name loses that association, even if it's as emotionally powerful as "Jaguar" or "Pan American World Airways," it will become essentially valueless.

In the last few years, even such brands as IBM, Sears, General Motors, and American Express have slipped badly—and not necessarily because their products were getting worse. In most cases they were improving—just not as fast as their competitors Intel, Microsoft, Wal-Mart, Toyota, and AT&T Universal Card were.

The purpose of this chapter is to show how to practice customer

153

value management and produce the market-perceived quality you need in the very big job of creating and managing a power brand. Marketers have long known that both creating and sustaining brand power were important. Yet even the best brand marketers have only in the past few years focused on how to benefit fully from the power brands that they have created. You have to manage *both* the quality of the product itself *and* the system that helps customers to perceive that quality:

- Procter & Gamble has finally begun to change the marketing mix for fast-moving consumer package goods away from its decades-long trend of emphasis on promotions that make the customer more price sensitive and discourage loyalty. It is now leading the way toward a pricing, advertising, and promotion mix that builds brand loyalty and equity for the marketer and results in lower-cost logistics systems for its distribution chain.
- Gillette has shifted its product development and marketing communications away from the economy end of the shaving business back toward the premium end with the introduction of its Gillette Sensor razor and its Gillette Series men's grooming products.

In this chapter we'll look at how the best brand marketing executives are coming to understand not only the creation of power brands, but also how to nourish them and keep them from slipping down the fair-value curve toward the generic, house brand, unbranded, economy end of the spectrum. They are beginning to understand the research—much of it previously unpublished—that supports their new way of doing business. Careful studies over the past twenty-five years have confirmed that the brands that achieve superior profitability are those that convince customers they stand for superior products.

As we showed in Chapter 1, studies based on the overall Profit Impact of Market Strategy (PIMS) database demonstrate that profit margins correlate closely with perceived quality.[1] In this chapter we focus only on the brands and businesses in the PIMS consumer database, which contains data on over eight hundred consumer products.[2]

Brands with superior quality (market-perceived quality ratio greater than 1.24) earn net margins nearly four times as high as those earned by brands perceived to be inferior (ratio less than 0.76). We show this data in Exhibit 7–1. (See the description of PIMS database in Chapter 3.)

In this chapter we'll try to describe the mechanism that produces a power brand. Any knowledgeable executive who has either (1) created a high-quality product, or (2) identified an unmet customer need can achieve a dominant competitive position and thus extraordinary profits.

The Wrong Way to Understand Brands

Before we look at the right way to build a brand, we need to understand what's wrong with old ways of thinking. In recent years many marketers have treated a brand as something other than a way of tapping into the power of market-perceived quality—as a guarantee of sales or cash flow, for instance. When people do that, all the benefits of a brand can quickly prove illusory.

Even so quality-conscious a company as Ford Motor fell into this old way of thinking in its multibillion dollar purchase of Jaguar. Neither Ford nor Jaguar had the resources to keep Jaguar competitive in quality with Japanese brands like Toyota's Lexus and Nissan's

EXHIBIT 7–1

Market-perceived quality boosts margins

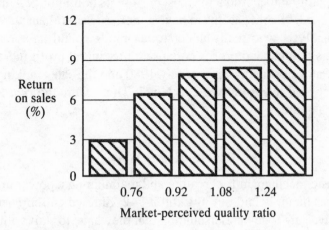

Information: PIMS database (consumer products).

Infiniti, which Ford knew were going to be launched shortly after Ford's purchase. The result: Jaguar ceased to mean top quality to luxury car purchasers within a year or two.

The market value of a storied name doesn't just disappear when it ceases to provide superior value to customers for a few years, and if Ford ever does succeed in producing superior cars under the Jaguar name again, the market's memory of the Jaguar will make them easier to sell and perhaps increase the price premium they command. But the brand has to mean quality, or it is valueless. As we write this, Ford is losing $400 million a year on Jaguar.

Management "experts" have actually encouraged brand mismanagement. Despite dozens of examples of brands that have ultimately lost all market value when they ceased to stand for quality, pundits have in the past been enamored with the short-term benefits of "milking" a brand. They've failed to point out the foolishness of undermining what the brand essentially is.

In the classic Schlitz Brewing Co. case, for example, managers in the 1970s launched a cost-cutting campaign that reduced the quality of its beer. They substituted corn syrup and hop pellets for traditional ingredients and shortened the brewing cycle by 50 percent. They bragged to analysts about their shortcuts.

When Schlitz achieved higher returns than Anheuser-Busch, the brewer of higher-cost Budweiser, in 1973, *Forbes* congratulated Schlitz managers and implicitly criticized Anheuser's: "Does it pay to build quality into a product if most customers don't notice?" the magazine asked. "Schlitz seems to have a more successful answer."[3]

As analysts who really understood brands would have expected, Schlitz's volume and profits collapsed after initial profit increases in 1973. Sales declined 40 percent by 1980 and the sales ranking of the Schlitz brand fell from No. 2 to No. 7. Those were the *real* fruits of ignoring quality.

The Right Way

The basic mechanism for creating and maintaining a power brand, on the other hand, is laid out in Exhibit 7–2. Shrewd entrepreneurs and executives are today understanding that they have to start with a clear

EXHIBIT 7–2

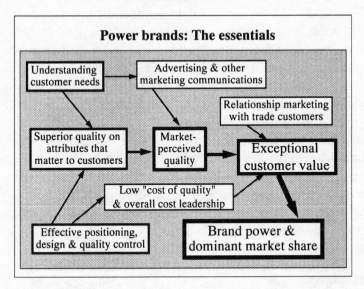

Power brands: The essentials

Understanding customer needs

Advertising & other marketing communications

Relationship marketing with trade customers

Superior quality on attributes that matter to customers

Market-perceived quality

Exceptional customer value

Low "cost of quality" & overall cost leadership

Effective positioning, design & quality control

Brand power & dominant market share

sense of the desires of a well-defined group of customers. They then must design and produce products, and supply the associated services, that meet those needs exceptionally well.

Effective quality-control measures must ensure that these competitors "do things right the first time" in delivering those products and services.

The proper goal is to achieve superior quality in areas that will matter most to the customer together with costs no higher—perhaps even lower—than those of lower-quality competitors. Though this is difficult, the PIMS database shows that most leading brands achieve it.

When Ford Motor Co. has built a program around principles like these—as it did in the creation of the Ford Taurus and the Ford Explorer—it has achieved enormous success. When it hasn't followed these principles, it has experienced the kind of disaster it is now seeing with Jaguar.

Other companies are now making the steps shown in Exhibit 7–2 top priorities. When Alfred Zeien became chairman of Gillette in

1991, one of his first moves was to delay the introduction of the new Gillette Series line of men's toiletries until product designers could demonstrate clear superiority to the competition in customer tests. They succeeded. For example, after R&D tinkered further with the formula for the new Gillette Series shaving gel, it beat S.C. Johnson's Edge, the previous market leader, on forty-five of forty-seven product attributes, including lather thickness and quality, beard preparation, shaving closeness, and smoothness.

Creating a product shown to be superior in controlled tests isn't enough, however. As we showed in Chapter 5, it can be difficult to convey products' real, important advantages through advertising and other marketing communications. But it is only when the customer *perceives* the quality and the exceptional value that dominant market share is achieved and a power brand is created.

Historically, companies have usually performed this effort in one or two markets first. Recently, however, companies are learning to develop products such as Toyota's Lexus and Gillette's shaving goods by evaluating customer desires in a dozen or more markets from the start. The achievement of superior market-perceived quality in one market almost always means that the product has characteristics that could lead to superior market-perceived quality in other markets. But companies need separate market-perceived quality analyses for at least the top half-dozen markets. They will usually reveal that the brand has strengths promotable in all those markets, possibly with a single global advertising campaign. (Dove soap uses the slogan, "One-quarter cleansing cream" in American, Australian, French, German, and Italian campaigns.[4] At the same time, however, market-perceived quality analyses in different countries will also reveal special needs in some markets. (German speed limits exceed those of the United States and Japan, so car makers must design "global" vehicles to achieve *Autobahn* speeds.)

The profit potential of a global power brand is awesome. And the developers of all the successful brands discussed so far in this book, such as AT&T Universal Card Services, Milliken carpet tile, and Perdue chicken, have followed the basic pattern described above.

The mechanism seems simple. But how many businesses are able to navigate these steps? More important, how many are really trying?

Choosing Where You Will Dominate

Perhaps the single most important step in creating a power brand (or strengthening an existing brand) is developing *quality of positioning*. That means choosing just what part of customers' lives you intend to dominate.

Some marketers fail to understand the importance of this step. Indeed, frequently "analysts" argue that a particular market is becoming homogeneous and that every competitor must become like every other. Remember all the talk about the development of "financial supermarkets" a few years ago? Supposedly, all financial services organizations would have to offer all kinds of financial services. But how many companies that tried to become "financial supermarkets" actually made money?

Similarly, in the mid-1980s every large computer or communications organization was told that the fields of computers and communications were merging. That was true. But the conclusion drawn was that every company would have to offer both computers and communications. A great battle for dominance was predicted among IBM, AT&T, and NEC. Companies like Xerox, Digital Equipment, and Unisys pondered how they would enter the war.

Marketing expert Larry Light, who was then president of the Ted Bates International advertising agency, saved Xerox a pile of money by warning executives not to fight on that battlefield. "In the battle for the computers and communications market, where is Xerox?" he asked. "Number 4? Number 5? That's not a very good market position."

Instead, Light urged Xerox to position itself where it could be Number 1: in the creation and processing of documents. So Xerox began to think of itself as "The Document Company." From desktop copiers to large systems that turn a floppy disk into a bound book, Xerox made itself the leader. By building on that leadership, Xerox navigated a period of vicious change in the information industry, ending with a stronger-than-ever brand.

The same principle can apply to smaller markets and smaller companies: Decide where you can be Number 1, then do everything necessary to achieve that positioning. Mars, the candy company, has strengthened the Snickers brand by deciding it would be the preeminent "source of quick energy" for adults. Snickers' advertising appeals to adults and shows off the peanuts in the bar as a subtle reminder that there is nutrition in the candy as well as good taste.

Even tiny companies often succeed by defining a niche and becoming share leaders there. In a town near my home, for example, an entrepreneur has established a company that sells uniforms to police, firemen, and emergency medical personnel. He knew that every member of the uniformed services in the surrounding towns receives an allowance of several hundred dollars each year to purchase uniforms.

He carefully analyzed what these uniformed personnel wanted, then consistently provided it. The result: He dominates uniform sales in his area.

Communicate the Quality You've Produced

Just because you've achieved high quality doesn't mean the world will beat a path to your door. In fact, many companies produce high-quality products, yet never adequately tell customers about them. Studies on the PIMS database demonstrate that advertising is essential to make people perceive what you've accomplished.

The PIMS database contains information on market-perceived quality, profitability, advertising, and promotional spending. Moreover, it contains data on how much individual companies spend on advertising and promotion *relative to their competitors.*

We've used this data to study the effects of advertising. We've shown that advertising usually improves relative-perceived quality and, by doing so, increases profitability. In fact, we've shown brands that spend a much larger than average share of their sales on advertising earn an average return on investment of 32 percent while brands that advertise much less than their competitors average only 17 percent. That's an enormous gap.

We've demonstrated a strong positive correlation between spending a larger portion of the sales dollar than competitors on advertising and achieving high perceived quality (Exhibit 7–3). Improvements in perceived quality in turn lead to high market share (Exhibit 7–4). And both superior perceived quality *and* heftier advertising budgets each seem independently to help brands achieve price premiums (Exhibit 7–5).

EXHIBIT 7–3

Superior quality and heftier advertising go together

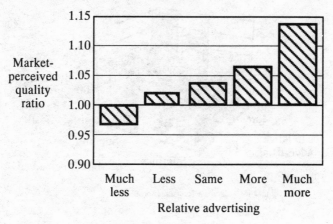

Information: PIMS database (consumer products).

EXHIBIT 7–4

Improving quality boosts market share

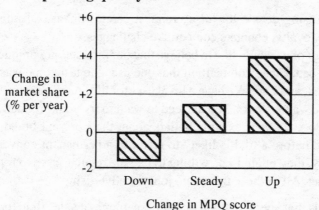

Information: PIMS database (consumer products).

EXHIBIT 7–5

Superior quality and heftier advertising
yield price premiums

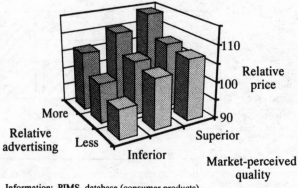

Information: PIMS database (consumer products).

The result: Companies that spend a larger share of their incomes on advertising tend to earn much more than companies that spend less.

Both personal experience and data like these have recently caused some of America's leading businesspeople to renew their commitments to advertising. For example, Edwin Artzt, chief executive of Procter & Gamble, has become a tireless campaigner for aggressive advertising both inside his company and in the business world as a whole. Artzt declares eloquently:

> Advertising does a lot for a brand. it creates image, informs, cements loyalty, counters competitive challenges. . . .
>
> Most of us would like to believe that our products are unique—so much better than competition that one use, one taste, one washing, one box, and Zap! We have a loyal user for life. As you know, that's not the way it works. People need to want to try your product. They need to have their existing beliefs about their present brand challenged before a trial is likely to result in a permanent conversion. Ideally, they ought to be willing to pay the regular price to try your product. All of those things are jobs for advertising.[5]

Brands that spend a much larger percentage of sales than their competitors on advertising have market-perceived quality ratios 17 percent greater than brands that spend a much smaller percentage of their sales dollar on advertising.

Admittedly, it's often difficult to judge just *how much* of the correlation between advertising and perceived quality is due to advertising itself. To some extent, companies with better products simply have more to say in advertising. So they're more likely to spend money saying it.

But we can measure the impact of advertising more directly by looking at how advertising affects market share over time—after controlling for other factors that could be causing changes in share. And when we did that, we found strong evidence that companies with high-quality products can increase profitability by increasing ad spending.

In one study, we looked at 314 fast-moving consumer goods businesses over a four-year period. We examined how changes in market share correlated with changes in spending on media advertising, changes in spending on sales promotions, changes in spending on the company sales force, new product introductions, relative quality improvements, the growth of the served market, and other factors.[6]

We found that increases in advertising expenditures were closely correlated with gains in market share *even after adjusting for the effects of all other factors.*

. . . And Don't Let Promotions Cheapen Your Product

Executives like Artzt find they must struggle constantly to put advertising findings like those of the PIMS database into practice. For many managers, even in companies with a long tradition of aggressive advertising like Procter & Gamble's, heavy advertising spending is just not "natural."

Consider how most managers mix advertising with promotions such as cents-off coupons. Price promotions produce quick short-term results. A manager can see the benefit immediately. Promotions also please most wholesalers and retailers. (Although they don't please Wal-Mart, which likes to offer everyday low prices and has finally acquired enough clout in the marketplace to convince some suppliers to change their marketing mix.)

In the United States from 1981 to 1991, the percentage of packaged goods manufacturers' advertising and promotion budgets spent on advertising fell from about 44 percent to 26 percent. Promotions like cents-off coupons and special discounts to distributors rose to make up the difference.[7]

The PIMS database shows that the long-run result of that trend, unless executives like Artzt are able to reverse it, is likely to be declines in both perceived quality and profitability. While research on the PIMS database documents a strong positive correlation among advertising, perceived quality, and profitability, increased use of cents-off coupons, special price breaks, and other sales promotion shows no statistically significant correlation with market share changes at all.

Exhibit 7–6 shows how companies with differing market positions tend to divide their advertising and promotional spending: Market leaders are the companies that emphasize advertising.

In another study, we divided the fast-moving consumer goods businesses in the PIMS database into three groups:

- Those that spent a significantly larger than average percentage of their marketing budget on promotions (average promotional spending for this group was 77 percent of the marketing budget)

EXHIBIT 7–6

Market leaders spend to build the franchise

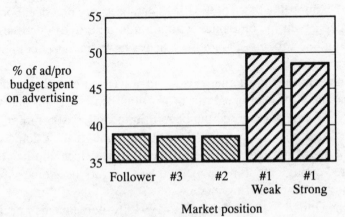

Information: PIMS database (consumer non-durable products).

- Those that split their budgets more or less evenly between advertising and promotions
- Those that spent the bulk of their budgets (an average of 66 percent) on advertising

We found companies that emphasized promotion were far less profitable than those that emphasized advertising. The average return on investment for the promotionally oriented businesses was 18.1 percent. The average for the mixed businesses was 27.3 percent. And the average for the advertising-oriented businesses was 30.5 percent (Exhibit 7–7).[8]

To cash in once you've properly positioned your product in the marketplace, you must emphasize advertising. Why spend millions of dollars to create a product that justifies a premium price, and then give the benefits away through promotions?

Promotions ensure that most of your units are sold not at the premium price you deserve, but at a discounted promotional price. Big, periodic promotions train customers to avoid buying your brands at your "regular" price and stock up at discounted prices. Thus, promotions not only reduce your net revenues, they also disrupt your distri-

EXHIBIT 7–7

Profitability, market rank, and the advertising/promotion mix

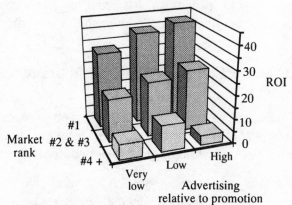

Information: PIMS database (consumer non-durable products).

bution system by causing irrational surges and slack periods. That increases shipping and storage costs.

Yet for many years even Procter & Gamble tended to emphasize promotion. Procter & Gamble started to learn how wasteful this was as top executives worked with Wal-Mart, a customer whose emphasis on consistently low prices discourages promotional discounting. Wal-Mart executives pointed out P&G had designed superior brands but put unsustainably high price premiums on them. Wal-Mart buyers had to concentrate buying when promotional prices were offered. This wasted both Wal-Mart's and P&G's resources.[9] Under the banner of "relationship marketing," P&G has worked closely with 190 of its largest 300 customers to reduce inventory and costs over the past several years.

Procter & Gamble cut back sharply on promotions and put part of the savings into lower regular prices—prices that included more realistic premiums over inferior competitors, and could be kept more stable. Much of the rest of the savings went into increased advertising.

But achieving high market-perceived quality through heavy, intelligent use of advertising is a constant struggle. Artzt says:

> Belief in advertising is not like breathing. It doesn't come naturally.
> It must be taught. It must be nurtured, and above all, it must be disciplined. Top management must chart the course and see that it is followed."[10]

Procter & Gamble is developing a program that every would-be market leader should learn from. It's requiring every manager, no matter what his or her job, to take an internship in advertising.

Market Share, Perceived Quality, and Brand Success

To complete the picture of how power brands are born and how they should be managed, we need to think about how to manage market share and about the role that market-share thinking should play in management decision making. This is important for two reasons:

- On one hand, merely achieving high market share—even if you don't do it by producing and marketing a superior-quality

product—can have enormous benefits, especially in industries that devote unusually large shares of their revenues to R&D and marketing, such as computer software and cosmetics.
- On the other hand, a misreading of some of the early results from what became the PIMS database has encouraged some businesspeople to overemphasize market share—adopting "market share at any cost" as a goal, and sometimes ruining companies in the process.

When we began careful analysis of corporate strategies in the late 1960s and early 1970s, our initial conclusions emphasized the importance of market share over quality. That was because the methods that we used to measure quality at the time were not as accurate as the metrics that we developed as the PIMS program evolved. It wasn't until the late 1970s, when we developed a methodology for tracking customer-perceived quality, that the paramount importance of quality for profitability became clear.

Today, managers of branded products still need to understand that market share can drive profitability. Dominant market share is often vital to make the essential steps to building a power brand work, as described in the previous sections. High market-share businesses— even those with merely average perceived quality—tend to enjoy economies of scale, to achieve better turnover of inventory and receivables, and can perform more research and development than low-share businesses. Moreover, many customers prefer to do business with them because customers perceive less risk in purchasing from them.

Indeed, even with today's improved methods of measuring market-perceived quality, the statistical correlation between profitability and market share is slightly stronger at any single point in time than the correlation between profitability and market-perceived quality.

But this data is only a kind of "snapshot." Market-perceived quality is a more important measure of competitiveness and thus of long-term profit potential than market share for two key reasons:

- First, most market leaders had to develop quality leadership first to achieve their large share position. Superior quality is the base upon which market leadership is usually built.

- Second, over all the time periods for which we have data, businesses that begin with a large share of the market tend to lose share. By contrast, those that begin with superior market-perceived quality tend to hold or gain share.

Thus, market share is often a lagging indicator of a company's performance. Quality is both a leading indicator and the ultimate key to success.

Sometimes you can create a power brand with quality that is merely average. You can create a product to serve a market that hadn't been served before, for example, and protect your product with patents. Or if you are a pioneer in a rapidly growing market, aggressive advertising and marketing may help you win a dominant position like the position Lotus 1-2-3 won in the computer spreadsheet market.

Moreover, in industries that devote unusually large shares of their revenues to R&D and marketing, even a high-quality producer must be especially careful to avoid winding up in a poor market-share position. A high-quality cosmetics company, for instance, will have difficulty giving its product the advertising support it needs if some other firm has much higher market share.

The PIMS database shows the enormous benefits of market share in R&D and marketing-oriented businesses. In manufacturing businesses, the difference in return on investment between Number 1 businesses and businesses ranked Number 5 or worse is 12 points. But in R&D and marketing-intensive businesses, the difference between Number 1 businesses and Number 5 or worse businesses is an incredible 26 points.

No. 1 businesses in such fields earn returns on investment of 36 percent, Number 2 businesses earn 23 percent, Number 3 businesses earn 17 percent, Number 4 businesses earn 16 percent, and Number 5 or worse businesses earn only 10 percent. Thus, market-share-oriented strategies—such as heavy advertising to gain an early lead in a rapidly expanding niche—are particularly important in R&D and marketing-intensive industries.

But never forget that quality is king—that you succeed in the marketplace because your name is synonymous with excellence to people in your served market. If you forget this, your strategy will ultimately fail.

The most effective way to gain market share is simply to provide a product your customers like better than the competition's. Exhibit 7–8 shows how dominant businesses tend to have superior market-perceived quality scores while follower businesses tend to have inferior scores.

Many market-share-oriented strategies that fail to emphasize quality are doomed to disaster. When Frank Lorenzo patched together America's largest airline from mergers that combined Texas Air, Continental, People Express, and Eastern, the result was an unwieldy monster. It did achieve some economies of scale, as connections among the parts of the system were arranged to make it easy for people to board Texas Air-affiliated carriers and take them to any other part of the United States. But the patchwork of organizational cultures couldn't deliver the excellence that quality-oriented, culturally consistent airlines like American and Delta had achieved. Texas Air's perceived quality score relative to its competitors, had it bothered to calculate it, would have been terrible. Eventually, the entire company fell apart.

EXHIBIT 7–8

**Market leadership is based on
superior market-perceived quality**

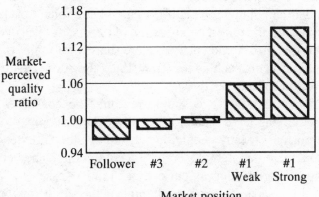

Information: PIMS database (consumer products).

Wielding Brand Power Wisely

Even true power brands can't raise their relative prices forever *unless at the same time they continually increase their relative-perceived quality*. Quality leaders who raise their prices without also increasing relative-perceived quality will eventually give up market share. We see this happening in the supermarket, where dominant brands raised relative prices dramatically in the 1980s while doing little to improve relative perceived quality: In the 1990s, the shares of the top three brands in disposable diapers, salad dressings, baking mixes, household cleaners, popcorn, barbecue sauces, dishwashing detergent, and canned cat food all show significant declines.[11]

On the other hand, even a quality leader can increase its profitability further by further increasing its lead in market-perceived quality. The reinvigoration of Gillette—one of the world's most important brands—shows what can happen when a company understands what a brand is.

Since the nineteenth century, Gillette had succeeded because its name was synonymous with quality. Sponsoring the World Series in the 1950s, the company proudly proclaimed Gillette was the "Only Way to Get a Decent Shave."

In some Third World languages, the word "Gillette" *is* the word for razor.

But in the early 1970s, Gillette's strength was sapped by diversification into fields where it couldn't be the quality leader. And competitors attacked its heart: Disposable razors offered a "decent shave" and were sold at less than $2 per half-dozen. Gillette fought back with its own disposable and took a good portion of the disposables market, but the disposable razor trend cut even more sharply into sales of $3-and-up shaving systems such as the Trac II and the Atra. This threw the market for blades into decline.

Profit margins slid. The simple reason: The consumer was no longer perceiving large quality differences among competitors in the shaving business. Many people, inside and outside Gillette, believed that razors were inevitably becoming a commodity. They concluded the company should sharply cut overhead in its "cash cow" shaving business. Four separate takeover attempts in the 1980s sought to force the company to do exactly that.

But the critics didn't understand the real problem. It was that Gillette had lost sight of what its franchise was.

It was natural that Gillette's margins would decline when it failed to make clear that it had products of superior quality and failed to develop new ones. The battle in marketing disposables—a significant innovation that inevitably would cost Gillette some profits—had caused the company to lose sight of the quality advantages it still possessed. The Trac II and Atra shavers still gave many men a better shave than any disposables. But the noise of promotion of Gillette's "Good News" disposables obscured that fact.

Recently the company has begun to practice superior brand stewardship. As early as 1979 it had begun development of the new Sensor razor—a process that would take more than a decade. Next, starting in Europe, it refocused its marketing. Leaving its disposables to sell themselves, it began putting all its marketing money into shaving systems that used replaceable cartridges.

In November of 1992, Robert J. Murray, executive vice president of Gillette's North Atlantic Group, gave a seminar at Boston College where he described how this new focus on superior quality positioning reversed the trend of the wet shaving market away from its slide toward the economy end.

> The revitalization of the Gillette brand began in 1988, when we embarked on a new mission with the clear objective of establishing Gillette as "the premier male grooming authority.'. . .
>
> We set out to accelerate the growth of value in the blade market, by encouraging consumers to trade up from disposables to better-performing shaving systems.
>
> Toward this end, we implemented a total international business program that reoriented blade and razor displays at retail, modernized the Gillette brand logotype, and developed a powerful image-building advertising campaign—"The Best a Man Can Get," that emphasized the *emotion* surrounding the shaving experience.
>
> And we significantly increased advertising expenditures to give the Gillette brand a greater share of voice and presence with consumers.
>
> In Phase Two, we cultivated this momentum into a reaffirmation of Gillette's technological leadership by bringing Gillette Sensor to market, revolutionizing the way men shave forever.

As a result, the razor-and-blade business again began to deliver excellent profits.

When Gillette introduced the Sensor in 1990, men demonstrated emphatically that the availability of a "decent shave" at a lower price didn't keep them from spending money for superior relative-perceived quality. The Sensor's blades float on tiny springs to conform better to the contours of the shaver's face. Protected by seventeen patents, the manufacture of the Sensor blade cartridge demands a machine that can make ninety-three precise laser welds per second. Initial sales exceeded company projections by 30 percent and might have been even higher if the company had been able to meet the demand.[12]

The company abandoned businesses where it couldn't become the leader in relative-perceived quality. But in other businesses, it proved the significance of its clear understanding of the meaning of brand stewardship. It scored successes with its Braun small appliances, Oral-B toothbrushes, and PaperMate Flexgrip pens that were smaller but essentially similar to its success with the Sensor. It made each product the perceived-quality leader in its niche.

As we write this, Gillette has just rolled out the Gillette Series—fourteen men's toiletry items from shaving gel to deodorant. Each has been demonstrated in user tests to be superior in perceived quality and will be sold at a premium price. Thinking globally, Gillette has merged its North American and Western Europe regions into one huge North Atlantic Group because it recognized that the nature of all the markets in the North Atlantic was becoming increasing similar. Gillette Series toiletries were receiving $125 million in advertising and promotion in their first year.

The Gillette Series may not succeed. It must battle against companies like S. C. Johnson, maker of the shaving gel Edge, and Procter & Gamble. Competitors in men's toiletries are quite capable of introducing their own new formulas, and they may understand the advertising and promotion of toiletries better than Gillette. Thus, they may achieve market-perceived quality even better than Gillette's.

But the success of Gillette's essential approach to managing its brand is already clear. Sensor received many awards and accolades around the world. It was named product of the year by both *Business Week* and *Fortune* magazines in 1992. In 1993 the women's version,

EXHIBIT 7–9
Gillette's Sensor and Sensor for Women Increase Gillette's Quality Lead and Capture a Larger Market Share

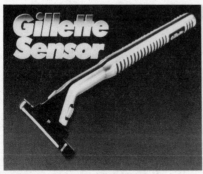 

Photographs courtesy of The Gillette Company.

Lady Sensor, was listed in *Business Week* as the best design for that year (Exhibit 7–9).

Today Gillette sales and profits are at record levels, return on equity is a whopping 40 percent, and some analysts are forecasting 20-percent-a-year profit increases. Those are remarkable achievements for a big company whose businesses are all more or less mature and easily dismissed as "commodities."

Marketers can create brand power and superior returns in almost any industry—if they focus on becoming market-perceived quality and customer value leaders.

Contrasting two tools

Tool: Price-performance
curve

Tool: Customer-value
map

Focus: Technology strategy

Focus: Marketing strategy

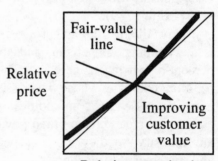

Price

Price-performance
curve

Advancing
technology

Performance

Relative
price

Fair-value
line

Improving
customer
value

Relative perceived
quality

CHAPTER 8

Assessing Competing Technologies and Nurturing a Long-Term Winner

How did Michelin, a French tire company, become Number 1 in the world even though Japanese, U.S., and German companies—not French companies—dominate the world automobile market? Why did endoscopic surgery replace traditional open surgery for gallbladder removal so quickly? Where are similar techniques likely to create big opportunities in the future? Why did chains like McDonalds so thoroughly displace Howard Johnson's in the restaurant business? How did Sonoco Products replace paper bags with plastic in grocery stores?

Most important, how can you manage your technologies and your technological positioning so that you will provide better customer value in the future than any competitor? When you learn to do that, you'll have made a major step toward the practice of true customer value management.

Customer value analysis provides a key to all these questions. Any organization's *future* success depends not only on using a technique like customer value analysis to diagnose its *current* position against the competition, but also on using the same methods to assess competing technologies, analyze how customers will perceive new products, and manage the discovery and introduction of technologies for the future. Indeed, in the fast cycle-time markets of the 1990s, you can't rely solely on historical data to assess how customers will perceive your products next month, let alone next year.

175

This chapter focuses on assessing and developing competing technologies and introducing the right ones at the right times. We'll show how to anticipate and control the positioning of your new products and how customers will perceive them.

If you apply the tools of customer value analysis to these issues better than your competitors, you'll become a *market-driving company*—which is even better and more profitable than being a market-driven company.

Becoming #1 in the Tire Business—Globally

Twenty-five years ago, if you could have envisioned the emerging global tire market as it exists today, you might have predicted that a U.S., German, or Japanese company would become Number 1 in the world. Instead, a French tire company—Michelin—has risen to the top. How did Michelin grow and prosper while Uniroyal's tire business withered and Firestone disappeared as an independent company? The answer is that Michelin's commitment to radial tires wasn't luck. It was based on a sophisticated understanding of customer value.[1]

Just twenty-five years ago almost all companies designed and produced tires using "bias technology." In all kinds of tires, rayon, nylon, polyester, or steel cords provide strength. In bias tires, each layer of cords runs diagonally (i.e., "on the bias") across the fabric belts that make up the tire's body. The diagonal in each layer runs in the opposite direction from the diagonal in the previous layer. In the United States—the leading market for automobiles and therefore tires—Goodyear, Goodrich, Firestone, Uniroyal, Armstrong, and Continental dominated the tire business.

In Europe, Michelin had become the leader in radial tires—tires in which the cords run directly from one wall of the tire to the other without criss-crossing. Michelin sold radials throughout Europe.

U.S. companies weren't concerned about Michelin. In business strategy thought, the Boston Consulting Group was encouraging people to focus on market share and "pricing down the experience curve." The more you manufactured, this doctrine taught, the more you would know about manufacturing. Therefore, your costs would be lower than your competitors', and your position would grow ever stronger. This framework either minimized the importance of quality differences or assumed that more experienced companies would always use their experience to become quality leaders.

Following this doctrine U.S. tire companies focused on maximizing their shares of the enormous domestic market. U.S. auto makers hadn't designed their cars to use radial tires. Radials represented just 3 percent of the domestic market, sold mainly for European imports and to some extent to owners of high-performance cars who didn't mind the rougher ride radials gave with U.S. suspension systems. So U.S. car companies dismissed Michelin as an unimportant competitor.

By dismissing Michelin and focusing on short-term market share, U.S. tire companies ignored several key questions that strategic teachings of the time failed to deal with:

1. Wasn't the tire market splitting into two different segments, a performance segment and an economy segment? Answer: "Yes, there is is the huge, traditional, bias-tire segment that emphasizes economy and the new, radial segment that stresses performance."
2. Which segment is growing and which is declining in unit volume? "The radial segment is growing pretty fast and the bias segment is sluggish." (An effort to draw a value map would have shown that the premium radial tires were in a superior value position to the right of the fair-value line.)
3. What share does Michelin have in the radial segment? "Oh, I guess they have almost 100 percent, but it's only three percent of the tire market. Several U.S. companies have U.S. market share that is much larger."
4. Is share of the U.S. market the relevant gauge? "Maybe we should also consider sales in Europe."
5. Which segment has the higher margins? "I'm not sure because we don't make radial tires here. The technology is complicated and the equipment is very expensive." (A customer value analysis would have forced consideration of the possibility that the premium product was sold at higher margins.)
6. How are the margins in the bias segment? "Terrible."

A quick review of customer value in the early days of radials reveals why the margins of U.S. tire companies went south from "terrible." First, a simplified quality profile of radial versus bias technology shows that on the key quality attributes—durability, safety, ride, and handling—radial tires clearly outperformed bias tires on three of these criteria (Exhibit 8–1). As noted above, radials gave a rougher ride on U.S. suspension systems.

The customer value profile shows radials received a relative-perceived quality ratio of 1.20. This means that customers perceive radials' overall quality score to be 20 percent better than bias tires. The "price competitiveness" score, shown at the top of Exhibit 8–1, was 7.2 for radials and 8.0 for bias tires. So radials had an 11 percent disadvantage in price competitiveness because radials were perceived to be more expensive.

Rather than drawing a value map right away, we'll calculate the *customer value ratio.* Assume that the weight that the average customer places on price is twice the weight on quality. The customer value ratio equals the weight on quality times the market-perceived quality ratio plus the weight on price times the price satisfaction ratio. Thus, using the quality and price ratios from Exhibit 8–1:

EXHIBIT 8–1
Quality Profile: Radial vs. Bias Tires

Quality Attributes	Performance			Importance Weight	Weight × Ratio
	Radial	Bias	Ratio		
Price satisfaction	7.2	8.0	0.90		
Relative price			1.11		
Safety	9	7	1.29	40	52
Ride	7	8	0.86	30	26
Handling	8	6	1.50	10	27
Durability	9	6	1.50	10	15
	Sum of weights			100	
	Relative-perceived quality—score:				120
	Relative-perceived quality—ratio: 1.20				

Note: In this simplified example, radials score 20 percent better on overall quality

Customer Value Ratio = 0.33 × 1.2 + 0.66 × 0.9

$$0.40 \quad + \quad 0.60 \quad = 1.0$$

A customer value ratio of 1.0 means that customers perceive the value of the two competing products to be the same. In this illustration we selected the relative weights of quality and price so that the weighted advantage that radials had in quality was exactly offset by the weighted disadvantage that radials had in price competitiveness.

But the weight customers put on quality in the purchase decision across the spectrum of tires from economy to premium was probably more like the solid line shown on the value map in Exhibit 8–2. Customers at the premium end of the fair-value curve tended to place more weight on quality while those shopping at the economy end placed less weight on quality. The fair-value line in Exhibit 8–2 is drawn with 40 percent of the weight on quality on the left side and 50 percent of the weight on quality on the right side. This put Michelin in a superior customer-value position. With 50 percent weight on quality in the premium segment, Michelin's customer value ratio was

EXHIBIT 8–2

Customer value map: Radial vs. bias tires

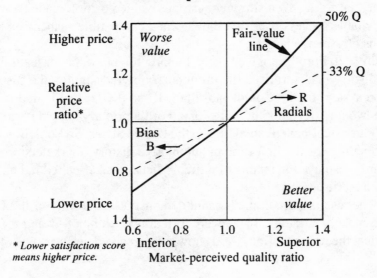

* Lower satisfaction score means higher price.

Customer Value Ratio = 0.5 × 1.2 + 0.5 × 0.9 =
              0.60   +   0.45   = 1.05

Even in the early days, before U.S. car companies redesigned their suspension systems, radials could be seen to have a real advantage in customer value, if the tire companies had carefully compared the two technologies.

Unlike, say, the software business, the tire business won't grow with technological innovation. The market is limited by the number of cars on the road and the yearly production of new cars. Thus in the tire market, introduction of the new radial technology did not expand the market for tires. It redistributed sales from one technology to another. It actually reduced the market for replacement tires because radials got better mileage.

In 1970, Michelin had introduced steel-belted radials to the United States. Radials weren't entirely new, and the technology wasn't mysterious. Several of the U.S. companies made radial tires in their European subsidiaries.

But steel and textile-belted radials introduced in the 1960s had gained only trivial market share. The reason for their failure to rapidly penetrate the market was simple: The tires were not compatible with the suspension systems on American cars. Radial tires "ran rough," and few consumers were willing to tolerate the discomfort. Radials' potential for an even stronger customer value position made them an inevitable success. But first they needed compatible suspension systems on American cars.

In 1970 Ford Motor Company, looking for a new, better feature for its luxury line, surprised the tire industry by redesigning the suspension system on the Continental Mark III so that a steel-belted radial tire would "run smooth." Firestone, Ford's primary supplier, did not produce steel-belted radial tires in the United States. So Ford turned to Michelin. For the first time in automotive history, marketers prominently displayed the name of a tire, "Michelin steel-belted radial," in car advertisements.

The results were dramatic, and demonstrated the folly of the U.S. tire-makers' strategy. If we were to redraw Exhibits 8–1 and 8–2 to reflect the new situation, we'd show the perceived performance of radials improving substantially on "ride"—probably resulting in a change in the perceived performance ratio of radials versus bias on "ride" from 0.86 to 1.20. The overall quality advantage of radials thus increased from approximately 20 percent to approximately 30 percent. The customer value advantage would double from 5 percent to 10 percent. All U.S. car manufacturers soon redesigned their suspension systems to be compatible with radial tires.

U.S. tire manufacturers were unprepared. Firestone's hasty response resulted in the infamous "Firestone 500" fiasco—a steel-belted tire that was alleged to fall apart! Within three years, radial tires mushroomed from a 3 percent share of the market to almost 30 percent. Within ten years, U.S. companies shut down over one-third of the U.S. bias tire producing capacity.

The reason the battle went as it did becomes clear when one considers the customer value positions of the tire technologies coupled with the suspension system change. The arrows in Exhibit 8–2 show how the redesign of U.S. suspension systems improved the market-perceived quality and value position of radials and worsened the market-perceived quality and value positions of bias tires.

Michelin's steel-belted radial was in a perfect position to attack the belted bias position as soon as U.S. auto manufacturers made their cars compatible with it. U.S. companies could not respond with a steel-belted tire of their own. Although "radial technology" was well understood, the companies had not carried out the analyses that would have enabled them to understand its importance to their futures. The technology of bonding wire to rubber was only practiced in Europe. Manufacturing experts had to transfer the knowledge from European divisions—a time-consuming process that inevitably involved problems.

U.S. fiber manufacturers helped by developing new synthetic fibers. Combined with existing radial technology, these fibers resulted in tires that could compete with the steel-belted radial. By 1980 several different kinds of radial tires, using different types of fibers, carved out their own "niches" in the marketplace. Steel-belted radials remained at the premium position. Tires with a synthetic textile fiber, such as Du Pont's Aramid, ran a close second. Glass fiber radials were positioned at the lower end of the radial segment—the lowest-priced radials, but higher in price and performance than the belted bias tire.

Michelin, as the market leader in radials, had an overwhelming advantage. As the company that introduced the premium steel-belted tire, its name could often command a price premium. It gained an enormous amount of market share. In 1991, Michelin finally passed Goodyear to become the Number 1 tire company in the world.

The fall of its U.S. rivals was ignominious. Uniroyal had to leave the tire business to focus on chemicals. And Firestone was sold to a once-tiny company founded in 1931 by Japanese entrepreneur Kanichiro Ishibashi. When Ishibashi started the company, the name Firestone was a symbol of American economic power like "Ford" and "Edison." Ishibashi means "stone bridge" in Japanese. By calling his company "Bridgestone," he had been virtually advertising his products as knock-offs of the great American brand Firestone. But this knock-off company not only rode the growth of the Japanese auto industry, but handled the transition to radials better than the American companies. Half a century after its founding, the knock-off took over the original, and tire industry analysts commented that when Bridgestone acquired Firestone, "They only had to change half the name."

The lessons of the tire industry's experience are many. One important lesson is that a customer value analysis—or any analysis of your competitive position—*must* include any small foreign competitors and any small competitors with new technology. It makes no sense to exclude a foreign competitor who has pioneered what could turn out to be the next-generation technology and at the same time include the Number 4 and Number 5 domestic competitors who use technology just like yours. Include at least your top two current competitors and each small competitor who has the potential to drive your market in the future.

In addition, when a new technology appears on the scene, whether in your own lab or in a competitor's product, do a customer value analysis that compares it directly with the existing technology. Below, we'll describe how to do this in more detail.

Today, even with the Bridgestone-Firestone combination, Michelin is on top. And they are certainly not there because the French automobile industry conquered the global market and pulled them along.

THE CUSTOMER VALUE MAP AND THE PRICE-PERFORMANCE CURVE

Research and development people often display the difference between competing technologies on a "price-performance curve." A good example is the set of price-performance curves for original-equipment passenger car tires prepared by Richard Klavans and shown in Exhibit 8–3.[2] In this example, he plotted the absolute price of different kinds of tires in 1980 dollars versus performance measured by miles per tire. The circles represent positions of the different tire technologies—bias tires, belted bias, glass-belted radials, textile-belted radials, and steel-belted radials—in 1972 and 1980. The size of each circle reflects the market share of its technology in each period.

The traditional price-performance curve resembles our customer value map, but it obscures some important aspects of any competitive struggle. To create a price-performance curve, technologists focus on absolute technical performance in one powerful dimension (miles per tire, in this case). If the tire that gives fewer miles also gives a better ride, there's no way to show that on the price-performance curve.

The customer value map, by contrast, focuses on customer-perceived performance on *all* the quality attributes that count in the purchase decision. For tires, it will include safety, ride, handling, and durability. Ideally, it should also include customer service attributes. (How well does the manufacturer service its distributors? How good is warranty coverage?)

Another difference between the price-performance curve and the customer value map is that the price-performance curve uses the estimated market transactions price while the customer value map uses perceived price competitiveness, as learned from interviews with customers.

A third difference is that the customer value measures are scaled *relative to competitors*. Therefore, it makes it possible to draw comparisons across businesses or technologies in different markets. It would have allowed Goodyear to ask the question:

"How does the value map position of radials compare with the value map position of successful new technologies in the past?" (See a comparison of endoscopic versus traditional open surgery for the gallbladder and hernia-repair markets below.) By contrast, the price-performance curve typically uses absolute price and performance scales. The focus is simply on how a single competitive arena evolves, and few comparisons between different arenas can be made.

Endoscopic Surgery:
Customer Value as a Tool to Attack a Leader

Another battle between old and new technologies pits traditional surgery, in which doctors cut large incisions in patients, against endoscopic surgery, in which a doctor makes a tiny cut and inserts a slender, tubular instrument called a trochar into the body to perform the surgery. The competition between United States Surgical Corporation (USSC) and the Ethicon Endo-Surgery business of Johnson & Johnson to supply endoscopic equipment for gallbladder operations and to be first to market with equipment for other endoscopic procedures has heated up dramatically since 1990. J&J is using customer value analysis to understand the market and decide where to advance. It therefore has powerful advantages over USSC despite USSC's first-to-market lead.

Conversion from open surgery to minimally invasive procedures began in the late 1980s when Leon Hirsch, founder of USSC, began to promote a new endoscopic procedure for gallbladder removal. Traditional open surgery required a cut several inches long in the abdominal cavity. It required a hospital stay of several days plus an extended at-home recovery of six to eight weeks. When President Lyndon B. Johnson underwent the procedure in the 1960s, virtually every American newspaper carried the photo of the president raising up his shirt to show the American people his large scar.

Today surgeons perform most gallbladder operations laparoscopically. Instead of making a single large incision, the surgeon inserts

EXHIBIT 8–3a

Technological advance shifts the price-performance curve

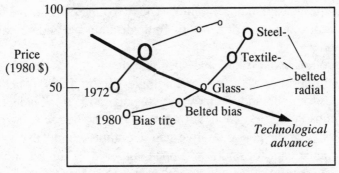

Source: "Formulating a Quality Improvement Strategy," *The Journal of Business Strategy,* Winter 1985, by Bradley T. Gale and Richard Klavans. Copyright © Journal of Business Strategy.

EXHIBIT 8–3b

Contrasting two tools

Tool: Price-performance curve

Focus: Technology strategy

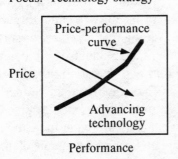

Tool: Customer-value map

Focus: Marketing strategy

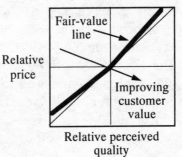

three trochars into the abdominal cavity. A trochar is shaped somewhat like a test tube with a knife at the leading end. The knife punc-
tures a small opening through the abdominal wall. The surgeon then
inserts one trochar for a video camera that guides a surgeon as he or
she watches its signal on a monitor. The two other trochars are used to
insert endoscopic instruments to find, disconnect, and remove the
gallbladder.

We compare the traditional/open and new/endoscopic procedures
in a quality profile of the two technologies (Exhibit 8–4). The quality
attributes for gallbladder removal are the operation time, the length of
stay in hospital, the complication rate, the at-home recovery period,
and the size of the post-operative scar. Columns 2 and 3 show typical
performance data for endo- and open surgery. Column 4 shows the
performance ratio of the endoscopic to the open procedure.

For gallbladder operations, endoscopic surgery is superior to open
surgery on all five attributes. Endo-surgery uses a muscle-splitting
technique whereas traditional surgery involves muscle cutting. This
leads to the real payoffs of endo-surgery—a short stay in the hospital,
a short at-home recovery period, minimal pain, and a small post oper-
ative scar. In addition, traditional surgery costs $5,000–10,000 but
endo-surgery costs only $3,000–6,000. Thus, endo-surgery has vastly
superior quality and dramatically lower price—an unbeatable advantage. The conversion from traditional to endo-surgery for gallbladder
operations has been dramatic. Both USSC and Ethicon Endo-Surgery
supply the medical instruments for endoscopic procedures, and are
promoting them throughout the world.

While USSC pioneered the field, J&J soon saw its potential for explosive growth. Not only could the company take market share from
USSC in the removal of gallbladders, it could encourage surgeons to
convert other traditional open surgical procedures to endo-surgery.

Ethicon had for decades been the leading manufacturer of surgical
supplies such as sutures. In 1991, under the guidance of Ethicon president Bob Croce, J&J split Ethicon into two operating organizations.
The suture business continued to be headquartered in Somerville,
New Jersey, with Frank Ryan taking over from Croce as president.
The Ethicon Endo-Surgery business, headquartered at the Cincinnati
factory that made endoscopic equipment, became a separate operating
unit in January 1992. William Weldon became president of U.S. oper-

EXHIBIT 8–4

Quality profile: Gallbladder operations
Endo-surgery versus traditional surgery

Quality attributes:*	Endo	Traditional	Ratio	Relative weight	Weight times ratio
Latent: _____					
Desired: Pill that dissolves the gallbladder					
		Performance			
At-home recovery	1–2 weeks	6–8 weeks	3.0	40	120
Hospital stay	1–2 days	3–7 days	2.0	30	60
Complications rate	0–5%	1–10%	1.5	10	15
Postoperative scar	0.5–1 inch	3–5 inches	1.4	05	07
Operation time	1/2–1 hour	1–2 hours	2.0	15	30
Basic: _____		Sum of quality weights:		100	
		Market-perceived quality score:			232

*Current attributes ordered from pacing to fading.

Note: In this example the ratios are not calculated directly from performance measures shown in columns one and two. They are based on performance scores from 1 to 10 that are linked to the performance data shown.

ations for Ethicon Endo-Surgery. Croce moved to J&J corporate headquarters in New Brunswick, New Jersey where he was named a corporate officer and also named J&J's first global general manager, in charge of the worldwide Ethicon Endo-Surgery business. The new J&J management team for endo-surgery was now ready to compete around the globe in providing instruments for emerging surgery procedures.

Preparing for the split in 1991, Ethicon's endo-surgery marketing group established "procedure development" teams to link its marketing and new product development efforts more directly to procedures where endo-surgery could develop a competitive advantage. In Ethicon's traditional business, the company marketed sutures, needles, and other traditional products. Previously, sutures, mechanical products, and endo-surgery products had all been marketed through the same sales organization.

Dave Clapper, who was then vice president of the new endo-surgery marketing group, realized that endo-surgery called for a totally new approach. Separate marketing teams would work on each procedure—gall bladder removal, hernia repair, bowel resection, hysterectomy, and so on. J&J would conduct customer value analyses on each procedure where endo-surgery could potentially replace a traditional technique. It would introduce the endo-surgery techniques commercially wherever it could develop methods that really offered more value than the old-fashioned ways.

USSC had had a tremendous "first to market" lead in the gallbladder procedure. But Ethicon pioneered in bringing endo-surgery to hernia repair. Ethicon ran its first education courses on hernia repair for surgeons in Cincinnati in the fall of 1991. We show the advantages of endo- versus open surgery for hernia repair in Exhibit 8–5.

The quality attribute list is similar to that of gallbladder surgery. For hernia repair, endo-surgery performs better on all attributes except "operation time," where open surgery is somewhat shorter. On the price side, however, endo-surgery costs roughly $3,400 or about 20–30 percent more than traditional surgery ($2,700). But since third-party insurers usually pay the surgical bill, most patients aren't extremely price sensitive. USSC followed closely behind J&J in entering the hernia-repair field.

We show the positioning of endoscopic versus open surgery for both gallbladder removal and hernia repair on a customer value map (Exhibit 8–6). Endoscopic surgery has a much bigger advantage over open surgery for removing gallbladders than for repairing hernias. That's why USSC had focused on gallbladders first and that's why the conversion from open to endoscopic occurred so quickly for gallbladders. But the advantage for hernia repair is still considerable.

By analyzing all the surgical procedures where the new method can develop a competitive edge on a single customer value map, and then assessing the overall market potential based on the current and potential surgical case load, Johnson & Johnson can pinpoint which procedures to target.

In general, any company can analyze a new technology versus an old technology for each of several potential market segments and summarize the results on a customer value map to pinpoint segments where the new technology has the largest advantage in providing better customer value.

USSC, the market leader today, appears to be taking a less well-thought-out approach. It apparently believes that with Johnson &

EXHIBIT 8–5
Quality Profile: Hernia Repairs
Endo-surgery vs. Traditional Surgery

Quality Attributes	Performance			Relative Weight	Weight × Ratio
	Endo-surgery	Traditional	Ratio		
Time back to work and nor-mal activity	7 days	22 days	2.00	40	80
Hospital stay	11 hours	18 hours	1.50	30	45
Operation time	108 min-utes	85 minutes	0.90	10	09
Complications*					
Short-term	9	5	1.80	10	18
Severe pain	1%	5%			
Moderate pain	15%	37%			
Mild pain	66%	42%			
None	38%	36%			
Long-term	10	5	2.00	10	20
Severe pain	1%	1%			
Moderate pain	1%	10%			
Mild pain	32%	41%			
None	73%	62%			
Sum of weights				100	
Relative-perceived quality score:					172
Relative-perceived quality ratio:					1.72

*Percentages of patients reporting complications following surgery.

In this example some of the ratios are not calculated directly from the performance data. They are estimated based on performance scores from 1 to 10. Endo-surgery scores 72 percent better than traditional surgery.

Based on information from MarketLab Research, Inc.

EXHIBIT 8–6

Customer value map: Endo vs. open surgery

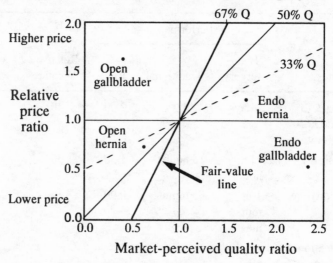

Johnson attacking its position in endo-surgery, it must continue an attack on Johnson & Johnson's position in traditional surgical products. So even though explosive growth in endoscopy is straining the resources and management abilities of both USSC and J&J Ethicon, USSC has set out to learn how to market needles and sutures like those J&J and Davis & Geck have made for decades. It's unclear how USSC can ever become the quality leader in this market.

Ethicon has responded to USSC's entry by sharpening its focus on customer needs. When USSC found itself with excessive inventories of suture and needle products, Wall Street grew worried. After hitting a peak of $134 in December 1991, USSC's stock price plunged from its previously smooth, exponential growth trend. During the first half of 1992 it fell into the $60–70 range (Exhibit 8–7).

Despite the wobble in USSC's stock price, chairman Leon Hirsch has certainly cashed in on his earlier pioneering efforts. Hirsch used several prior years of options to buy stock in 1992 for a profit of $58.5 million. Hirsch's options to buy stock at a specific price set in the late 1980s became very valuable as U.S. Surgical soared 770% from the end of 1987 through the end of 1992. In addition, as reported in *USA Today* in March 1993, USSC executive vice president Turi Josefsen,

EXHIBIT 8–7

"After years of smooth sailing, a wobble develops"

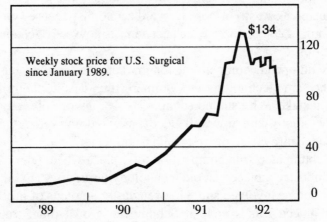

Weekly stock price for U.S. Surgical since January 1989.

$134

120

80

40

0

'89   '90   '91   '92

Source: *New York Times,* 16 August 1992. Copyright © 1992. The New York Times Company. Reprinted by permission.

Hirsch's wife, also cashed in options for a profit of $25.5 million. A successful pioneer can earn enormous payoffs.[3]

But in the summer of 1993 USSC's stock price was languishing in the twenty to thirty dollar range and the options that Leon Hirsch got in 1991 to buy 2.75 million shares at $62 each were worthless for the time being. Johnson & Johnson's use of customer value analysis to improve its positioning and its procedure development teams shows the right way for an early follower to aggressively invest in improved customer value and dramatically increase its share of an explosive new technology. We'll look in greater depth at some of Johnson & Johnson's methodology in Chapter 10.

We have used the historical competition between open and endo-surgery to illustrate how the tools of customer value analysis can be applied to competing technologies. These same tools can be used to analyze the current battle between reusable and disposable endoscopic instruments. They can also be used to size up the emerging battle between equipment that currently produces two-dimensional images and stereoscopic camera systems that improve the quality of endo-surgery by providing three-dimensional images.

"Schumpeterian" Competition

Competition between technologies is often far more exhilarating than competition among companies using the same basic systems. Joseph Schumpeter, an Austrian-born Harvard economist, focused on this exciting form of competition, which economists now call "Schumpeterian competition."[4]

To Schumpeter, competition for market share among businesses using the same technology was uninteresting, despite the billions of dollars at stake. Why should economists—or anyone else outside the industry—really care how well Goodyear was doing versus Goodrich, Firestone, Uniroyal, Armstrong, and Continental?

To Schumpeter, true competition took place when a new technology or industry replaced an old technology or industry (Exhibit 8–8). This, of course involved shifts in even vaster amounts of profit. Railroads replaced canals and, in Schumpeter's own time, trucks displaced railroads. Transistors replaced tubes in electronics. More recently, minicomputers thrived at the expense of mainframes only to be knocked off by the personal computer. McDonalds devastated Howard Johnson's as automobiles and fast-paced life styles caused fast food to replace slow food.

Baxter-Travenol pioneered in the PVC bags containing medical solutions, and thus displaced McGaw's glass bottles. When a nurse dropped a glass bottle of solution, she used to have to clean up a big mess. Today when a nurse drops a PVC bag, he or she merely picks it up. Sonoco Products, Inc., backed Ohio entrepreneur Gordon Dancy and replaced much of the paper grocery bag industry's business with Sonoco's plastic grocery bags, as we'll see below.

The list of examples of Schumpeterian competition gets longer each year. The Apple Power Book 170 computer that I bought in 1991 was no longer on the market in November 1992. With the explosive interest in cycle-time reduction—triggered by the prime-mover advantages of being first to market with a unique attribute or product—the list of new technologies replacing old will soon get longer every month!

And yet many businesspeople can't conceive how *they* and their products can be replaced. Think about it—your business too could go the way of the bias tire, the vinyl record, the wooden tennis racket, or the black and white overhead transparency.

EXHIBIT 8–8

Schumpeterian Competition: New Technologies Replace Old

| Market/Industry | Pioneer | Technology | | Displaced/Damaged |
		New	Old	
Tires	Michelin	Radial	Bias	Firestone, Uniroyal
Auto bumpers	General Electric	Plastic	Metal	US Steel
Transportation		Trucks	Railroads	
Aircraft propulsion		Jet engine	Propeller	
Gallbladder removal	USSC	Endo-surgery	Open surgery	Many open products
Hernia repair surgery	Ethicon	Endo-surgery	Open surgery	Many open products
Grocery bags	Sonoco Products	Plastic	Paper	Paper companies
Containers	Baxter Travenol	PVC	Glass	McGaw
Coatings for beverage containers	Glidden	Water-based	Solvent-based	Dexter, Mobile
Restaurants	McDonalds	Fast food	Slow food	Howard Johnson's
Computers	DEC	Mini	Mainframe	IBM
Computers	Apple	Personal computer	Mini	DEC
		Word processor	Typewriter	IBM

(cont.)

193

EXHIBIT 8–8 (cont.)

Market/Industry	Technology			
	Pioneer	New	Old	Displaced/Damaged
Telephone		Cordless	Corded	
Communications		Fax	Telegram	
Telecommunications		Fiber optics	Copper wires	
Radio components		Transistors	Tubes	
Radio sound		Stereo	Mono	
Home entertainment		Television	Radio	
Television		Color	Black and white	
Recordings		Tape	Vinyl	
		CD	Tape	
Water sports		Wind surfing	Inner tube	
Tennis rackets		Metal	Wood	
		Composite	Metal	
Carpet	Milliken	Tiles	Rolls	

Customer Value Analysis Chooses and Nurtures a Winner: The Polysack Case

A seemingly unlikely arena for Schumpeterian competition was the grocery bag industry.[5] Charles Coker, chief executive and principal shareholder of Hartsville, South Carolina's Sonoco Products Company, had made his fortune producing low-tech items such as paper tubes and cones on which nearby textile companies wound their thread. Sonoco Products had converted the industry from old wooden cones to less expensive paper cones and had also played a role in the conversion of containers from metal cans to paper cans.

In the early 1980s, Sonoco executives heard of a unique opportunity with the potential to become quite large: the plastic grocery sack. Ohio entrepreneur Gordon Dancy teamed up with Sonoco executive F. Bennett Williams to propose replacing an American staple, the brown-paper grocery bag, with thin, high-density polyethylene bags.

The high-density technology had originated in Europe and was catching on in Canada. Dancy argued that his bags, which he called Polysacks, would be cheaper and easier to handle than paper. Moreover, he envisioned that at some point high-density polyethylene, which faced competition from a low-density technology, would prove to be the low-cost technology. Based on this conviction, he had set up his own small company—far too small ever to manufacture plastic bags profitably without a major infusion of capital.

Dancy, an expert in manufacturing technology, was sure his product had technical superiority. It was stronger than both traditional paper bags and competing plastic sacks. Williams, a senior Sonoco executive responsible for new business development, was impressed by Dancy's sales pitch and by Sonoco's own tests of the bags. Williams and Dancy were totally committed to success. They planned to grab a large share of the market, confidently expecting that brown paper bags would quickly disappear.

Sonoco Products had been a member of the Strategic Planning Institute for several years and had analyzed several of its core businesses using the PIMS database and models. In addition, we had conducted in-house seminars at Sonoco on quality profiling and "Using Quality As a Strategic Weapon." Thus Sonoco became one of the first organizations to use the methodology that became customer value analysis.[6]

The company asked us to work with it in evaluating the competitive potential of the Polysack technology. In addition to showing how customer value analysis can help organizations nurture the right technology for the future, the Sonoco experience illustrates the pitfalls of any kind of technological change.

Sonoco sent researchers into supermarkets where they talked to store managers, checkout personnel, and shoppers. They pointed out the different product attributes of paper and plastic bags, and noted that consumers rated Sonoco's sacks superior to competition on overall strength, wet strength, and carrying ease. Store managers responded positively to the plastic sacks' lesser space in inventory and lower cost.

Paper bags, on the other hand, stood up better to be filled. They involved no retraining of employees and no risk. Sonoco had constructed a customer value analysis of plastic versus paper technology based on product attributes and price. This early analysis showed that Polysack's advantages clearly outweighed those of paper. So Sonoco decided to enter the plastic bag business. It bought Dancy's company and made him Sonoco's Polysack product manager.

In retrospect, we realize they began with the assumption that consumers' needs were homogeneous—an assumption that didn't prove correct.

Things didn't go as planned. By 1984, plastic bags had gained only a 17 percent share of the grocery bag market. Despite attaining a one-third share of the plastic bag portion—nearly 6 percent of the national market for grocery bags—Polysack's sales were only $16 million and the business was an unprofitable cash drain. This was primarily because of the huge training force needed to continually train checkout employes due to high employee turnover. Some senior executives expressed serious doubts about plastic sacks.

Sonoco executives learned some of the reasons things were going wrong. Shoppers and checkout clerks were accustomed to paper bags. Store managers doubted that the shoppers and clerks preferred plastic sacks and feared that switching to plastic would hurt business. Stores that did try plastic bags simply carried them in addition to paper bags. Checkout clerks found that the newfangled plastic sacks were difficult to use and slowed down the checkout process.

With Polysack stumbling, the business was at a critical juncture. Williams and Dancy were under pressure.

Should Sonoco pursue this business or not? To help address the issue, Sonoco set out to analyze Polysack against information in the PIMS database for similar businesses. Working with Strategic Planning Institute vice president Phillip Thompson, the company came away with three crucial new insights:

- First, successful start-up businesses are often unprofitable for approximately four years.
- Second, to succeed, start-ups must translate technological quality advantages into measurable customer-perceived quality advantages. Many experience difficulties in doing this, but those who succeed create big winners.
- Third, customer service is often the key to customer-perceived quality and value, and thus to market penetration and long-term profitability (as we saw from the PIMS evidence at the beginning of Chapter 6).

With this in mind, Bob Kearns, then Sonoco's director of market research, and Lois DuBois, a former SPI employee who had joined Sonoco's planning group, began a sizable West Coast study to talk in depth with grocery-chain executives. The object was to determine why Sonoco was winning or losing orders for plastic bags. This study shed further light on what was going wrong and how to improve the marketing and customer service processes. As F. Bennett Williams puts it:

The profile of the customers making up the $16 million in sales was the puzzle to solve. We had some sales in nearly all the chains. These sales were their "test stores" where the sack was to be evaluated.

In theory each chain had said, "We'll test in these stores for X days [usually 90 days]. If the test goes well we will expand chain-wide, if it goes poorly we will take plastic out."

Universally the tests went well. Almost as often, no expanded usage occurred. When asked why they did not quit using plastic in the test stores, the chain-store buyers said they couldn't take them out because the customers liked them too much. But they gave no reason why they didn't expand.

In this atmosphere of selling tests and incurring high training costs, we did have a few chains that had expanded their usage to all of their stores. The breakthrough insight that was gotten from our field research was the differences in the decision-making process between those chains that continued to successfully test for years with no action and those that acted on the test results.

The action always came when the test was "ordered," "controlled," or "motivated" by senior line or operations managers. The nonaction tests were always directed by staff such as purchasing, public relations, environmental or industrial engineering, etc.

In addition it was shown that the successfully expanded situations had their own training departments where Sonoco trained the trainer and did not have to do extensive in-store training and retraining.

To us this was "compelling" insight. Therefore our customer service program was redirected at those executives whom we identified as being the "correct" decision maker in each chain. Our total sales effort was shifted away from purchasing, etc., to line management.

In addition to the training programs for their trainers, we supplied the training tools for their trainers. Maybe more importantly we developed a series of tools for the executive himself to monitor daily usage among his stores and between his chain and other chains successfully using the program.

This change in emphasis and technique changed the Polysack program from "spinning our wheels" to a high-speed vehicle on a fast track.[7]

The Polysack story is a classic case of nurturing the success of a new technology by carefully determining *why orders are won or lost.* The breakthrough insights from field research dealt with:

1. Who should be the customers' decision maker?
2. Which market segment can we serve best? Where can we provide the best value?

Notice from Williams's summary that it was not just a matter of understanding how the decision maker thinks. In most chains where plastic bags were tested the decision maker was a staff person who gave no reason why they did not expand the use of plastic chain-wide after a successful test. From Sonoco's perspective, these people were the wrong decision makers. Sonoco's marketers and sales force needed to understand who *should* make the purchase decision and take steps to assure that line management, the right people from Sonoco's perspective, made the decisions on the testing and use of plastic bags.

Sonoco's marketers also needed to understand two very different market segments. Successfully expanded chains had their own training departments. This meant Sonoco's customer service activities could be designed to train the trainers and provide them with training tools. Targeting this market segment proved to be more cost effective than trying to serve segments where Sonoco had to provide the continuing training services directly.

The research on the PIMS database and Kearns's insights from in-depth field research created this major change in Sonoco's point of view. Previously, the company had thought of bags as a commodity. It had believed that since Polysacks gave better performance (strength and lightness) for a lower price, they would inevitably sell. But early on Sonoco hadn't helped store managers and grocery customers to *perceive* the difference in performance. And it hadn't considered customer service as a major quality attribute in the grocery bag business at all.

The West Coast study identified the right decision makers and pinpointed a focused service opportunity. Sonoco already knew that grocery chains needed a training program that would teach clerks how to use the plastic sacks to speed up—rather than slow down—the checkout process. If trained clerks, using plastic sacks, could check customers out faster, the managers would gladly carry both plastic and paper, and give the consumer a choice. The segmentation finding led Sonoco to focus on chains that had their own training programs.

Sonoco developed its train-the-trainer program and made it available to large supermarket chains. Using Sonoco's program, chains could introduce stands to hold the plastic bags, train baggers to use the stands, and hold rallies to show how quickly baggers could place grocery items in the plastic sacks. The chains bought in. High-density polyethylene became a key factor in the grocery bag market. Maintaining its one-third share, Sonoco's Polysack sales grew from an unprofitable $16 million in 1984 to a highly profitable $105 million in 1988.

The initial customer value analysis had accurately shown the technology opportunity. But superior product technology alone had not been enough. Polysack became a winner only when it clearly understood why orders were won or lost, targeted the right decision makers, focused on the market segment that it could serve best, and addressed all the key attributes that counted in the purchase decision—which included customer service as well as product superiority.

Creating and Monitoring Innovation and Linking It to Success

As the Sonoco case shows, understanding why orders are won or lost, what customers need, and how they make purchase decisions is crucial for the successful introduction of a new technology. The R&D effort must understand what the customer values from the beginning, so researchers work on the right objectives. This will make their innovation activity effective.

Moreover, an effective link between technology strategy and business strategy is the most important issue for many companies. To move quickly from concept to successful business, a business system of interrelated processes (technology development, manufacturing, selling, delivery, and service) must be developed simultaneously with the product.

For an established business, it is also important to monitor the innovation effort, the speed of new-product development time relative to competitors, and the proportion of sales from new products. We show some key conceptual relationships that connect innovation activity to competitive advantage in Exhibit 8–9.

Many aspects of technological progress can't be "managed" in traditional ways. 3M Corporation is one of America's most innovative firms, partially because it creates "an internal free market for innovation." It is argued that three rules are responsible for 3M's success:

1. Managers are told that new products should account for at least 25 percent of their division's revenues every five years.
2. Researchers are encouraged to spend up to 15 percent of their time on projects they're personally interested in, even if they aren't what their boss has assigned them to do.

EXHIBIT 8–9

Tracing the links from innovation to profitability and growth

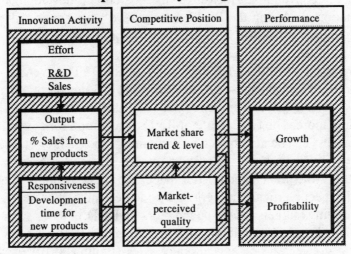

3. 3M has no central source of innovation funding; if one part of the company rejects your idea, you can try to sell it to another.[8]

Most companies that compete on science monitor their business units on three key measures. R&D as a percentage of sales (or of value-added) is a measure of innovation *effort.* Cycle time for developing new products reflects innovation *leadership and responsiveness to anticipated customer needs.* The percentage of sales from products introduced in the last three to five years measures the *output* or commercial success of a business's innovation efforts.

These guides may be too gross to measure what truly distinguishes an excellent R&D program from a mediocre one. In addition to decentralism, excellent R&D programs are genuinely customer-driven. Part of the strategic navigation system at all levels of any business should be Pareto analyses of customers' complaints: What is it that customers *don't* like? Also, what are the quality attributes on which customers report *all* competitors are performing poorly? Areas of customer dissatisfaction point to opportunities for product improvements—and areas where competitors can beat you if you fail to act. They often tell you where the competitive battles will be won or lost in the future.

But the conventional measures of research and development are also important. Using the PIMS database we have empirically analyzed the linkages shown in Exhibit 8–9 and produced some important insights.

How much should a company spend on R&D? The average business in the PIMS database spends 2 percent of sales on product and process R&D, but the evidence suggests that it would benefit by spending more. The typical rate of R&D expenditure for any individual business can be determined by examining "look-alike" businesses that are similar in degree of vertical integration, market growth rate, and other structural characteristics that affect R&D spending. (As one would expect, vertically integrated businesses and businesses in rapidly growing markets tend to spend more on R&D.)

Our studies show that innovation activity pays off. Businesses with either a greater rate of new product sales (Exhibit 8–10) or rising

EXHIBIT 8–10

R & D leads to more sales from new products

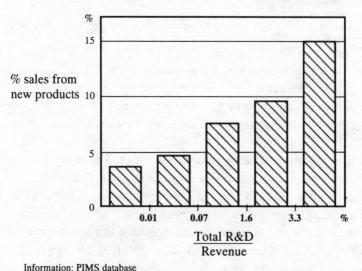

Information: PIMS database

market-perceived quality tend to gain market share and achieve higher long-term internal rates of return on their investments.[9]

But R&D costs and the expenses of new product launches are investments in the future, while accounting standards require businesses to treat them as current expenses. Thus, new product effort reduces the current year's earnings, and the short-term correlation between profitability and new product activity is negative. Some managers thus underinvest in innovation, especially where executive compensation packages are tied to profitability as accountants measure it.

As we would expect, innovation effort leads to innovation output. Heavy R&D spenders obtain 15 percent of their sales from products less than three years old while light R&D spenders receive only 4 percent of their sales from such products (Exhibit 8–11).

Naturally, shorter product development cycles also help new product sales (Exhibit 8–12). In addition, development time for new products is positively correlated with the market-perceived quality of a business relative to its competitors. Being first to market is a key purchase criterion in many markets.

EXHIBIT 8–11

New product activity leads to gains in market share

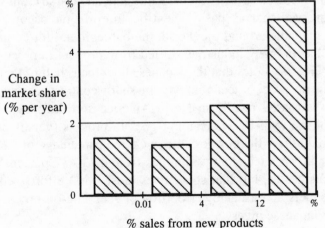

% sales from new products

Information: PIMS database

EXHIBIT 8–12

Shorter product development cycles yield more sales from new products

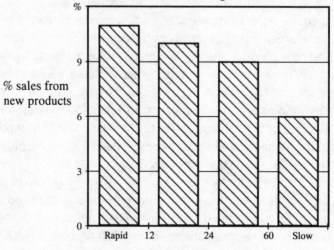

% sales from new products

Development time for new products (months)

Information: PIMS database

Are you spending your R&D for the right purposes? Many companies seem to misdirect their funds. Kim Clark and Ralph Gomory have each observed that as basic scientific information becomes more readily available around the world, the battleground for commercial success has in many industries shifted from product to process technology. Gomory notes that the Japanese now focus half of their R&D spending on process technology.[10] In sharp contrast, among PIMS businesses (based mostly in North America and Europe) only one fourth of the total R&D spending goes to process (versus product) technology. Over the business life cycle the percentage of R&D that goes for process technology doubles from 18 to 37 percent among PIMS businesses, but that still leaves most R&D effort focused on new products and a far lower portion of spending on process R&D than the Japanese invest.

As you develop a new technology, whether it is for product or process, customer value analysis is the best tool for judging whether the enormous cost of actually introducing the technology is worthwhile. For process technologies, a customer value analysis can focus on the benefits of the technology to the process's internal customers.

The bottom-line results of the research are that companies can generally improve their competitive position by:

- developing a flexible "free market for innovation" within the organization
- analyzing customer complaints and product attributes on which customers tell you all competitors are performing poorly, to get a hint of customer's future wants
- ensuring that research and development funding decisions aren't biased—and new products underfunded—because of internal measurement systems that emphasize the short-term costs of creating new products more than the long-term benefits
- shortening cycle times for developing new products and bringing them to market
- tracking the portion of sales from new products and demanding that a high rate be achieved
- making sure that process R&D receives adequate funding
- conducting careful, forward-looking customer value analysis of new technologies when they are developed or introduced by competitors

A strategic navigation system that monitors innovation activity, combined with the tools of customer value analysis to assess competing technologies and bring the best to market promptly, can focus a company on future customer needs and keep it in a market driving position.

PART FOUR

The Tools and Metrics of Customer Value Analysis

Chapter 9

The Seven Tools of Customer Value Analysis

Chapter 10

Putting the Power of a Whole Organization in a Single Room—
The War Room Wall and Strategic Navigation

Chapter 11

Aligning Your Quality Initiatives with the Goal
of True Customer Value Management

The seven tools of customer value analysis

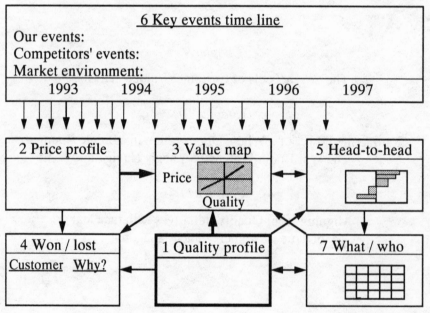

CHAPTER 9

The Seven Tools
of Customer Value Analysis

To compete in the 1990s you need to know more than you've ever known before. To *win,* your entire management team needs to know more than your competitors about your:

customers

markets

competitors

technologies

processes

And your team needs to use that knowledge better.

"Management by fact" is the path to competitive advantage. Yet many companies cannot really manage by fact. Executives from different parts of the business speak different languages. The result: The team fails to achieve a fact-based consensus, and "the boss" ultimately makes decisions based on his or her own subjective criteria. Often some team members don't even understand a decision well enough to implement their part of it.

In this chapter and the next, we'll show how to manage information to achieve *customer value management.* Thus these chapters are, in a sense, the climax of the book.

In Chapters 1 and 2 we discussed what it takes to compete today. In Chapters 3 through 8 we've shown how a handful of companies have understood market-perceived quality and customer value and won victories for customers, employees, and stockholders as a result.

We've used each of the tools of customer value analysis at least once in the last six chapters. And we've shown that some companies are using these tools to serve their customers.

Now we're ready to present a clear basic description of the methods. We will show that a few essentially simple tools enable an organization to navigate strategically even in confusing times like the 1990s.

In this chapter we'll first review what you're trying to accomplish, then summarize the *seven tools of customer value analysis* that, as a group, keep you in touch with customers and tell you what you should do to deliver value. We'll also tell where the tools came from. Then in the next chapter we will show how to use the *war-room* approach to manage business-unit team meetings and how to create a comprehensive *strategic navigation system* that makes competitive information available in a usable form.

With these tools and methods, any company can manage itself strategically. And any company can win.

Understanding the Path to Competitiveness

Why do most Western companies fail to use information well? Look at Exhibit 9–1, the "path to competitiveness" that we first introduced in Chapter 2. This exhibit displays the two key dimensions of the problem.

The first dimension of the problem, illustrated on the bottom axis, is the independent functional "fiefdoms" into which most organizations are divided. The people who work in marketing or manufacturing or R&D pass ideas up and down hierarchically without communicating to the other pieces of the organization.

What traps companies in this mode? Why don't they turn themselves into teams that unite to think through the problems of serving customers? Key difficulties include:

- Executives' lack of training outside their functional areas
- The lack of any common language or metrics of strategy shared among the parts

EXHIBIT 9–1

The path to competitiveness

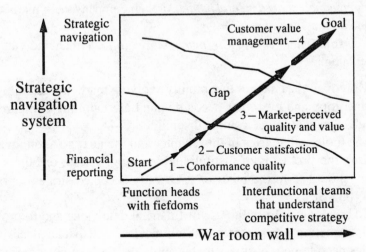

* The lack of connection between the management systems used in the different parts of the company. (The evaluation measures a marketing person uses mean nothing to an engineer, and vice versa.)

The second dimension of the failure to use information is that business teams as a whole usually receive only financial data. They don't receive information about customers, markets, technologies, and competitors. This is illustrated on the vertical axis of Exhibit 9–1.

Managers introduce additional data at team meetings, of course. But the team rarely sees crucial nonfinancial information in a form that the members can understand and digest. If an executive wants data produced by a nonfinancial department (other than his or her own) he or she probably has to send someone to the office that produced the data. Usually, no one bothers.

No one agrees on what are the key nonfinancial measures (customer satisfaction, market-perceived quality, productivity, innovation . . .). Organizations invest large amounts in market research. But few pull their market-research and other nonfinancial data together in ways that enable them to act on it effectively.

Arie P. de Geus noted in a seminal article:

Institutional learning is the process whereby management teams *change their shared mental models* of their company, their markets, and their competitors.

   Institutional learning is much more difficult than individual learning.[1]

Moreover, the changes that rapidly evolving markets, technologies, competitors, and customer needs demand are daunting compared to the changes that affect a single discipline.

The tools and metrics in this chapter and the next go a long way to solving the problems of institutional learning. These, or others like them, should form the basis of "generally accepted strategic principles" (GASP).

To break away from the use of financial data alone and to provide the information necessary for institutional learning to take place, companies need to help business teams apply the tools of customer value analysis. They need to adopt a war-room approach to meetings that will ensure that the best available data is widely understood and utilized. And they need a comprehensive strategic navigation system to make all crucial competitive data widely available. If they take these steps, the organization can navigate strategically and be the customer's best servant.

Starting in Chapter 2, we've shown how customer value analysis can help an organization understand its marketplace and, more important, take steps to win in that marketplace. Now it's time to summarize customer value analysis and the complete set of customer value analysis tools.

Look at Exhibit 9–2. It displays in miniature a comprehensive analysis of customer value using the seven tools of customer value analysis. The seven tools it uses are:

1. The market-perceived quality profile
2. The relative price profile
3. The customer value map
4. The won/lost analysis
5. A head-to-head area chart of customer value
6. A key events time line
7. A what/who matrix

We'll discuss each of these in turn.

EXHIBIT 9–2

The seven tools of customer value analysis

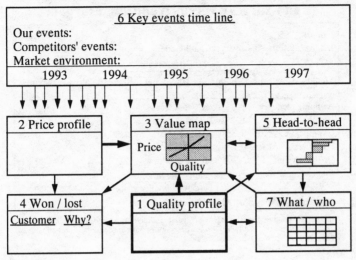

1. The Market-Perceived Quality Profile

The market-perceived quality profile is the heart of a customer value analysis. We discussed how to create it in Chapter 2, and we've shown ways of using it in each of the last few chapters.

Exhibit 9–3 shows a market-perceived quality profile for gall-bladder operations that we presented in Chapter 8. We've shown in the past few chapters that market-perceived quality profiles can provide profoundly important information on everything from chicken to multimillion-dollar telephone switching systems.

Creating the market-perceived quality profile involves several steps:

1. In forums such as focus groups, ask customers in the targeted market—both your customers and competitors' customers—to list the factors other than price that are important in their purchase decisions.
2. Establish how the various quality attributes are weighted in the customer's decision, usually by simply asking customers to tell you how they weight the various factors, distributing 100 points among them.

EXHIBIT 9–3

Quality profile: Gallbladder operations
Endo-surgery versus traditional surgery

Latent: _____					
Desired: Pill that dissolves the gallbladder					
		Performance			
Quality attributes:*	Endo	Traditional	Ratio	Relative weight	Weight times ratio
At-home recovery	1–2 weeks	6–8 weeks	3.0	40	120
Hospital stay	1–2 days	3–7 days	2.0	30	60
Complications rate	0–5%	1–10%	1.5	10	15
Postoperative scar	0.5–1 inch	3–5 inches	1.4	05	07
Operation time	1/2–1 hour	1–2 hours	2.0	15	30
Basic: _____	Sum of quality weights:			100	
	Market-perceived quality score:				232
*Current attributes ordered from pacing to fading.					

Note: In this example the ratios are not calculated directly from performance measures shown in columns one and two. They are based on performance scores from 1 to 10 that are linked to the performance data shown.

3. Ask well-informed customers—both yours and your competitors'—how you and your competitors perform on the various quality attributes. Then for each attribute, divide the score of the product or service you are studying by the scores of competitors' products. That gives you the performance ratio on that attribute. Multiply each ratio by the weight of that attribute. And add the results to get an overall market-perceived quality score.

The market-perceived quality score is the single most useful indicator of how well you are performing overall for customers in your targeted market.

The quality attributes in Exhibit 9–3 are ordered by their stage in the attribute life cycle, ranging from pacing to fading. This ordering works well in dynamic markets where the key quality attributes change rapidly.

In other circumstances, a different presentation of the attributes works better: Sometimes, for instance, it is useful to cluster the core product attributes into one group and the customer service attributes into another. Brand image may be broken out as a third group.

For dynamic markets, it is best to order attributes by their stage in the attribute life cycle, which we described in Exhibit 6–7. The stages of the attribute life cycle are:

- *latent:* customers don't even recognize their desire
- *desired:* customers recognize their desire, but no competitor is meeting it
- *unique:* only one competitor has this attribute
- *pacing:* the emphasis on this attribute is increasing
- *key:* these are the attributes where competition is centered
- *fading:* the market is placing less emphasis on this attribute
- *basic:* all competitors have this attribute, so it doesn't enter into the supplier selection decision; but it can become important if one supplier fails to perform.

When an attribute is in the unique stage, the one supplier who offers the attribute typically gets a high performance score while its competitors receive a 1 on a scale of 1 to 10.

Even though latent, desired, and basic attributes don't carry weight in the current decision of which supplier is selected, it is a good idea to provide space for them and to list them on the quality profile as shown in Exhibit 9–3. Desired attributes are known but not yet delivered. They can be listed and we can track the race to see who will be first to market. Latent attributes are not yet known (by the customer, anyway), but we should provide a space on the quality profile to remind us that competitive advantage in the future will depend in large part on who does the best job of discovering and delivering quickly on latent attributes.

Basic attributes can quickly become key attributes if any supplier in the marketplace has difficulty delivering them. For example, a few years ago a medical supplies company had a problem assuring that the solutions it sold to hospitals were sterile. Its products were off the market for several months. So it's wise to keep the basic attributes on the attribute list as a reminder of what will happen if you fail to deliver on one of them.

Advancing technology can also bring a basic attribute back into the supplier selection decision if some segment of the market desires a

next-generation level of performance on what had been a basic attribute.

In many businesses, each brand will tend to be the performance
leader on at least one attribute. In luxury cars BMW, which is perceived to be the performance leader in driveability, is more competitive in the market segment where people emphasize driver/car performance. Lincoln Continental, perceived to be the performance leader
in "large and roomy," leads among very tall people and those who
frequently carry six passengers. The Japanese brands Lexus and
Acura are relatively trouble-free. By entering the luxury car market
with superior, trouble-free performance, they have made this the single most important quality attribute in the luxury-car market. According to a small-sample survey I recently conducted, trouble-free is almost 50 percent more important than the second most important
attribute.

Diversified companies like Sonoco Products use the market-
perceived quality ratio not only to understand how individual businesses stack up against competitors in a single market. They also use
it to gauge the relative competitive strength of sister businesses in a
sector or even of radically different businesses in a corporate portfolio.

2. The Market-Perceived Price Profile

The market-perceived price profile is the second of the major tools of
customer value analysis. It is illustrated in Exhibit 9–4.

The construction of the market-perceived price profile is exactly
like the construction of the market-perceived quality profile. But instead of asking customers to list the factors that affect their perception
of a product's quality, you ask them to list the factors that affect their
perception of the product's cost to them. Then you ask them to tell you
the weights they put on each and to rate how they perceive the different competitors' performance on each price attribute.

A price profile may be unnecessary in some industries, where the
price is clearly understood. But in most businesses it's extremely important. Exhibit 9–4 is a price profile for a luxury automobile. This is
a more complete price profile than the version introduced in Chapter
2, because it shows not only the relative price ratio calculated from

EXHIBIT 9–4

Market-perceived price profile: Luxury cars

Price satisfaction attributes: 1	Importance weights: 2	Satisfaction scores:		
		Acura 3	Others 4	Ratio 5 = 3/4
Purchase price	60	9	7	1.29
Trade-in allowance	20	6	6	1.00
Resale price	10	9	8	1.13
Finance rates	10	7	7	1.00
	100			
Price satisfaction score:		8.3	7.0	
Price competitiveness score:				1.18
Relative price ratio (from satisfaction data)				0.85
Transactions prices ($000): a		Acura b	Others c	Ratio d = b/c
Perceived		32.8	40.0	0.82
Actual		35.2	40.0	0.88

customer satisfaction data, but also several other metrics. For a discussion of these other metrics, see "Relative Price Metrics," below.

Typically the quality leader commands a price premium relative to other suppliers. If the perceived price premium is greater than the actual price premium, the quality leader must take steps to inform the market that the price differential is not as great as they think it is.

But what's most important is to make sure that if you're producing a premium product, your lead in perceived quality is sufficient to give you a lead in customer value despite your higher price.

3. The Customer Value Map

The next tool, the customer value map, gives you the clearest picture of how the customer's decision is made among several contending suppliers. Exhibit 9–5 repeats the luxury car value map originally presented in Chapter 2, based on data from *Consumer Reports* and the relative price ratios calculated from market-perceived price profiles.

The customer value map is an exceptionally powerful tool. It shows

RELATIVE PRICE METRICS

Note that the "price score" of a product in a customer value analysis is not simply the price paid for one product divided by the price paid for the other. A thorough analysis requires at least two price metrics. Many companies use at least three.

The first, and easiest to learn from research with customers, tracks customers' perceptions of price competitiveness—their "price satisfaction." At AT&T, for instance, in the same interviews where customers are asked to rate AT&T equipment, installation, and overall quality as either "poor, fair, good, or excellent," customers also rate their satisfaction with AT&T prices as "poor, fair, good, or excellent." The *price competitiveness score* or price satisfaction score is AT&T's score divided by its competitors' score. The *relative price ratio* is the reciprocal of the price competitiveness score—the price satisfaction score of the company being studied divided by the price satisfaction score of its competitor. This is useful when you create value maps, because people find it easier to understand a map where a higher number represents a higher price.

The second measure is how high customers *perceive the competition's actual prices to be* relative to yours. For instance, AT&T interviewed customers and found they perceived MCI's prices to be some 20 percent lower than AT&T's.

The third price metric is the *actual relative prices* at which real transactions take place. This is not always easy to calculate, since different companies may sell under differing terms and conditions. But you have to calculate how much you really receive from your customers relative to how much your competitors really receive from theirs.

You can conduct a customer value analysis using only perceived prices on actual prices, but most companies that do customer value analysis track all three measures.

Here's how AT&T uses them: First, it plots perceived relative price versus the actual relative price for different customer groups. Then it diagnoses where it needs to act to change unfavorable perceptions. When AT&T long distance was only 5 percent more expensive but was perceived to be 20 percent more expensive, AT&T obviously had to take steps to tell its customers the truth.

You can also trace the larger relationships among price satisfaction, relative-perceived price, and quality. Suppose you are producing a premium product, for instance. Consider the following scenario:

1. The competition follows a strategy of pricing 15 percent below you;
2. Customers correctly perceive the price differential to be 15 percent.
3. Your surveys show that this translates into a 20 percent disadvantage in price satisfaction—your price satisfaction score divided by your competitor's price satisfaction score is .80.
4. Price satisfaction carries 40 percent of the weight and non-price attributes 60 percent in the customer-value equation.

To position your product in a superior value position you must achieve an overall market-perceived quality rating that is more than 13⅓ percent superior. (In other words, your overall market-perceived quality ratio must be greater than 1.133.) Here's how that's calculated:

Customer value = (Relative overall quality score × Quality weight) + (Relative price competitiveness score × Price weight)

Your relative price competitiveness score is .80, which reflects your 20 percent disadvantage on the price competitivenes score. Therefore to achieve a customer value rating of 1.0, you would need a market-perceived quality ratio of 1.133:

Customer value = 1.133 × .60 + .80 × .40

With a 13⅓ percent superior rating in overall quality and a 20 percent disadvantage in price competitiveness, the relative customer values offered by the two competitors are equal.

EXHIBIT 9–5

Luxury cars: Customer value map

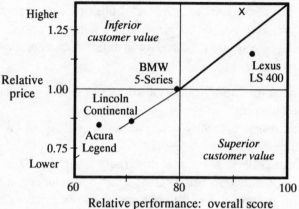

Note: Data for relative performance based on
Consumer Reports ratings, April 1993, p. 228.

you who is likely to gain market share, and why. Companies tend to gain market share when they are below and to the right of the fair-value line.

A company can also use the customer value map to compare the value positioning of each of its businesses. Exhibit 9–6 shows a value map for a large corporation's portfolio of business units. (We cannot name the corporation for confidentiality reasons.)

This kind of map probably tells more about the business as a whole than any other single exhibit—even more than a one-page financial statement. This particular map reveals a sizable cluster of business units receiving premium prices that are not fully supported by superior perceived quality. Several thoughts occurred to the company's president as he reviewed his corporate value map. Most of the business units had achieved superior perceived-quality relative to the competition. Perhaps some of his businesses were able to charge higher price premiums because they were part of a portfolio in which the superior perceived quality of each business spilled over onto sister businesses.

However, he could see his company was vulnerable. This president

EXHIBIT 9–6

A value map of your business units can pinpoint strengths and weaknesses

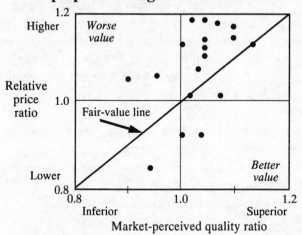

Adapted from *The PIMS Principles,* by Robert D. Buzzell & Bradley T. Gale; copyright © 1987 by The Free Press.

decided to launch a dramatic market-perceived quality improvement program to fully support its premium price.

4. The Won/Lost Analysis

The next tool is straightforward, but few organizations regularly use it. It is a won/lost analysis of recent competition. When executives are asked if they use a "won/lost" analysis to track the outcome of major competitive confrontations, the frequent responses are, "We already do that," or, "We tried that, and it didn't work." So I ask them to show me their won/lost analysis.

There's rarely a careful analysis to show. Frequently the only won/lost analysis is an informal understanding that the last competitive struggles the organization won were won because, "We did a heck of a job of salesmanship." The last few losses were lost because, "The other guys cut their prices to the bone."

A worthwhile won/lost analysis requires greater care. When you "did a heck of a job of salesmanship," what were the key points you made that turned the tide in your favor? Those may be important clues to the quality attributes that will drive your targeted market in the future.

Many companies do lose a few sales battles to dying competitors who "cut prices to the bone"—operating below the survival level in order to keep their production lines busy a little while longer. But more commonly when the competition wins a battle on price, either the competition has learned to deliver at lower cost than you, or the potential customer didn't believe your salespeople when they discussed the quality attributes that *should* have made your product worth more.

Either way, a careful won/lost analysis is an extraordinarily valuable tool for understanding customer value.

For mass-market products where you don't speak individually to each purchaser, an analysis of the different segments of the market where you are gaining or losing share, and why, can serve the same purpose. For example, for luxury automobiles two obvious segmentation analyses are older versus younger customers and male versus female customers.

The won/lost analysis is especially crucial for start-up businesses, which may not yet have enough customers to make a customer-value and market-perceived-quality tracking system practical. As IBM reorganized into "lines of business" in 1991 it shifted focus from hardware to software and services. This spawned embryonic business-to-business software products with fewer than 100 "installs." For these businesses there is no huge customer base. But for each serious sales opportunity it is vital to know why the customer decided to buy or not buy the software and why they decided to buy from IBM or a competitor.

On the other hand, in certain market segments where major pieces of business are won or lost as suppliers court large-volume buyers, won/lost analysis can play a special role. For example, there are two key segments of the market for nicotine patches designed to help people give up smoking. The segment composed of individual doctors who prescribe patches for patients is obviously very fragmented. By contrast, the segment of providers who supply patches for an entire HMO or large corporation is much more concentrated. It is important to know how the first dozen HMOs and large companies select a supplier, who wins the contracts and why.

Won/lost analyses are also crucial when a new competitor enters the market. In defending its dominant position in surgical sutures, the Ethicon division of Johnson & Johnson conducted especially careful analyses to understand why some hospitals decided to try the products of its rival, United States Surgical Corporation, how they judged performance head-to-head during the trial, why they decided to convert to USSC or stay with Ethicon, and why they might decide to switch back.

5. The Head-to-Head Area Chart of Customer Value

The head-to-head area chart of customer value is a graphic display of where you are doing well and where you do worse against a single competitor (Exhibit 9–7). This kind of chart is crucial in helping you decide where you need to improve performance and how you should try to shift importance weights or focus on segments where the importance weights favor you.

Exhibit 9–7 is a head-to-head area chart of customer value repre-

EXHIBIT 9–7

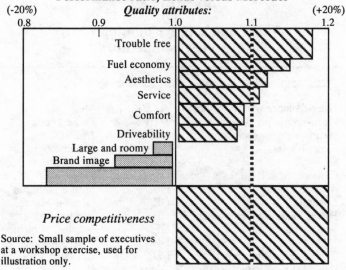

Head-to-head area chart of customer value
Performance ratio, Lexus versus Mercedes

| (-20%) | *Quality attributes:* | (+20%) |

| 0.8 | 0.9 | 1.0 | 1.1 | 1.2 |

Trouble free
Fuel economy
Aesthetics
Service
Comfort
Driveability
Large and roomy
Brand image

Price competitiveness

Source: Small sample of executives
at a workshop exercise, used for
illustration only.

senting views about the quality of two makes of luxury cars. The opinions are those of a small sample of executives at a recent workshop.

The horizontal dimension shows how much the targeted market perceives Lexus's performance to be better or worse than a key competitor. On "trouble free" Lexus's performance is 8.6 and Mercedes's is 7.3. So the performance ratio of Lexus versus Mercedes on trouble free is 1.18. This means that Lexus's performance score on trouble free is 18 percent better than Mercedes's score. The thickness of the bars in Exhibit 9–7 reflects how important each component of customer value is in the targeted market. Respondents placed about two thirds of the weight on quality and one third on price. "Trouble-free" accounts for 19 percent of the weight of the quality attributes.

The quality attributes are plotted in order of Lexus's performance versus its competitor. In this example, Lexus has a performance advantage versus Mercedes on many quality attributes and a big performance edge on price as well. Certain segments will place more weight on safety. This will make Mercedes, which is perceived to be the quality leader in safety, more competitive in the safety-conscious segment.

In many markets, the focus of competition is between the top two or three competitors, as shown in Exhibit 9–8.

EXHIBIT 9–8

Many markets are dominated by two key competitors

Targeted market	Top competitors	
Long-distance phone service	AT&T	MCI
Lipid-regulating drugs	Merck	Parke-Davis
Instruments for endo-surgery	USSC	J&J Ethicon
Razor blades	Gillette	Schick
Soap	P&G	Lever
Carbonated soft drinks	Coca Cola	Pepsi
Aircraft engines	GE	Pratt & Whitney
Locomotives	GE	General Motors
Power generation equipment	GE	Westinghouse
Washers & dryers	GE	Maytag, Whirlpool
Light bulbs	GE	GTE Sylvania
Construction equipment	Caterpillar	Komatsu
Regional newspaper, Boston	Globe	Herald

The battles between Number 1 and Number 2 in these kinds of markets are always interesting, and shifts in competitive advantage can be captured on head-to-head area graphs of customer value which complement the quality profile and reveal more detailed insights than the position of just two competitors on a customer value map.

6. The Key Events Time Line

The key events time line (Exhibit 9–9) is a vitally important strategic planning tool that few organizations use.

It enables you to develop a better understanding of how your actions and your competitors' actions change the market's perception of performance on each quality attribute, and how these actions also shift the relative importance weights of key quality attributes. It is vital for learning to recognize that changes in the customer value you provide really do affect market share.

One of the most dramatic events to hit the luxury car market in the last decade was the long awaited entry of a Japanese competitor. Honda Motors entered that market with a new, separate division and

EXHIBIT 9–9

Key events time line: Cholesterol drugs

Feb. 1982	Parke-Davis launches Lopid
Jan. 1987	Lopid promotes "long-term safety" as a key attribute
Sep. 1987	Merck launches Mevacor as a cholesterol-lowering drug
Feb. 1988	National Cholesterol Education Program Guidelines - 1
Aug. 1989	Statistics from Helsinki Heart Study released showing Lopid increased HDL, improved lipid balance, and reduced coronary heart disease
1990–92	Lopid repositioned as a "lipid-regulating" drug
Jan. 1991	Framingham Heart Study publishes new risk equation focused on mix of good vs. bad cholesterol instead of total (combined level of good and bad) cholesterol
1992	Two new cholesterol-lowering drugs, Pravachol and Zochor launched—Lopid holds share, Mevacor slips
June 1993	NCEP Guidelines - 2: Measure HDL for all adults

brand—Acura—in 1986. For many years Japanese cars had out-performed U.S. and European economy and intermediate models on being trouble free. Acura brought this key advantage to the luxury car market, and quickly captured the "economy" end of the luxury car market. Toyota Motors entered at the top-quality end of the luxury car market with Lexus in 1988. It wasn't quite at the typical premium end of the fair-value line because it came in with superior quality and an average, rather than a premium price.

BMW made efforts to improve performance on "trouble free" while also improving on driveability. Cadillac completely revamped the way in which it designs new models and brings them to the market.

Instead of trying to match Lexus on price, Mercedes initially chose to respond by focusing on new, higher performance models. But, as a *New York Times* article noted in the summer of 1992, investors are uneasy about Daimler-Benz because Mercedes has faced a slowdown, losses and layoffs in the 1990s.

> The slowdown at Mercedes stems from a lingering recession in Europe, the United States and Japan, and problems with the new line of Mercedes luxury sedans, called the S class, introduced in early 1991.
>
> The German auto media are critical of the S Class, calling it too big, too heavy, too expensive and too cramped. The car is 17 feet long, weighs almost 5,000 pounds and costs $60,000 to $135,000. Because of the small back seat, it can hold only three large adults in reasonable comfort.[2]

Finally, in another key event, Mercedes announced in the *Wall Street Journal* on September 23, 1993, that it was cutting prices.

> Mercedes-Benz of North America, Inc., trying to position itself as a "value" player in a sluggish U.S. market for luxury cars, said it's cutting prices as much as 14.8 percent on some of its best-selling automobiles for the 1994 model year.
>
>   . . . Mercedes-Benz AG said the price of its six-cylinder-powered E320 sedan would start at $42,500, a 14.8 percent cut from a year ago, when the vehicle, known then as a 300E sedan, sold for

$49,900. The name changes are part of a new, simpler classification system Mercedes is introducing this year.[3]

The next day, the *Wall Street Journal* carried a two-page ad proclaiming "To all those who think a sensible Mercedes-Benz is an oxymoron. Introducing the new E-Class." Five days later another two-page *Wall Street Journal* ad noted, "It will send the competition back to our drawing board. . . . The New E-Class starting at $42,900." On October 20, 1993, a *Wall Street Journal* reporter summarized these new initiatives in "Mercedes-Benz Tries to Compete on Value." As the author noted, "this year's model, the C-Class sedans are symbols of a new phase for Mercedes-Benz as it tries to shed its old and arrogant ways."[4]

At Parke-Davis, the key events time line helped the brand team to understand the changing positioning of Lopid in the market for lipid-regulating drugs (Exhibit 9–9). Lopid had entered the market in February of 1982 and become the market leader. During the 1980s most of the focus was on lowering total cholesterol rather than improving the mix of good versus bad cholesterol. As it turned out when the market finally realized the importance of raising good cholesterol, Lopid's great strength was its relative efficacy in raising HDL cholesterol. But its brand name "Lopid" connotes the ability to lower total cholesterol rather than to raise good cholesterol.

Anticipating Merck's entry with a new drug, Parke-Davis converted to a safety focus in its promotion in January of 1987. Merck entered in September of 1987 with Mevacor, which outperformed Lopid on lowering total and LDL (bad) cholesterol, but wasn't as efficacious as Lopid at boosting good cholesterol.

The National Cholesterol Education Program Guidelines, which emphasized total cholesterol and LDL cholesterol, were published in February of 1988. Other key events included the publication of scientific studies that began to clarify the different roles of different kinds of cholesterol. Statistics from the Helsinki Heart Study, which found that Lopid improved the lipid balance and reduced the rate of coronary heart disease relative to a control group taking placebos, were released in the *Journal of the American Medical Association,* in 1988. The shift from using a measure of total cholesterol to using a measure of the mix of good and bad cholesterol in the Framingham Heart Study risk equation was a key event when published by the Framingham research team in January of 1991. Practicing physicians sharpened their knowledge of the roles of good versus bad cholesterol as risk indicators and began to develop a clearer understanding of the relative efficacy of Lopid versus Mevacor on each of the elements of total cholesterol. As these events took place, physicians began to shift weight away from simply lowering total cholesterol toward boosting good (HDL) cholesterol and reducing bad (LDL) cholesterol. The triglyceride consensus released in 1992 was a benchmark event that further integrated and disseminated the stream of scientific findings. National cholesterol guidelines issued by the U.S. government in 1993 also proved to be a key event for the cholesterol-lowering and lipid-regulating segments of the market for cardiovascular drugs.

The General Business Systems unit of AT&T achieved a much deeper understanding of their market-perceived quality and customer value data in 1990 when they linked the results of a key-events time-line study, carried out by an outside group, to the monthly trends in their perceived performance versus competitors on several quality attributes. Key events included new product launches, pricing changes, shifts in customer service policies and a victory in an anti-dumping case against a Japanese competitor.

7. A What/Who Matrix

A what/who matrix (Exhibit 9–10) is the method for tracking who is responsible for the actions that will make success in customer value possible. The what/who matrix indicates which processes determine our performance versus competitors for each quality attribute. For a specific competitor, it should also indicate who "owns" the process that is most responsible for influencing our performance versus competitors. This process owner is responsible for coordinating the different processes and functions required to improve performance versus competitors.

But be careful when preparing a "who-does-what-by-when" set of action steps. Determine to what extent a performance advantage or disadvantage is "perceived" or "real." Suppose you sell a product that contains fluid and you find that customers perceive that you have more leaks than competitors. How do you fix it?

First, find out if you really have proportionately more leakers.

EXHIBIT 9–10

What/who matrix: Luxury cars
What process drives performance? Who owns it?

Quality attributes	Designing	Assuring conformance	Manufacturing	Selling & servicing	Distributing	Marketing
Trouble free	X	X	☒	X	X	
Comfort	☒	X				
Safety	☒	X	X	X		
Driveability	☒	X				
Service				☒	X	
Aesthetics	X					☒
Brand image	X			X		☒

Then, determine where the problem occurs. Perhaps the manufacturing process is OK but the products are damaged in transit. If so, it won't do any good to put the director of manufacturing in charge of fixing the problem.

Suppose, however, that you conduct a careful study and find that your performance is actually better than the competition—you have fewer leakers—but the customers think you have more! In this case you must disseminate the evidence to your sales force and the customer in a clear, convincing fashion.

The Significance of Customer Value Analysis

Some of the milestones in developing metrics for strategic navigation are displayed in Exhibit 9–11. The merchants of Venice invented double-entry bookkeeping in the fifteenth century. A mathematical treatise, *Summa de Arithmetica, Geometria, Proportioni et Proportionalita*, published by Luca Pacioli five centuries ago, summarized their methods and laid the foundation for the income statement and balance sheet.

To collect taxes and protect investors, the Internal Revenue Service

EXHIBIT 9–11

Milestones in measurement for strategic navigation

AT&T: Market-perceived quality, relative price, customer value

PIMS: Metrics for market attractiveness, competitive position, operating effectiveness and financial results [Multi-industry database of business units]

GE: Share, quality, productivity + P&L, BS [Industrial and consumer-durable-goods SBUs]

Nielsen: Market size and share [Consumer package goods]

P&L and balance sheet   From GAAP toward GASP
→

Pacioli	A.C. Nielsen	G.E.	Schoeffler	Customer
Venice	Chicago	Measurements	Buzzell & Gale	value
		task force	*The PIMS Principles*	analysis
1490s	1930s	1950s	1970s–1980s	1990s

(IRS) and Securities and Exchange Commission (SEC) monitor the financial reporting of corporations. The Financial Accounting Standards Board (FASB), enhances the comparability of financial statements.

But no agency has set out to design the information system that a business needs to successfully navigate its way in the competitive marketplace. The Baldrige guidelines developed at the National Institute of Standards and Technology are a step in this direction, but, unlike the institute that created them and sets standards on everything except measures of competitive position, the Baldrige guidelines, by design, are not prescriptive. Companies are encouraged to use a customized approach to winning in the marketplace and to write up that approach in their Baldrige application.

The pieces for a strategic navigation system and the metrics of customer value analysis have been evolving over the last sixty years—a short time span by accounting standards. During the 1930s, A. C. Nielsen began to track the sales of categories of fast-moving consumer packaged goods through the distribution system to the household end user. Once marketers knew the volume of sales in a category, they could calculate their market share by dividing their sales in the category (coffee, razor blades, shaving cream) by the total sales. This breakthrough set the stage for development of additional nonfinancial metrics.

The next major steps in creating a science of strategic management were taken by General Electric. Again, necessity was the mother of invention. GE competed in many different markets against many tough competitors. (Note the number of markets in Exhibit 9–8 where General Electric is one of the top two competitors.) GE needed a facts-based method, more dependable than "gut feel," to decide which businesses to invest in and which to leave.

In the 1950s, GE had about fifty different lines of business. Therefore it needed fifty general managers. But the company found business schools focused on individual disciplines like sales, manufacturing, personnel, accounting and finance. They had few executive courses for general managers. One result was that GE established its famed executive education center in Crotonville, New York, to develop these general managers. (The situation in business schools has improved somewhat and will continue to improve as executive educators and graduate business schools scramble to make their curriculums more relevant and to head off any trend toward customized, in-company executive education centers).

In the 1970s, GE went on to invent the disciplines of strategic planning and strategic management. Under Fred Borch and Jack McKitterick, GE came up with the concept and definition of a "served market" and a "natural business unit," which partners at McKinsey & Co. later repackaged as a "strategic business unit."

One key GE initiative is central to our story. One of McKitterick's major researchers, as we've indicated previously, was Sidney Schoeffler, the economist and certified public accountant that GE had enticed away from the University of Massachusetts economics department during the 1960s.

Schoeffler's seminal contribution was to combine data received from GE's financial people (P&L—including purchases and value added—and balance sheet) with data from operations (value added, capacity utilization, headcount), marketing (market share, product quality, percent of sales from new products), and other sources for each of GE's ninety or so nondefense related "departments."

Sid used statistical analyses to understand why some GE businesses were highly profitable while others were not. He built his findings into a profit optimization model (called "PROM") that GE planners and executives used to challenge the strategic plans of GE's operating units and, more importantly, to sharpen the strategic thinking of GE's operating managers.

The work fascinated many other companies and their executives came to swap ideas with GE corporate planners in what might be considered an early form of benchmarking.

Then, as GE became increasingly interested in service industries, top executives decided to allow Schoeffler a leave of absence to set up a multicompany, multiindustry research program modeled on the GE business database. Schoeffler was to validate the work that he had pioneered at GE and extend the analysis to sectors of the economy where GE had no experience.

Sid had been my advisor when I earned a masters degree in economics at the University of Massachusetts, and I had worked with him at GE's corporate planning operation during summers in the late 1960s while completing a doctoral program at Rutgers. Sid asked me to join Harvard Business School professor Bob Buzzell and him to establish the Profit Impact of Market Strategy (PIMS) program at the Marketing Science Institute in Cambridge, Massachusetts. We held a kickoff meeting at the Harvard Business School in the fall of 1971. By 1975, companies were asking the PIMS team to help their business units use the metrics we'd developed to improve their competitive positions. Since this work went beyond the scope of the Marketing Science Institute, we set up the Strategic Planning Institute in 1975 as the home for our research, executive education, and consulting. The product of all this was to build upon and extend Schoeffler's influential work on the importance of market share, capital intensity, productivity, relative quality, and other key variables in determining profitability.

Customer-value analysis developed out of this research tradition. At the PIMS program, we had inherited two components of a customer value metric from GE that we eventually refined, expanded, and integrated. One measured a business's quality versus competitors from the customer's point of view. The questionnaire asked a product-line business unit to classify the portion of its sales that came from products that were viewed by customers as "superior," "equivalent," or "inferior" to competition. We then calculated relative quality as the percent superior minus the percent inferior. If 45 percent of your sales came from products viewed as superior and 25 percent came from products viewed as inferior, your score was 45 minus 25 or 20. This metric correlated with market share and profitability, but it didn't yield much insight into how to improve relative quality or business performance.

Moreover, it didn't work for businesses or brands that had just one product. I remember a phone call from a brand manager, an SPI member, who was validating his proposed strategy against the experiences of businesses in the PIMS database. He had only one product. When he came to the relative quality question, he realized that he had only three possible entries: 100 percent superior, 100 percent equivalent, or 100 percent inferior. He felt that consumers viewed his brand as somewhat better than competitors, but he was reluctant to enter "100 percent superior" because this would wildly overstate his advantage.

Working with people from participating companies, we then evolved a quality profiling chart somewhat similar to those we have used to calculate market-perceived quality throughout this book. The market-perceived quality methodology has been carefully developed since 1980.

I developed the market-perceived quality ratio metric introduced in Chapter 2 in 1992, and applied to the Strategic Planning Institute for permission to use the PIMS database to study how this quality ratio is related to measures of competitive position and business results. The results of this research appear in Chapters 1, 7, and 12. Like other key strategic navigation data—market share and growth rates, for instance—the market-perceived quality ratio is easy to calculate, track, and interpret once you have gathered the necessary data.

The other component of a customer value metric that we inherited from GE was the actual relative transactions price of a business versus its competitors. This important and powerful piece of information ultimately became part of the broader relative price profile described above. Unfortunately, it didn't enable us to calculate a clean, easy-to-interpret metric for customer value. The customer value metric introduced in this book, also developed in 1992, uses relative-perceived price performance (on a scale of 1 to 10) as the price metric.

All this means something significant: Practitioners now have a consistent set of customer value metrics that are easy to interpret. In Chapter 4 we showed how customer value is a leading indicator of market share. In Chapter 7 we showed how market-perceived quality is the key to positioning power brands. In Chapter 12, we'll also show, with detailed data, that market-perceived quality is directly linked to business results across all kinds of businesses and markets.

Market-perceived quality and the other information displayed by the seven tools of customer value analysis are crucial to understanding, planning, and adapting strategy. A summary of what the best companies do as they strive to provide superior value for their targeted markets is shown in Exhibit 9–12. For comparison we contrast the ordinary and best elements of various systems businesses use to measure and improve customer value.

Note, however, that I don't say this information is crucial to "implementing" or "executing" a "long-range" strategy. There was a period during the 1970s and early '80s when executives thought that strategic plans were powerful and strategy implementation was weak.

EXHIBIT 9–12

Striving for superior customer value:
What the best companies do

Elements	Ordinary	Best
Quality attributes	Internal phrases Static Product only	Customer's words Dynamic, future Product & service
Price attributes	None	Three price metrics
Importance	Ratings	Relative weights
Sample	Own customers	Targeted market
Performance	Our company	Versus competitors
Metrics	Ineffective	Link to results
Alignment to market	Weak	Comprehensive

But executives now realize that a strategically well-managed business is one where executives think and manage strategically every day, not one with a neat, detailed, long-range plan. Most long-range plans really can't be implemented because the market environment and competitive conditions change too quickly.

Larry Bossidy, then vice chairman of the board and executive officer of General Electric and now CEO of Allied Signal, summarized GE's transition from strategic planning to strategic thinking and true strategic management masterfully in a 1987 speech.

> . . . I want to make it clear that when we deserted strategic planning, we most emphatically did not abandon strategic thinking or strategic management. . . . This discipline is a vital, continuous, flexible process consisting of:
>
> - Gathering information
> - Setting direction
> - Marshaling resources
> - Identifying objectives
> - Analyzing performance
> - And, most importantly, modifying objectives, revising resource commitments, and changing direction as appropriate.
>
> There is nothing ad hoc or seat-of-the-pants about this form of management. In fact, it is much more intellectually demanding of the leader who employs it, since the "Plan" is never put to bed, as it was in the strategic planning era, but rather is constantly tested and revised based on events in the real world.
>
> The key to strategic management is strategic thinking. Relevant strategic thinking focuses not on finding some elusive optimum but on understanding the forces that influence the success of the business.
>
> Strategic thinking begins with the familiar: strategic analysis. One examines market evolution; who buys which product; how much do they buy, why, and how much are they willing to pay? 101 stuff until you seek the factors that could turn the world upside down. . . .
>
> The next step is to understand competition. What is their position in terms of capital, product breadth, geographic coverage, technology, etc.? How well do they do what they do? Are we as good or bad

as we think? Why? Again pretty elementary ideas. The challenge, however, is to understand the radical steps the competitors can take to upset the competitive equilibrium: GE buying CGR; BBC merging with ASEA; Chrysler buying American Motors, and what these steps mean. A crucial element of management behavior these days depends on an understanding of the competitive environment. A realistic in-depth understanding facilitates the ability to either plot your own strategy or to devise defenses for those of your competitors. A comprehensive knowledge of the competitive environment also breeds an understanding of the enormous value of a strategic first strike because it is understood that although most strategic developments are replicable, follow-ons are not of the same value.

In the book *Islands in the Stream,* Hemingway describes how an argument between a genteel New Yorker who had sailed his yacht to the island, and an alcoholic fishing boat captain, progressed to a fight. Hopelessly outclassed, the New Yorker soon conceded, only to be savagely beaten. Hemingway's point was that prep school rules don't apply in the alley. So it is in business. Fierce competitors press every advantage. Realistic appraisals of a situation and tough, prompt decision-making prevent one from waking up on the dock, bloody and beaten. . . .

Strategic thinking identifies and synthesizes the forces which affect your business, while strategic management uses strategic thinking to set business objectives and to communicate this direction to the organization. . . .

In my view, any enterprise where complete knowledge of the business is shared by a large number of its people is on the track to success."[5]

It's hard to disagree: The extent to which managers learn to think strategically ultimately determines their success.

For most, today, that's a long way away. Many companies are just beginning to face up to the challenge of providing an infrastructure that will allow a business-unit management system to work. In the past several years, AT&T (1989), Pitney Bowes (1990), IBM (1991), Xerox (early 1992), Polaroid (mid-1992), and Digital Equipment (late 1992) have all attempted to reorganize into more coherent business units.

"BIAS INDEX" COMPENSATES FOR OVERREPRESENTATION OF YOUR OWN CUSTOMERS IN SURVEY SAMPLES

Many companies obtain monthly data on customer satisfaction and perceived price from sources that tend to overrepresent their own customers. Others carry out random sample surveys, but the monthly sample sizes are small and the proportion of their own customers in the samples varies from month to month.

This often leads to misleading analyses, because your own customers' perceptions frequently differ from those of competitors' customers. They may weight various product or customer service attributes differently. They probably have a higher opinion of your product/service offering than competitors' customers. And they often view your pricing policies differently than competitors' customers as well.

The biggest problem occurs when the extent of the bias fluctuates from month to month. Then executives may spend hours trying to correct "problems" that aren't problems at all.

The following "bias index" allows you to adjust for shifts in market-perceived quality or market-perceived price scores that may be caused by changes in the bias of the samples. Simply calculate:

$$\text{Bias index} = \frac{\%\text{ of your customers in sample} - \text{Your market share}}{\text{Your market share}} \times 100$$

Suppose, for example, you sell agricultural chemicals to farmers and your market share is 30 percent. If you use a random sample survey and your customers make up 36 percent of the respondents, your bias index is 20 percent in your favor. If your customers make up only 20 percent of the respondents, your bias index is 33 percent against you.

Some researchers control for the effects of random variation by using a moving average of three months or quarters. But this averages the effects of bias across time periods and lengthens competitive response time. The effects of bias, caused by over-representation or underrepresentation of your customers in any sample time period, on your relative-perceived quality scores can be calibrated and removed each month or quarter. This approach reduces the cycle time for competitive response.

But their efforts represent only a small part of the solution to the problem. Companies need operating managers who understand competitive strategy and work as a cooperative team. Then they'll be on the "interfunctional teams that understand competitive strategy" side of the horizontal axis and the "strategic navigation" end of the vertical axis of Exhibit 9–1. And then they can consistently deliver what customers want.

Most companies today are at the lower left in Exhibit 9–1. Function heads run fiefdoms, and managers rely almost exclusively on financial data to understand the organization as a whole. They need to find their way to the upper right.

To me, the best way to begin this journey toward competitiveness is to work on assuring that complete knowledge of the business is shared by a large number. Applying the seven tools of customer value analysis is the best possible start. Then designing a strategic navigation system for your business and using the war-room approach for business-unit team meetings, which we will discuss in the next chapter, will catapult your organization to true customer value management.

The war room panel for managing customer value

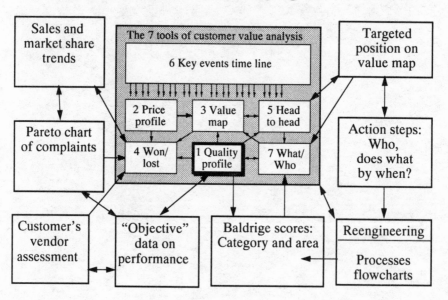

CHAPTER 10

Putting the Power of Your Whole Organization in a Single Room: The War-Room Wall and Strategic Navigation

---

Now we have a standard set of tools for understanding and improving value. But all-purpose tools, by themselves, can't make an organization a winner. We need a system to help management utilize the data.

To create such a system, adopt the war-room method of conducting business meetings, create a *war-room wall* that will help the business team absorb all the crucial facts about the business, and build a *strategic navigation system* that will make the important strategic information available and useful. This chapter will tell you how.

What Is a "War-Room Wall"?

The war room is one of the oldest and best-proven of management devices. It's certainly older than financial accounting. Every organization needs at least one war room. And many need dozens of war rooms where parts of the business can be understood and managed.

As we discussed in Chapter 2, successful generals universally use a war room because it is the only way to deal with a problem that generals share with executives: too much of (mostly) the wrong kind of data. In the war room the general and his staff assemble and analyze all the key information needed for formulating and implementing strategy. They select the information that's relevant to their problems, and put it up on the war-room wall. Because it's all on the wall, each

241

member of the team can study the parts he or she needs to understand. Each can discuss questions with other members without taking the time of others who may not be interested in or need to understand a particular topic.

For a business, the war-room wall displays the crucial information about the customers, markets, competitors, technologies, and processes that can drive or prevent success.

Locate the main war-room wall in a resource-rich room where the business-unit general manager and his team meet regularly. The tools of customer value analysis (see Exhibit 9–2) are at the core of the war room wall. Using these tools helps a business-unit team to answer the competitive strategy questions listed in Exhibit 10–1, which most of today's management systems cannot handle.

In addition to the seven tools of customer value analysis, the war-room wall may contain:

- *A Pareto chart of complaints:* pinpointing the most frequent reasons why customers complain
- *A plot of market share trends:* tracking your progress versus competitors
- *Customer retention rates:* indicating the percentage of customers retained year to year
- *New-customer win rates:* tracking the percentage of new customers won each period
- *Market segment analysis:* showing how the weights on quality attributes differ by market segment
- *Report card from customer:* giving feedback from one or more major, leading-edge customers
- *List of latent/emerging attributes:* showing what will drive the market in the future
- *New product launch schedule:* targeting the commercialization of new goods and services
- *Cycle time for new products:* tracking how long it takes versus competitors
- *Cycle time for delivery:* tracking how long it takes versus competitors
- *Technological substitution curve:* tracking how fast a new technology is displacing the old technology

EXHIBIT 10–1
Does Your Current Management System
Enable You to Answer These Questions?

---

1. How do our customers and noncustomers select among competing suppliers?
2. What are the key quality attributes (purchase criteria)?
3. How important is each criterion (relative weights)?
4. Which criteria are increasing or decreasing in importance?
5. How do the weights differ by market segment?

6. How do we perform on each criterion?
7. How does each of our competitors perform on each criterion?
8. How do customers (ours and competitors') size us up versus each of our key competitors?
9. How is our perceived performance versus competitors changing?
10. What process determines our performance versus competitors? Who owns it?

11. Why are orders/customers won or lost?
12. Who are we winning orders from—who are we losing them to—why?
13. How does each set of competitors' customers size us up head-to-head versus that competitor?
14. How can we improve our performance versus competitors?
15. How can we shift the importance weights in our favor?
16. Which segments should we target?
17. How will customers size up the new versus the old technology?
18. Which of the new technologies will win?

- *Technology profile:* identifying the technologies that underpin your products and markets and where you stand on each technology versus competitors
- *Core competencies list:* identifying your key skills as an organization
- *Latest Baldrige assessment:* telling where your organization is strong and where it is weak

- *Baldrige estimates on competitors:* showing competitors' strengths and weaknesses.
- *A list of action steps:* that the business team is taking to improve customer value and achieve its targeted position of providing superior customer value

Exhibit 10–2 is a mock-up of a war-room wall panel focused on providing superior customer value. It contains several of the exhibits listed above, clustered around the seven tools of customer value analysis in the center. Examine this collection of data. Imagine how it can be used to make sense of, and to improve, a business.

Executives can gain a clear understanding of how the customer selects among competing providers in your marketplace. They can think through why orders and customers are won or lost. The quality profile (near the center of the exhibit) tells how customers perceive the organization's performance versus competitors. The "head-to-head" charge of customer value (to the right and above the quality profile) provides a graphic display of how you stand up against one key competitor. A customer's vendor assessment reveals how that company sizes up alternative suppliers. Objective data on performance (from

EXHIBIT 10–2

The war room panel for managing customer value

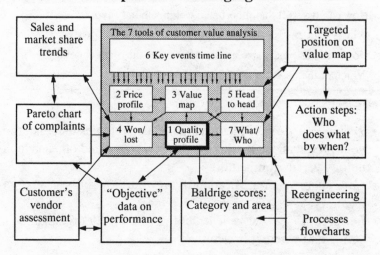

engineering studies, benchmarking, competitive intelligence, or third-party rating services) tell where you're ahead and where you're behind. They may indicate gaps between the perceptions displayed in the other charts and reality.

A comparison of the data from these different sources allows the interfunctional management team to learn more about its markets, customers, and competitors. It reduces the level of "noise" in the data that prevents alignment and positive action. It increases the likelihood that managers will hear the signals in the data that pinpoint which actions have a good chance of paying off in the marketplace.

At the same time, the displayed thinking on the right half of Exhibit 10–2 reveals where the business wants to position itself on the value map, and how the team intends to get there. It's vitally important for teams to remind themselves of what they've already decided.

And as all this information is acted on, the customer value tracking system at the center of Exhibit 10–2 (especially the quality profile, the price profile, the value map, and the key events time line) will allow the team to continuously monitor their progress toward its targeted customer value position—or movement away from it.

Exhibit 10–3 is a mock-up of another war-room wall panel—this

EXHIBIT 10–3

The internal view of quality
**Initiatives and tools for improving processes
and reducing failure rates and costs**

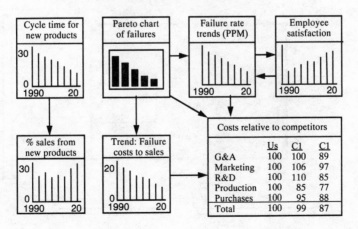

Costs relative to competitors			
	Us	C1	C1
G&A	100	100	89
Marketing	100	106	97
R&D	100	110	85
Production	100	85	77
Purchases	100	95	88
Total	100	99	87

one focused on internal metrics. Companies that have concentrated on conformance quality have most of the ingredients for this internal view (Pareto chart of failures, failure rate trends, trends of costs of poor quality, yield rates, etc.). But when this data is viewed next to the customer quality and value data shown in Exhibit 10–2, the team can for the first time think wisely about its meaning. The what/who matrix and "who does what by when" list of action steps begin to spring to life.[1]

The Traditional Meeting Room vs. the War Room

Unfortunately, most business meeting rooms have little of this information. And the team cannot easily refer to what is present because it is buried in books and papers. In short, our meeting rooms are not designed for action learning or for creative problem solving.

The typical meeting room is rectangular, with a table in the center (Exhibit 10–4). The general manager sits at the head of the table, and a presenter shows visual aids one at a time on a screen near the foot of the table.

EXHIBIT 10–4

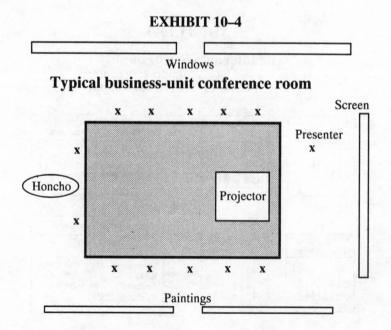

Windows

Typical business-unit conference room

Paintings

No one can practice the science and art of displayed thinking in this room. Information cannot be efficiently communicated. In fact, businesspeople perform thousands of absurdly wasteful scenarios in this kind of conference room every day.

The executives who meet here are among the busiest people in the world. But the meetings typically don't start until the top executive arrives. If he is late, the executives shuffle nervously or make small talk.

Once a presentation is under way, listeners often don't know how to react. Sometimes they don't understand the material well enough to respond usefully to it. But they don't want to displease the boss. So they swivel their necks between the presenter and the boss, hoping to react in a way that will please the him (or her). They are like people at the net watching a tennis match. It's amazing that companies that conduct meetings this way ever reach wise decisions.

By contrast, consider a meeting conducted in a war room such as that shown in Exhibit 10–5. This war room draws not only on the work of the Strategic Planning Institute and of Market-Driven Quality Inc., but also on concepts of the team meeting room and displayed thinking

EXHIBIT 10–5

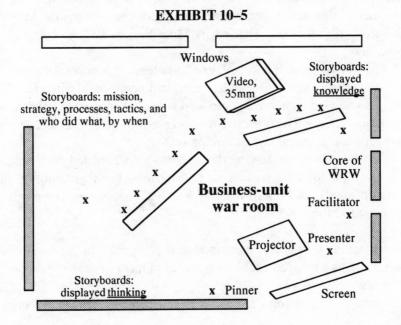

developed by former Walt Disney executive Mike Vance based on his Disney experiences.

Storyboards cover most of the wall space in this kind of room. Meetings really begin as soon as the first participant wanders in. Anyone in the room can absorb new knowledge about the marketplace and about the business's progress from the storyboards; as soon as two executives are present, they can begin working together to deepen their understanding. So the meeting builds as early arrivers enter, cluster around a storyboard, and begin to interact.

When the meeting gets into full swing, people take turns playing the roles of presenter, facilitator, and "pinner"—the person in charge of effectively adding new information to the storyboards.

Members participate in each presentation with all the information on the war-room wall as background. The presenter makes some of the connections between his topic and the overall strategy of the organization, but his teammates are in a position to make many more.

The facilitator coordinates the flow of ideas. Participants state their questions, suggestions, and proposed action steps and then write them on five-by-eight-inch index cards in heavy, readable letters. The "pinner" pins each card in the appropriate place on a storyboard. By adding more cards to the storyboard, the pinner displays the thinking of the group for all to see. That's why Mike Vance calls this "displayed thinking."

The war-room wall is "displayed knowledge." A powerful meeting occurs—and is likely to lead to successful decisions—when the displayed knowledge of a war-room wall is used to support the displayed thinking process. The objective data on the war-room wall is essential to keeping managers' team-thinking realistic.

On the other hand, having the war-room wall loaded with crucial data won't help as much as it could if each team member interprets the data differently and doesn't share ideas with associates. The meeting room in Exhibit 10–5 helps everyone:

- filter out the "noise" and pinpoint the "signals" in the data
- learn as a team and achieve better alignment in strategic thinking
- create clear action steps and a commitment to carry them out

Creating a War-Room Wall Forces
You to Improve Your Systems

Creating the displays for the war-room wall often forces you to improve your organization's systems. Each organization should include not only the seven tools of customer value analysis on its war-room wall, but also additional data and tools to meet its own needs.

One important tool, as listed above, is a Pareto chart of customer complaints. At the Ethicon surgical sutures business, for instance, we found that we needed three such Pareto charts:

- one for product-inquiry complaints about medical instruments and materials (the kind of complaints that must be recorded and reported to the U.S. government)
- one for logistics complaints
- one for general customer inquiries and complaints

The process of creating the charts resulted in important improvements for Ethicon's customers. When we met with the person responsible for the complaints that must be reported to the government, we found that they were in good order, organized on a computer, and therefore easy to analyze. We learned that the person who maintained this database had long known it could be a vital resource for the organization as a whole. And he had deeply desired better ways to communicate its usefulness. But he felt he had no way to reach his superiors.

The logistics complaints would be handled by J&J Hospital Supply, the unit that helps businesses in the J&J professional sector deliver their products to hospitals.

But complaints and inquiries that did not relate to the performance of a product or to logistics (including complaints about pricing, customer service, surgeon education and training, etc.) were not easy to chart. The reason was that no system had been set up to use these complaints for process improvement. Customer service representatives handled them by telephone. They weren't tracked systematically. We not only started a system to track these complaints, we also set up a mechanism to analyze and eliminate their causes. The smaller flow of complaints would then be captured, analyzed, and reported on the war-room wall.

A Global Business Is More Complex

"Think global, act local" is a phrase that I picked up from my colleague Larry Light, the brand strategist, during one of our discussions at the Strategic Planning Institute. Many markets, as we showed in Chapter 9, are dominated by two or three competitors (see Exhibit 9–8). Many are global, and more arenas are shifting from national to global each year. Acting locally is relatively easy if there is no global strategy within which your region must play a role. But how does an international, interfunctional global business team think globally and coordinate a global strategy while still encouraging regional or national managers to adjust the strategy and tactics to meet the needs of their local markets?

By now my answer should be no surprise. You begin by applying the seven tools of customer value analysis to each of the major national or regional markets of your global business. The customer value metrics and other competitive strategy and business results data can then be summarized in a global business strategy matrix (Exhibit 10–6).

EXHIBIT 10–6

Global business, competitive strategy matrix

	USA/Can.	Fran./Germ./Italy/UK	Japan	Global
Sales: Market Ours Global comp. Local comp.				
Share: Ours Global comp. Local comp.				
MPQ ratio: Us Global comp. Local comp.				
Price: Us Global comp. Local comp.				

The global matrix for competitive strategy shows the size and rate of growth of each major national or regional market. It captures your market share versus the market shares of the leading global and local competitor in each market. Finally it presents data on your market-perceived quality and price relative to these same key competitors. These data are just the tip of the iceberg of what you can design into the global business matrix.

In addition to the global business matrix, a portable, global war-room wall for interactive strategy sessions would include:

- a storyboard cluster of the seven tools of customer value analysis for each geographic region
- a customer value map of your portfolio of geographic regions that shows your global business position (versus your leading global competitor) in the various geographic regions
- a plot of your position versus the leading global competitor with your relative market share on the vertical axis and your market-perceived quality on the horizontal axis
- a storyboard of Pareto charts of customer complaints from the different regions
- a matrix of Baldrige scores for each category and subcategory by national market
- a plot showing where each of the regions is on the technological substitution curve when a new technology is displacing an old technology on a global basis (airlines converting from propellers to jets, surgeons converting from open to closed procedures, recorded music shifting from vinyl to tape to CD)
- a matrix of key events and strategies (new product introduction, price change, advertising campaign, etc.) planned by you and key competitors, by national market with the dates of these events in the cells
- a chart showing new product cycle time to market for each of the regions
- a chart tracing the attribute and product life cycles as they roll out from the lead market to the rest of the world
- a matrix indicating special roles each region is to play (a particular region may serve as a window on new technology, may

be a place where you disrupt a competitor's price structure in his home market, may teach you how to operate in a heavily regulated market, may serve as a window on a market that leads in fashion, may be an emerging region you need to conquer before competitors get established, etc.)

LESSONS FROM GENERAL SCHWARZKOPF, PRIME MINISTER CHURCHILL, AND THE CLINTON CAMPAIGN: IT MAY NOT TAKE A HERO—BUT YOU DO NEED A WAR ROOM

As events unfolded in Operation Desert Storm, General Norman Schwarzkopf relied on his war room to determine what the Allies could and could not do. The war room revealed to General Schwarzkopf that the Allies were not in a position to carry out every act that politicians wanted.

Schwarzkopf followed in a long line of successful leaders of large organizations. At the start of World War II, Prime Minister Winston Churchill recalled the success of a strategic navigation system he had developed during World War I and advocated a similar system:

> A central body which should grip together all Admiralty statistics, and present them to me in a form increasingly simplified and graphic. I want to know at the end of each week everything we have got, all the people we are employing, the progress of all vessels, works of construction, the progress of all munitions. . . . The whole should be presented in a small book such as was kept for me . . . at the Ministry of Munitions in 1917 and 1918. Every week I had this book, which showed the past and the weekly progress, and also drew attention to what was lagging. . . .

Churchill used this information to create an underground war room near 10 Downing Street in the West End of London. The walls displayed data on the number of bombs dropped, the amount of energy produced, and other important facts about each side. Churchill referred to the statisticians and economists who supplied this data as "my own sure, steady source of information, every part of which was integrally related to all the rest."[2]

Bill Clinton's presidential campaign success owed a great deal to the war room the Clinton team set up in Little Rock to maintain a clear understanding of all the top problems the campaign faced.

The Clinton team has set up a similar war room in the White House. It remains to be seen how successful this will be—the U.S. government and the world are probably too complex to be managed from a single war room. It would be better if members of Clinton's team ensured that leaders in each part of the government used the war-room meeting style and developed good strategic navigation systems for their own parts of the government.

Carrying the War Room Around the World

The war-room concept should never be confined to a single physical wall. Indeed, perhaps every person in the company should see and work with some subset of the information on the war-room wall.

To facilitate knowledge and sharing of best practices, most businesses need a portable global version of their war-room wall. Once the exhibits for the master war-room wall have been produced, it is a simple matter to copy them, roll them up in a tube (a modern briefcase?) and take them to national marketing strategy meetings in Miami, Manchester, Frankfurt, Paris, Milan, and Tokyo. Why should people have to sit through one-exhibit-at-a-time presentations (often made in the presenter's or listener's second- or third-best language) of national marketing plans at global meetings with no backdrop of displayed knowledge and no build-up of displayed thinking? The war-room approach helps you break away from function heads running functional fiefdoms and national business-unit heads running national fiefdoms. By communicating information better, it creates an interfunctional, global team competing to give customers superior value.

Protecting Confidentiality

Some of the war-room exhibits can be distributed throughout the organization. But in most organizations, some war-room-wall information is inevitably confidential. How will you protect it?

Address this issue when you first decide to create a war room. You need the same kind of hierarchy of access privileges for competitive strategy information that you have for financial data.

Most organizations now realize they have historically communicated too little about their financial situation to rank-and-file employees. If the rank and file hears nothing about the financial situation of the organization, it won't understand why it needs to work smarter to improve performance. And if only a small amount of information is forthcoming, the data may not be trusted.

Still, some data needs to remain confidential. Reports delivered to directors cannot be delivered to the entire world. Obviously AT&T might not have wanted the world to know that its internal measures of technical quality showed MCI catching up in the late 1980s—until AT&T had corrected the problem and regained the lead.

Organizations first need to define what competitive strategy information must be limited to certain levels of the organization. Then, they need a strategy for making information really usable to those who should use it while keeping it from those who shouldn't see it.

One approach, practiced at Parke-Davis, is to keep the war room locked, and only allow authorized people to meet in it. Confidential exhibits can be omitted when the war room is "packed up" and taken on the road. Divisions and regional offices can have their own war rooms with only data their executives are authorized to review.

Alternatively, the war-room wall can display only data available to all employees. Many companies have decided that the overwhelming majority of company data should be widely available. Under this approach, all employees can visit the room to better understand competition. If executives need a few confidential exhibits for their meetings, they can be brought to the war room for those meetings and kept under lock and key afterwards.

Whatever you do, don't let confidentiality fears prevent you from making important data clearly visible to the people who should use it. Data in a confidential book may seem important. But in fact few people will understand data unless it is clearly displayed. And when no one understands data, it is not likely to do your organization much good.

Creating a Complete Strategic Navigation System

A strategic navigation system is a larger collection of data from which the knowledge on the war-room wall is selected. Your strategic navigation system is what ultimately enables you to be a future-oriented, market-driving company.

A well-organized strategic navigation system gives you data that focuses on how the game will be won, rather than just reporting the score. It is what Winston Churchill called the "sure, steady source of information" that helps executives form a "just and comprehensible view." Companies need strategic navigation systems *both customized* to meet the individual needs of each business unit *and standardized* so that accurate comparisons can be made across business units.

The data in the strategic navigation system may be communicated principally through a book, published monthly or quarterly, perhaps with separate editions for different levels of the company so that sensitive data is not widely distributed. Better yet, as at United Technologies, the strategic navigation system can be a well-designed computer information system that carries up-to-date data, both financial and nonfinancial.

Naturally, the core tools of customer value analysis are at the heart of the strategic navigation system, as they take a prominent place on the war-room wall. The strategic navigation system must supply all the data necessary so the organization can create the tools of customer value analysis. So the metrics of customer value analysis, ten of which are listed in Exhibit 10–7, are central to core of a strategic navigation system.

Almost all these have been discussed in previous chapters. Customer retention will be discussed in Chapter 11 and the alignment index will be introduced in Chapter 14.

While the customer value metrics play a dominant role in aligning your organization to its targeted market, however, your strategic navigation system must also track any other competitive strategy data that the organization wants to include on the war-room wall. And it should

EXHIBIT 10–7

The metrics of customer value analysis

Newer:
1 Market-perceived quality ratio
2 Price metrics
3 Weight on quality versus price
4 Slope of fair-value line
5 Customer value ratio
6 Alignment index

Older:
7 Customer satisfaction
8 Repurchase ratio
9 Recommend ratio
10 Customer retention/loyalty

also monitor a larger array of indicators from which both top managers and others can choose metrics that may be crucial indicators of their own progress.

Questions to Ask in Creating the Strategic Navigation System

A few pages ago we talked about "thinking globally and acting locally." It's also important to "think corporate and act business unit." That means adopting the following principles for the creation of the strategic navigation system:

- First, identify *standardized* corporate metrics for market-perceived quality and other measures of competitiveness and business success.
- Second, have each business identify *customized* quality attributes, on which they will track their performance and the performance of competitors.

The corporate metrics can be the metrics in Exhibit 10–7. You will use the performance on the attributes chosen by each business unit to calculate performance on the corporate metrics.

The pioneers who worked on GE's measurements task force in the 1950s developed a set of standardized metrics for market position, customer-perceived quality, productivity, growth, and profitability. These metrics were used across GE's wide range of products and markets, and they eventually formed the foundation of the PIMS database. By contrast, McKinsey consultants preferred to identify "critical success factors" for each individual business.

Both approaches have disadvantages. But the approach we outlined above captures the best of both. The strategic navigation system should focus on the needs of individual business units. But our approach makes it unnecessary for each business unit to design its own strategic navigation system. (What sector executive wants to review a portfolio of related businesses that provide comparable metrics for profitability and seven different metrics for the customer's view of quality?) The strategic navigation system should be designed to meet the needs of the individual business units first, and also meet corporate needs as well.[3]

The strategic navigation system must include a much wider array of data than the war-room wall. In creating the war-room wall, you want to avoid information overload. You only want to include information on the wall that will clearly benefit meeting participants.

The strategic navigation system will supply the data from which individual management teams will choose the indicators they will use for their own war rooms. To decide what information to include, ask:

- What information should appear on the war-room wall of each part of our business?
- What data will help us understand where we stand on each of the categories of the Baldrige Award criteria?
- How can different operating units synthesize their war-room wall analyses to gain further insights? Should these analyses be communicated to others through the strategic navigation system?
- Which of the data are we already calculating? What new data do we need to produce to clearly understand our position?

A Checklist for a Strategic Navigation System

As discussed in Chapter 2, strategic navigation systems for large organizations should include most of the data on the following list. Data required to create the seven tools of customer value analysis are marked with an asterisk (*); naturally other strategic navigation system data will be used to create other exhibits for the war-room wall:

- How customers think—including the latest information on their desires and needs*, key attributes*, and weights*
- From customers: satisfaction on each key attribute*, complaints, willingness to recommend, repurchase intention and retention, new customer win rate, perceived prices*
- From competitors' customers: satisfaction on each key attribute*, complaints, willingness to recommend, repurchase intention and retention, perceived prices*
- Market perceived quality and customer value relative to competitors (calculated from the above), and actual transactions prices*
- Failure rates, productivity, capital intensity and cost, each compared with competitors
- Employee satisfaction, employee turnover
- Innovation, cycle time for new products, percent of sales from new products, responsiveness, cycle time from order to delivery, and on-time performance versus competitors
- Description of the internal and external measurement systems, including bias indices
- Market share, market share ratio to leading competitor, profitability, growth, and shareholder value.

In planning the strategic navigation system, you should also ask the following questions:

- How good is our competitive strategy data relative to that possessed by competitors?
- How often must each piece of data be updated? Who will be responsible for each part of the process of updating the strategic navigation system and the war-room wall?
- How will we handle data security issues?
- What barriers will we encounter in making the strategic navigation system and war-room wall concepts work for us?

One common barrier: some employees have information that they perceive makes them indispensable. They like to keep it to themselves except when they can emphasize their importance by sharing it. Think through how you will overcome this kind of attitude.

But if such issues are well-managed, the strategic navigation system and the war-room wall will enable an organization to achieve excellent customer value management.

Leading the Way at J&J and the Ethicon Division

Johnson & Johnson and especially its Ethicon division, which we introduced in Chapter 8, tell a great deal about how to use the tools of customer value analysis, war-room walls and strategic navigation systems.

In 1990 Bob Croce, a former Ethicon marketing vice president who was then president of the division, circulated a paper I had written on "The Role of Marketing in Total Quality Management." Jerry Cianfrocca, director of J&J's Quality Institute, invited me to speak and to facilitate four quality profiling sessions at a meeting of the Johnson & Johnson, U.S., Quality Council.

Jerry then invited me to meetings with the Quality Institute staff and representatives of J&J operating companies. Thus, I had a good opportunity to understand what was happening at the company. At one meeting, Jerry was preparing to classify Quality Institute training programs into three categories: skill development, team building, and motivation/culture. I suggested we use a three-by-three classification matrix. We used Jerry's classifications for the rows. For the columns we used: "internal focus," "external focus" (that is, focus on customer and target-market), and programs that improved "both" internal operations and performance as perceived by the target market.

We discussed and classified each activity into the matrix. After we'd classified some two-dozen programs, one at a time, a staff member looked at the matrix and exclaimed, "My God—everything is in the left column!" That was the "internal focus" column (Exhibit 10–8).

That helped us realize why some J&J operating companies thought they didn't benefit from Quality Institute services. To a large extent J&J had been stuck in Stage One, conformance quality, with a focus on internal operations and manufacturing improvement.

J&J went on to launch a new quality effort that came right from the

EXHIBIT 10–8

Classifying education programs
at the J&J Quality Institute

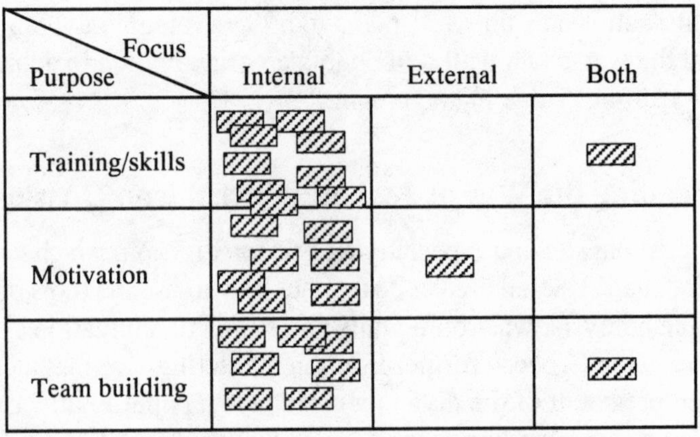

Purpose \ Focus	Internal	External	Both
Training/skills	▨▨▨		▨
Motivation	▨▨▨	▨	
Team building	▨▨▨		▨

top. In the "Signature of Quality" document announcing this thrust, CEO Ralph Larsen stressed,

"Our goal is to be the best health care company in the world in everything we do through a process of market-driven continuous quality improvement."

Larsen demonstrated his commitment by appointing Jeff Nugent to the newly created position of corporate vice president for quality for J&J and establishing a quality council made up of J&J's top executives. Jeff named Cianfrocca as vice president for quality for the professional sector and subsequently brought in Kerry McCarter, a marketer, to be vice president for quality for the consumer sector. At the Malcolm Baldrige National Quality Award Quest for Excellence conference in February of 1991 (to celebrate the 1990 Baldrige winners), 140 of 1,400 participants came from J&J. The company launched a company-wide Baldrige-criteria-based effort in 1992.

Launching a Strategic Navigation System at Ethicon

Ethicon implemented a particularly wide-ranging, market-driven quality effort, jumping straight into Stage Three, the careful management of market-perceived quality and customer value. Bob Croce, Ethicon's president, took the lead. He put the development of a market-perceived quality and customer value tracking system in the hands of two very smart executives: Dave Murray, vice president for marketing, and Ken Driver, a former human resource executive whom he named director of quality administration, reporting directly to Croce.

Driver's charge was to move Ethicon up and to the right along the path we drew in Exhibit 9–1. He was to promote a strategic navigation system. And he was to help Ethicon managers become an interfunctional business unit team focused on the challenges we first mentioned in Chapter 8: leapfrogging United States Surgical Corporation in endoscopy and preventing USSC from successfully cracking the market for surgical sutures and needles, which Ethicon dominated.

Ken and I met with innumerable Ethicon managers and began to assemble competitive strategy data. We held quality profiling sessions with

- salespeople and regional sales directors
- a cross-functional team of people from operations and R&D
- product managers and new-product development managers
- the Ethicon internal board that reported to Croce, and Croce himself

We also attended medical conventions and worked with market researchers. We talked to surgeons, nurses, and hospital administrators. We held focus groups to finalize a list of quality attributes.

In 1991 the Ethicon board recorded how they saw their performance. They thought surgeons found them far ahead of competition in sutures and far behind competition in endoscopy. At the time I sketched the data for sutures and endoscopy on the same exhibit so the board could see the contrast (Exhibit 10–9).

At each step, Ken involved more people, including people at each Ethicon plant. Ken had just come from a plant, and he realized the importance of involving the whole company. At times Dave Murray complained that we were creating the market-perceived tracking system and strategic navigation system "on the fly." And to some extent we were. No one can simply "install" a strategic navigation system designed outside the organization that is supposed to use it.

EXHIBIT 10–9

Head-to Head area chart of market-perceived quality Performance difference, Ethicon minus USSC

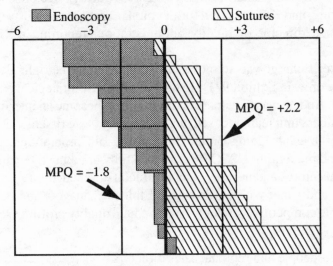

Source: Small sample of executives at a strategy meeting.

But we relied on the guiding principles of customer value management and worked to design a tracking system that would help all operating managers become better competitive strategists. Together with market researchers, we designed a random monthly survey of surgeons for each of Ethicon's three businesses (sutures, endoscopic products, and mechanical products).

Steve Petitt, Ethicon's quantitative market-research specialist, launched it as a formal tracking system in January of 1992. The initial results contained good news and bad news. In sutures, the Ethicon board thought that Ethicon was ahead of their competitors on all but one quality attribute. In endoscopy, on the other hand, they thought that surgeons perceived Ethicon to be behind USSC on all but one attribute. But when Petitt presented the first formal survey data, we found that the positive gap for sutures wasn't as big as the board had thought. Although USSC had only announced it was entering the suture business and hadn't yet shipped products, surgeons gave it high marks on some service-related quality attributes in sutures. Surgeons' perceptions revealed what Petitt called a "halo effect." But the surgeons didn't think that Ethicon was as far behind in endoscopy as the board had thought, either.

Ken's efforts to involve people and to share information throughout the organization at each step of the way were crucial to his success.

While we were putting the market-perceived quality tracking system in place, Bob Croce and his boss Frank Fitzpatrick were commencing a restructuring that was inevitably highly disruptive—splitting Ethicon into two separate operating companies. One company, headquartered in Cincinnati, would handle the new endoscopy technology and Ethicon's mechanical surgery products like surgical staplers (see Chapter 8). The other, remaining at the company's long-time headquarters in New Jersey, would handle its traditional surgical sutures business. The old management team had to be converted into two new teams.

The new organizations were put in place in two major chunks, one halfway through 1991 and the other at year-end. There were lots of other changes along the way. People moved from the suture business in Somerville to the endo/mechanical operation in Cincinnati. New executives arrived from other J&J operating companies. Some Ethicon people left. Of the six who met with me to kick off the market-perceived quality effort in January 1991, only three remained at Ethicon eighteen months later and only one still held the same job. So without Ken's continuous efforts to involve people and bring new people up to date, the build-up of knowledge about the voice of the marketplace and a growing sense of how to use this knowledge could never have developed. In Cincinnati, Ethicon Endo-Surgery evolved and deployed its own market-perceived quality system.

Once the war room was put in place in early 1992, it was naturally much easier to bring new people up to speed. But Ken had to keep communicating carefully while he gathered and in many cases arranged for the creation of the data that would fill the war room.

Clear Knowledge from Surgeons Wins Market Share

As discussed in Chapter 8, customer value analysis played a key role in determining which surgical procedures Ethicon should help surgeons do endoscopically. During 1992, Ethicon Endo-Surgery also dramatically improved its overall market-perceived quality score versus USSC. Key events included

- being first to market in the hernia repair segment in the fall of 1991
- rounding out its endoscopy product line
- hiring and training a sales force dedicated to endo and mechanical products in early 1992
- opening the Ethicon Endo-Surgery Institute in Cincinnati in May 1992.

Ethicon's share of the worldwide endoscopy market has been estimated as 9 percent in 1990, 17 percent in 1991, 25 percent in 1992, and 35 percent in 1993.

Meanwhile Ethicon's suture business began to widen its market-perceived quality advantage versus USSC and Davis & Geck. The newly split organization developed new sales training and accelerated new product development to answer the new products from USSC that claimed such benefits as increased needle sharpness.

The War-Room Wall

In Somerville, Ken Driver had a wall knocked out between two offices to create the "war room" one floor below the president's office. The latest market-perceived quality information is posted there every month. The room also contains relative perceived quality profiles by customer group. The key segments are:

- USSC-supplied surgeons "loyal to USSC"
- USSC-supplied surgeons who "might switch"
- Surgeons who "don't know" who their supplier is
- Ethicon-supplied surgeons who "might switch"
- Ethicon-supplied surgeons who were "loyal to Ethicon"

Needless to say, the customer value position of Ethicon versus USSC gets greater as we look across the customer segment spectrum from the segment loyal to USSC toward the segment loyal to Ethicon. More important, the quality profile charts reveal the reasons why the scores differ. This information has become a monthly input to the Ethicon marketing process.

The war room also contains data on perceptions of hospital admin-istrators and purchasing people, plus price data, value maps, current Pareto charts of complaints, and flow charts of key processes. Won/lost analyses, a head-to-head chart of customer value, key events time lines, and what/who matrices have been created for particular meetings. Recently, the organization has developed charts that track changes in the perceptions of each segment of the market over time. All the strategic navigation system data collected by the market-ing department is distributed throughout the organization once a month.

The war room also contains data on market-share changes, based on tracking from an outside research firm. But these data from outside have problems typical of research-firm market-share information. Some instruments are sold as both stand-alone items and as parts of kits. As a result, the research-firm data didn't give accurate market-share data by instrument. And misleading data suggested that market share and market-perceived quality weren't closely correlated. After a careful analysis, the market research team managed to adjust the market-share tracking system for changes in both direct sales and kit sales. And the correlation between market-perceived quality and mar-ket share became clear.

Early in 1993, Ken Driver reviewed the 1992 data with members of the whole suture marketing team in an ad hoc war room at the Ethicon's annual marketing meeting. Ken displayed on a storyboard the knowledge of how Ethicon's performance versus Davis & Geck and USSC, as perceived by surgeons, had shifted from month to month in 1992. He displayed the shifts in individual quality attributes as well as the overall market-perceived quality score.

Then, he asked members of the marketing team to develop a time line of key marketing events in 1992. They identified new-product launches, informative displays at medical conventions, news stories, price changes, sales force campaigns, and so on. They began to map the items on the "events time line" to the changes in perceived perfor-mance versus competition on the storyboards. Members of the team uttered several "Ah-ha's" as they jointly made the connections be-tween the marketing initiatives and their impact on perceived perfor-mance versus competitors and later market share. But the most valu-able part of this analysis was yet to come.

Ken then asked them to state their marketing plans for 1993 and how they would affect Ethicon's market-perceived quality. This triggered a remarkably creative process of identifying gaps in the current plans and designing ways to communicate the superior performance of Ethicon's product/service offering more effectively. The team was using the war-room method to monitor and improve how the marketing process changed surgeons' perceptions of Ethicon's performance versus its competitors.

Customer Satisfaction Moved from a Slogan to a Science at Ethicon

The result of improved market-perceived quality was a stronger-than-ever market leader in needles and sutures and dramatic increases in endo-surgery market share. As discussed in Chapter 8, Ethicon's customer value management contributed to a dramatic decline in USSC's stock price. And it led to a dramatic increase in the competitive position and value of the Ethicon businesses.

To a large extent, Ethicon is able to navigate strategically because it has the tools to do so. Creating them wasn't simple. But it was certainly worthwhile.

From the experience of Ethicon and other organizations who have adopted the war-room approach and developed strategic navigation systems to support it, we find support for the strategic principles we first proposed in Chapter 2. To summarize, it's worthwhile to repeat them:

1. Companies succeed by providing superior *customer value.*
2. Companies should track the customer value they provide through a method like *customer value analysis.*
3. Companies should use a method of business planning that allows for *action learning,* such as the *war-room* method of conducting business meetings.
4. Companies need a comprehensive *strategic navigation system* to provide data on *both* financial performance and customer value performance.

These strategic principles merit general acceptance. The techniques in Chapters 9 and 10 allow people to *act* on them.

Contrasting the house of quality with the tools of customer value analysis

	House of quality	Tools of customer value
Focus	Design	Competitiveness
Unit analyzed	New product	Ongoing business
Functions covered	Several	All
Attributes covered	Product	Product and customer service
Attributes linked to	Engineering characteristics	Processes and owners
Importance scores	Ratings	Relative weights
Voice of customer	One shot, up front	Continuous tracking
Metrics for	Engineering characteristics	Market perceived quality, price, customer value, weight of quality vs. price, customer satisfaction

CHAPTER 11

Aligning Your Quality Initiatives with the Goal of True Customer Value Management

---

Most companies have dozens of quality initiatives under way. Often, that's good.

But usually the quality initiatives don't add up to a coherent strategic approach. Employees feel top management is zigzagging from one "quick fix" to another.

Whenever anything new is proposed, managers react almost defensively. The most common refrain is that they can't take on the new idea because "We need to digest what we already have on our plates."

That refrain usually indicates a problem. It means that what's on those plates has been presented in a way that is indigestible. No one understands what's underway as a comprehensive strategic package designed to serve customers better. So no one can evaluate whether the proposed new initiative would complement and strengthen the existing bundle.

In Chapters 9 and 10 we described the tools and metrics you need to implement customer value management. We tried to show that the seven tools of customer value analysis are more than just a collection of useful devices. They also reinforce one another to help a business team understand its competitive position and develop action steps to achieve success.

The purpose of this chapter is to show how businesses can avoid the "zigzag" feeling—how executives can prevent employees from feeling that each new initiative is the "quality flavor of the month" that they can more or less ignore. This chapter will show how to put your existing initiatives together with customer value analysis and a strategic navigation system in a balanced diet for the organization as a whole.

First, we'll show how to cluster and align quality initiatives—the tools of customer value analysis as well as other useful tools—so the entire organization understands how they relate to a progression through the stages to true customer value management.

Second, we'll look at several widely implemented quality initiatives that are not part of customer value analysis as we've introduced it in this book. We'll show how each relates to the progression to true strategic management. And we'll show that people working on most of these initiatives can increase their effectiveness and influence by integrating their current activities with the market-driven quality tools and metrics we have discussed here. Specifically, in this chapter we will compare the following widely used techniques to the ideas developed in the previous chapters:

1. Competitive benchmarking
2. The house of quality and quality function deployment
3. Customer retention analysis
4. Customer satisfaction measurement
5. Service quality gap analysis (ServQual)

Aligning Quality Initiatives Toward True Customer Value Management

Many companies falter in total quality management because they adopt numerous different initiatives without showing how all the pieces fit together. This is the underlying cause of the feeling that the company is jumping from one flavor-of-the-month to the next.

Obviously quick-fix programs don't work. They aren't "fixes" at all—if they were, the company wouldn't need to keep trying another quick fix.

Moreover, people don't really commit themselves to initiatives that they feel will soon be supplanted. So even potentially good initiatives are undermined by their apparent flavor-of-the-month status.

Thus, it's imperative that top management not only understand each individual quality initiative, but also understand how it fits into the total thrust toward competitiveness. But even this isn't enough. Managers must ensure that *everyone* in the organization sees how the pieces fit into the whole.

This is not an easy task. Many specialists like to develop and sell their own narrow slice of the total quality management pie, often as if it were a complete package. They tend to obstruct the big picture.

Exhibit 11–1 fits the pieces together. Common quality initiatives are clustered into seven categories:

- Statistics and internal operations
- People
- Processes
- Customers
- Awards and certification
- Targeted market and competitors
- Comprehensive alignment

"X"s indicate which stages in the path to customer value management each initiative focuses on. Initiatives that we will link to the customer value philosophy in this chapter are marked with an asterisk (*).

Most organizations aren't pursuing the full array of initiatives listed in Exhibit 11–1, so they can easily produce a simpler chart of their own. Ideally, this chart will show how each initiative relates to the four stages. Thus, it will show that your initiatives represent a coordinated approach to continuous improvement.

But if your chart shows you are neglecting one of the four stages—whether you are a service company that has never created a conformance-quality system or a large manufacturer that isn't developing the comprehensive alignment necessary for true strategic management—the chart will suggest where you need to change.

You don't have to use exactly this kind of chart. But you *do* have to show how the different pieces of your quality program relate to one another. Exhibit 11–3 is an example of a chart that unified aspects of the quality program at a Baldrige award winner. At the Conference Board's regional Baldrige conference in Dallas in June of 1993, Dean Clubb, representing Texas Instruments' award-winning Defense Sys-

EXHIBIT 11-1

Are Your Quality Initiatives "Flavors of the Month" or Components of an Integrated Approach to Competitiveness?

Focus and Initiatives:	Stage			
	1 Conformance Quality	2 Customer Satisfaction	3 Market-Perceived Quality & Value	4 True Strategic Management
Comprehensive Alignment				
Strategic navigation system			X	X
War-room approach			X	X
Policy deployment			X	X
Allocate capital to achieve superior customer value positions			X	X
Align people and processes with targeted market segments			X	X
Targeted Market and Competitors				
Seven tools of customer value analysis		X	X	
*Competitive benchmarking			X	
*House of quality	X		X	

272

EXHIBIT 11-1 (cont.)

Focus and Initiatives:	1 Conformance Quality	2 Customer Satisfaction	3 Market-Perceived Quality & Value	4 True Strategic Management
			Stage	
Awards and Certification				
Baldrige assessment	X	X	X	
Deming prize	X	X		
ISO 9000 (see Chapter 13)	X			
Customers				
*Customer retention		X	X	X
Customer delight		X		
*Customer satisfaction		X		
*Serve quality gap analysis	X	X		
Service blueprinting	X	X		
Processes				
Reengineering	X	X	X	
Concurrent engineering	X	X	X	
Design for manufacturing	X	X	X	

273

EXHIBIT 11-1 (*cont.*)

Focus and Initiatives:	Stage			
	1 Conformance Quality	2 Customer Satisfaction	3 Market-Perceived Quality & Value	4 True Strategic Management
Processes (cont.)				
Cycle time reduction	X	X	X	
Workout	X		X	
People				
Interfunctional cooperation	X	X	X	X
Empowerment	X	X	X	
Involvement and commitment	X	X		
Quality improvement teams	X	X		
Statistics and Internal Operations				
Six Sigma	X			
Zero defects	X			
Cost of poor quality	X			
Statistical process control	X			

*This chapter will link the five initiatives marked by an asterisk to the customer value philosophy.

tems and Electronics Group, noted, "We had a lot of initiatives in place and were accused of the flavor-of-the-month approach in the mid 1980s. We were missing a process that pulled it all together."

To understand how people in that organization must have felt, see Exhibit 11–2.

After many revisions and a lot of hard work, the TI quality team finally put together the overall framework for their program shown in Exhibit 11–3.

The rest of this chapter discusses how five widely used quality initiatives relate to the tools and metrics of customer value analysis as discussed so far in this book. These linkages should help you understand how you can create your own unified perspective.

Competitive Benchmarking

Competitive benchmarking is widely used to improve competitiveness. It consists of carefully studying other organizations' performance in an aspect of your business, with a view to improving your own performance.

EXHIBIT 11–2

TI customer satisfaction through total quality

Six sigma

Supplier quality improvement   Supplier certification   Worldclass
                                                                leadership
    Just-in-time manufacturing   Customer
Quality improvement teams   satisfaction   Lean production

          Malcolm Baldrige   Design for manufacturing
    Deming   process   Quality function deployment
Q&R bluebook
        People   Business process management
     involvement
                    Total cycle time   Benchmarking
  Continuous
    improvement   Operator/process certification   Policy deployment

Customer   Cell teams   Concurrent engineering
    #1   Effectiveness teams   Design of experiments

Crosby quality   Self-directed   Self-managed
  college   Statistical process control   work teams   work teams

Juran training   **Total quality roadmap**

| 1980 | 1990 | Vision 2000 |

Source: Texas Instruments DSEG, courtesy of G. Dean Clubb.

EXHIBIT 11–3

Total quality management strategy

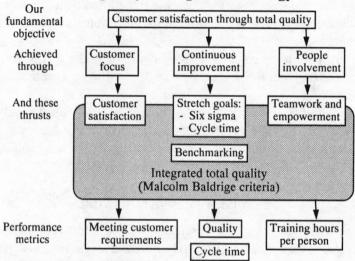

Source: Texas Instruments DSEG, courtesy of G. Dean Clubb.

Benchmarking can clearly make an important contribution to the achievement of market-perceived quality leadership. Indeed, if you don't know how other world leaders perform on each of the major functions in your business and you don't know the quality of results they achieve, how can you understand what it will take to become the market-perceived quality leader?

But many organizations don't think strategically when they benchmark. As a result, they gain only a tiny fraction of benchmarking's benefits, they fail to move toward market-perceived quality leadership, and they don't achieve strategic excellence.

Some companies, for example, focus on cost reduction almost to the exclusion of improving market-perceived quality and revenues. Moreover, most benchmarking studies focus on a single process or function. A business is an integrated system of processes and functional units, yet most organizations don't think about how to benchmark themselves as a whole business against other whole businesses. And when they benchmark individual processes or functional units, they don't think about how to integrate those processes or functions into an improved understanding of the whole.

One stumbling block with traditional benchmarking is that it requires the cooperation of other companies. It is difficult for competitors to cooperate.

In a sense, the market-perceived quality profiling that is the first tool of customer value analysis is a kind of benchmarking. It benchmarks how customers view your product and your customer-service performance versus each of your toughest competitors. But this kind of competitive benchmarking can take place without the cooperation of the competitors.

The market-perceived quality profile also provides the basic background essential to getting the most out of any other kind of benchmarking project. Indeed, before visiting another company to benchmark one of its functions or processes, everyone involved should understand:

- the market-perceived quality profile of your business
- its position on the value map
- the market-perceived quality profile and the position on the value map that your business is trying to achieve

Sometimes it may be impossible for *everyone* to understand all this. If your organization is currently in an inferior position on the value map and the benchmarking project involves a salesperson, for example, you may not want him or her to know all the bad news. However, it's always possible to tell employees enough so they can effectively think about the company's strategic needs. And that's what they need to do effective benchmarking.

Moreover, to be most useful your benchmarking projects should also involve another of the tools of customer value analysis: the what/who matrix. You should examine major processes that affect customers' perceptions of quality and value, asking:

- What does my business do that most influences customer purchase decisions?
- What are the critical drivers of market-perceived quality and value?
- Are customer perceptions of relative performance consistent with objective measures of relative performance?
- Who in the organization is responsible for each event that must occur for us to become market-perceived quality and value leaders?

The answers to these questions will enable you to produce the matrix (see discussion of Exhibit 9–10).

Each group within your organization should be responsible for benchmarking the performance of other organizations that are perceived to be leaders in their functions.[1]

Good benchmarking focuses not only on reducing errors and waste, but also on the effectiveness of your company's units in delivering a high-value product. Bad benchmarking focuses solely on the efficiency of the processes of the functional units, without careful analysis of what those processes are supposed to deliver to the marketplace.

AT&T, for example, has a system that links benchmarking activities to the processes that drive performance. At leading AT&T businesses, the approach is:

- Understand the needs and perceptions of the markets that you serve.
- Pinpoint which processes drive your performance and benchmark them against competitors on the quality attributes and subattributes that drive customer value and market share.
- Benchmark the processes that have a major impact on your competitive position against the "best of breed."

Who should carry out this market-driven benchmarking? The people who are going to have to implement the changes. The business general manager and the interfunctional team of people who directly report to the business general manager play the most important role.

Everyone who will play a role in the benchmarking process should start by completing the same questionnaire that customers in the targeted market complete when the market-perceived quality profile is being prepared:

- How important is each quality attribute (expressed as a percentage of 100)?
- Which attributes are increasing or fading in importance?
- How do they think customers perceive their business's performance and that of competitors on a scale of 1 to 10 on each of the attributes.

They should review the results of market research only after their individual and collective opinions have been gathered. A spreadsheet of how much weight each one places on each attribute—and another of how each thinks customers view your performance relative to competitors will help the managers understand what to look at to improve in the benchmarking process.

Without an exercise like this, the odds of getting the most important insights from benchmarking are poor. And even if someone in the organization does get the right insights, it will be hard to implement them because the organization won't understand what its strategic priorities should be.

If they are carried out well, on the other hand, quality profiling, market research, and benchmarking can jointly create an enormously powerful wave of organizational learning that will have a profound impact on competitiveness and business results.

The House of Quality and Quality Function Deployment

The "house of quality" is the central new-product-design tool of a management approach known as *quality function deployment* (QFD), which originated in 1972 at Mitsubishi's Kobe shipyard.

The house of quality is a conceptual map that allows people from different parts of the organization to work together in planning and designing a new product. A generic house of quality, adapted from one published by Hauser and Clausing in the *Harvard Business Review,* is shown in Exhibit 11–4.[2]

The house of quality helps a new-product team to link the attributes that customers want in a product to the engineering characteristics required. Actually, General Electric used a similar, earlier approach called a "quality map" to achieve these links as early as 1961.[3] Japanese companies developed several related ideas, and these ideas came to the United States during the 1980s as the house of quality and quality function deployment.

In essence, a completed house of quality is a structured panel of displayed knowledge from the targeted market and displayed thinking about how to design a better product. The house of quality contains eight basic components. The first three components—attributes, importance ratings, and performance scores—represent displayed knowledge from the targeted market. Components four through eight

EXHIBIT 11–4

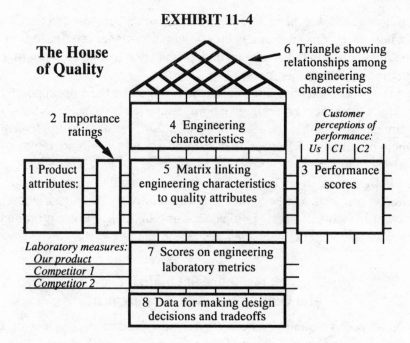

represent the team's displayed thinking about how to design a better product.

How do the house of quality and each of its components relate to the tools and metrics of customer value analysis, to the war-room wall, and to a strategic navigation system as discussed in this book? How does the house of quality fit into the progression to customer value management?

Look at Exhibit 11–5. It contrasts the house of quality with the tools of customer value analysis described in Chapter 9.

Basically, the house of quality is designed to be used on a "one-shot" basis to facilitate communication among marketing, engineering, and manufacturing during the design phase of a new product. By contrast, the tools of customer value analysis are used on an ongoing basis to help the whole interfunctional management team navigate its way to competitiveness in the marketplace. Customer value analysis covers both customer service and product attributes, while the house of quality usually deals only with product attributes. Moreover, a

EXHIBIT 11–5

Contrasting the house of quality with the tools of customer value analysis

	House of quality	Tools of customer value
Focus	Design	Competitiveness
Unit analyzed	New product	Ongoing business
Functions covered	Several	All
Attributes covered	Product	Product and customer service
Attributes linked to	Engineering characteristics	Processes and owners
Importance scores	Ratings	Relative weights
Voice of customer	One shot, up front	Continuous tracking
Metrics for	Engineering characteristics	Market perceived quality, price, customer value, weight of quality vs. price, customer satisfaction

customer value analysis includes price and the weight that customers put on quality versus price, as well as performance.

In short, the house of quality produces customer-driven new-product designs, while customer value analysis helps you continuously run your business in a customer-driven way. The house of quality is an essential tool for creating customer satisfaction and achieving leadership in market-perceived quality, and is an essential underpinning to true customer value management. Virtually all companies that face complex engineering problems in new products should use it.

However the house of quality, as it is normally implemented in the United States, does not itself produce a truly strategic approach to management. Not only does it usually focus only on products rather than customer service, but it is so complex that it is unlikely ever to be used except as part of the inevitably complex task of designing a new product.

Understanding the Differences

In principle, it would be possible to create a new kind of house of quality that would incorporate elements of customer value analysis and form part of the war-room wall of a company practicing true strategic management. We could call the conventional house of quality a "design house of quality" and the new house of quality, incorporating elements of customer value analysis, the "dynamic house of quality." Since the dynamic house of quality would incorporate the elements of customer value analysis, it would provide the benefits of customer value analysis.

Companies that have already made the traditional house of quality a central element of their corporate cultures may actually want to develop the dynamic house of quality on their war-room walls as a way of introducing customer value analysis techniques.[4] But the purpose of the discussion below is to illustrate the difference between what the (conventional) house of quality—the "design house of quality"—accomplishes and what customer value analysis accomplishes.

Let's discuss the first six basic components of the house of quality illustrated in Exhibit 11–4. We will describe how you would convert a conventional house of quality used for product design into a new dynamic house of quality, designed to produce the benefits of customer value analysis, as we cover some of the basic components.

Product Attributes

Some descriptions of the house of quality refer to the product attributes as "customer attributes." This is not meant to imply that these attributes describe the customer. They are really the attributes that the customer wants built into the product. The adjective "customer" is used to distinguish the source of these attributes from the sources of attributes used in older design approaches, where the desired product attributes came from engineers or executives.[5]

The typical house of quality deals with primary, secondary, and tertiary product attributes, but excludes customer service attributes. For complicated products, where the design house of quality is most valuable, the number of attributes at each stage of the attribute tree diagram can become quite large. This is appropriate during the product design process, where all details should be considered.

By contrast, the market-perceived quality profile includes customer service attributes. But the customer value analysis as used by the senior members of the business unit team typically uses fewer attributes than the design house of quality. The goal is to keep the market-perceived quality profile simple enough so that it reflects how customers actually choose among competing suppliers and everyone can understand it. Managers at lower levels may track larger numbers of secondary and tertiary attributes in the areas they are responsible for.

To create the dynamic house of quality that would give you the advantages of customer value analysis, you need to include customer service attributes and relative price metrics in the analysis.

Importance Ratings

Most house of quality analyses that I've seen are based on surveys that ask customers how important each attribute is on a scale of 1 to 5 or 1 to 10. These surveys yield data that can be used to rank the importance of the attributes. But the average importance scores obtained by this approach are biased toward being equal. They are not relative importance weights that can be used to calculate an overall weighted performance score of the product attributes.

Even the traditional house of quality would work better if surveys asked customers to distribute a constant sum of, say, 100 points among the various primary attributes. To create the dynamic house of quality that tracks the performance of the business as a whole over time, you need not only the 100 points distributed among the various primary attributes, but also an expanded list of quality attributes that includes customer service attributes. Or you can obtain relative weights indirectly through statistical analysis of how well the individual quality attributes correlate with an overall score of quality that you track as well.

Because the traditional house of quality doesn't have true importance weights that add up to 100, no one can calculate a relative perceived quality score from the data in the traditional house of quality. But when you include importance weights that add to 100, you can calculate overall relative quality scores. This is vital for the dynamic house of quality. It enables you to track changes in this score over time and trace them back to changes in the performance scores and weights. Like an income statement, your dynamic house of quality, which now contains the full equivalent of a market-perceived quality profile, will have a bottom line. And you can perform variance analysis that explains why the bottom line changes.

Performance Scores

Most companies that use the house of quality utilize performance scores from a sample of the targeted market that is biased toward their own customers. Whether or not you are creating a dynamic house of quality, helpful insights can be obtained by separating the respondents into two groups—your customers and your competitors' customers. Further insights can be gleaned by analyzing how the performance scores and importance weights differ by market segment. This can help the team to design a family of products that meet the different needs of the segments.

Engineering Characteristics, Linked to Quality Attributes and Related to One Another

The classic teaching example for the traditional house of quality shows how to use the tool to design a car door. Customers want a door that doesn't leak water, has no wind noise, doesn't rattle or let in road noise, and is easy to close. The engineering characteristics that affect the performance scores on these quality attributes are listed across the top of the house of quality. These include flexible sealing material, foot-pounds of pressure required to close the door, metal thickness of the inner and outer door panels, and so on.

The heart of the house of quality is the matrix showing the links from engineering characteristics to quality attributes. Symbols are placed in the cells of this matrix to show whether the engineering characteristic has a strong, medium, or weak impact on the performance of each attribute. If the engineering characteristic has no impact on an attribute, that cell in the matrix is left blank.

Designing the perfect door is not simple because customer desires can lead to engineering characteristics that are in conflict. Most car buyers say they want a door that closes easily. But they also do not want to get wet when driving in a rainstorm. These two desires are in conflict, because doors that seal tightly enough to keep out water require a good slam to close properly. The triangular roof at the top of the house relates the various engineering characteristics to one another to check for conflicts (or reinforcing effects). Designers place symbols in the diamonds of the triangle to indicate whether there is a positive or negative correlation between pairs of engineering characteristics. This is where the leaks-versus-door-closing problem becomes clear.

Shifting from a design house of quality to a dynamic house of quality will dramatically change how these sections of the "house" work because you will be adding customer service attributes. Thus, you'll now have to show the interplay between product design and customer service design and delivery. Companies like Toyota, Komatsu, and Canon designed and manufactured cars, heavy construction equipment, and copiers that had lower failure rates than their competitors'. Like Honda's Acura Legend and Toyota's Lexus 400, they were able to penetrate their targeted markets by shifting weight in the supplier selection decision onto this "hassle free—minimum repair" attribute where they had opened up a performance advantage. This shifted weight away from customer repair and service systems and thereby hurt competitors who had built more elaborate service systems.

The traditional design house of quality focuses on the link between product attributes and engineering characteristics. Other matrices that are part of the full quality function deployment system link engineering characteristics in turn to parts characteristics, process operations, and production requirements. With the seven tools of customer value analysis we use the what/who matrix to go directly from perceived performance versus competitors on key quality attributes to the processes that determine performance versus competitors, the processes owners, and what these owners need to do to improve relative performance. The full house of quality clearly adds clarity in dealing with a complex product.

When you add customer service attributes to the list of product attributes, you must also add service design characteristics to the list of engineering characteristics. At this point a house of quality may get too complicated if you try to include tertiary attributes along with primary and secondary attributes. Perhaps tertiary attributes can be analyzed in "cabins" or "in-law apartments" separate from the main house of quality. (Tertiary attributes are usually more actionable than primary or secondary attributes and should not be dropped from the analysis.)

The Benefits of Comparing Engineering
and Customer Measures of Quality

Once a design team has displayed desired product attributes from the targeted market (components 1–3) and linked them to engineering characteristics (components 4–6), it can add the displayed knowledge of component 7—objective metrics on engineering characteristics—at the bottom of the house. Companies often test and then reverse engineer their competitors' products to assess relative performance objectively. Once objective measures are known, the team can eventually move to establish target values for each engineering characteristic to redesign a product.

This part of the house of quality allows a team to check to see if customers' perceptions of relative performance on quality attributes are consistent with the objective measures of relative performance on engineering characteristics. If, for example, the door requiring the least energy to open is perceived as hardest to open, then perhaps the measures are faulty or the car is suffering from an image problem that is skewing consumer perceptions.

In one study of pickup trucks, Ford found that its perceived acceleration was inferior to a competitors'. But objective measures showed that its acceleration was superior. This prompted a careful study. The discoveries reveal that customers perceived superior acceleration because:

- Toyota's exhaust system was louder
- On the Toyota truck, there was a slight pause before acceleration started
- The seat in the Toyota deflected backwards slightly when acceleration started.[6]

Ford considered design changes as well as marketing communications to address the problem. You want your performance advantage to be real—but you *also* want it to be perceived.

In the analytical system put forth in this book, differences between perceived relative performance from a quality profile and objective measures of relative performance would be analyzed on the war-room wall as discussed in Chapter 10. (In the Parke-Davis case discussed in Chapter 5, for example, we found that customer perceptions of relative efficacy differed from the scientific evidence, and the organization developed ways to move these perceptions closer to scientific evidence through a war-room-like meeting process.) But the house of quality is also an excellent tool for exposing conflicts between perception and reality that should be considered in the product-design process.

Quality Function Deployment and Related Tools

Quality function deployment begins with the house of quality, but three additional matrices convey the customer's voice through to the manufacturing process. The house of quality links the quality attributes to engineering characteristics. Then a second matrix links engineering characteristics to component parts. Next, a third matrix links component parts to manufacturing processes. Finally, a fourth matrix links manufacturing processes to the supplies and materials required to make the parts. These are all extremely useful in achieving a leadership position in market-perceived quality.

Many other tools focus on process improvements to improve quality and/or reduce cost:

- Quality mapping, value engineering, workout [used at General Electric][7]
- Cost time profiles, process mapping, value edge analyses [used at Westinghouse]
- Service blueprinting, process improvement, reengineering, and value-chain analysis.

All can play crucial roles in achieving customer satisfaction and market-perceived quality leadership. But none, by itself, gives you a truly strategic approach to management. They should be part of a package of initiatives including customer value analysis so that the company as a whole can be managed to maximize the customer value produced.

Customer Loyalty and Retention

Frederick Reichheld, a successful consultant, has developed an important contribution to strategic management called "customer-retention analysis." He points out that attracting and retaining the right customers is better than achieving the same level of sales while constantly losing old customers and gaining new ones. It's easier to retain a customer than to attract a new customer, he notes. Beyond the extra effort required to make the initial sale, moreover, companies face costs associated with training new customers and establishing ways to interact that often make the profit per customer increase with the number of years a customer has used the product or service. Yet many businesses put far more effort into selling (to noncustomers) than they do into learning how to retain the customers they have.

Customer value analysis should lead companies to practice customer retention. Winning customers by providing superior quality (achieving a position that is below the fair-value line but at the high end of the value map) attracts customers who are inherently more loyal. They buy superior products and customer services. By contrast, customers who instinctively buy on price, or are trained to buy on promotions, tend to wander from supplier to supplier looking for the one who is most desperate and therefore most willing to cut price.

But it's also important to understand why you lose the customers that you still lose. "Customers won/lost analysis" remains vital. It's one thing to lose a customer because he goes out of business, moves, or stops using your product or service. But it is a much more serious problem to lose a customer because he or she has switched to a competitor. Many studies of lost customers stop at a pie chart of the reasons why customers left, using categories like those just mentioned, instead of zooming in on the customers that were lost to competitors and discovering which competitor won them and why. By continuously probing the decision-making of customers who switch to competitors, you can maintain an early warning system for detecting instances where a competitor may have surpassed you on some of the key quality attributes that drive customers' supplier selection decisions. At this point, customer retention analysis blends into quality profiling of customers lost.

Thus, Reichheld's work provides an important complement to customer value analysis. He reminds us of the important strategic point that a company with a portfolio of branches, like a retail bank, typically finds that the branches with the highest customer retention ratios also are the most profitable. To improve the performance of a portfolio of branches using customer retention analysis, organizations then try to determine what criteria people use when they decide to stay with their current bank or to close out their account. They then compare the performance of the high-retention banks versus the low-retention banks. In a sense, Reichheld is teaching a special type of segmentation analysis—the people you are already doing business with are a different segment of the market from the people you're not now doing business with. They may base their decisions on different attributes, and they certainly weight attributes differently from non-customers in their purchase decisions. Reichheld points out that high-retention customers are especially profitable customers. He recommends an internal type of benchmarking where typical branches learn from the best practices of their top-performing sister branches.

Reichheld also notes that customer loyalty and retention depend on the kind of customers you attract, how you attract them, the kind of employees you attract, and how you compensate them.

> People who buy because of a personal referral tend to be more loyal than those who buy because of an advertisement. Those who buy at the standard price are more loyal than those who buy on price promotion.[8]

Customer retention scores and brand-switching data are excellent contributions to a strategic navigation system. Results of customer retention analyses should be placed on the war-room wall near the market-perceived quality profile chart and the won/lost analysis.

"Customer Satisfaction" Measurement

Today, most companies employ some kind of customer satisfaction measurement system. In many cases it's been introduced or dramatically revised in the past few years.

Such systems vary enormously in usefulness. Some are rudimentary surveys that actually discourage people from working on quality improvement. Such systems encourage managers to make meaningless statements, like "Surveys show an overwhelming share of our customers are satisfied."

The response to this kind of statement should always be "Satisfied compared to what?" No matter how much trouble a company is in, some set of questions can usually cause 70 percent or more of its customers to say they are "satisfied."

The best customer satisfaction measurement systems, on the other hand, provide sophisticated information about how a business is positioned versus competitors in its targeted market.

Fortunately, virtually any customer satisfaction measurement system can be modified to create a state-of-the-art system that can drive true customer value management.

Refer back to Exhibit 9–12, "Striving for superior customer value: What the best companies do." It describes the best customer satisfaction measurement systems. The objective in moving toward true strategic management should be to upgrade the existing customer satisfaction measurement system so that it does everything that the best systems do.

Let's consider a typical customer satisfaction measurement system and how it might be upgraded. Usually, the customer satisfaction survey gathers data on a large number of individual "satisfiers" and on some overall satisfaction measure. (For example, in addition to asking how customers feel about product quality, repairs, billing, and the like, the survey probably asks them a question such as, "How do you feel about your experience with Company X taken as a whole?") The survey often asks the customers to answer all these questions with ratings on a five-point scale, for example:

Very satisfied

Satisfied

Neutral

Dissatisfied

Very dissatisfied

In many customer-satisfaction surveys, the individual "satisfiers" are confused and overlapping. The customer may be asked his or her level of satisfaction with "customer service," "repair," and "friendliness of personnel," for example. In such a case, there is usually no way for people in the company to judge whether a poor score on "friendliness of personnel" indicates problems in the customer service department, the repair department, or both.

Sometimes "price satisfaction" is listed among the individual satisfiers, sometimes it is not. Some companies ask customers to consider price when they answer the overall satisfaction question and others leave it out. Some include a "value" question (AT&T's traditional "worth what paid-for" question). Some include questions about both price satisfaction and value.

Exhibit 9–12 provides insights for modifying these diverse customer satisfaction measurement systems toward what the best companies do. For example, suppose your survey asks about a confused, overlapping set of individual "satisfiers" based on phrases your managers or engineers use to discuss your product rather than the words customers themselves typically use. You should develop a hierarchical structure for the satisfiers you ask about in the system, and you should describe them with the words customers themselves use.

Suppose you wanted to ask about "customer service," "repair," and "friendliness of personnel" in a way that would provide genuine strategic insight, for example. You would deal with "friendliness of personnel" hierarchically—as a subattribute of both "customer service" and "repair." In other words, you would ask about the friendliness of the customer service personnel when you asked about customer service and friendliness of the repair personnel when you asked about repairs. Thus, you would obtain actionable data.

Many systems use customer satisfaction metrics that are inefficient (because they disregard some important data) and ineffective (because they don't allow managers to link the results of the customer satisfaction questions to business results). A commonly used metric, for example, is the percentage of customers who are "satisfied." A company may focus on the percentage of customers who check one of the top two boxes in the survey ("very satisfied" or "satisfied"). As we showed in Chapter 4, this combined two-box score is inefficient and ineffective because it treats a very satisfied respondent the same as a satisfied respondent. The repurchase intentions of these two groups may differ dramatically. The top-two-boxes approach is also inefficient because it fails to use the information about how many respondents checked each of the three boxes at the bottom.

You can quickly improve such a system by reporting the percentages in all five categories and focusing the reports on the percentage "very satisfied." Increases in the percentages of customers "very satisfied" are very likely to indicate an increase in market-perceived quality and competitive position.

You should also emphasize the percentages saying they are "dissatisfied" or "very dissatisfied." Significant numbers in these categories—and especially any increase in the numbers in these categories—usually indicate a substantial problem in your system.

A more difficult task is upgrading your customer satisfaction measurement system so you understand the segments of your targeted market better. Most customer satisfaction systems focus solely on the customers of the business sponsoring the survey. They neglect customers of competitors and noncustomers of the product/service. As we showed above, it's important to pay particular attention to your own customers, because retaining your current customers is highly profitable. But surveys that neglect the competition's customers cannot answer the question, "How do we become more competitive?"

So it's a straightforward project to modify these systems so that you can focus on performance versus competitors, analyze competitors' customers, and use the sample bias metric (see the description in Chapter 9) to gauge how much your customer satisfaction metrics are biased in your favor relative to what the scores would have been if they were based on a fully representative sample of customers in the targeted market.

In short, a management team and a market research department, working together, can improve most customer satisfaction measurement systems. The improved systems can become essential contributors to customer value management. And dramatic improvements can be achieved fairly quickly.

Service Quality Gap Analysis ("ServQual")

"Service Quality Gap Analysis" was developed by three academic researchers, Valerie Zeithaml, A. Parasuraman, and Leonard Berry. It is often abbreviated "ServQual." ServQual looks at customer service only and provides a framework for examining whether customer service is meeting customers' expectations.

The ServQual technique may be something of a problem for a business unit organization advancing toward customer value management. We've shown in this chapter that most of the important quality techniques can provide strong support for a unified approach to quality and customer value. But often the ServQual methodology, as it is typically deployed, can't help advancement beyond a narrow conformance-quality or customer- satisfaction orientation.

In any kind of organization, Ziethaml and colleagues recommend that service quality be measured along five general dimensions:

Empathy

Assurance

Responsiveness

Reliability

Tangibles[9]

They conduct customer interviews to determine, for each of the dimensions, both customers' expectations of service and their perceptions of the service your organization is actually delivering. Thus, they pinpoint gaps between "expected service" and "service delivered," and they identify opportunities for improvement. If, for example, research shows that your customers perceive that your customer service doesn't have the reliability they expect, the ServQual team will recommend you provide training and make management changes that will increase reliability. The ServQual research team has also developed a model that links service-quality deficiencies to common deficiencies within companies. It's designed to provide further insights on closing the gaps.

The ServQual framework can be thought of as a methodology for bringing the principles and benefits of Stage One of the quality movement, "conformance quality," to the management of customer service. While "product specifications" are usually written precisely, "service standards" are often vague or unspecified. "Defects" are hard to recognize and measure in customer service activities. If a customer service representative speaks unfeelingly to you, for example, is that a "defect"? Instead of looking at "defects," Ziethaml and colleagues measure "gaps" between perceived and expected performance by comparing actual service to a service standard. Surveys indicate whether customers are getting less "empathy" than they expected. If a survey at a bank branch indicates that tellers scored poorly on "empathy," they could be trained to act more empathetically.

If we think of the bank branch as an isolated outpost, this works well, just as "zero defects" techniques work well when we think of the factory as an isolated outpost whose only job is to produce according to specifications. However, the ServQual technique can cause confusion in an organization that is trying to manage market-perceived quality and customer value in a truly strategic way. Often, the actual service dimensions on which customers make their decisions are not fully captured in the "empathy, assurance, responsiveness, reliability, tangibles" framework. And the use of that framework in a large part of the organization is likely to confuse efforts to manage strategically.

The customer value analysis approach differs from the ServQual approach in two ways.

First, customer value analysis does not use a *standard* set of dimensions of service excellence. Instead, we ask customers how they actually make their purchase decisions. Then, we choose the quality attributes we will track based on what *customers* in the target market say causes them to decide between one provider and another. For endoscopic medical instruments, for instance, customers say "surgeon education and training" is a key attribute of customer service. That's not fully captured in "empathy, assurance, responsiveness," and so on.

Like conformance quality techniques, measures based on ServQual's five dimensions of service quality have an important advantage: You can often act on them without involving the whole organization.

Conversely, the five ServQual dimensions are probably unable to provide an actionable framework for guiding your organization as a whole. When you interview customers in *your* own marketplace and learn the quality attributes on which they say they base their decisions, you get information that is: (1) based on how customers actually make their decisions, (2) specific to the market that you serve, and (3) actionable by the whole organization.

Possibly the five standard ServQual dimensions may have the advantage of allowing you to pool data across different businesses for analysis and comparison. As we discussed in Chapter 3, companies such as Milliken frequently need to create a list of service dimensions that they can use to compare the performance of different businesses in their portfolio.

However, usually "empathy, assurance, responsiveness, reliability, and tangibles" are not good choices of dimensions for comparing service performance across different businesses. Usually it's better, for instance, to compare the quality of "sales," "installation," "repair," and "billing" services across many businesses. If Business A scores better than Business B on "installation" but worse than Business B on "repair," you know that this information should be communicated to the people doing the repairs for Business A. But what do you do if it turns out that Business A scores better than Business B on "empathy" but worse on "assurance"? Empathy and assurance might be subattributes of each of the major functional categories of service. If this is the case, it's not clear which function within Business B needs to improve empathy. Moreover, in some cases other subattributes might be preferable in your industry.

If you are using the ServQual format and the dimensions both match what customers say is important and also give you the insight you need into customer purchase decisions, stay with them. If, however, the data from the standard ServQual analysis either don't match what customers say is important or aren't actionable in your business, you should customize your attribute list based on what customers tell you is important.

ServQual analysis also differs from the customer value analysis approach in one other way, of course. Customer value analysis focuses on performance versus competitors while the ServQual model focuses on performance versus "expectations."

As Professor Berry noted at the Conference Board's 1990 Quality Conference, if you gather the data on competitors' performance using the ServQual framework, you can also easily calculate relative ServQual scores versus competitors. Berry said that for a particular served market, the customers' expectations are roughly the same for you and your competitors.

If you look at ServQual scores versus competitors, the performance "versus expectations" feature actually drops out. You wind up with performance rating ratios just like those in customer value analysis. When the five generic service-quality ratios are calculated versus competitors, they are analogous to the market-perceived quality ratios that are the focus of the quality profiling model.

Still, ServQual focuses on five standard dimensions of the customer service portion of the quality attributes, while customer value analysis focuses on all the actual purchase criteria that customers use in your targeted market.

For strategic management, it's always better to find out the purchasers' actual criteria (and the words they themselves use to describe them). The ServQual standards, in the context of assessing your business's overall performance on key purchase criteria, will be most suitable as subattributes used to measure service performance in particular departments or your organization.

Deploying the Metrics and Tools of Customer Value Analysis

We've shown in this chapter that any organization can pull its diverse quality efforts together into a coherent package, and that most existing quality efforts can fit nicely into a move toward true strategic management based on customer value analysis.

But to effectively use the metrics and tools of customer value analysis, or any set of tools designed to achieve total quality management and true strategic management, you need a formal, structured process. This is where many U.S. companies fail. My guess is that most companies get only 20 percent of the possible benefit from their existing market research and competitive intelligence activities, for example.

To improve the percentages in your company and achieve true strategic management, follow the strategic principles discussed in the earlier chapters, especially Chapters 2, 9, and 10. To unify your efforts:

- First, create a chart like Exhibit 11–1 that describes your existing quality efforts and those that you are currently contemplating introducing.
- Second, benchmark yourself against what the best companies do as they strive to provide superior customer value to their targeted markets. Identify gaps and develop action steps to close them.
- Third, develop a what/who matrix that shows what process determines your performance versus competitors on each quality attribute and who owns that process.
- Fourth, list the subattributes for each key quality attribute and develop a what/who matrix for each subattribute.

- Fifth, align your internal operating metrics with the quality attributes and subattributes from the targeted market.
- Sixth, display your knowledge about customers, markets, competitors, technologies, and processes so that your people can act on it.
- Seventh, keep the knowledge up to date with your strategic navigation system.

If you do this, you will be well on the way to producing a properly structured process that drives the voice of the targeted market deep into your organization—to your people and their processes—and also gives you ways to respond powerfully to that voice. Thus, you will align your processes and people ever more closely with their targeted markets, and you will win.

PART FIVE

The Payoff from Providing Superior Quality and Value

Chapter 12

Here's the Proof: Superior Quality Drives
the Bottom Line and Shareholder Value

Chapter 13

Learning from the Malcolm Baldrige National Quality Award

Chapter 14

Comprehensive Alignment: Key to True Competitiveness

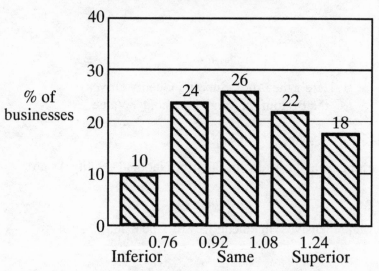

Market-perceived quality positions of PIMS businesses

% of businesses

Market-perceived quality (ratio)

Which businesses produce the best financial results?

Source: PIMS database

CHAPTER 12

Here's the Proof: Superior Quality Drives the Bottom Line and Shareholder Value

Ask any CEO: To convince skeptics about the effectiveness of total quality management, market-perceived quality, and customer value, we need strong evidence that superior quality drives the bottom line and creates shareholder value.

There's only one reliable way to produce such evidence: We need reliable measures of quality, profitability, and shareholder value over a considerable time period for a large number of businesses in many different industries and markets. Then we need to show that quality and profitability are, in fact, correlated. In addition, we should try to trace the relationships that cause this correlation, using data on business costs, sales growth, market shares, and so on.

Happily, the Profit Impact of Market Strategy (PIMS) database contains the information we need, and it includes 2,746 business units that have supplied the kind of data we want for at least four years.[1] (For a description of the PIMS database, see Chapter 3).

In this chapter, we will show in detail how market-perceived quality drives the bottom line: Strong evidence demonstrates high-quality businesses in the real world achieve price premiums and increase their market shares. But their direct costs are, on average, no higher than those of their lower-quality competitors.

As a result, we'll show, high-quality businesses achieve far higher profits than producers of lower-quality goods or services. We'll also show that quality leads to far higher cash flows and much greater shareholder value.

We've already demonstrated in earlier chapters how companies like AT&T, Milliken, Parke-Davis, Sonoco Products, and Johnson & Johnson have achieved bottom-line success using the definitions and measures of quality described in this book to drive their businesses. This chapter will demonstrate that when quality as defined here has been achieved in hundreds of organizations, similar bottom-line results have occurred.

And it will also suggest that large companies can develop further profitable insights by assembling and analyzing a proprietary competitive-strategy database made up of financial and nonfinancial metrics for their own businesses, brands, or regions. Such a database will show them

- problems and opportunities that exist across their operating units
- additional insights into how to improve performance versus competitors throughout their own organization

A Reliable Way to Study Quality and Profitability

If the relationship between quality and profitability is so clear and strong, why hasn't it been better documented in the past? The reason is that it is more difficult to study the relationship between quality and profitability than you might imagine.

Let's start by asking what level of organizational unit we should look at. It is often easiest for researchers to obtain cooperation of people in a single function within a business unit (e.g., the marketing department, manufacturing, etc.). But studies of such units can tell us little about the relationship between quality and profitability. Individual functional units have no bottom line.

It's also fairly easy for researchers to obtain data on whole corporations, at least if they are publicly held. But can meaningful research on the relationship between quality and profitability be carried out with such data? Unfortunately, the answer is usually "No."

Many large corporations are made up of dozens of business units with vastly different levels of market-perceived quality and profitability. Even a corporation whose main business is easily identified, such as General Motors, contains numerous business units that do not make cars and achieves varying levels of quality among the business units that do make cars.

The *business unit* is the organizational level appropriate for studying the relationship between quality and profitability. First, most business units have measures of profit. Their market-perceived quality ratios, as defined in Chapter 2, can be calculated. And the Strategic Planning Institute has also developed measures of the market value of a privately held business unit.

But before the creation of the PIMS database, none of this information was available in a systematic format suitable for studying how market-perceived quality drives the bottom line.

Now, business-unit-level information can be obtained from the PIMS database, which contains confidential information on business units that are not publicly held. The information is disguised—you couldn't learn any secrets about individual PIMS businesses from the database. But with the names of the businesses hidden from us, we can ask the computer to what extent market-perceived quality and other variables from these business units are correlated with profitability and other key measures of business success. That's what we did to provide the data for this chapter. The analysis reported here is based on businesses with at least four years of data in the PIMS database.

The Market's Definition of Quality

Throughout this book we have recognized that if we want to understand why orders are won or lost among competitors and to calibrate how quality differences lead to profitability differences among businesses, we must define quality from the *market's* point of view. The market-perceived quality ratio versus competition, as described in Chapter 2 (or the market-perceived quality score, which is simply 100 times the ratio), is a clear and simple way of understanding the customer's definition of quality and measuring whether companies have achieved it. To achieve superior market-perceived quality you must simply outperform your competitors on quality attributes that customers weight heavily.

The PIMS database includes such market-perceived quality scores.

Since real data from the PIMS database are confidential, in Chapter 2 we used numbers from the classic Perdue case to illustrate how to calculate market-perceived quality and to show how it relates to customer satisfaction metrics. These Perdue statistics are not proprietary and are not part of the PIMS database.

The database contains real, confidential statistics from real businesses. The numbers from the Milliken/PIMS carpet tile case study described in Chapter 3, for instance, are the kind of data that are in the database. The background information includes quality profiles based on field research with customers—in Milliken's case, with building owners, designers, and carpet dealer/installers. The market-perceived quality data entered with carpet-tile financial and competitive strategy data into the PIMS research database by the case team is based on the Milliken team's overall assessment of how all customers in the served market (both Milliken and non-Milliken customers) view Milliken's performance versus competitors.

Evidence That Superior Quality Drives the Bottom Line

AT&T's research described in Chapter 4 demonstrated that changes in customer value—either in quality, price, or both—were followed in only a few months by changes in customer perceptions and, only a few months after that, by changes in market share.[2] For the large number of businesses in the PIMS database, does this relation mean that higher market-perceived quality will lead to better business results?

To study the question, we have classified PIMS businesses into five categories based on their overall market-perceived quality ratio:

Ratio	Category
0.76 or less	Inferior quality
From 0.76 to 0.92	Somewhat worse quality
From 0.92 to 1.08	About the same quality
From 1.08 to 1.24	Somewhat better quality
Greater than 1.24	Superior quality

The percentage of the businesses in the four-year database of 2,746 that falls in each of these five categories is shown in Exhibit 12–1.

EXHIBIT 12–1

Market-perceived quality positions of PIMS businesses

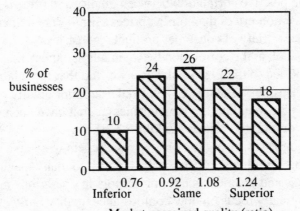

Market-perceived quality (ratio)
Which businesses produce the best financial results?

Source: PIMS database

Superior Quality Leads to Higher Selling Prices

The first dimension of the quality-and-business-results issue we'll examine is: To what extent are customers willing to pay extra for higher-quality products?

This is a good example of the kind of question the PIMS database answers better than other data sources. Some researchers had previously attempted to determine whether higher quality commands higher prices. After surveying research to date, however, Harvard Business School professor David Garvin concluded that no such correlation could be demonstrated.[3] How could this be? Unfortunately, most research was carried out without using the PIMS database. So researchers did not have access to data on actual selling prices and quality levels of the products of a large sample of businesses.

Generally, researchers have had to use data from sources such as *Consumer Reports,* which carries out evaluations of product quality and also reports the list prices of the products evaluated. Such studies have shown little correlation between quality and list price.

But that shouldn't surprise you if you've ever shopped for a car using *Consumer Reports.* Dealers inevitably offer much greater discounts on models *Consumer Reports* criticizes than on those the magazine praises. If the data were readily available, it would presumably show that the positive correlation between quality and price is greater for real transaction prices than for list prices. Similar phenomena may exist in a wide variety of consumer products industries.

When we look at the correlation between quality and actual selling prices as reported to the PIMS database, we find that the relationship is powerful. Businesses that have achieved a superior quality position earned prices 8 percent higher than businesses that have been shoved into an inferior quality position (Exhibit 12–2).

This finding is surprising not only to researchers who have studied the same subject with less reliable data, but also to many manufacturing executives and business school professors in operations management who typically focus on how conformance quality *reduces costs.*

But it is not surprising to an old marketer like Frank Perdue. Frank has a saying:

People will go out of their way to buy a better quality product— and you can charge them a toll for the trip.

EXHIBIT 12–2

Superior quality earns price premiums

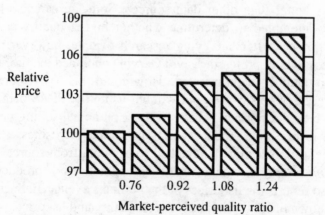

Relative price (y-axis: 97, 100, 103, 106, 109)

Market-perceived quality ratio (x-axis: 0.76, 0.92, 1.08, 1.24)

Information: PIMS database.

Perdue Farms has earned premium prices in the supermarkets across the eastern seaboard.

Yet Achieving Superior Quality Costs No More

On the other hand, superior quality doesn't mean higher costs (Exhibit 12–3).

Businesses with inferior quality positions actually have higher relative direct costs than businesses in any other position. But in contrast to the strong systematic relationship between quality and price shown in Exhibit 12–2, there seems to be no consistent relationship between the amount you spend to produce a product and the quality you achieve.

The data in Exhibit 12–3 is the net result of at least two offsetting effects: First, superior *conformance quality* reduces cost. If you have systems to ensure that you do things right the first time, you'll spend less because you'll do less rework. As a result, many quality-control analysts and consultants expect a high-quality producer to have *lower* costs than a low-quality producer.

EXHIBIT 12–3

Superior quality doesn't mean higher cost

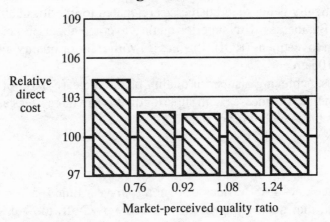

Information: PIMS database.

But second, achieving superior quality *as customers perceive it* is frequently more than just achieving excellent conformance quality. It requires using better, more expensive ingredients (real vanilla instead of artificial vanilla) or adding features (a standard air bag) that lead us to expect that products with high market-perceived quality will have high relative direct cost. As Exhibit 12–3 shows, these two opposing effects just about cancel each other out. In contrast to the steep relationship between quality and price, using the same scale, the relation between quality and cost is almost flat.

As we'll discuss below, this calls for a rethinking of much business school teaching about corporate strategy: Strategy courses typically teach businesspeople to decide whether they will focus on producing a premium product or a low-cost, price-competitive product, and then manage their businesses accordingly. But these data show that companies clearly can provide high quality at competitive cost. We will come back to this strategy issue below when we examine how relative direct cost and market-perceived quality jointly affect business results.

The Bottom Line

Next, let's look at the bottom line. Since high-quality businesses get higher prices yet have no higher costs than their competitors, we naturally expect they'll earn higher profits.

Exhibit 12–4 shows that the difference is vast. Businesses with superior market-perceived quality positions show bottom-line results dramatically better than businesses relegated to inferior quality positions. Businesses with superior quality average about 30 percent return on investment (ROI). Businesses with inferior quality average a mere 10 percent.

Thus, achieving a superior quality position clearly pays off on the bottom line. Businesses with superior quality are three times as profitable as those with inferior quality.

Market Share Change

If we look at PIMS businesses over a four-year time span, moreover, we find that quality *improvement* clearly pays off, too—if you improve faster than competitors. Businesses in the PIMS database that

EXHIBIT 12–4

Superior quality drives profitability

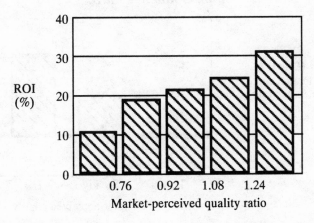

ROI
(%)

Market-perceived quality ratio

Information: PIMS database.

improved their overall market-perceived quality ratio gained market share at the rate of 4 percent per year (Exhibit 12–5). By contrast, businesses that didn't change market-perceived quality managed to gain at 2 percent per year, and those that declined in market-perceived quality didn't gain any share.

Note that we are looking at a four-year time span and only businesses that survived the four years are around to put their experience into the database. That's why it is natural that no category of businesses showed a loss in market share: Many of the businesses that were going out of business during the four years were losing market share and probably declining in profitability as well. These businesses didn't complete the four-year span and didn't wind up in the database. This "survivor effect" is important to consider when evaluating research that simply looks at a single group of businesses, rather than comparing two different groups. As Exhibit 12–5 suggests, a group of businesses drawn at random from a database that only contains survivors will tend to show a market-share gain.

But the completeness of the PIMS database allows us to show not only that businesses that improved quality relative to competitors

EXHIBIT 12–5

Improving quality — vs. competitors — boosts market share

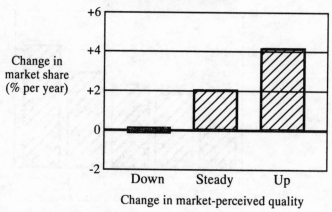

Change in market-perceived quality

Information: PIMS database.

gained share, but also that they gained share *at a faster rate* than businesses that slipped in quality relative to competitors.[4]

How Much Quality Advantage Does a Leader Need?

How big is the quality advantage of market leaders over followers? To answer this question, we've identified "strong" and "weak" market leaders and determined how their quality ratios differ from businesses ranked 2, 3, or 4 and worse. ("Weak market leader" may sound like an oxymoron, but Sears would have been an example a few years ago. In our terminology, a weak market leader is simply a business that is Number 1 in its industry but does not dominate it. To qualify as a strong market leader, a business must have a market share that is at least 50 percent greater than that of its biggest competitor.)

Strong market leaders' performance scores on quality attributes are about 15 percent higher than their competitors' scores (Exhibit 12–6). Weak market leaders outperform their competitors' customer satisfaction scores by some 6 or 7 percent. Business ranked Number 2 in their targeted markets tend to score below the market leader but above the more distant followers. Overall, their market-perceived quality scores

EXHIBIT 12–6

Market leadership is based on superior quality

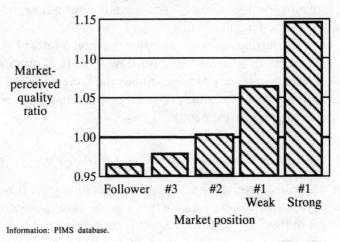

Information: PIMS database.

average just about 1.0. As we move down in market rank, businesses tend to fall further behind their competitors in perceived performance on key quality attributes.

Superior Quality Also Drives Cash Flow and Shareholder Value

For many years financial economists have worked to show that sole reliance on profitability to measure success tends to stunt a company's growth. Emphasizing current profits—sales-minus-cost— encourages managers to inadequately manage inventories, receivables, and other components of investment and to underinvest in research and development, for instance.

Today, companies are tracking measures of cash flow and shareholder value. Some companies are trying to move toward "economic" rather than "accounting" measures of financial performance as the basis for executive compensation. AT&T's 1992 decision to switch from measured operating income (MOI) to "economic value added" in 1993, as the basis for incentive compensation, is a recent example.

Quality and Cash Flow

The crippling impact of inferior quality on a business's ability to generate cash shows up clearly in Exhibit 12–7. Businesses pushed into inferior quality positions experience negative cash flow rates that amount to fully 2 percent of sales.

By contrast, businesses with superior perceived quality generate about 2.4 percent of sales as free cash flow. (We measure operating cash flow here as after-tax earnings minus the increase in net investment. This is equivalent to after-tax earnings, plus depreciation, minus the increase in gross investment.)

Shareholder Value and Internal Rates of Return

Of course, unlike profitability, a positive operating cash flow is not necessarily desirable. Many businesses *should* have a negative cash flow because they are investing to build competitive position in rapidly growing markets.

The measure that financial economists really prefer is "internal rate

EXHIBIT 12–7

Inferior quality cripples cash generation

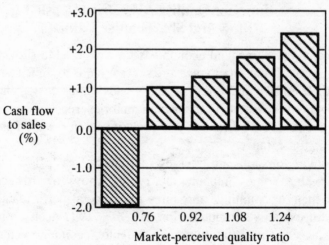

Cash flow to sales (%)

Market-perceived quality ratio

Information: PIMS database.

of return"—the measure that takes into account not only short-term profits but also changes in the market value of the business. A rapidly growing business can have negative operating cash flow as it builds for the future, yet achieve an excellent internal rate of return if it dramatically improves its market value. Shareholder value analysis focuses on both operating cash flow and the change in market value.

To decide whether managers are creating value for shareholders you need to know not only operating cash flows during a specific time period, but also a business's market value at the beginning and end of that period. Thus, a business's internal rate of return—perhaps the most important measure of business success—is hard to calculate if the business's shares are not traded on the open market.

At the PIMS program in 1987, however, we developed a market-value model that enables PIMS to estimate the value of a business that is not publicly held. To do this, we used financial data that are normally available at the business-unit level. If we have these data—profitability, trend of profitability, rate of sales growth, rate of R&D spending, and degree of capital intensity—we can make a good estimate of the internal rate of return the business is achieving.[5]

Using this model to estimate the values of businesses, we found once again that the payoff from achieving high quality is enormous. Businesses with inferior quality have an approximate market-value-to-investment multiple of about 1.5 (Exhibit 12–8, investment is measured at book value). By contrast, businesses that achieve superior quality have multiples of about 2.7 or 2.8.

So what would happen to your business's market value if you leapfrogged from a position of inferior quality to a superior position? Our estimates show that the change would be likely to result in an immediate 80 percent increase in the business's market value, because the market-value-to-investment multiple would move from 1.5 to 2.7. Merely pulling ahead from an "about the same" quality position to a superior position can improve market value by about 35 percent.

Actually, such a move would have an even greater impact on market value because it would also tend to help the business gain market share. Thus there is good reason to expect that internal rates of return will increase enormously if relative quality improves.

EXHIBIT 12–8

Superior quality makes a business more valuable

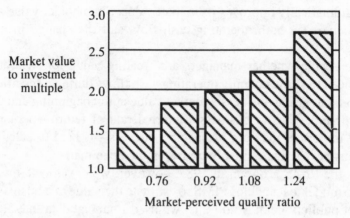

Information: PIMS database.

Better Quality and Cost Competitiveness: Can a Business Achieve Both?

As we mentioned earlier, most business school strategy courses encourage managers to choose *either* a "high-end," quality-oriented strategy *or* a "mass market," price-competitive strategy. Based on the discovery that high-quality producers don't, on average, have higher costs, we have to ask: Does this make sense?

Let's look at the data. Splitting the PIMS businesses on relative direct cost and market-perceived quality reveals that many businesses achieve both better quality *and* cost competitiveness (Exhibit 12–9a). In fact there are more businesses in the better-quality, same- or lower-cost quadrant than there are in any other quadrant in Exhibit 12–9a.

Thirty-one percent of the businesses (860 of the 2,746) are perceived as providing better quality while operating at direct costs that are the same or even lower than their competitors'! Of these 860 businesses, 439 have relative direct costs about the same as competitors'. And 421 have costs that are *lower* than competitors'.

Not surprisingly, businesses that achieve better quality and competitive costs capture a larger share of their targeted market (Exhibit 12–9b):

EXHIBIT 12–9a

Better quality and cost competitiveness: Many businesses achieve <u>both</u>

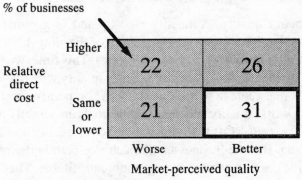

% of businesses

Relative direct cost

Higher — 22 | 26
Same or lower — 21 | 31

Worse   Better
Market-perceived quality

Information: PIMS database.

EXHIBIT 12–9b
Businesses that achieve both capture a larger market share

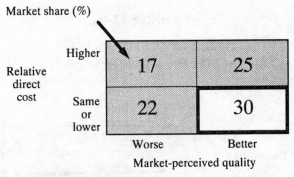

Market share (%)

Relative direct cost

Higher — 17 | 25
Same or lower — 22 | 30

Worse   Better
Market-perceived quality

Information: PIMS database.

• If we just compare businesses that achieve better quality at higher cost to businesses that have worse quality at the same or lower costs than their competitors, we find that the businesses

with better quality capture a slightly larger market share (25 percent) than those with worse quality and competitive costs (22 percent).
- But the large number of businesses with both better quality *and* competitive costs capture a 30 percent market share.

With better quality, competitive costs, and larger market share, businesses in the lower right quadrant of Exhibit 12–9 naturally achieve higher profitability (Exhibit 12–9c). This time, we find that if we compare businesses that achieve better quality with higher costs to businesses that achieve worse quality with competitive costs, we find those with worse quality and competitive costs are slightly more profitable (22 percent ROI) than those with better quality and high costs (20 percent). But the businesses that achieve both better quality and competitive cost are overwhelmingly more profitable: They achieve a full 30 percent return on investment.

Finally, when we look at the ratio of market value to sales, we find that businesses with better quality and competitive costs are worth significantly more than businesses in the other quadrants. The estimated market-value-to-sales multiple is 57 percent higher for businesses with better quality and competitive costs than it is for businesses with worse quality and higher costs (107 versus 68, Exhibit 12–9d).

EXHIBIT 12–9c

**Businesses that achieve both
are more profitable**

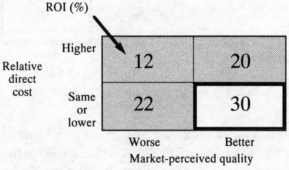

Information: PIMS database.

EXHIBIT 12–9d

Businesses that achieve both are worth more

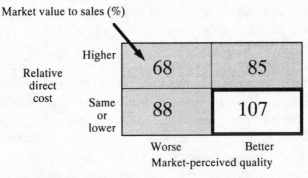

Market value to sales (%)

	Worse	Better
Higher	68	85
Same or lower	88	107

Relative direct cost

Market-perceived quality

Information: PIMS database.

The Payoff from Total Quality Management

Taken together, these new research findings represent powerful evidence that market-perceived quality drives business results. The market-perceived quality score is a quality metric that is easy to use and interpret. And the data show it is closely linked to profitability, price premiums, market-share gain, cash flow, and market value. Furthermore, while some business school academics taught throughout the 1980s that it is almost impossible to achieve both better quality and competitive costs, the evidence shows that practitioners in excellent companies have managed to achieve both. This is certainly the goal of world-class, highly competitive companies.

Perhaps we can't convince every skeptic. But we have strong evidence that superior quality drives the bottom line and shareholder value.

Creating Your Own Proprietary Competitive-Strategy Database

You don't have to have a huge portfolio of operating businesses or brands to carry out simpler forms of this kind of research. The method of measuring quality we've discussed so far can serve as the basis for building a proprietary competitive strategy database in any company that has at least two or three dozen businesses or brands.

CEOs, strategists, marketers, and quality executives yearn for conclusive evidence that superior quality drives business results. Naturally, they also seek new ways to differentiate their performance and drive their markets. This chapter contains powerful evidence, perhaps the most powerful yet assembled. But by creating your own database you can create similar evidence that may be far more persuasive in your own corporation and more relevant to the problems it confronts. More importantly, a proprietary database will give you new insights about your company's strengths and weaknesses as customers see them, from data of business units across your company. The most powerful analysis package is not only to have your own proprietary competitive strategy database, but also to validate your findings and proposed strategies against the much richer experience of a much larger sample of businesses like the PIMS database.

Since the Baldrige award criteria first appeared in 1988, many companies have gathered statistics on customer satisfaction, customer satisfaction relative to competitors, and Baldrige scores for most operating units. You can combine this nonfinancial data with your data on business-unit results to calculate the strength of the relationships between quality and business results for the markets you serve.

The ingredients needed appear in Exhibit 12–10. If your company has much of the data listed, you can begin compiling your proprietary competitive strategy database immediately. Once your database is in good order you will be in a position to carry out competitive strategy benchmarking studies against businesses in comparable databases, if you so choose. You'll be surprised how much extraordinarily useful insight comes from your own database even before you've worked out all the problems involved in making it easy to use.

Moreover, some insights cut across several business units in a company. (At the Strategic Planning Institute we first discovered this working with six businesses of Baxter Travenol that sold solutions to hospitals in PVC bags.[6] The customer-service attributes turned out to be the same for all six businesses. By improving processes that determined perceived performance, the Travenol team improved the market-perceived quality of all six businesses.)

EXHIBIT 12–10

Diagnose your company's proprietary, competitive-strategy database

Do we have this data by business unit?

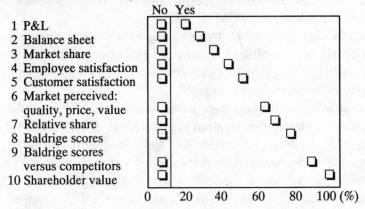

 1 P&L
 2 Balance sheet
 3 Market share
 4 Employee satisfaction
 5 Customer satisfaction
 6 Market perceived:
   quality, price, value
 7 Relative share
 8 Baldrige scores
 9 Baldrige scores
   versus competitors
10 Shareholder value

Following the Travenol engagement, the Strategic Planning Institute worked with a fast moving consumer package goods company. A combined team from the company, PIMS, and a market research firm found that analyzing customer satisfaction data for a dozen brands at once proved to be far more insightful than assembling the results of a dozen ad hoc market research studies. The consistency designed into this study helped to improve the company's knowledge of the entire set of related categories as well as how consumers perceived each powerful, stand-alone brand versus its competitors. It also clarified communication among sister brands and between brand managers and category executives. At the conclusion of the study, the company hired two top researchers from the market research firm to carry out follow-up research and brand-positioning studies.

Some companies like 3M also use such insights and examples from their in-house customer satisfaction database to align sales-force and customer-service training with the voice of the marketplace.

The Benefits of a Standardized
Quality Measurement System

Many U.S. CEOs want to strengthen American competitiveness. As more companies make the links between market-perceived quality, Baldrige scores, and business results, we will have more evidence to convince or silence the TQM skeptics.

But the abstract goal of "strengthening America's competitiveness" isn't nearly as compelling to most chief executives as the opportunity to protect the jobs of their employees (and their own jobs as well) and achieve bottom-line improvements.

Companies can now encourage and coach each business or division to develop a strategic navigation system that is *customized* (as it is in the PIMS database) to reflect the specific quality attributes that customers in the targeted markets use (or will use) to select among competing suppliers. At the same time, a thoughtful company can develop *standardized* metrics (like those in the PIMS database) for market-perceived quality, price, and customer value that facilitate communication, quality improvement, and competitive advantage, as well as research insights, across groups of businesses and entire corporations.

Companies like GE that once carried out ad hoc studies of markets within the United States have been conducting forward-looking, systematic, global studies of competitive arenas targeted by their megabusinesses to pave the way for market leadership. By contrast, as many former market leaders have shown recently, *responding* to the changing needs of the marketplace is a strategy that may get you there too late. The research in this chapter, and the insights you can gain by better understanding the continuing shifts in your own competitive position, let you drive the *dynamics* of your marketplace so you can win in the future.

Baldrige award criteria framework:
Dynamic relationships

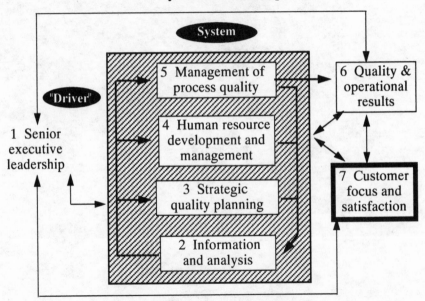

Source: *1994 Baldrige Award Criteria*, National Institute of Standards and Technology, Gaithersburg, Maryland.

CHAPTER 13

Learning from the Malcolm Baldrige National Quality Award

The Malcolm Baldrige National Quality Award has become the most influential source of U.S. management thinking since the end of World War II.

Some criticize it. Consultants like W. Edwards Deming and Phil Crosby dismiss it. Tom Peters challenges the focus of the award. Others note—rightly in some cases—that winners haven't achieved quality in all of the aspects of their businesses that are most crucial to customers. And some winners have shown very modest financial success.

Clearly, "quality specialists" who support the Baldrige award aren't perfect. Some become so fixated on idealized engineering processes that they fail to ask what really makes a customer happy. Moreover, pursuit of the Baldrige award—or any prize—cannot be an ideal driver of competitive strength. A simple, focused understanding of *creating value for customers* is the right strategic focus for an organization.

But I don't bash the Baldrige award process. On the contrary, I think that learning from the Baldrige award is crucial to competitive success today. Why? The reason is simple: Because the Baldrige award provides the most complete description in the world of *what an organization capable of consistently delivering superior value to customers should look like.*

Many people, including Dr. J. M. Juran, worked with NIST to develop and establish the award (Exhibit 13–1). The Baldrige award's designers have worked hard to go beyond technical definitions of "quality" and focus on real customer wants. I personally am pleased at the progress so far. No doubt evolution toward increased understanding of customer satisfaction relative to competitors will continue for several more years.

But without prescribing particular solutions to the issues an organization faces, the Baldrige criteria list those issues with a clarity available nowhere else. Yes, the criteria still do a far more complete job of addressing the issues of conformance quality than of addressing market-perceived quality and customer value. But they form a better

EXHIBIT 13–1
Juran's presence helped to launch the
Baldrige National Quality Award

From the left: William Verity, the Secretary of Commerce who succeeded Malcolm Baldrige, with Dr. J. M. Juran and Dr. Bradley T. Gale at the White House kickoff ceremony in April, 1988. Photograph courtesy of National Institute of Standards and Technology, Gaithersburg, Maryland.

picture of an effective organization than the Deming Prize criteria in Japan or the ISO 9000 (discussed below) standard widely used in Europe. And certainly they present a far better picture than any offered so far by those who attack the award.

In this chapter we'll look at the Baldrige award and compare it with the Deming Prize in Japan, the European Quality Award, and ISO 9000. We'll show its strengths and acknowledge its limitations.

More important, we'll try to show what the pursuit of the Baldrige award can and can't do for an organization—and what you can gain by assessing your organization based on the Baldrige award's criteria.

What the Baldrige Award Criteria Do

The Baldrige Award criteria for 1994 appear in Appendix A. They do a good job of describing an excellent organization. Excellence starts with and is driven by *leadership* (section 1 of the Baldrige criteria). The excellent company has a system to achieve quality that consists of:

- *information and analysis* to drive quality throughout the organization (section 2 of the criteria)
- *strategic quality planning* processes that give direction to improvement efforts (section 3 of the criteria)
- *human resource development and management* that enable the company to achieve the potential of its workforce (section 4 of the criteria)
- systematic *management of process quality* (section 5 of the criteria) that ensures excellent, ever-improving results.

Quality and operational results (section 6 of the criteria) are the internal measures of success. *Customer focus and satisfaction* (section 7 of the criteria) is the ultimate goal.

If your organization is failing in the marketplace, you shouldn't focus first on analyzing yourself using the Baldrige criteria. You'll get quicker results if you first use the tools of customer value analysis to understand just what you're failing to do for your targeted customers. What are the main criteria on which they judge you? Where are you doing worse than the competition? Where are the leverage points that can enable you to dramatically improve marketplace perceptions—and to do so quickly?

But the Baldrige criteria provide enormous benefits for an organization that has already done that, has started to improve, and is hitting barriers to further progress. If you're finding that you can't quite achieve what you know your people should be able to do, then it's time to take a good look at your organization through the lens of the Baldrige criteria. A self-assessment will reveal why your organization isn't performing as it should. A drive to win the prize can force people to improve.

Alternatives to the Baldrige Criteria

Numerous alternatives to the Baldrige criteria exist. But people who study them carefully tend to come away with a greater appreciation for just how useful the Baldrige criteria are.

The Deming Prize Criteria

The most obvious alternative to the Baldrige criteria are the criteria the Union of Japanese Scientists and Engineers uses to judge the Deming Prize in Japan. The Deming Prize was a model for the Baldrige award; Curt Reimann and others closely studied the Deming system.

But even the simplest review of the Deming Prize criteria will show they are not a suitable alternative to the Baldrige criteria. The Baldrige criteria can be seen as an expression of the West's penchant for systematic analysis of large issues; the Deming criteria illustrate Japan's preference to leave things a little bit more vague. Rather than a systematic description of the management elements a company needs to deliver superior quality as customers will perceive it, the Deming Prize criteria are a fairly simple checklist. Here is the first section of the criteria as printed in Kaoru Ishikawa's book, *What Is Total Quality Control?*[1]

I. Policy and Objectives

   1. Policy with regard to management, qualilty, and quality control
   2. Methods for determining policy and objectives
   3. Appropriateness and consistency of the contents of objectives
   4. Utilization of statistical methods . . .

It is difficult for anyone not closely associated with the people who produced these guidelines to know just what they mean. How can you tell whether an organization has achieved "appropriateness and consistency of the contents of objectives"?

The Baldrige criteria listed in Appendix A allow anyone to evaluate an organization. With a little bit of training, people who have never met anyone at the National Institute of Standards and Technology can apply the criteria competently.

These Deming criteria, on the other hand, are designed to be used by a tight-knit group—the counselors associated with the Union of Japanese Scientists and Engineers in Japan. Outsiders can never know just what JUSE is looking for.[2]

In America, many winners of the Baldrige award have had little contact—and in some cases none at all—with the consultants involved in designing the prize system.

In Japan, by contrast, companies that hope to win the Deming Prize work with JUSE-affiliated "counselors" to do so. There is little chance either of figuring out how you stand on the Deming Prize criteria without help of a JUSE counselor or of winning the prize by relying on counselors outside the JUSE network.

Thus the Deming Prize criteria, however much JUSE may have accomplished in Japan, will never serve as a suitable basis for people outside JUSE to objectively evaluate organizations.

The European Quality Award

The European Quality Award, presented annually starting in 1992 by the European Foundation for Quality Management in Eindhoven, the Netherlands, draws on the experience of the Baldrige award process much as the Baldrige award draws on the experience of the Deming process. Its criteria resemble the Baldrige criteria except that one criterion of excellence is a company's success in achieving its planned financial targets.

At first glance, this seems eminently sensible. Any CEO committing to quality initiatives seeks evidence that these initiatives pay off in strong financial results. Moreover, nobody who is part of an award-granting process, in America or elsewhere, wants to see companies win quality awards and yet achieve poor financial results. By including financial results in the award criteria the Europeans appear to eliminate the confusion and even embarrassment that may occur when companies with mediocre recent financial results get an award.

But using financial results as an award criterion has other effects as well:

- First, superior financial performance in a given time period is due to a host of factors, including luck. Adding financial results as an award criterion may shift the focus away from measuring the causes of excellent performance for customers (which in the long run determines financial performance) and toward rewarding luck. That would shift the function of the award away from transferring the know-how of excellence toward simply reminding people that a little luck always helps. The prescription "be lucky" doesn't really help companies or society as a whole.
- Second, as we saw in Chapters 4 and 12, market-perceived quality is a leading indicator of market share and financial performance. By including financial results in the award criteria, the award's focus shifts from the present and future toward the past.

The issues are complicated. The award design teams on both sides of the Atlantic have discussed them thoroughly. They have come to different conclusions, and it will be interesting to see which continent's award winners achieve better financial performance in the years *after* they win the award.

The European Quality Foundation broke new ground in an important way by giving awards not only to *organizations* that practice quality, but also to academic theses, articles, and television broadcasts. Roy Peacock, program manager for the award, says the foundation's "first priority is to influence the educational infrastructure from nursery schools to the postgraduate level."

Whether the foundation will succeed is not clear. But so far, still in its early stages, the European Quality Award has not achieved a level of attention in Europe comparable to the attention the Baldrige award receives in the United States.

Exhibit 13–2 shows the European Quality Award's framework.

EXHIBIT 13–2

The European Quality Award: Assessment model

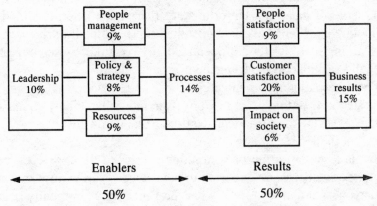

Reprinted courtesy of the European Foundation for Quality Management.

The European Quality Foundation is naming several winners of the "European Quality Prize" every year, then choosing one of them as "the most successful exponent of Total Quality Management in Western Europe." This makes the award more of a competition for the top spot and less of a simple "search for several of the best." The foundation presented the first European Quality Award for a company in 1992 to Rank Xerox, the British-based affiliate of Xerox Corp. Rank Xerox was one of several companies that first received the "European Quality Prize," and then Rank Xerox was named the best of the entire group. Milliken & Co. won the top prize in 1993.

Time will tell how the European community reacts to this process. But skeptics can question whether the European Quality Foundation can really pick "the most successful exponent of Total Quality Management in Western Europe" every year. In sum, the European Quality Award represents a highly worthwhile initiative, but one that does not yet challenge the Baldrige award model for significance or usefulness. And while the U.S. and European quality awards do differ, they also overlap enormously, and both will no doubt help companies to improve quality and competitiveness.

The ISO 9000 Standard

While the European Quality Award has achieved only modest attention, another set of criteria have played a far more influential role in Europe: the International Organization for Standardization's ISO 9000 series of standards. Unfortunately, these criteria don't seem to be promoting excellence at all. Unlike the criteria of the Baldrige award, the Deming Prize, or the European Quality Award, they seem to promote old-fashioned, Stage One conformance quality.

The International Organization for Standardization (ISO) represents standard-setting organizations from more than ninety countries. Delegates from the American National Standards Institute (ANSI) represent the United States.

While a global group of committees designed the ISO 9000 program, the standards are expected to have special force in Europe and for anyone who hopes to sell what the European Community designates as "regulated products" in Europe. Under systems that European bureaucrats are developing, "regulated products"— products which the bureaucrats decide affect health, safety, or the environment—would be required to meet requirements described in EC directives. The directives, in turn, are expected to demand certification that the products were made under a quality system in conformity with ISO 9000 standards.[3]

Unfortunately, the ISO standards not only don't accomplish what the Baldrige criteria accomplish, but they actually seem likely to create more bureaucracy than quality.

Unlike the Baldrige criteria, the ISO standards describe the specifics of a quality system in considerable detail. Consider the following excerpt from the standards:

4.5.1 Document Approval and Issue
The supplier shall establish and maintain procedures to control all documents and data that relate to the requirements of this Standard. These documents shall be reviewed and approved for adequacy by authorized personnel prior to issue. This control shall ensure that:

a) the pertinent issues of appropriate documents are available at all locations where operations essential to the effective functioning of the quality system are performed;

b) obsolete documents are promptly removed from all points of issue or use. . . .[4]

Such minute regulation encourages bureaucratic confusion. You can imagine the problems when certification people try to determine in tens of thousands of companies whether "obsolete documents are promptly removed from all points of issue or use." An essentially good principle—that organizations shouldn't leave old documents in places where they can confuse people—is sure to cause vast amounts of wasted effort when it becomes a bureaucratic mandate.

The Baldrige criteria, by contrast, in Section 5.2 on Process Management, allow considerable flexibility. The "areas to address" in this section simply ask applicants to describe

> how the company maintains the quality of production and delivery processes in accord with the product and service design requirements. Include: (1) the key processes and their requirements; (2) key indicators of quality and operational performance; and (3) how quality and operational performance are determined and maintained, including types and frequencies of in-process and end-of-process measurements used.

Thus, the Baldrige criteria allow a company to apply any workable system for ensuring process quality; examiners need not involve themselves in the minutiae of checking whether obsolete documents are removed unless they conclude that is crucial to understanding whether the particular organization's system really works.

The ISO 9000 system is made worse by the industry of consultants that the standards have spawned. As of mid-1993, European governments had not actually required products to conform to ISO 9000. In fact, Richard C. Buetow, the director of quality at Motorola and an opponent of the ISO 9000 standards, says of ISO 9000 certification that Motorola has "not faced a customer yet who has said, 'If you don't get it, we won't do business with you.'"

But people who make their living helping companies get ready for certification have a profound interest in spreading the idea that no one can do business in Europe without certification. One quality executive suggested that the ISO 9000 standards had become, "an employment act for otherwise unemployable quality people."

The very concept of ISO 9000 is highly questionable. If the Baldrige criteria were made the basis of a quasi-governmental certification program, they too might lead to incentives for bureaucrats to ask bureaucratic behavior. In June 1993, Motorola's Buetow issued an extremely perceptive statement on the standards, which is reprinted here on pages 334–335.

If you want to use the Baldrige criteria to qualify your suppliers, fine. Perhaps there's even a niche for an independent, nonprofit organization to score suppliers for such evaluations. But don't expect the government or any quasi-governmental agency to organize appropriate evaluations except possibly for highly standardized products or for the government's own suppliers.

ISO 9000 may have beneficial effects in helping the nations of Europe better understand the quality of each others' goods. But it is certainly spawning an enormous bureaucracy—one that raises costs without any clear corresponding benefits for most customers.

How to Use the Baldrige
Criteria to Improve Your Business

No standards should be applied slavishly to any organization. But the Baldrige criteria contain both a clarity that is absent from the Deming Prize criteria and enormous flexibility that is not present in criteria of ISO 9000.

If the Baldrige criteria are the best description of a quality organization, then, how do you use them to improve the organization where you work?[5]

As described above, they will work best if you don't focus excessively on them. Use the tools of customer value analysis, or other, similar methods, to describe *what* your organization should be doing for its customers.

Customer value analysis forces you to start by focusing on Section 7 of the Baldrige criteria: Customer Focus and Satisfaction. The subsections of Section 7 are shown in Exhibit 13–3. You can see how customer value analysis addresses all these issues. It enables you to understand current customer expectations and gives you a framework for understanding future customer expectations (Subsection 7.1); it provides a framework for overall customer relationship management (Subsection 7.2); it helps you evaluate your commitment to customers (Subsection 7.3); it determines customer satisfaction effectively (Subsection 7.4); it tells you your customer satisfaction results in a highly

EXHIBIT 13–3

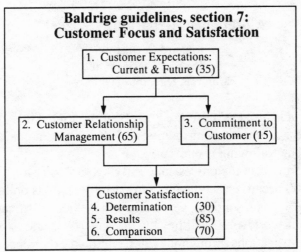

Courtesy of National Institute of Standards and Technology, Gaithersburg, Maryland.

usable format (Subsection 7.5), and it gives you a customer satisfaction comparison (Subsection 7.6).

Customer needs should always drive a company. And most companies can achieve considerable improvement in their competitive position just by using customer value analysis to identify what is important and focusing management attention on getting it done.

But once you've done that, you'll also encounter frustrating barriers. The organization won't respond to your desires or the market's desires as you would like. That's why you should also use the Baldrige criteria to audit each part of your organization. This will show you opportunities to increase your ability to do what your customer value analysis indicates you *should* be doing.

Section 1, Leadership, will help you identify ways in which the messages from your executives are failing to support the actions you know need to be performed. Section 2, Information and Analysis, will point out areas where you don't know how to improve because you lack the data necessary to understand your own processes and the best practices that should be your models.

Section 3, Strategic Quality Planning, will force you to evaluate and improve the process by which you plan your responses to custo-

MOTOROLA, INC.
A Statement Regarding ISO 9000

Richard C. Buetow
Senior Vice President and
Motorola Director of Quality

Motorola is often asked: "Are you obtaining ISO 9000 certification and . . . what is your opinion of ISO 9000 as a quality system?" The following is our reply:

Motorola is in the process of certifying particular locations to ISO 9000 because a segment of our customer base is obliging us to do so. We presently have obtained ISO 9000 certification in 25 of our worldwide facilities (as of May 1993) and expect 13 more certifications throughout 1993. Our own experience shows it to be of very limited value and it is expensive. In turn, we have informed our supply base that Motorola will not require ISO 9000 as a requirement to do business with us. Motorola will make its purchases based on excellence in product and service, not on compliance to a system of standards. Motorola will neither recommend nor discourage any of its suppliers regarding ISO 9000 certification. Each supplier must make that decision based on other customer obligations.

We are critical of how ISO 9000 is being used and misrepresented. The unfortunate mandating of a static, partial quality system as a requirement to do business which does not address the actual quality of product or service sends the wrong message as to the real requirements and actions necessary to serve one's customers. Some recently certified companies, through advertisements, imply that a customer can be assured of high standards, reliable product and service as a result of ISO 9000 certification. This is false! ISO 9000 certification has no direct connection to a product or service. There are no quality measurements or minimum standards required for certification. ISO 9000 represents the old paradigm of an internal, overlay quality program implying that quality costs money. Over time, quality programs of this type fail to provide the required improvement to maintain competitiveness.

The new quality system paradigm, which Motorola has observed through worldwide benchmarking of best-in-class companies and which we have experienced over the last six years, is that quality is not a cost, it is a savings. A successful quality system is customer focused and driven. Quality is not an assignable task, it must be rooted and institutionalized within every step of the business process. A living, dynamic quality system required for today and tomorrow involves all employees, continuous improvement, life long training, metrics, reach out goals, documented and audited results and empowerment. Empowerment moves decision making to those involved with each issue. There is little place for a static and sometimes adversarial set of procedures to be adjudicated by a non-involved third party. Trust must become implicit within the workforce. Quality is everyone's responsibility; continuous improvement is mandatory.

ISO 9000 certification, for many companies, has a high probability of becoming a "tranquilizer." With ISO 9000, one can certify poor quality processes and practices and ship product or provide services that fall far short of what is required to compete effectively today and survive in the future. To maintain certification implies conformance to past practices, good and bad!

Businesses worldwide would be far better served to embrace the principles and framework as articulated in the award criteria expressed within the United States Malcolm Baldrige National Quality Award (MBNQA). Other countries have used the MBNQA award particulars as the foundation for their national awards. Its non- prescriptive assessment highlights the need for a customer focused, continuous improvement, total quality system. Each firm embracing its principles will deliver ever-improving value to its customers and, at the same time, will begin to experience internal operational excellence.

It would be most unfortunate, in this writer's opinion, to displace the momentum and progress that has been engendered by the massive interest and application of the Baldrige principles over the past six years by the distraction and implied threat that, without ISO 9000 certification, a firm cannot do business, and with certification, you have met the requirement. As I observe the discussions in the printed media, we are approaching that crossroad. The outcome is not clear.

mer needs. Section 4, Human Resource Development and Management, will force you to look carefully at each of five key issues:

Human resource planning and management

Employee involvement

Employee education and training

Employee performance and recognition

Employee well-being and satisfaction

Section 5, the Management of Process Quality, requires a careful examination of how you manage all the processes of your business, from design to delivery to support services such as finance and public relations. It also requires an examination of the quality of your suppliers and the quality of your own internal quality assessment methodology.

Section 6, Quality and Operational Results, includes examinations of the technical measures of product and service quality, the operational results of your organization, the trends in internal quality measures, and the trends in quality results of your suppliers.

By covering your entire organization so thoroughly, you will uncover numerous opportunities to improve so the organization responds better to customer and market needs.

As we pointed out in Chapter 10, the results of an analysis of your organization based on the Baldrige criteria can have an important place on the war-room wall. They will remind you of strengths you can use to serve customers even better and of the weaknesses you must overcome to stay competitive.

Baldrige Scores Versus Your Best Competitor

Ideally you should also display an analysis of where your main competitors stand on the Baldrige criteria. Working with research firms or on their own, some companies have found they can develop very credible estimates of their main competitors' positions. An estimate of your businesses' "Baldrige scores" *relative to your best competitor* will help you to clearly establish a link between your business's total quality management achievements and their business results (Exhibit 13–4).

EXHIBIT 13–4

Plot your company's business units in the Baldrige versus relative-Baldrige matrix

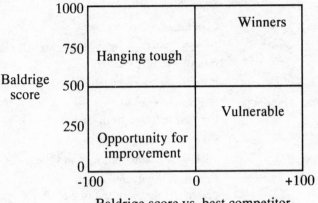

Baldrige score vs. best competitor

My hypothesis is that, looking across a company's portfolio of businesses, current business results will correlate more strongly with the relative Baldrige score than the absolute Baldrige score.

Businesses in the upper right corner of Exhibit 13–4 are true winners, outperforming the best competitor in world-class markets. Businesses in the lower right corner of Exhibit 13–4 are better than a group of weak competitors, but vulnerable to being wiped out by a new entrant with more effective management. Businesses in the upper left corner are hanging tough against world-class competitors. Their profit rates may not be terrific, but competitors would drive them out of business if they weren't unusually well run. Businesses in the lower left have, in Baldrige award terminology, the greatest "opportunity for improvement"—both in total quality management and in competitive position.

Contributions of Some Baldrige Winners

As you seek to improve your organization, consider methods developed by some important Baldrige winners, listed in Exhibit 13–5. They may be useful to solve your own organization's problems.

EXHIBIT 13–5
Some "Signature" Contributions of Baldrige Award Winners

Motorola	Six Sigma
Westinghouse	Value Edge
(nuclear fuel)	Cost time profile
Globe Metallurgical	Proactive response to customer's programs to improve vendor quality
Milliken	Relative-perceived quality tracking system
Xerox Business Products	Benchmarking Cascade teaching from the top
Cadillac	Concurrent engineering
Federal Express	Package-tracking information system
IBM Rochester	Customer involvement, early and often, in design and development of the AS/400 systems

AT&T Universal Card	Superior value positioning
	    Outstanding system for customer service
	    Low price—variable interest rate and no
	    annual fee for charter members

Granite Rock	Granite express: 24-hour automated system for dispensing rock accurately
Ritz-Carlton Hotel	Selecting, training, and empowering employees

The Wages of TQM: One Company's Evidence

Does effectiveness in approaching, deploying, and achieving TQM pay off? A large company that has developed a rigorous measurement system to assess quality can answer this question for itself.

Les Papay, while director of quality at IBM, created one example. He conducted a pioneering study that links Baldrige scores of IBM operating units to several business metrics, including the bottom line.

The goals of the Baldrige National Award Criteria Framework are:

Customer satisfaction

Customer satisfaction relative to competitors

Customer retention

Market-share gain

The Baldrige guidelines cover a business's approach to quality, the deployment of the approach, and the results achieved. So a Baldrige score is not a measure of how much a business spends on quality or how much of a quality effort it's making. The score is a measure of how effective a business is at approaching, deploying, and achieving quality.

Les selected all IMB operating units that scored over 500 on IBM's internal Baldrige examination and compared their performance with IBM's overall corporate performance (Exhibit 13–6).

Since the Baldrige award score includes points for customer satisfaction, employee satisfaction, and market-share gain as part of the overall scoring process, the observed relations between having Baldrige scores over 500 and outperforming the IBM average on these factors are definitional.

But Les's major finding relates to "operating profit growth." He has shown that IBM businesses that are effective in the approach, deployment, and results components of their quality improvement efforts

EXHIBIT 13–6
IBM Units That Scored Over 500 on Baldrige
Outperformed Their Sister Businesses

Measure	Performance Versus Total IBM	
Baldrige assessment (higher by definition)	+190	
	Positive Gap	Widening Gap
1. Customer satisfaction	yes	yes
Customer satisfaction versus best competitor	yes	yes
2. Morale (employee satisfaction)		
Nonmanager	yes	yes
Manager	yes	yes
3. Market share	yes	yes
Change in market share*	yes	
4. Revenue growth*	yes	yes
5. Operating-profit growth*	yes	yes

*1989 to third quarter, 1992.

Information: Laszlo Papay, Testimony to Congress, February 18, 1993.

dramatically outperform their low-scoring sister businesses on *improving the bottom line*. The results show that while IBM as a whole may be struggling, some parts of the company have learned to make money by serving customers well.[6]

Remember What the Baldrige Award Is Not

You can't expect the Baldrige award to do what it was not designed to do. It is an award for quality—not an award for customer value management or strategic management.

Total quality management, as we showed in Chapter 1, is a subset of the thoroughgoing strategic approach we call customer value management. Exhibit 13–7 shows what the Baldrige award covers and reminds you of what it does not.

EXHIBIT 13–7
Positioning the Baldrige National Quality Award:
What Lies Within or Outside Its Boundaries

Covered by Baldrige	*Not covered* by Baldrige
• Senior leadership of a business creates and implements clear quality values	• True strategic management at corporate level, e.g.: What business should we be in?
• Strategic quality planning	• Quality strategic management
• *Process* management and continuous improvement. (Gets at underlying *causes,* a big plus)	• Measures of *financial results*/performance, financial budgeting and control
• Actions based on facts, data, and analysis measures	• Consistency between capital investment and incentive compensation systems
• Defect and error prevention, design quality,	• Market segmentation and positioning quality
• Fast response	• Innovation and creation of new markets, products, and services
• Participation by all employees	• Making operating managers better teams and strategists
• Customer-driven quality	• Globalization

The Baldrige guidelines represent a consensus definition of total quality management. As new ideas come forward, the guidelines need to evolve. They should cover all that can be covered under the legislation that authorized the Baldrige award and judged by the Baldrige process and board of examiners. But there will always be some aspects of strategic management that are not covered. It's unlikely we would ever want a government-sponsored program judging companies on their procedures for leaving businesses where they can no longer make a profitable contribution, for instance.

The Baldrige Award and Your Company

Each company must deal differently with the Baldrige criteria. In some industries, a Baldrige-criteria audit may be of minimal value. For example, some software companies or advertising agencies may be so driven by innovation that a Baldrige-based analysis of their operations seems pedantic. If you run such a business, you should still think about the Baldrige criteria. Most such businesses waste enormous amounts of energy, and cause painful frustration for customers and employees alike, because they do not understand their own processes. But you probably don't want to put your staff through a Baldrige audit.

For most companies, however, a Baldrige analysis is more than just a helpful pointer. It is an indispensable report on what needs to be done to make an organization competitive for the long haul. It is a strong tool to help you deliver what the market is telling you it wants.

As Dr. Reimann noted near the end of his presentation at the Total Quality Forum Five:

> In closing, I emphasize again that total quality is not merely use of tools and techniques to reduce errors and associated costs. Total quality is primarily about customer-driven quality—enhancing value delivered to customers.[7]

Customer value management:
Creating quality and service that customers can see

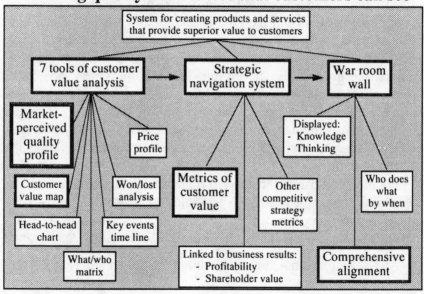

CHAPTER 14

Comprehensive Alignment: Key to True Competitiveness

As we've tried to show throughout this book, quality pays. And hundreds of organizations have achieved important successes in total quality management

But for all the rhetoric of the last decade and a half, only a handful of organizations have transformed their competitive positions. Although it's clear that companies who achieve leadership in market-perceived quality also create better jobs and superior profits, few companies are effectively acting to do so.

In this chapter, we'll ask why so many companies are failing. And then we'll describe the steps companies have to take to make certain that their efforts to provide value for customers will succeed.

Why Do TQM Efforts Fail?

To ensure success in anything, it helps to start by asking why the efforts of others in your field have failed. Then you can act to prevent yourself from failing in the same ways.

What are the best, surest, and most subtly effective ways to fail while attempting to use (or claiming to use) TQM?

In this book we've shown some of the ways.[1] A list appears in Exhibit 14–1.

Some organizations never really define their quality programs or

EXHIBIT 14–1
Top Reasons Why TQM Initiatives Fail

Pre-Stage One: Why No Change May Be Accomplished at All

1. Fragmented, partial approaches. "Empowerment" without a clear strategy is chaos.
2. Poor communication. Few people really understand the program.
3. Training not tied to real problems. No "action learning."

Stage One: Conformance Quality, Small Improvements Achieved, but Little Else

4. Internal focus: TQM effort not aimed at the customer.
5. Focus solely on cleaning up messes rather than delivering superior products and customer service.
6. Imposition of a rigid, predetermined TQM program on the organization.

Stage Two: "Customer Satisfaction." Real Improvements Achieved for Customers, but Not Enough to Create a Competitive Organization

7. Focus on our performance instead of how customers view our performance versus our competitors.
8. Market research neglects key determinants of customer satisfaction, or isn't adequately analyzed or communicated.
9. TQM effort not aligned with the whole targeted market.
10. TQM effort not connected to competitive strategy or business results.

Stage Three: Market-Perceived Quality, Performance Is Compared with Competitors, but Real Strategic Advantage Isn't Achieved

11. Companies adopt customer value slogans but don't carefully develop competitive metrics.
12. Segments within the targeted market are not clearly understood.
13. Customers won and lost are poorly analyzed, so key market-driving factors are poorly understood.
14. Inadequate quality effort in innovation and cycle time.

---

never communicate them to the organization as a whole. Or they fail to tie their quality training to the solution of real problems.

In many such cases, the programs never really get started. In the 1980s, General Motors epitomized this kind of problem. Despite pockets of high quality, the organization as a whole didn't understand how to change its products.

More commonly, quality programs do get started and do achieve real successes. However, organizations get stuck in one of the early stages of quality improvement. And even improvement efforts associated with those early stages succeed only in small parts of the company.

An internal focus or the imposition of a rigid, predetermined quality program from the outside generally leaves the organization stuck in Stage One, with a focus on conformance quality. Companies with such programs achieve some reductions in defect rates, but they have little else to show for their efforts. Improving conformance is important, of course—but it only pays big dividends if your specifications are better tuned to market needs than your competitors'.

For instance, IBM got stuck in Stage One. At a time when its customers were fleeing because competitors heard customer voices better and provided products more suited to their needs, IBM Chairman John Akers appeared on the cover of *Electronic Business* magazine in 1992 promoting a "Six Sigma" quality campaign.

"Six Sigma," an idea developed by Motorola, means reducing defect rates to a level equivalent to 99.9997% perfection.[2] The term comes from statistical analysis, where it refers to a deviation six times the standard deviation. The idea is that if processes are in such control that even a deviation six times the standard does not cause a problem, your organization is doing well.

"Six Sigma" is a good idea, especially for a company whose customers are complaining about excessive defects. But customers in IBM's markets weren't (generally) complaining about excessive defects; they found that IBM's whole approach just wasn't structured to meet their needs. And improved conformance quality couldn't do anything about that. A year later, IBM was losing money and Lou Gerstner had replaced Akers as CEO.

Other companies enter Stage Two, adopting the slogan, "customer satisfaction," but never really acquire a profound understanding of what customer satisfaction means. They don't analyze their performance versus competitors, or connect their TQM effort with a coherent competitive strategy.

These companies achieve real improvements for customers. But the improvements are not sufficient to make them truly competitive unless they compete in unusually sleepy markets. AT&T's struggles through the mid-1980s, discussed in the first part of Chapter 4, fell into this category. Happily, AT&T succeeded in advancing its program to Stages Three and Four and is using customer value analysis today to win in the marketplace.

Still other companies truly enter Stage Three, focusing on market-perceived quality versus competitors. But they never develop good competitive metrics like those we've discussed in this book. Or they don't understand the segments within their marketplaces, and fail to adequately analyze why customers are won or lost. Such companies are often good organizations, and they earn enough profits to stay in business. But they aren't what they could be.

There are other ways that companies in Stages Two or Three can fail, too. If their quality efforts don't sufficiently improve innovation and cycle time to let them keep up with their markets, even a good understanding of historical customer value analysis and market-perceived quality may not save them.

And finally, some companies accomplish all the elements of total quality management but fail to achieve a truly strategic approach to management. They neglect to use what they've learned about creating value for customers to drive wise decisions in the rest of their management systems. Their businesses produce a great deal of customer value, but they can't be said to be practicing true customer value management.

A good example of this, unhappily, has been Westinghouse. This is ironic, because Westinghouse's "Value Edge" tools are consistent with many of the ideas in this book, and Westinghouse *did* apply them to strategic management in most parts of its business. But the Value Edge tools, unlike the tools in this book, were not easily applied to some important businesses. Westinghouse did not apply them to its financial services unit, which wound up producing multibillion-dollar losses. Instead of learning how to be a leader in providing real value to the customers in their marketplaces, Westinghouse's financial services businesses created short-term paper profits by making questionable loans.

Achieving the Paradigm Shift to Competitiveness

When the quality effort is tightly linked to competitive strategy, on the other hand, the whole organization has a thorough knowledge of customers and competitors. It aligns its strategy and quality improvement efforts with the voice of the market. Once this focus is achieved, the bang-per-buck and employee satisfaction from other parts of a TQM system, namely,

- SPC tools
- Training
- Empowerment
- Conformance to specifications
- Teamwork
- Internal customer

increase dramatically.

To win in the 1990s, business units need a paradigm shift and a change in behavior and culture. The nature of the paradigm shift is shown in Exhibit 14–2. You can start to internalize the shifts you need by customizing this exhibit for your business unit or company.

Two Approaches to Alignment in the Business Unit

What do all of the "ways to fail" in Exhibit 14–1 have in common? In three words, they indicate *lack of alignment.*

People and processes in organizations that fail simply are not aligned to pursue the goal of serving customers in a unified way.

What do the points in the paradigm shift exhibit (Exhibit 14–2) have in common? The answer: *They are all ways of aligning the whole organization to address the market's real needs.*

This points to the real path to certain success. You need to align all managers, workers and processes in the business unit to fulfill the market's real needs.

There are two ways to attempt to align business units with customer needs:

1. "Cascade alignment," whereby the needs of external customers are communicated to employees who serve the external customer (salespeople, customer service employees) and then passed on to the internal employees who serve a chain of "internal customers."
2. "Comprehensive alignment," whereby the voice of your targeted market is communicated directly to every group within your organization.

Let's consider each in turn.

EXHIBIT 14–2
The Paradigm Shift Toward Competitiveness

From	To
1. Driven by financial marketplace	Driven by customer marketplace
• Financial results only	• Root causes of competitiveness
• Income statement as only tool	• Seven tools of customer value analysis
• Sales – Cost = Profit	• Customer value = Quality for price
• Financial data only	• Market and competitive strategy data
• Earnings per share	• Superior quality and larger share
• Financial control only	• Strategic navigation system
2. Short-term, financial focus ("steering by our wake")	Longer term, competitiveness focus
3. Long product-development cycle	Short product-development cycle
4. Technology, product-forward view	Market-back, competitive view
Conformance quality only	Market-perceived quality
Your customers only	Winning in the targeted market
Performance vs. average competitor	Performance versus best and emerging competitors
One functional issue at a time	War-room wall concept
5. Mega, administrative "business units"	BUs defined by competitive reality
6. Functional fiefdoms in mega BUs	Interfunctional business-unit teams
7. Traditional conference room	Business-unit war room

Cascade Alignment

When the total quality movement first moved from Stage One, conformance quality, toward Stage Two, satisfying customers, many companies faced a dilemma. How could employees make sure that they were doing "the right things right for customer satisfaction" if most employees never saw the customer and didn't really know how their work affected customers?

The creative solution was the idea that "everyone has a customer." Some are external customers—the ones who pay the bills. Others are "internal customers." Internal customers are part of a chain. An internal customer may serve another internal customer, who serves another internal customer, who finally serves the external customer. Clarifying the needs of internal customers improved internal communications and efficiency in many organizations.

But unfortunately, the challenge of providing superior value to customers in a targeted market is more complex than this cascade can really address. Much of the information about the external customer inevitably gets lost as it passes through the internal customer chain. In some cases, external customer needs are not just lost—they are displaced by the needs of internal customers who have selfish goals.

Thus, the internal-customer concept has a fatal flaw. And it is ultimately wrong to think that most employees "don't have external customers." It may seem like they don't, because they don't know who the external customers are, what they need, and how the customers view the organization's performance versus that of competing product suppliers and service providers. But they do.

The internal customer concept tends to shift the focus away from getting each part of the whole organization aligned directly with external customers, toward a focus on internal customers' needs. At the same time it may make people feel that the problem of focusing on the external customer is solved. This is a more subtle way to fail than just plain ignoring external customers. The lack of alignment remains, but you feel that it's been dealt with, so no further action is taken.

Comprehensive Alignment

Rather than relying on an uncertain chain of communications, a program to create *comprehensive alignment* clearly communicates the needs of the external customer directly into every group in your organization. By doing so, it greatly enhances the organization's effectiveness in meeting external customer needs.

Comprehensive alignment guards against information loss. It helps you manage internal customers who might otherwise encourage their "internal suppliers" to stray from the real needs of the external customer. If top management, middle management, and operations people all get clear, direct input from customers, it's far less likely that any group will neglect the real customer needs.

Most important, comprehensive alignment is exciting. It helps each person in your organization comprehend what they do, why it's important, and how it impacts the customer to make your organization more competitive. It energizes your people and builds their self esteem. They are no longer just cogs imprisoned in some internal customer's version of the true customer's need. You may still want to talk about "internal customers" and about ensuring that their needs are met. After all, even if everyone understands the needs of external customers, each individual still has to do his or her job in a way that supports the next person in the line. But the most important points are to achieve true knowledge of real customer needs throughout the organization and to create a deep desire to meet those needs.

How to Achieve Comprehensive Alignment

How, then, do you attain comprehensive alignment of your organization with the needs of customers in your targeted market?

Large companies often have more difficulty than small companies. Bureaucracy sets in. Successful large companies, like Johnson & Johnson and General Electric, are usually organized into many operat-

---

WHO IS REALLY IN CHARGE OF QUALITY?

Who is responsible for linking organizational change and quality improvement to business results? For anyone to achieve clear links between quality programs and business results, he or she needs responsibility for management of both. This really exists only at the business unit level (Exhibit 14–3). So the general manager of a business unit must have primary responsibility for quality.

Change efforts that focus on anything except the business unit will have difficulty showing results. They cannot effectively align the organization with the voice of the market and cannot directly link quality metrics to measures of business success.

EXHIBIT 14–3
Linking Quality and Competitive Position to Business Results

	Metrics for:	
Organizational Level	Competitive Position	Business Results
Corporation	No	Yes
Sector	No	Yes
Business unit	*Yes* (Market-perceived quality)	*Yes* (ROS, ROI, ROA)
Cross functional team	No	No
Function	No	No

ing companies or business units that focus on a few targeted markets. Yet even these operating units are enormous collections of people that must continuously struggle to stay ahead of small, quick competitors.

Large organizations are made up of many different groups. These groups can be classified into at least two kinds:

- Functional (marketing, R&D, engineering, manufacturing, sales, distribution, and customer service)
- Hierarchical (top management, middle management, operations, and front-line customer service providers)

To achieve comprehensive alignment, ask three questions about each group within the organization:

1. Are the people within the group closely aligned with each other in their ideas about how customers choose a supplier, or are their ideas widely dispersed?
2. Is the group's consensus idea of how customers make the supplier selection decision aligned with the real desires of customers in the targeted market?
3. Do people in the group know what they have to do to enable the organization to accomplish what they believe the customer wants?

If you can answer yes to each of these questions, then the group achieves comprehensive alignment: (1) members of a group hold similar views about customer needs and how customers perceive your performance versus competitors; (2) the group's tight consensus is aligned with the needs of your targeted market; and (3) the members of the group know what they have to do to enable the organization to deliver what the customer wants.

And only if each group in your organization fulfills these three requirements does your organization as a whole achieve comprehensive alignment. Accomplishing this is a difficult task.

Exhibit 14–4 shows four possible positions of groups with respect to the voice of the market.

Suppose, for example, a group communicates well internally, but its members receive misleading input, or no direct input, from the marketplace. Their opinions may be aligned with each other, but not with customers' needs. This places the group in the upper left corner of Exhibit 14–4.

Have you ever encountered a group like this? Perhaps it is the people who answer the phones when customers have a problem. Listening

EXHIBIT 14–4

**Achieving comprehensive alignment
with the voice of your targeted market**

Where does each group within your organization fall?

Widely shared	*Everyone pulling in the wrong direction*	*Comprehensive alignment*
Opinions of individuals within a group		
Wildly different	*Chaos*	*Average on target, but much offsetting energy*

Weak   Strong
Alignment of group's average opinion
with voice of targeted market

to customers' demands all day, they may believe the customer wants responsive attention more than anything else. So when the customer says he wants a repair truck "right away," these people valiantly promise to "do all they can" to get one there "within the hour." And they do all they can, too. They constantly push the repair people to address these urgent needs. But the repair people can't fulfill all the promises the telephone staff has made.

Now suppose that what customers *really* wanted most was *reliable* service. In reality, the unified, harmonious work of the telephone answering group is pulling the whole organization off course, making the repair service less reliable because promises can't be kept. This can sink a business.

First of all, you need to convey compelling information to all these groups about the perceptions that customers hold. As the new knowledge is absorbed, even a group in chaos will begin to center its opinion closer to the targeted market and to reduce the dispersion of individual opinions toward a consensus. It may well be easier to bring a chaotic group into alignment than to deal with a group that is off-target but tight-knit, like the telephone answerers. But all the groups need clear information.

A second essential step is to review compensation systems. If compensation systems reward something other than what the customer needs, few employees can be expected to sacrifice financial success for the customer. In many organizations, for example, engineers are rewarded mainly for improving in their engineering specialties. Is improvement in engineering specialties really what will help your engineers serve customers better?

By contrast, consider how compensation works at AT&T's Universal Card unit. Everyone in the organization is eligible for bonuses. But the bonuses are calculated on a group basis, based on whether the groups achieve targets in providing what customers have said they need. If the group achieves the target for 50 days out of 90 in a quarter, it will receive 5/9 of its possible bonus for that quarter.

Not every group can be compensated so directly for its contribution to meeting customer needs. But at minimum you can ensure that compensation systems don't pull in the opposite direction. Most people have worked at some time in a job where incentives—created by honest people trying to encourage excellence—pulled them away from serving the customer. Can you say for sure that the incentives in your organization don't do that today?

Where Does Your Organization Fall in the Alignment Matrix?

Exhibit 14–5 shows a quality profile created by a real group in a real company, and contrasts managers' perceptions with the actual perceptions of customers in the company's targeted market. The company is given the pseudonym Thingamajig Inc.

The data in Exhibit 14–5 show that the group (in this case the Thingamajig management team) tended to overemphasize reliability and efficiency and to underemphasize ease of installation and maintenance relative to what customers in the targeted market said was important. And the team also believed its performance versus their toughest competitor was better than customers thought it was.

In Exhibit 14–5, we use three alignment scores to show how

EXHIBIT 14–5

Quality profile of Thingamajig, Inc.: Group opinion vs. customer perception

Quality attributes	Importance weights			Performance ratio: Thingamajig vs. C1		
	Mgt.	Cust.	Diff.	Mgt.	Cust.	Diff.
Reliable operation	30	20	+10	1.1	1.0	+10%
Efficiency	20	10	+10	1.0	1.0	0
Durability/life	20	20	0	1.0	0.9	+11
Easy to maintain	10	20	–10	0.9	0.8	+13
Easy to install	10	20	–10	1.0	0.9	+11
Customer service	10	10	0	1.0	0.9	+11
	100	100				

Alignment scores:
Amount of weight not aligned:
- with customers   40
- within the group   30*
Weighted absolute performance difference   +11.2%
*Calculated from individual responses

misaligned this group is with real customers and with itself. The first compares the average importance weights that members of the group give with the average weights that customers in the target market give. Relative to customers, the Thingamajig group overweights some attributes (reliable operation) and underweights others (easy to install). Overall, of the 100 points of weight the Thingamajig management team has assigned, 40 points are not aligned with the weights as customers give them. The amount of weight misaligned is a metric that locates groups on the horizontal dimension of an alignment matrix like that shown in Exhibit 14–4.

A second metric can locate groups on the vertical dimension of the alignment matrix. After you've produced a quality profile as in Exhibit 14–5, comparing the group's opinions to customer's perceptions, calculate how much the average member of the group deviates from the group average. Take the average weights of the group as a whole as a reference point. Then, for each member of the group, calculate the amount of weight that differs from the group average.

Finally, the third alignment score shown in Exhibit 14–5 looks at how the group's view of its own company's performance compares with the views of customers in the targeted market. Take the performance ratios for Thingamajig versus its toughest competitor ("C1"), as given by both the group and the customers themselves. This particular Thingamajig team's consensus opinion is off by about 11 percent—they think they are doing 11.2 percent better than customers think they are doing.

If these three scores are calculated for every significant group in your business, you'll know how well the whole organization is aligned.

Remember: The voice of the marketplace must directly reach each group in an organization. Once you have the survey instrument for your quality profile, gather sample responses from the targeted market and several different employee groups. Then prepare quality profiles that compare each group's opinions with the actual perceptions from the marketplace as in Exhibit 14–5. The quality profiles should be linked to a quality tree that pays special attention to the subattributes the work of the group in question can influence.

At this point the group should hold a meeting with a facilitator who is not from the group to discuss how their opinions differ from customer perceptions. They should discuss why they differ, what the difference means, and what implications it has for serving the market and improving market-perceived quality and value.

After the first of these meetings, the group should have time to digest these perceptions, hear complaints, and study won/lost analyses. It should then meet again, probably a couple of months later, and discuss the latest market-research data. After a few such meetings, the group will have not only a set of clearly understood quality attributes, but also a clear understanding of the subattributes that it must take responsibility for. The links among the quality tree of attributes and subattributes, the internal operating metrics, and the what/who matrix of processes and process owners will become clear. And your business will align its actions to the needs of the marketplace.

Aligning Corporate Systems
with the Voice of the Marketplace

The final step in comprehensive alignment is to make sure that your major corporate systems (budgeting, strategic navigation, planning, capital allocation, performance review and reward) are aligned with the voice of the marketplace. If these systems become uncoupled, your company will never achieve the competitiveness that comprehensive alignment brings. The strategic navigation process is the system that helps you to couple your major corporate systems with each other and with the knowledge from your competitive arena (Exhibit 14–6).

Participative Action Learning

As we noted in Chapter 2, functional isolation runs deep in many companies. Shifting from a financially driven to a market-driven focus, and from functional fiefdoms to an interfunctional business team, does not come easily. It requires interfunctional cooperation and synergy, and a customer/market/competitor focus.

What's most difficult in all this is changing people's behaviors. In too many organizations, people attend classes, listen to speeches, learn to talk in slogans, then go back and do exactly what they had been doing.

EXHIBIT 14–6

Bringing strategic thinking and management to life: An executive information system for strategic navigation

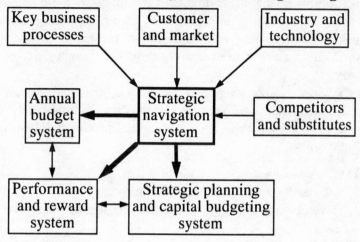

Most adults *learn by doing.* But as a *New York Times* article pointed out:

> In conventional management development, training is training, doing is doing and never the twain do meet. Would-be mechanics get cars to fix and aspiring cooks stir pots on the stove. Yet the briefcase crowd still gets plunked in classrooms and plied with theory.[3]

Action learning is the communication of information in a setting where the hearers can (and often must) put it to work right away. It is an essential component—probably the most important component other than customer value analysis—of creating the comprehensively aligned, new-paradigm organization. Action learning is relatively common in workgroup-level quality training. In such training, outside facilitators attempt to teach problem-solving tools in the context of solving a specific quality problem. When this is done well, the results have often been excellent. Indeed, the success of some such interventions has been a driving force in the quality movement.

But workgroup-level training can't produce a high-performance organization when the organization as a whole has not been aligned to meeting market needs. And paradoxically, facilitated action learning is far less common among senior executives than in workgroup-level teams. Companies that are trying it are getting easier to find, however (Corning, GTE, Westinghouse). General Electric routinely canvasses its business units for projects that they want tackled in the four-week action-learning courses for executives about to be promoted to general manager.

The key point underlying action learning is the idea that people are more likely to retain what they learn if they use it immediately. Consider these four approaches to achieving the paradigm shift towards competitiveness:

1. Hire consultants to solve the problem
2. Send employees to outside training courses
3. Develop customized, in-house training for the management team
4. Achieve change by using a facilitated action-learning process focused on the business unit's current problems and opportunities

Exhibit 14–7 rates each of these for relevance to the business's current problems and depth of involvement of the management team.

Sending someone to an outside training course (low strategic relevance, low team involvement) can increase skills. But when he returns, the culture that was there when he left often blocks any chance to use the skills.

Customized in-house training often results in the response, "This is interesting, but why are we doing this?"

"Solutions consulting" often involves hard work by savvy outsiders. They often come up with a credible strategy and "action plans." However, if the operating team hasn't been involved, they are not likely to implement it effectively. Solutions consulting isn't likely to create long-term improvement unless the consulting firm involves operating managers in developing strategies—a form of action learning that some leading consultants are just beginning to practice.

The quality profiling sessions we've discussed—at Milliken, Ethicon, Parke-Davis, and other organizations—are examples of fa-

EXHIBIT 14–7

Action learning: The best intervention approach to accelerate your progress on the path to competitiveness

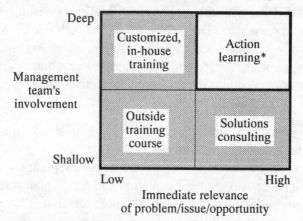

*Relevance and involvement yield synergy and action.

cilitated action learning. They teach a management team to use new concepts, tools, and information to solve burning business issues, with new insights about customers, noncustomers (how they make the purchase selection) and competitors (why orders are won or lost, from whom, to whom).

Customer value analysis is not the only technique that should be taught through facilitated action learning. Almost anything that is important enough to be taught to top managers should be taught this way. And the war-room method of conducting business meetings makes every meeting an exercise in action learning.

But customer value analysis, with market-perceived quality profiles that clearly indicate what the customers in the targeted market actually want, is probably the right place for action learning to start. It can identify the key issues. Then anyone who intends to teach a new technique should be able to use action learning, and in the process demonstrate to participants that it truly has power to overcome barriers that prevent your organization from serving its market as it should.

From War to Harmony:
Creating Strategists with Action Learning

Two of the intervention approaches shown in Exhibit 14–5 are issue-oriented: facilitated action learning and "solutions consulting." Each uses an outside resource. The difference is that action learning facilitation not only helps the team set the strategic direction and outline action steps for market-driven quality improvement, but, in sharp contrast to many interventions by consulting firms that focus on providing analysis and solutions, also:

- helps operating managers clearly understand markets, customers, and competitors
- assures interfunctional communication and cooperation
- yields a consensus strategic direction and action plan where all functions understand the whole and their part in it
- builds commitment to quality improvement, customer value, and strategy execution
- provides a strategic navigation system
- develops operating managers who think strategically and can anticipate shifting competitive environments
- facilitates communication between the business-unit team and sector and corporate executives, on the one hand, and operating managers within the business unit on the other

Achieving real competitiveness ultimately depends on business-unit management teams. Action learning moves your management from a group of warring function heads to a team of operating managers who think like strategists. So action learning is the intervention most likely to accelerate the paradigm shift that's needed.

What the Best Companies Do

To achieve a world-class, competitive organization, don't just follow the advice in this or any other book. And don't mimic a single role-model company. Instead, target a composite of what the best companies do.

Consider: Companies like General Electric and Gillette focus on how each business unit or product can outperform its competitors in meeting the needs of customers in its targeted market. "Outperform" means providing better customer value, superior market-perceived quality and lower costs. While the lowest costs are sought, actual prices may be higher or lower than the competition's—in the majority of cases price is targeted to be higher.

Their targeted markets are grouped into "competitive arenas" or "brand categories." The best companies choose whether to participate in a market based on their strategic intent and core capabilities.

Then, in many of the best companies, each business-unit team meets in a "war room" (or in the Walt Disney parlance, a "team center")—not in a "conference" room that is furbished and decorated like a dining room.

At companies like Motorola, the meeting doesn't start with a review of monthly financial statements. Instead, the meeting starts with a focus on quality. At dynamic companies in fiercely competitive markets, the meeting starts with an analysis of orders and customers won or lost, getting down to objective reasons why.

At AT&T, interfunctional business-unit teams increasingly use the tools and metrics of customer value and competitive analysis to fix problems and capitalize on opportunities. In contrast to the "non-prescriptive" Baldrige award guidelines, the AT&T Chairman's Quality Award has prescriptive guidelines that include the methodology of carrying out customer value analyses. The aim is to deploy world-class quality-improvement initiatives tightly coupled to AT&T's targeted markets and strategic-management systems.

In the best companies, action learning takes place at every meeting. Participants don't have an "everything-is-predetermined," "no surprises" attitude toward meetings. Like General Electric's famous no-holds-barred "workout" sessions, the meetings are creative and challenging.

At Ethicon the voice of the surgeon is monitored on a monthly basis.

At Xerox the "Leadership Through Quality" initiatives begun in 1983 have evolved to make their TQM efforts increasingly more effective. In 1991, Xerox tightly linked its Leadership Through Quality initiatives to corporate strategy and business results and shifted its span of vision from annual plans to a three- to five-year strategic time horizon.

Use customer value analysis to align your business comprehensively with your own market's needs. Use participative action learning to drive that alignment through your organization and help your organization to understand the problem-solving techniques that will make you truly competitive. Develop a good strategic navigation system, and practice the war-room method of business meetings. Learn why companies have failed. Learn what the best companies do, learn from their experience, and create your own best practices. If you do, your company can expect to achieve dramatic improvements in perhaps half the time that it took the quality and customer value pioneers.

Epilogue

What's Next?

The fastest, best way to master any new set of concepts is to apply them to your own situation. The purpose of this epilogue is to offer some ways you can start doing that with the tools and concepts in this book.

Exhibit E-1 lists a key action point or two from each chapter in this book—steps you can take immediately. The following pages describe methods of learning that may be especially useful for particular organizational units and types of people—managers in business units and small companies, top executives and staff people in multi-unit corporations, professionals serving businesses, and teachers of business.

Using This Book in a Business Unit or Small Company

The team that runs a business unit can use "action learning" to bring to life the customer value management system. To make the process more interesting, thorough, and fun, try this approach to role-playing: Form one interfunctional team that represents your business. Then form three others: two will role-play your best, toughest current competitors and a third will role-play the most threatening new competitor or the best new technology.

The team that represents your organization starts by outlining its current competitive position and steps that it intends to take. The

EXHIBIT E–1
Immediate Steps You Can Take to Learn From Each Chapter

Chapter	Action Points for Making Your Business More Competitive

1. Estimate the extent to which each of your business units understands and fully deploys the useful tools of each of the 4 stages to Customer Value Management. Establish current and targeted levels on a scale from 0 to 100 percent and develop steps to close the gaps within two years.

2. Begin to use each of the 7 tools of customer value analysis.

3. Deploy a systematic way of tracking perceived performance versus competitors and acting on the changing knowledge from customers.

4. Develop a measurement system for improving "customer value added" and reporting customer value metrics to top management and corporate directors.

5. Analyze your marketing communications to determine whether they are appropriately aligning customer perceptions with reality.

6. Do a customer value analysis to diagnose the product attributes that are in early stages of the attribute life cycle in your business. Where possible, supply feedback from customers directly to the individuals who provide the service.

7. Create a scenario: What would it take to build a new power brand in your industry or an industry closely related to yours? Then use marketing strategy and the marketing mix to position your own brands in a superior customer-value-building position.

8. Think of three new or improving technologies that might displace one of your key technologies. Then do a customer value analysis comparing your current technology with each of the three. Use this kind of insight to prevent yourself from being blind-sided by a new technology. New technologies displacing old is your toughest competitive threat.

9. Examine the tools of customer value analysis as an integrated system. Use it to practice what the best companies do as they strive to provide superior customer value for the marketplace.

10. Create a "first draft" of your war-room wall, then use both the war-room approach to team meetings and your strategic navigation system as stepping stones to comprehensive alignment with your targeted markets.

11. Create a chart that describes how all your total quality and customer value initiatives fit together. Use it to align them with the voice of the marketplace.

EXHIBIT E–1 *(cont.)*
Immediate Steps You Can Take to Learn From Each Chapter

Chapter   Action Points for Making Your Business More Competitive

12. Develop your own proprietary database of businesses, brands, or regions, and use it as a competitive strategy laboratory and tool for educating managers and validating strategies.

13. Adapt the Baldrige guidelines to meet your company's needs. Assess your quality system relative to competitors.

14. Study the tools and metrics of customer value analysis and plan how you will use them to align your business unit strategy and corporate systems with the voice of the marketplace.

team's role-playing competitors then describe what they will do to offset your competitive initiatives and what initiatives of their own they'll take. Your team (and also the people role-playing your competitors) will quickly learn to anticipate competitive responses and to search for action steps that produce defensible, lasting advantages.

Another good variation is to have a team role-play your *competitors' best customers.* How do they make the supplier-selection decision? Why do they buy from your competitors instead of your business? Why are they so willing to repurchase and recommend your competitor's products? How can you make investments that will place your business in the superior-value zone from their point of view?

While most companies strive for cycle-time reduction for the filling of orders and the introduction of new products, how many are reducing the response time to competitors' moves? Joseph P. Nacchio, who was named president of AT&T's consumer business in August 1993, is one executive who is reducing competitive response time. As reported in the *Wall Street Journal,*

Mr. Nacchio said he will deploy "Delta Force" tactics to assess quickly a rival's new offer to consumers and respond instantly. Yesterday he responded to a new international discount plan from MCI by matching the pricing and covering more countries.

"It took us 22 months to respond to Friends and Family" with the i Plan, he said. "This [response] came in five days. . . . You'll see more of that." He added: "I'm not going to lose customers to avoid competing on price."[1]

Your strategic navigation system is a key tool in reducing response time to competitors' moves. Use it to role-play competitive moves and responses. You'll find that it will quicken your organizational reflexes.[2]

Using This Book in the Multi-Unit Corporation

For a CEO trying to make his businesses and company more competitive, a key question is this: To what extent does each of our businesses understand and fully deploy the appropriate tools from each of the four stages of customer value management?

Ask each business unit team to use a grid like Exhibit E-2 to report their current and targeted levels on a scale from 0 to 100 percent. They can then develop action steps to close the gaps within two years.

Since the gap between your current and targeted positions will probably be greater for Stages Three and Four than for the earlier

EXHIBIT E–2

To what extent does our business understand and fully deploy the useful tools of each stage of customer value management?

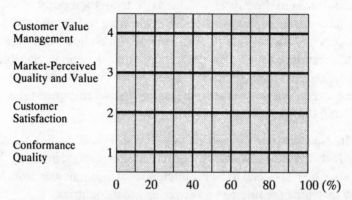

For each of the four bold horizontal lines, place a "C" for your business's current level of understanding and deploying the relevant tools, and a "T" for your targeted position in two years.

stages, you may want to probe these later stages in more detail (see Exhibit E–3).

For practitioners (and academics) who want to continue the process of moving "customer satisfaction" from a slogan to a customer-value science, we are beginning to develop networks to accelerate the pace (see Appendix C). The questionnaire in Appendix D provides a structured process for estimating your current and targeted position on each of the important elements of your customer value system. Use that questionnaire and Exhibit E–3 to diagnose how to improve your performance in Stage Three, market-perceived quality and customer value.

At the corporate level, on the other hand, one important step in closing the gap between current and targeted position in the principles of Stage Four, Customer Value Management, is for officers and directors to apply the tools of customer value analysis to major capital investment decisions. If all capital appropriation requests that arrive at the corporate center somehow manage to beat the corporate hurdle rate-of-return by a couple of percentage points, how do you decide which ones to fund and which ones to turn down?

Milliken has adopted a good principle: Investments should either

EXHIBIT E–3

To what extent does our business understand and fully deploy each element of a customer value management system?

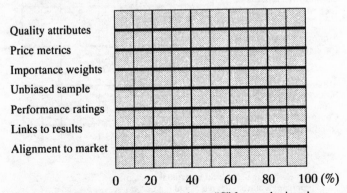

For each of the seven bold horizontal lines, place a "C" for your business's current level of understanding and deploying the relevant elements of customer value analysis, and a "T" for your targeted position in two years.

go into businesses that already have a superior customer value position or go to businesses that have strategies that will lead to a superior customer value position.

What fraction of your investments over the last five years were made in businesses that had a superior customer value position when the investments were made? How do you audit past capital investment decisions to see which ones actually beat the cost of capital and why? How do you track whether investments that were supposed to improve a business's competitive position actually improved its perceived quality, price satisfaction, and customer value relative to competitors?

The strategic navigation concept provides a key way to integrate corporate systems into a powerful customer value management tool. Are your company's systems closely integrated or operated as separate functional fiefdoms?

Typically, a CEO integrates all of the corporate systems in his or her head and tends to perceive that they are all closely coupled. But individual members of the top management team may not perceive this integration. Use a template like Exhibit E–4 to assess where gaps

EXHIBIT E–4

To what extent are our corporate systems closely coupled?

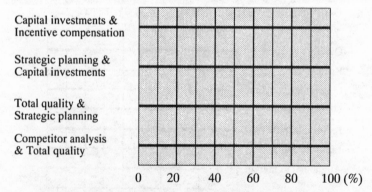

Capital investments &
Incentive compensation

Strategic planning &
Capital investments

Total quality &
Strategic planning

Competitor analysis
& Total quality

0   20   40   60   80   100 (%)

For each of the four bold horizontal lines, place a "C" for your company's current degree of linking corporate systems and a "T" for your targeted position in two years.

need to be closed. (If individual members of the top management team or the board of directors were to fill out Exhibit E–4, where do you think the biggest gaps would be?) Pinpoint the gaps perceived by individual executives (finance, technology, human resources, strategy, quality), and develop a consensus on where you are versus where you want to be and how to close the gap within two years.

Using This Book If You're a Professional Serving Businesses

If you're a business journalist, consultant, market researcher, educator or trainer, before you apply these concepts and tools to your customers' businesses, make sure that you apply them to your own.

How do people decide whether to renew their subscriptions to *Fortune, Forbes, Business Week, Inc. Magazine,* the *Economist,* the *Harvard Business Review* or the *Wall Street Journal*? Why do subscribers read your column rather than a competing column? Why are advertisers shifting to or from your magazine or journal?

How do companies select among competing market research firms? What product and customer service attributes do they use? How do they rate your performance versus other market research firms?

Why do students select your university over your competitors? Your functional specialty versus other specialties? Your course versus your colleagues' courses? Why did your training firm lose its last three potential customers to the same competitor?

Once you have applied the tools to your own service, you can provide enormous help to your customers by helping them to apply them too.

Using This Book in Courses

Teachers will think of many ways to use this book to teach marketing, strategy, and quality. For example, classes can be divided into three groups focused on markets in three different kinds of industries selected from a master list (see Exhibit E–5).

EXHIBIT E–5

Type of Industry	Possible Targeted Market
Consumer package goods	Razor blades, beer, hair spray
Consumer durables	Luxury cars, personal computers, CD players
Business to business products	Chemicals, office equipment
Business to business services	Market research, consulting, accounting, information management
Services provided to consumers	Airlines, movers, tax preparation
Retailers	Drug stores, grocery stores, department stores

Each group can then be split into three teams representing the three leading competitors. The teams can report to the class in a sequence similar to the one suggested above for business-unit teams.

Alternatively, almost any business newspaper or magazine article can be analyzed using the tools and metrics of customer value analysis.[3]

Or in executive education programs, students can role-play a board member who wants to know:

- where a business is now on the customer value map
- where it will wind up if its strategy and capital requests are approved.

Malcolm Baldrige National Quality Award: 1994 Award Examination Criteria and Guidelines

Permission to use pages 13 through 38 of the *1994 Award Criteria, Malcolm Baldrige National Quality Award,* has been granted by courtesy of the National Institute of Standards and Technology, Office of Quality Programs, Gaithersburg, Maryland.

1994 AWARD EXAMINATION CRITERIA

1994 AWARD EXAMINATION CRITERIA

1.0 Leadership (95 pts.)

The *Leadership* Category examines senior executives' *personal* leadership and involvement in creating and sustaining a customer focus and clear and visible quality values. Also examined is how the quality values are integrated into the company's management system, including how the company addresses its public responsibilities and corporate citizenship.

1.1 Senior Executive Leadership (45 pts.)

Describe the senior executives' leadership, personal involvement, and visibility in developing and maintaining an environment for quality excellence.

A   D   R
☑—☑   ☐

(See page 33 for a description of these symbols.)

AREAS TO ADDRESS

a. senior executives' leadership, personal involvement, and visibility in quality-related activities of the company. Include: (1) creating and reinforcing a customer focus and quality values; (2) setting expectations and planning; (3) reviewing quality and operational performance; (4) recognizing employee contributions; and (5) communicating quality values outside the company.

b. brief summary of the company's customer focus and quality values that serve as a basis for consistent understanding and communication within and outside the company

c. how senior executives regularly communicate and reinforce the company's customer focus and quality values with managers and supervisors

d. how senior executives evaluate and improve the effectiveness of their personal leadership and involvement

Notes:

(1) "Senior executives" means the applicant's highest-ranking official and those reporting directly to that official.

(2) Activities of senior executives (1.1a) might also include leading and/or receiving training, communicating with employees, benchmarking, customer and supplier interactions, and mentoring other executives, managers, and supervisors.

(3) Communication by senior executives outside the company [1.1a(5)] might involve: national, state, and community groups; trade, business, and professional organizations; and education, health care, government, standards, and public service/charitable groups. It might also involve the company's stockholders and board of directors.

1.2 Management for Quality (25 pts.)

Describe how the company's customer focus and quality values are integrated into day-to-day leadership, management, and supervision of all company units.

A   D   R
☑—☑   ☐

AREAS TO ADDRESS

a. how the company's customer focus and quality values are translated into requirements for all managers and supervisors. Describe: (1) their principal roles and responsibilities within their units; and (2) their roles and responsibilities in fostering cooperation with other units.

b. how the company's customer focus and quality values (1.1b) are communicated and reinforced throughout the entire work force

c. how overall company and work unit quality and operational performance are reviewed. Describe: (1) types, frequency, content, and use of reviews and who conducts them; and (2) how the company assists units that are not performing according to plans.

d. how the company evaluates and improves managers' and supervisors' effectiveness in reinforcing the company's customer focus and quality values

Notes:

(1) Communication throughout the entire work force (1.2b) should emphasize the overall company approach and deployment. Some of this communication may be done by senior executives, as addressed in Item 1.1.

(2) The evaluation (1.2d) might utilize employee input or feedback on managers' and supervisors' leadership skills in reinforcing a customer focus and quality values.

1.3 Public Responsibility and Corporate Citizenship *(25 pts.)*

Describe how the company includes its responsibilities to the public in its quality policies and improvement practices. Describe also how the company leads as a corporate citizen in its key communities.

A   D   R

AREAS TO ADDRESS

a. how the company integrates its public responsibilities into its quality values and practices. Include: (1) how the company considers risks, regulatory and other legal requirements in setting operational requirements and targets; (2) a summary of the company's principal public responsibilities, key operational requirements and associated targets, and how these requirements and/or targets are communicated and deployed throughout the company; and (3) how and how often progress in meeting operational requirements and/or targets is reviewed.

b. how the company looks ahead to anticipate public concerns and to assess possible impacts on society of its products, services, and operations. Describe briefly how this assessment is used in planning.

c. how the company leads as a corporate citizen in its key communities. Include: (1) a brief summary of the types and extent of leadership and involvement in key communities; (2) how the company promotes quality awareness and sharing of quality-related information; (3) how the company seeks opportunities to enhance its leadership; and (4) how the company promotes legal and ethical conduct in all that it does.

d. trends in key measures and/or indicators of improvement in addressing public responsibilities and corporate citizenship. Include responses to any sanctions received under law, regulation, or contract.

Notes:

(1) The public responsibility issues addressed in 1.3a and 1.3b relate to the company's impacts and possible impacts on society associated with its products, services, and company operations. They include business ethics, environment, and safety as they relate to any aspect of risk or adverse effect, whether or not these are covered under law or regulation.

(2) The term "targets" as used in Item 1.3 and elsewhere in the Criteria refer to specific performance levels, based upon appropriate measures or indicators.

(3) Major public responsibility or impact areas should be addressed in planning (Item 3.1) and in the appropriate process management Items of Category 5.0.

(4) Health and safety of employees are not included in Item 1.3. They are covered in Item 4.5.

(5) The corporate citizenship issues appropriate for inclusion in 1.3c relate to actions by the company to strengthen community services, education, health care, environment, and practices of trade or business associations. Such involvement would be expected to be limited by the company's available human and financial resources.

(6) If the company has received sanctions under law, regulation, or contract during the past three years, include the current status in responding to 1.3d. If no sanctions have been received, so indicate. If settlements have been negotiated in lieu of potential sanctions, give explanations.

2.0 Information and Analysis (75 pts.)

The *Information and Analysis* Category examines the scope, management, and use of data and information to maintain a customer focus, to drive quality excellence, and to improve operational and competitive performance.

2.1 Scope and Management of Quality and Performance Data and Information (15 pts.)

Describe the company's selection and management of data and information used for planning, day-to-day management, and evaluation of quality and operational performance.

A	D	R
☑	☑	☐

AREAS TO ADDRESS

a. criteria for selecting data and information for use in quality and operational performance improvement. List key types of data and information used and briefly outline the principal roles of each type in improving quality and operational performance. Include: (1) customer-related; (2) product and service performance; (3) internal operations and performance, including business and support services, and employee-related; (4) supplier performance; and (5) cost and financial.

b. how reliability, consistency, and rapid access to data are assured throughout the company. If applicable, describe how software accuracy and reliability are assured.

c. how the company evaluates and improves the scope and management of data and information. Include: (1) review and update; (2) shortening the cycle from data gathering to access; (3) broadening access to all those requiring data for day-to-day management and improvement; and (4) aligning data and information with process improvement plans and needs.

Notes:

(1) Item 2.1 permits the applicant to demonstrate the breadth and depth of its data. Applicants should give brief descriptions of the data under major headings such as "internal operations and performance" and subheadings such as "support services". Note that information on the scope and management of competitive and benchmark data is requested in Item 2.2.

(2) Actual data should not be reported in Item 2.1. These data are requested in other Items. Accordingly, all data reported in other Items should be part of the base of data and information to be described in Item 2.1.

(3) Improving the management of data and information (2.1c) might also include company mechanisms and/or incentives for units to contribute and to share data and information.

2.2 Competitive Comparisons and Benchmarking (20 pts.)

Describe the company's processes, current sources and scope, and uses of competitive comparisons and benchmarking information and data to support improvement of quality and operational performance.

A	D	R
☑	☑	☐

AREAS TO ADDRESS

a. how competitive comparisons and benchmarking information and data are used to help drive improvement of quality and operational performance. Describe: (1) how needs are determined; and (2) criteria for seeking appropriate competitive comparisons and benchmarking information — from within and outside the company's industry.

b. brief summary of current scope, sources, and principal uses of each type of competitive comparisons and benchmarking information and data. Include: (1) customer-related; (2) product and service quality; (3) internal operations and performance, including business and support services and employee-related; and (4) supplier performance.

c. how competitive comparisons and benchmarking information and data are used to improve understanding of processes, to encourage breakthrough approaches, and to set "stretch" targets

d. how the company evaluates and improves its overall processes for selecting and using competitive comparisons and benchmarking information and data to improve planning and operational performance

Notes:

(1) Benchmarking information and data refer to processes and results that represent superior practices and performance and set "stretch" targets for comparison.

(2) Sources of competitive comparisons and benchmarking information might include: (1) information obtained from other organizations through sharing; (2) information obtained from the open literature; (3) testing and evaluation by the company itself; and (4) testing and evaluation by independent organizations.

2.3 Analysis and Uses of Company-Level Data *(40 pts.)*

Describe how data related to quality, customers and operational performance, together with relevant financial data, are analyzed to support company-level review, action and planning.

A   D   R

AREAS TO ADDRESS

a. how customer-related data and results (from Category 7.0) are aggregated with other key data and analyses and translated via analysis into actionable information to support: (1) developing priorities for prompt solutions to customer-related problems; and (2) determining key customer-related trends and correlations to support reviews, decision making, and longer-term planning

b. how quality and operational performance data and results (from Category 6.0) are aggregated with other key data and analyses and translated via analysis into actionable information to support: (1) developing priorities for improvements in products/services and company operations, including cycle time, productivity and waste reduction; and (2) determining key operations-related trends and correlations to support reviews, decision making, and longer-term planning

c. how the company relates overall improvements in product/service quality and operational performance to changes in overall financial performance to support reviews, decision making, and longer-term planning

d. how the company evaluates and improves its analysis for use as a key management tool. Include: (1) how analysis supports improved data selection and use; (2) how analysis strengthens the integration of overall data use for improved decision making and planning; and (3) how the analysis-access cycle is shortened.

Notes:

(1) Item 2.3 focuses primarily on analysis for company-level purposes, such as reviews (1.2c) and strategic planning (Item 3.1). Data for such analysis come from all parts of the company. Other Items call for analyses of specific sets of data for special purposes. For example, the Items of Category 4.0 require analyses to demonstrate effectiveness of training and other human resource practices. Such special-purpose analyses are assumed to be part of the overall information base of Category 2.0, available for use in Item 2.3. These specific sets of data and special-purpose analyses are referred to in 2.3a and 2.3b as "other key data and analyses."

(2)"Actionable" means that the analysis provides information that can be used for priorities and decisions leading to allocation of resources.

(3) Solutions to customer-related problems [2.3a(1)] at the company level involve a process for: (1) aggregation of formal and informal complaints from different parts of the company; (2) analysis leading to priorities for action; and (3) use of the resulting information throughout the company. Note the connections to 7.2e, which focuses on day-to-day complaint management, including prompt resolution.

(4) The focus in 2.3a is on analysis to improve customer-related decision making and planning. This analysis is intended to provide additional information to support *such decision making and planning that result from day-to-day customer information, feedback, and complaints.*

Examples of analysis appropriate for inclusion in 2.3a are:
* *how the company's product and service quality improvement correlates with key customer indicators such as customer satisfaction, customer retention, and market share;*
* *cross-comparisons of data from complaints, post-transaction follow-up, and won/lost analyses to identify improvement priorities;*
* *relationship between employee satisfaction and customer satisfaction;*
* *cost/revenue implications of customer-related problems and problem resolution effectiveness;*
* *rates of improvements of customer indicators;*
* *customer loyalty (or positive referral) versus level of satisfaction; and*
* *customer loyalty versus level of satisfaction with the effectiveness of problem resolution.*

(5) The focus in 2.3b is on analysis to improve operations-related decision making and planning. This analysis is intended to support *such decision making and planning that result from day-to-day observations of process performance.*

Examples of analysis appropriate for inclusion in 2.3b are:
* *how product/service improvement priorities are determined;*
* *evaluation of the productivity and cost impacts of improvement initiatives;*
* *rates of improvement in key operational indicators;*
* *evaluation of trends in key operational efficiency measures such as productivity;*
* *comparison with competitive and benchmark data to identify improvement opportunities and to set improvement priorities and targets.*

(6) The focus in 2.3c is on the linkages between improvements in product/service quality and operational performance and overall financial performance for company goal and priority setting. Analyses in 2.3c might incorporate the results of analyses described in 2.3a and 2.3b, and draw upon other key data and analyses.

Examples of analysis appropriate for inclusion in 2.3c are:
* *relationships between product/service quality and operational performance indicators and overall company financial performance trends as reflected in indicators such as operating costs, revenues, asset utilization, and value added per employee;*
* *comparisons of company financial performance versus competitors based on quality and operational performance indicators;*
* *allocation of resources among alternative improvement projects based on cost/revenue implications and improvement potential;*
* *net earnings derived from quality/operational performance improvements;*
* *comparisons among business units showing how quality and operational performance improvement have improved financial performance; and*
* *contributions of improvement activities to cash flow and/or shareholder value.*

3.0 Strategic Quality Planning (60 pts.)

The *Strategic Quality Planning* Category examines the company's planning process and how all key quality and operational performance requirements are integrated into overall business planning. Also examined are the company's short- and longer-term plans and how plan requirements are deployed to all work units.

3.1 Strategic Quality and Company Performance Planning Process

(35 pts.)

Describe the company's business planning process for the short term (1-3 years) and longer term (3 years or more) for customer satisfaction leadership and overall operational performance improvement. Include how this process integrates quality and operational performance requirements and how plans are deployed.

A	D	R
☑—	—☑	☐

AREAS TO ADDRESS

a. how the company develops strategies and business plans to address quality and customer satisfaction leadership for the short term and longer term. Describe how plans consider: (1) customer requirements and the expected evolution of these requirements; (2) projections of the competitive environment; (3) risks: financial, market, technological, and societal; (4) company capabilities, such as human resource and research and development to address key new requirements or market leadership opportunities; and (5) supplier capabilities.

b. how strategies and plans address operational performance improvement. Describe how the following are considered: (1) realigning work processes ("re-engineering") to improve customer focus and operational performance; and (2) productivity and cycle time improvement and reduction in waste.

c. how plans are deployed. Describe: (1) how the company deploys plan requirements to work units and to suppliers, and how it ensures alignment of work unit plans and activities; and (2) how resources are committed to meet plan requirements.

d. how the company evaluates and improves: (1) its planning process; (2) deploying plan requirements to work units; and (3) receiving planning input from work units

Notes:

(1) Item 3.1 addresses overall company strategies and business plans, not specific product and service designs. Strategies and business plans that might be addressed as part of Item 3.1 include operational aspects such as manufacturing and/or service delivery strategies, as well as new product/service lines, new markets, outsourcing, and strategic alliances.

(2) Societal risks and impacts are addressed in Item 1.3.

(3) Productivity and cycle time improvement and waste reduction (3.1b) might address factors such as inventories, work in process, inspection, downtime, changeover time, set-up time, and other examples of utilization of resources such as materials, equipment, energy, capital, and labor.

(4) How the company reviews quality and operational performance relative to plans is addressed in 1.2c.

3.2 Quality and Performance Plans

(25 pts.)

Summarize the company's specific quality and operational performance plans for the short term (1-3 years) and the longer term (3 years or more).

A   D   R

☑—☑   ☐

AREAS TO ADDRESS

a. for planned products, services, and customer markets, summarize: (1) key quality requirements to achieve or retain leadership; and (2) key company operational performance requirements

b. outline of the company's deployment of principal short-term quality and operational performance plans. Include: (1) a summary of key requirements and associated operational performance measures or indicators deployed to work units and suppliers; and (2) a brief description of resources committed for key needs such as capital equipment, facilities, education and training, and new hires.

c. outline of how principal longer-term (3 years or more) quality and operational performance requirements (from 3.2a) will be addressed

d. two-to-five-year projection of key measures and/or indicators of the company's quality and operational performance. Describe how quality and operational performance might be expected to compare with key competitors and key benchmarks over this time period. Briefly explain the comparisons, including any estimates or assumptions made regarding the projected quality and operational performance of competitors or changes in benchmarks.

Notes:

(1) The focus in Item 3.2 is on the translation of the company's business plans, resulting from the planning process described in Item 3.1, to requirements for work units and suppliers. The main intent of Item 3.2 is alignment of short- and long-term operations with business directions. Although the deployment of these plans will affect products and services, design of products and services is not the focus of Item 3.2. Such design is addressed in Item 5.1.

(2) Area 3.2d addresses projected progress in improving performance and in gaining advantage relative to competitors. This projection may draw upon analysis (Item 2.3) and data reported in results Items (Category 6.0 and Items 7.5 and 7.6). Such projections are intended to support reviews (1.2c), evaluation of plans (3.1d), and other Items.

4.0 Human Resource Development and Management (150 pts.)

The *Human Resource Development and Management* Category examines the key elements of how the work force is enabled to develop its full potential to pursue the company's quality and operational performance objectives. Also examined are the company's efforts to build and maintain an environment for quality excellence conducive to full participation and personal and organizational growth.

4.1 Human Resource Planning and Management *(20 pts.)*

Describe how the company's overall human resource management, plans and processes are integrated with its overall quality and operational performance plans and how human resource planning and management address fully the needs and development of the entire work force.

A   D   R

AREAS TO ADDRESS

a. brief description of the most important human resource plans (derived from Category 3.0). Include: (1) development, including education, training and empowerment; (2) mobility, flexibility, and changes in work organization, work processes or work schedules; (3) reward, recognition, benefits, and compensation; and (4) recruitment, including possible changes in diversity of the work force. Distinguish between the short term (1-3 years) and the longer term (3 years or more), as appropriate.

b. how the company improves key personnel processes. Describe key improvement methods for processes such as recruitment, hiring, personnel actions, and services to employees, including support services to managers and supervisors. Include a description of key performance measures or indicators, including cycle time, and how they are used in improvement.

c. how the company evaluates and improves its human resource planning and management using all employee-related data. Include: (1) how selection, performance, recognition, job analysis, and training are integrated to support improved performance and development of all categories and types of employees; and (2) how human resource planning and management are aligned with company strategy and plans.

Notes:

(1) Human resource plans (4.1a) might include one or more of the following:
- *mechanisms for promoting cooperation such as internal customer/supplier techniques or other internal partnerships;*
- *initiatives to promote labor-management cooperation, such as partnerships with unions;*
- *creation and/or modification of recognition systems;*
- *creation or modification of compensation systems based on building shareholder value;*
- *mechanisms for increasing or broadening employee responsibilities;*
- *creating opportunities for employees to learn and use skills that go beyond current job assignments through redesign of processes;*
- *creation of high performance work teams;*
- *education and training initiatives; and*
- *forming partnerships with educational institutions to develop employees or to help ensure the future supply of well-prepared employees.*

(2) The personnel processes referred to in 4.1b are those commonly carried out by personnel departments or by personnel specialists. Improvement processes might include needs assessments and satisfaction surveys. Improvement results associated with the measures or indicators used in 4.1b should be reported in Item 6.3.

(3) "Categories of employees" (4.1c) refers to the company's classification system used in its personnel practices and/or work assignments. It also includes factors such as union or bargaining unit membership. "Types of employees" takes into account other factors, such as work force diversity or demographic makeup. This includes gender, age, minorities, and the disabled.

(4) "All employee-related data" (4.1c) refers to data contained in personnel records as well as data described in Items 4.2, 4.3, 4.4, and 4.5. This might include employee satisfaction data and data on turnover, absenteeism, safety, grievances, involvement, recognition, training, and information from exit interviews.

(5) The evaluation in 4.1c might be supported by employee-related data such as satisfaction factors (Item 4.5), absenteeism, turnover, and accidents. It might also be supported by employee feedback.

4.2 Employee Involvement
(40 pts.)

Describe how all employees are enabled to contribute effectively to meeting the company's quality and operational performance plans; summarize trends in effectiveness and extent of involvement.

A   D   R

<table>
<tr><td>☑</td><td>—</td><td>☑</td><td></td><td>☑</td></tr>
</table>

AREAS TO ADDRESS

a. how the company promotes ongoing employee contributions, individually and in groups, to improvement in quality and operational performance. Include how and how quickly the company gives feedback to contributors.

b. how the company increases employee empowerment, responsibility, and innovation. Include a brief summary of principal plans for all categories of employees, based upon the most important requirements for each category.

c. how the company evaluates and improves the effectiveness, extent, and type of involvement of all categories and all types of employees. Include how effectiveness, extent and types of involvement are linked to key quality and operational performance improvement results.

d. trends in key measures and/or indicators of the <u>effectiveness</u> and <u>extent</u> of employee involvement

Notes:

(1) The company might use different involvement methods and measures or indicators for different categories of employees or for different parts of the company, depending on needs and responsibilities of each employee category or part of the company. Examples include problem-solving teams (within work units or *cross-functional); fully-integrated, self-managed work groups; and process improvement teams.*

(2) Trend results (4.2d) should be segmented by category of employee, as appropriate. Major types of involvement should be noted.

4.3 Employee Education and Training *(40 pts.)*

Describe how the company determines quality and related education and training needs for all employees. Show how this determination addresses company plans and supports employee growth. Outline how such education and training are evaluated, and summarize key trends in the effectiveness and extent of education and training.

A   D   R

<table>
<tr><td>☑</td><td>—</td><td>☑</td><td></td><td>☑</td></tr>
</table>

AREAS TO ADDRESS

a. how the company determines needs for the types and amounts of quality and related education and training for all employees, taking into account their differing needs. Include: (1) linkage to short- and long-term plans, including company-wide access to skills in problem solving, waste reduction, and process simplification; (2) growth and career opportunities for employees; and (3) how employees' input is sought and used in the needs determination.

b. how quality and related education and training are delivered and reinforced. Include: (1) description of education and training delivery for all categories of employees; (2) on-the-job application of knowledge and skills; and (3) quality-related orientation for new employees.

c. how the company evaluates and improves its quality and related education and training. Include how the evaluation supports improved needs determination, taking into account: (1) relating on-the-job performance improvement to key quality and operational performance improvement targets and results; and (2) growth and progression of all categories and types of employees.

d. trends in key measures and/or indicators of the <u>effectiveness</u> and <u>extent</u> of quality and related education and training

Notes:

(1) Quality and related education and training address the knowledge and skills employees need to meet their objectives as part of the company's quality and operational performance improvement. This might include quality awareness, leadership, project management, communications, teamwork, problem solving, interpreting and using data, meeting customer requirements, process analysis, process simplification, waste reduction, cycle time reduction, error-proofing, and other training that affects employee effectiveness, efficiency, and safety. In many cases, this might include job enrichment skills and job rotation that enhance employees' career opportunities. It might also include basic skills such as reading, writing, language, arithmetic, and basic mathematics that are needed for quality and operational performance improvement.

(2) Education and training delivery might occur inside or outside the company and involve on-the-job or classroom delivery.

(3) The overall evaluation (4.3c) might compare the relative effectiveness of structured on-the-job training with classroom methods. It might also address how to best balance on-the-job training and classroom methods.

(4) Trend results (4.3d) should be segmented by category of employee (including new employees), as appropriate. Major types of training and education should be noted.

4.4 Employee Performance and Recognition
(25 pts.)

Describe how the company's employee performance, recognition, promotion, compensation, reward, and feedback approaches support the improvement of quality and operational performance.

A   D   R

☑——☑   ☑

AREAS TO ADDRESS

a. how the company's employee performance, recognition, promotion, compensation, reward, and feedback approaches for individuals and groups, including managers, support improvement of quality and operational performance. Include: (1) how the approaches ensure that quality is reinforced relative to short-term financial considerations; and (2) how employees contribute to the company's employee performance and recognition approaches.

b. how the company evaluates and improves its employee performance and recognition approaches. Include how the evaluation takes into account: (1) effective participation by all categories and types of employees; (2) employee satisfaction information (Item 4.5); and (3) key measures or indicators of improved quality and operational performance results.

c. trends in key measures and/or indicators of the <u>effectiveness</u> and <u>extent</u> of employee reward and recognition

Notes:

(1) The company might use a variety of reward and recognition approaches — monetary and non-monetary, formal and informal, and individual and group.

(2) Employee satisfaction (4.4b) might take into account employee dissatisfaction indicators such as turnover and absenteeism.

(3) Trend results (4.4c) should be segmented by employee category, as appropriate. Major types of recognition, compensation, etc., should be noted.

4.5 Employee Well-Being and Satisfaction *(25 pts.)*

Describe how the company maintains a work environment conducive to the well-being and growth of all employees; summarize trends in key indicators of well-being and satisfaction.

A   D   R

☑——☑   ☑

AREAS TO ADDRESS

a. how employee well-being factors such as health, safety, and ergonomics are included in quality improvement activities. Include principal improvement methods, measures or indicators, and targets for each factor relevant and important to the company's employee work environment. For accidents and work-related health problems, describe how root causes are determined and how adverse conditions are prevented.

b. what special services, facilities, activities, and opportunities the company makes available to employees to enhance their work experience and/or to support their overall well-being

c. how the company determines employee satisfaction. Include a brief description of methods, frequency, and the specific factors for which satisfaction is determined. Describe how these factors relate to employee motivation and productivity. Segment by employee category or type, as appropriate.

d. trends in key measures and/or indicators of well-being and satisfaction. Explain important adverse results, if any. For such adverse results, describe how root causes were determined and corrected, and/or give current status. Compare results on the most significant measures or indicators with appropriately selected companies and/or benchmarks.

Notes:

(1) Special services, facilities, activities, and opportunities (4.5b) might include: counseling; recreational or cultural activities; non-work-related education; day care; special leave; safety off the job; flexible work hours; and outplacement.

(2) Examples of specific factors for which satisfaction might be determined (4.5c) are: safety; employee views of leadership and management; employee development and career opportunities; employee preparation for changes in technology or work organization; work environment;

teamwork; recognition; benefits; communications; job security; and compensation.

(3) Measures or indicators of well-being and satisfaction (4.5d) include safety, absenteeism, turnover, turnover rate for customer-contact employees, grievances, strikes, worker compensation, and results of satisfaction determinations.

(4) Comparisons (4.5d) might include industry averages, industry leaders, local/regional leaders, and key benchmarks.

5.0 Management of Process Quality *(140 pts.)*

The *Management of Process Quality* Category examines the key elements of process management, including design, management of day-to-day production and delivery, improvement of quality and operational performance, and quality assessment. The Category also examines how all work units, including research and development units and suppliers, contribute to overall quality and operational performance requirements.

5.1 Design and Introduction of Quality Products and Services *(40 pts.)*

Describe how new and/or modified products and services are designed and introduced and how key production/delivery processes are designed to meet both key product and service quality requirements and company operational performance requirements.

A   D   R

☑——☑   ☐

AREAS TO ADDRESS

a. how products, services, and production/delivery processes are designed. Describe: (1) how customer requirements are translated into product and service design requirements; (2) how product and service design requirements, together with the company's operational performance requirements, are translated into production/delivery processes, including an appropriate measurement plan; (3) how all product and service quality requirements are addressed early in the overall design process by appropriate company units; and (4) how designs are coordinated and integrated to include all phases of production and delivery.

b. how product, service, and production/delivery process designs are reviewed and validated, taking into account key factors: (1) overall product and service performance; (2) process capability and future requirements; and (3) supplier capability and future requirements

c. how designs and design processes are evaluated and improved so that new product and service introductions and product and service modifications progressively improve in quality and cycle time

---

Notes:

(1) Design and introduction might address modifications and variants of existing products and services and/or new products and services emerging from research and development or other product/service concept development. Design also might address key new/modified facilities to meet operational performance and/or product and service quality requirements.

(2) Applicants' responses should reflect the key requirements for their products and services. Factors that might need to be considered in design include: health; safety; long-term performance; environment; measurement capability; process capability; manufacturability; maintainability; supplier capability; and documentation.

(3) Service and manufacturing businesses should interpret product and service design requirements to include all product- and service-related requirements at all stages of production, delivery, and use.

(4) In 5.1a(2), company operational performance requirements relate to operational efficiency and effectiveness — waste reduction and cycle time improvement, for example. A measurement plan should spell out what is to be measured, how measurements are to be made, and performance levels or standards to ensure that the results of measurements will show whether or not production/delivery processes are in control.

(5) Results of improvements in design should be reported in 6.1a. Results of improvements in design process quality should be reported in 6.2a.

5.2 Process Management: Product and Service Production and Delivery Processes

(35 pts.)

Describe how the company's key product and service production/delivery processes are managed to ensure that design requirements are met and that both quality and operational performance are continuously improved.

A   D   R

☑—☑   ☐

AREAS TO ADDRESS

a. how the company maintains the quality and operational performance of the production/delivery processes described in Item 5.1. Describe: (1) the key processes, their requirements, and how quality and operational performance are tracked and maintained. Include types and frequencies of in-process and end-of-process measurements used; (2) for significant (out-of-control) variations in processes or outputs, how root causes are determined; and (3) how corrections of variation [from 5.2a(2)] are made, verified, and integrated into process management.

b. how processes are improved to achieve better quality, cycle time, and operational performance. Describe how each of the following is used or considered: (1) process analysis/simplification; (2) benchmarking information; (3) process research and testing; (4) use of alternative technology; (5) information from customers of the processes — within and outside the company; and (6) stretch targets.

Notes:

(1) Manufacturing and service companies with specialized measurement requirements should describe how they assure measurement quality. For physical, chemical, and engineering measurements, describe briefly how measurements are made traceable to national standards.

(2) Variations [5.2a(2)] might be observed by those working in the process or by customers of the process output. The

latter situation might result in formal or informal feedback or complaints. Also, a company might use observers or "mystery shoppers" to provide information on process performance.

(3) Results of improvements in product and service production and delivery processes should be reported in 6.2a.

5.3 Process Management: Business and Support Service Processes
(30 pts.)

Describe how the company's key business and support service processes are designed and managed so that current requirements are met and that quality and operational performance are continuously improved.

A   D   R

AREAS TO ADDRESS

a. how key business and support service processes are designed. Include: (1) how key quality and operational performance requirements for business and support services are determined or set; (2) how these quality and operational performance requirements [from 5.3a(1)] are translated into delivery processes, including an appropriate measurement plan.

b. how the company maintains the quality and operational performance of business and support service delivery processes. Describe: (1) the key processes, their requirements, and how quality and operational performance are tracked and maintained. Include types and frequencies of in-process and end-of-process measurements used; (2) for significant (out-of-control) variations in processes or outputs, how root causes are determined; and (3) how corrections of variation [from 5.3b(2)] are made, verified, and integrated into process management.

c. how processes are improved to achieve better quality, cycle time, and overall operational performance. Describe how each of the following are used or considered: (1) process analysis/simplification; (2) benchmarking information; (3) process research and testing; (4) use of alternative technology; (5) information from customers of the business processes and support services — within and outside the company; and (6) stretch targets.

Notes:

(1) Business and support service processes might include units and operations involving finance and accounting, software services, sales, marketing, public relations, information services, purchasing, personnel, legal services, plant and facilities management, basic research and development, and secretarial and other administrative services.

(2) The purpose of Item 5.3 is to permit applicants to highlight separately the improvement activities for functions that support the product and service design, production, and delivery processes addressed in Items 5.1 and 5.2. The support services and business processes

included in Item 5.3 depend on the applicant's type of business and other factors. Thus, this selection should be made by the applicant. Together, Items 5.1, 5.2, 5.3, and 5.4 should cover all operations, processes, and activities of all work units.

(3) Variations [5.3b(2)] might be observed by those working in the process or by customers of the process output. The latter situation might result in formal or informal feedback or complaints.

(4) Results of improvements in business processes and support services should be reported in 6.3a.

5.4 Supplier Quality
(20 pts.)

Describe how the company assures the quality of materials, components, and services furnished by other businesses. Describe also the company's actions and plans to improve supplier quality.

A   D   R

AREAS TO ADDRESS

a. how the company's quality requirements are defined and communicated to suppliers. Include a brief summary of the principal quality requirements for key suppliers. Also give the measures and/or indicators and expected performance levels for the principal requirements.

b. how the company determines whether or not its quality requirements are met by suppliers. Describe how performance information is fed back to suppliers.

c. how the company evaluates and improves its own procurement processes. Include what feedback is sought from suppliers and how it is used in improvement.

d. current actions and plans to improve suppliers' abilities to meet key quality, response time, or other requirements. Include actions and/or plans to minimize inspection, test, audit, or other approaches that might incur unnecessary costs.

Notes:

(1) The term "supplier" refers to providers of goods and services. The use of these goods and services may occur at any stage in the production, delivery, and use of the company's products and services. Thus, suppliers include businesses such as distributors, dealers, warranty repair services, contractors, and franchises as well as those that provide materials and components.

(2) Generally, suppliers are other-company providers of goods and services. However, if the applicant is a subsidiary or division of a company, and other units of that company supply goods/services, this relationship should be described as a supplier relationship.

(3) Determining how quality requirements are met (5.4b) might include audits, process reviews, receiving inspection, certification, testing, and rating systems.

(4) Actions and plans (5.4d) might include one or more of the following: joint planning, partnerships, training, long-term agreements, incentives, and recognition. They might also include supplier selection. "Other requirements" might include suppliers' price levels. If this is the case, suppliers' abilities might address factors such as productivity and waste reduction.

5.5 Quality Assessment
(15 pts.)

Describe how the company assesses the quality and performance of its systems and processes and the quality of its products and services.

A   D   R

AREAS TO ADDRESS

a. how the company assesses: (1) systems and processes; and (2) products and services. For (1) and (2), describe: (a) what is assessed; (b) how often assessments are made and by whom; and (c) how measurement quality and adequacy of documentation of processes are assured.

b. how assessment findings are used to improve: products and services; systems; processes; supplier requirements; and the assessment processes. Include how the company verifies that assessment findings are acted upon and that the actions are effective.

Notes:

(1) The systems, processes, products, and services addressed in this Item pertain to all company unit activities covered in Items 5.1, 5.2, 5.3, and 5.4. If the assessment approaches differ appreciably for different company processes or units, this should be described in this Item.

(2) Adequacy of documentation should take into account legal, regulatory, and contractual requirements as well as knowledge preservation and knowledge transfer to help support all improvement efforts. Adequacy should take into account completeness, timely update, useability, and other appropriate factors.

6.0 Quality and Operational Results *(180 pts.)*

The ***Quality and Operational Results*** Category examines the company's achievement levels and improvement trends in quality, company operational performance, and supplier quality. Also examined are current quality and operational performance levels relative to those of competitors.

6.1 Product and Service Quality Results *(70 pts.)*

Summarize trends and current quality levels for key product and service features; compare current levels with those of competitors and/or appropriate benchmarks.

AREAS TO ADDRESS

a. trends and current levels for the key measures and/or indicators of product and service quality

b. comparisons of current quality levels with that of principal competitors in the company's key markets, industry averages, industry leaders, and appropriate benchmarks

Notes:

(1) Key product and service measures are measures relative to the set of all important features of the company's products and services. These measures, taken together, best represent the most important factors that predict customer satisfaction and quality in customer use. Examples include measures of accuracy, reliability, timeliness, performance, behavior, delivery, after-sales services, documentation, appearance, and effective complaint management.

(2) Results reported in Item 6.1 should reflect all key product and service features described in the Business Overview and addressed in Items 7.1 and 5.1.

(3) Data reported in Item 6.1 are intended to be objective measures of product and service quality, not the customers'

satisfaction or reaction to the products and/or services. Such data might be of several types, including: (a) internal (company) measurements; (b) field performance (when applicable); (c) proactive checks by the company of specific product and service features (7.2d); and (d) data routinely collected by other organizations or on behalf of the company. Data reported in Item 6.1 should provide information on the company's performance relative to the specific product and service features that best predict customer satisfaction. These data, collected regularly, are then part of a process for monitoring and improving quality.

(4) Bases for comparison (6.1b) might include: independent surveys, studies, or laboratory testing; benchmarks; and company evaluations and testing.

6.2 Company Operational Results *(50 pts.)*

Summarize trends and levels in overall company operational performance; provide a comparison with competitors and/or appropriate benchmarks.

A   D   R

AREAS TO ADDRESS

a. trends and current levels for key measures and/or indicators of company operational performance

b. comparison of performance with that of competitors, industry averages, industry leaders, and key benchmarks

Notes:

(1) Key measures of company operational performance include those that address productivity, efficiency, and effectiveness. Examples should include generic indicators such as use of manpower, materials, energy, capital, and assets. Trends and levels could address productivity indices, waste reduction, energy efficiency, cycle time reduction, environmental improvement, and other measures of improved overall company performance. Also include company-specific indicators the company uses to track its progress in improving operational performance. Such

company-specific indicators should be defined in tables or charts where trends are presented.

(2) Trends in financial indicators, properly labeled, might be included in Item 6.2. If such financial indicators are used, there should be a clear connection to the quality and operational performance improvement activities of the company.

(3) Include improvements in product and service design and production/delivery processes in this Item.

6.3 Business and Support Service Results *(25 pts.)*

Summarize trends and current levels in quality and operational performance improvement for business processes and support services; compare results with competitors and/or appropriate benchmarks.

A   D   R

□—□   ☑

<table>
<tr><td colspan="2">AREAS TO ADDRESS</td></tr>
<tr><td>a.</td><td>trends and current levels for key measures and/or indicators of quality and operational performance of business and support services</td></tr>
<tr><td>b.</td><td>comparison of performance with appropriately selected companies and benchmarks</td></tr>
</table>

Notes:

(1) Business and support services are those covered in Item 5.3. Key measures of performance should reflect the principal quality, productivity, cycle time, cost, and other effectiveness requirements for business and support services. Responses should reflect relevance to the company's principal quality and operational performance objectives addressed in company plans, contributing to the results reported in Items 6.1 and 6.2. Responses

should demonstrate broad coverage of company business and support services and work units. Results should reflect the most important objectives for each service or work unit.

(2) Comparisons and benchmarks for business and support services (6.3b) should emphasize best practice performance, regardless of industry.

6.4 Supplier Quality Results *(35 pts.)*

Summarize trends in quality and current quality levels of suppliers; compare the company's supplier quality with that of competitors and/or with appropriate benchmarks.

A   D   R

□—□   ☑

<table>
<tr><td colspan="2">AREAS TO ADDRESS</td></tr>
<tr><td>a.</td><td>trends and current levels for key measures and/or indicators of supplier quality performance</td></tr>
<tr><td>b.</td><td>comparison of the company's supplier quality levels with those of appropriately selected companies and/or benchmarks</td></tr>
</table>

Notes:

(1) The results reported in Item 6.4 derive from quality improvement activities described in Item 5.4. Results should be broken down by major groupings of suppliers and reported using the principal quality measures described in Item 5.4.

(2) Comparisons (6.4b) might be with industry averages, industry leaders, principal competitors in the company's key markets, and appropriate benchmarks.

7.0 Customer Focus and Satisfaction (300 pts.)

The *Customer Focus and Satisfaction* Category examines the company's relationships with customers, and its knowledge of customer requirements and of the key quality factors that drive marketplace competitiveness. Also examined are the company's methods to determine customer satisfaction, current trends and levels of customer satisfaction and retention, and these results relative to competitors.

7.1 Customer Expectations: Current and Future

(35 pts.)

Describe how the company determines near-term and longer-term requirements and expectations of customers.

A   D   R

AREAS TO ADDRESS

a. how the company determines *current and near-term requirements* and expectations of customers. Include: (1) how customer groups and/or market segments are determined or selected, including how customers of competitors and other potential customers are considered; (2) how information is collected, including what information is sought, frequency and methods of collection, and how objectivity and validity are assured; (3) how specific product and service features and the relative importance of these features to customer groups or segments are determined; and (4) how other key information and data such as complaints, gains and losses of customers, and product/service performance are used to support the determination.

b. how the company addresses *future requirements* and expectations of customers. Include: (1) the time horizon for the determination; (2) how important technological, competitive, societal, environmental, economic, and demographic factors that may bear upon customer requirements, expectations, preferences, or alternatives are considered; (3) how customers of competitors and other potential customers are considered; (4) how key product and service features and the relative importance of these features are projected; and (5) how changing or emerging market segments and their implications on current or new product/service lines are considered.

c. how the company evaluates and improves its processes for determining customer requirements and expectations

Notes:

(1) The distinction between near-term and future depends upon many marketplace factors. The applicant's response should reflect these factors for its market.

(2) The company's products and services might be sold to end users via other businesses such as retail stores or dealers. Thus, "customer groups" should take into account the requirements and expectations of both the end users and these other businesses.

(3) Product and service features refer to all important characteristics and to the performance of products and services that customers experience or perceive throughout their overall purchase and ownership. These include any factors that bear upon customer preference, repurchase loyalty, or view of quality — for example, those features that enhance or differentiate products and services from competing offerings.

(4) Some companies might use similar methods to determine customer requirements/expectations and customer satisfaction (Item 7.4). In such cases, cross-references should be included.

(5) Customer groups and market segments (7.1a,b) should take into account opportunities to select or <u>create</u> groups and segments based upon customer- and market-related information.

(6) Examples of evaluations appropriate for 7.1c are:
* *the adequacy of the customer-related information;*
* *improvement of survey design;*
* *the best approaches for getting reliable information — surveys, focus groups, customer-contact personnel, etc.; and*
* *increasing and decreasing importance of product/service features among customer groups or segments.*

The evaluation might also be supported by company-level analysis addressed in 2.3a.

7.2 Customer Relationship Management *(65 pts.)*

Describe how the company provides effective management of its interactions and relationships with its customers and uses information gained from customers to improve customer relationship management processes.

A   D   R

AREAS TO ADDRESS

a. for the company's most important contacts between its employees and customers, summarize the key requirements for maintaining and building relationships. Describe how these requirements are translated into key quality measures.

b. how service standards based upon the key quality measures (7.2a) are set and used. Include: (1) how service standards, including measures and performance levels, are deployed to customer-contact employees and to other company units that provide support for customer-contact employees; and (2) how the performance of the overall service standards system is tracked.

c. how the company provides information and easy access to enable customers to seek assistance, to comment, and to complain. Include the main types of contact and how easy access is maintained for each type.

d. how the company follows up with customers on products, services, and recent transactions to seek feedback and to help build relationships

e. how the company ensures that formal and informal complaints and feedback received by all company units are resolved effectively and promptly. Briefly describe the complaint management process.

f. how the following are addressed for customer-contact employees: (1) selection factors; (2) career path; (3) deployment of special training to include: knowledge of products and services; listening to customers; soliciting comments from customers; how to anticipate and handle problems or failures ("recovery"); skills in customer retention; and how to manage expectations; (4) empowerment and decision making; (5) satisfaction; and (6) recognition and reward

g. how the company evaluates and improves its customer relationship management processes. Include: (1) how the company seeks opportunities to enhance relationships with all customers or with key customers; and (2) how evaluations lead to improvements such as in service standards, access, customer-contact employee training, and technology support; and (3) how customer information is used in the improvement process.

Notes:

(1) Requirements (7.2a) might include responsiveness, product knowledge, follow-up, ease of access, etc. They do not include product and service requirements addressed in Item 7.1.

(2) "Service standards" refers to performance levels or expectations the company sets using the quality measures.

(3) The term "customer-contact employees" refers to employees whose main responsibilities bring them into regular contact with customers — in person, via telephone, or other means.

(4) In addressing "empowerment and decision making" in 7.2f, indicate how the company ensures that there is a common vision or basis to guide the actions of customer-contact employees. That is, the response should make clear how the company ensures that empowered customer-contact employees have a consistent understanding of what actions or types of actions they may or should take.

(5) In addressing satisfaction (7.2f), consider indicators such as turnover and absenteeism, as well as results of employee feedback through surveys, exit interviews, etc.

(6) Information on trends and levels in measures and indicators of complaint response time, effective resolution, and percent of complaints resolved on first contact should be reported in Item 6.1.

(7) How feedback and complaint data are aggregated for overall evaluation and how these data are translated into actionable information, should be addressed in 2.3a.

7.3 Commitment to Customers *(15 pts.)*

Describe the company's commitments to customers regarding its products/services and how these commitments are evaluated and improved.

A   D   R

AREAS TO ADDRESS

a. types of commitments the company makes to promote trust and confidence in its products/services and to satisfy customers when product/service failures occur. Describe these commitments and how they: (1) address the principal concerns of customers; (2) are free from conditions that might weaken customers' trust and confidence; and (3) are communicated to customers clearly and simply.

b. how the company evaluates and improves its commitments, and the customers' understanding of them, to avoid gaps between customer expectations and company performance. Include: (1) how information/feedback from customers is used; (2) how product/service performance improvement data are used; and (3) how competitors' commitments are considered.

Note: *Examples of commitments are product and service guarantees, warranties, and other understandings, expressed or implied.*

7.4 Customer Satisfaction Determination *(30 pts.)*

Describe how the company determines customer satisfaction, customer repurchase intentions, and customer satisfaction relative to competitors; describe how these determination processes are evaluated and improved.

A   D   R

AREAS TO ADDRESS

a. how the company determines customer satisfaction. Include: (1) a brief description of processes and measurement scales used; frequency of determination; and how objectivity and validity are assured. Indicate significant differences, if any, in processes and measurement scales for different customer groups or segments; and (2) how customer satisfaction measurements capture key information that reflects customers' likely future market behavior, such as repurchase intentions or positive referrals.

b. how customer satisfaction relative to that for competitors is determined. Describe: (1) company-based comparative studies; and (2) comparative studies or evaluations made by independent organizations and/or customers. For (1) and (2), describe how objectivity and validity of studies are assured.

c. how the company evaluates and improves its overall processes and measurement scales for determining customer satisfaction and customer satisfaction relative to that for competitors. Include how other indicators (such as gains and losses of customers) and customer dissatisfaction indicators (such as complaints) are used in this improvement process.

Notes:

(1) Customer satisfaction measurement might include both a numerical rating scale and descriptors assigned to each unit in the scale. An effective (actionable) customer satisfaction measurement system is one that provides the company with reliable information about customer ratings of specific product and service features and the relationship between these ratings and the customer's likely future market behavior.

(2) The company's products and services might be sold to end users via other businesses such as retail stores or dealers. Thus, "customer groups" or segments should take into account these other businesses as well as the end users.

(3) Customer dissatisfaction indicators include complaints, claims, refunds, recalls, returns, repeat services, litigation, replacements, downgrades, repairs, warranty work, warranty costs, misshipments, and incomplete orders.

(4) Company-based or independent organization comparative studies (7.4b) might take into account one or more indicators of customer dissatisfaction as well as satisfaction. The extent and types of such studies may depend upon factors such as industry and company size.

7.5 Customer Satisfaction Results *(85 pts.)*

Summarize trends in the company's customer satisfaction and trends in key indicators of customer dissatisfaction.

AREAS TO ADDRESS

a. trends and current levels in key measures and/or indicators of customer satisfaction, including customer retention. Segment by customer group, as appropriate. Trends may be supported by objective information and/or data from customers demonstrating current or recent (past 3 years) satisfaction with the company's products/services.

b. trends in measures and/or indicators of customer dissatisfaction. Address the most relevant and important indicators for the company's products/services.

A   D   R

Notes

(1) Results reported in this Item derive from methods described in Items 7.4 and 7.2.

(2) Information supporting trends (7.5a) might include customers' assessments of products/services, customer awards, and customer retention.

(3) Indicators of customer dissatisfaction are given in Item 7.4, Note 3.

7.6 Customer Satisfaction Comparison *(70 pts.)*

Compare the company's customer satisfaction results with those of competitors.

AREAS TO ADDRESS

a. trends and current levels in key measures and/or indicators of customer satisfaction relative to competitors. Segment by customer group, as appropriate. Trends may be supported by objective information and/or data from independent organizations, including customers.

b. trends in gaining and losing customers, or customer accounts, to competitors

c. trends in gaining or losing market share to competitors

A   D   R

Notes:

(1) Results reported in Item 7.6 derive from methods described in Item 7.4.

(2) Competitors include domestic and international ones in the company's markets, both domestic and international.

(3) Objective information and/or data from independent organizations, including customers (7.6a), might include survey results, competitive awards, recognition, and ratings. Such surveys, competitive awards, recognition, and ratings by independent organizations and customers should reflect comparative satisfaction (and dissatisfaction), not comparative performance of products and services. Information on comparative performance of products and services should be included in 6.1b.

SCORING SYSTEM: APPROACH, DEPLOYMENT, RESULTS

The system for scoring applicant responses to Examination Items and for developing feedback is based upon three evaluation dimensions: (1) Approach; (2) Deployment; and (3) Results. All Examination Items require applicants to furnish information relating to one or more of these dimensions. Specific factors associated with the evaluation dimensions are described below. Scoring Guidelines are given on page 34.

Approach

"Approach" refers to how the applicant addresses the requirements given in the Examination Items. The factors used to evaluate approaches include *one or more* of the following:

- appropriateness of the methods, tools, and techniques to the requirements

- effectiveness of use of methods, tools, and techniques

- degree to which the approach is systematic, integrated, and consistently applied

- degree to which the approach embodies effective evaluation/improvement cycles

- degree to which the approach is based upon quantitative information that is objective and reliable

- evidence of unique and innovative approaches. This includes significant and effective adaptations of approaches, tools, and techniques used in other applications or types of businesses

Deployment

"Deployment" refers to the extent to which the applicant's approaches are applied to all relevant work units and activities given in the responses to Examination Items. The factors used to evaluate deployment include *one or more* of the following:

- appropriate and effective use of the approach in key processes

- appropriate and effective use of the approach in the development and delivery of products and services

- appropriate and effective use of the approach in interactions with customers, employees, suppliers of goods and services, and the public

Results

"Results" refers to outcomes in achieving the purposes given in the Examination Items. The factors used to evaluate results include *one or more* of the following:

- current performance levels

- performance levels relative to appropriate comparisons and/or benchmarks

- rate of performance improvement

- demonstration of sustained improvement and/or sustained high-level performance

- breadth and importance of performance improvements

Item Classification and Scoring Dimensions

Award Examination Items are classified according to the kinds of information and/or data applicants are expected to furnish.

The three types of Items and their designations are:

1. Approach/Deployment

2. Results

3. Approach/Deployment/Results

Approach and Deployment are linked to emphasize that Items requesting information on Approach always require information to convey Deployment — consistent with the specific requirements of the Item. Although Approach and Deployment dimensions are linked, feedback to the applicant would reflect strengths and/or areas for improvement in either or both dimensions.

Results Items depend primarily on data. However, the evaluation factor, "breadth and importance of performance improvements", is concerned with how widespread and how significant an applicant's improvement results are. This is directly related to the Deployment dimension. That is, if improvement processes are widely deployed, there should be corresponding results. A score for a Results Item is a composite based upon overall performance, also taking into account the breadth and importance of performance improvements.

Approach/Deployment/Results Items focus mainly on Approach/Deployment. The results requested are those most directly derived from the Approach/Deployment and hence most important for use in the evaluation of the effectiveness of the Approach/Deployment. Such results are used in process improvement.

"Relevance and Importance" as a Scoring Factor

The three evaluation dimensions described above are all critical to the assessment and feedback processes. However, evaluations and feedback must also consider the relevance and importance to the applicant's business of improvements in Approach, Deployment, and Results. The areas of greatest relevance and importance are addressed in the Business Overview, and are a primary focus of Items such as 3.1, 5.1, and 7.1.

SCORING GUIDELINES

SCORE	APPROACH/DEPLOYMENT
0%	■ no systematic approach evident; anecdotal information
10% to 30%	■ beginning of a systematic approach to the primary purposes of the Item ■ early stages of a transition from reacting to problems to a general improvement orientation ■ major gaps exist in deployment that would inhibit progress in achieving the primary purposes of the Item
40% to 60%	■ a sound, systematic approach, responsive to the primary purposes of the Item ■ a fact-based improvement process in place in key areas; more emphasis is placed on improvement than on reaction to problems ■ no major gaps in deployment, though some areas or work units may be in very early stages of deployment
70% to 90%	■ a sound, systematic approach, responsive to the overall purposes of the Item ■ a fact-based improvement process is a key management tool; clear evidence of refinement and improved integration as a result of improvement cycles and analysis ■ approach is well-deployed, with no major gaps; deployment may vary in some areas or work units
100%	■ a sound, systematic approach, fully responsive to all the requirements of the Item ■ a very strong, fact-based improvement process is a key management tool; strong refinement and integration — backed by excellent analysis ■ approach is fully deployed without any significant weaknesses or gaps in any areas or work units

SCORE	RESULTS
0%	■ no results or poor results in areas reported
10% to 30%	■ early stages of developing trends; some improvements *and/or* early good performance levels in a few areas ■ results not reported for many to most areas of importance to the applicant's key business requirements
40% to 60%	■ improvement trends *and/or* good performance levels reported for many to most areas of importance to the applicant's key business requirements ■ no pattern of adverse trends *and/or* poor performance levels in areas of importance to the applicant's key business requirements ■ some trends *and/or* current performance levels — evaluated against relevant comparisons *and/or* benchmarks — show areas of strength *and/or* good to very good relative performance levels
70% to 90%	■ current performance is good to excellent in most areas of importance to the applicant's key business requirements ■ most improvement trends *and/or* performance levels are sustained ■ many to most trends *and/or* current performance levels — evaluated against relevant comparisons *and/or* benchmarks — show areas of leadership and very good relative performance levels
100%	■ current performance is excellent in most areas of importance to the applicant's key business requirements ■ excellent improvement trends *and/or* sustained excellent performance levels in most areas ■ strong evidence of industry and benchmark leadership demonstrated in many areas

1994 EXAMINATION RESPONSE GUIDELINES

Introduction

This section provides guidelines and recommendations for writing the Business Overview and for responding to the requirements of the 28 Examination Items of the Award Criteria. The section consists of four parts: (1) Description of the Business Overview; (2) Description of an Examination Item; (3) Guidelines for Preparing the Business Overview; and (4) Guidelines for Responding to the Examination Items.

Description of the Business Overview

The Business Overview is an outline of the applicant's business, addressing what is most important to the business and the key factors that influence how the business operates.

The Award Examination is designed to permit evaluation of any kind of business. However, individual Items and Areas to Address may not be equally applicable or equally important to all businesses, even to businesses of comparable size in the same industry. The Business Overview is intended to "set the stage" for the Examiners' evaluation. It should help Examiners to understand what is relevant and important to the applicant's business.

The Business Overview is used by the Examiners in all stages of the application review. For this reason, this Overview is a vital part of the overall application.

Description of an Examination Item

Writing an application for the Award requires responding to the requirements given in the 28 Examination Items. Each Item and its key components are presented in the same format as illustrated in the figure below.

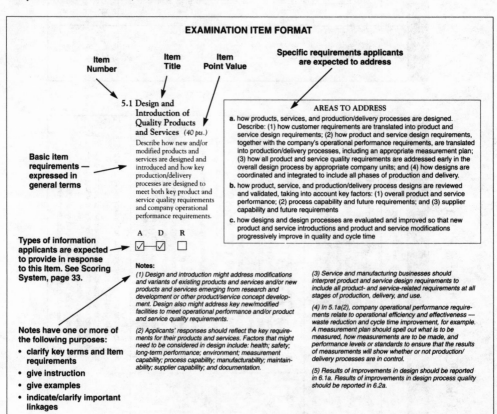

EXAMINATION ITEM FORMAT

Item Number

Item Title

Item Point Value

Specific requirements applicants are expected to address

5.1 Design and Introduction of Quality Products and Services *(40 pts.)*
Describe how new and/or modified products and services are designed and introduced and how key production/delivery processes are designed to meet both key product and service quality requirements and company operational performance requirements.

Basic item requirements — expressed in general terms

A   D   R
☑ — ☑ — ☐

Types of information applicants are expected to provide in response to this Item. See Scoring System, page 33.

AREAS TO ADDRESS

a. how products, services, and production/delivery processes are designed. Describe: (1) how customer requirements are translated into product and service design requirements; (2) how product and service design requirements, together with the company's operational performance requirements, are translated into production/delivery processes, including an appropriate measurement plan; (3) how all product and service quality requirements are addressed early in the overall design process by appropriate company units; and (4) how designs are coordinated and integrated to include all phases of production and delivery.

b. how product, service, and production/delivery process designs are reviewed and validated, taking into account key factors: (1) overall product and service performance; (2) process capability and future requirements; and (3) supplier capability and future requirements

c. how designs and design processes are evaluated and improved so that new product and service introductions and product and service modifications progressively improve in quality and cycle time

Notes:

(1) Design and introduction might address modifications and variants of existing products and services and/or new products and services emerging from research and development or other product/service concept development. Design also might address key new/modified facilities to meet operational performance and/or product and service quality requirements.

(2) Applicants' responses should reflect the key requirements for their products and services. Factors that might need to be considered in design include: health; safety; long-term performance; environment; measurement capability; process capability; manufacturability; maintainability; supplier capability; and documentation.

(3) Service and manufacturing businesses should interpret product and service design requirements to include all product- and service-related requirements at all stages of production, delivery, and use.

(4) In 5.1a(2), company operational performance requirements relate to operational efficiency and effectiveness — waste reduction and cycle time improvement, for example. A measurement plan should spell out what is to be measured, how measurements are to be made, and performance levels or standards to ensure that the results of measurements will show whether or not production/delivery processes are in control.

(5) Results of improvements in design should be reported in 6.1a. Results of improvements in design process quality should be reported in 6.2a.

Notes have one or more of the following purposes:

• clarify key terms and Item requirements
• give instruction
• give examples
• indicate/clarify important linkages

Guidelines for Preparing the Business Overview

A Business Overview fully responsive to the Examiners' requirements should describe:

- the nature of the applicant's business: products and services
- principal customers (consumers, other businesses, government, etc.) and their special requirements. Special relationships with customers or customer groups should be noted.
- a description of the applicant's major markets (local, regional, national, or international)
- key customer quality requirements (for example, on-time delivery or low defect levels) for products and services. Include all important quality requirements. Briefly note significant differences in requirements among customer groups or markets, if any.
- the applicant's position (relative size, growth) in the industry and key factors in the competitive environment
- the applicant's employee base, including: number, type, educational level, bargaining units, etc.
- major equipment, facilities, and technologies used
- types and numbers of suppliers of goods and services. Indicate the importance of suppliers, dealers, and other businesses, and any limitations or special relationships that may exist in dealing with such businesses.
- the regulatory environment within which the applicant operates, including occupational health and safety, environmental, financial regulations, etc.
- other factors important to the applicant, such as major new thrusts for the company, major changes taking place in the industry, new business alliances, etc.

If the applicant is a subsidiary or division of a company, a description of the organizational structure and key management links to the parent company should be presented. Also include percent of employees and relationships of products and services.

The Business Overview must be limited to four pages. These four pages are not counted in the overall page limit.

Guidelines for Responding to the Examination Items

1. Read the entire Award Criteria booklet.

   The main sections of the booklet provide an overall orientation to the Criteria and how applicants' responses are evaluated.

2. Understand the meaning of "how".

   All Items that request information on Approach include Areas to Address that begin with the word "how". Responses to such Areas should provide as complete a picture as possible to enable meaningful evaluation and feedback. Responses should outline key process details such as methods, measures, deployment, and evaluation factors. Information lacking sufficient detail to permit an evaluation and feedback, or merely providing an example, is referred to in the Criteria booklet as anecdotal information.

3. Understand the meaning of measures and/or indicators.

   All Items calling for results require data using "key measures and/or indicators". Measures and indicators both involve measurement related to performance. When the performance can be measured directly, such as cycle time and on-time delivery, the term "measure" is used. When the overall performance may not be evaluated in terms of one type of measurement, and two or more measurements are used to provide ("indicate") a more complete picture, the term "indicator" is used. For example, innovation success is not easily described in terms of a single measurement. Patents and patent citations provide two measurements which are indicators of innovation success, but completing the picture requires other indicators, such as cycle time for bringing new products to market and market share gain from introduction of innovative products or services.

4. Note the distinction between data and results.

   There is a critical distinction between data and results — a distinction that is often misunderstood. Data are numerical information; results are the outcomes of activities. Data could be used as inputs to activities, as well as outcomes of activities. Results Items require data to demonstrate progress and achievement. Approach/Deployment Items, focused on processes, may benefit from data to provide a clearer and more complete picture of key aspects of Approach and/or Deployment. For example, a company may use self-directed work teams in its approach. It may report that 5 such teams involving 75 percent of the people on the shop floor undertook 11 projects during the past year to reduce scrap and rework. These data are input data giving deployment information related to the approach (self-directed work teams). These teams reducing scrap and rework by 17 percent is a result.

5. Understand specific Item requirements.

Review each Item classification and the specific requirements given under Areas to Address and in Item Notes.

6. Gather and organize relevant information for a response.

Most of the Items require summaries of information gathered from different parts of the company.

7. Select relevant/important information.

In preparing Item responses, focus on information that is *both* directly responsive to the Item requirements and to key business requirements spelled out in the Business Overview. Information and data included should be relevant and important to both the Item and to the applicant's business.

8. Anticipate assessment and feedback.

A well-written response is one that lends itself to Examiner or other feedback. A response that facilitates assessment gives clear information on how (approach) and on the relevant use (deployment) of the approach. Anecdotal information or information lacking overall context should not be given as it is usually not possible to prepare meaningful feedback. Examples are, of course, helpful but examples often do not convey a picture of overall approach and deployment. If examples are used, make certain that they illustrate a more complete response already presented.

9. Make responses concise.

The application page limits (85 pages for companies in the Manufacturing and Service Categories and 70 pages for companies in the Small Business Category) do not permit lengthy narrative or inclusion of information not directly responsive to Item requirements. For this reason, applicants are urged to make all responses concise and factual. Statements should be supported with data whenever appropriate.

10. Cross-reference when appropriate.

Although applicants should seek to make individual responses self-contained, there may be instances when responses to different Items are mutually reinforcing. In such cases it is appropriate to reference responses to other Items, rather than to repeat information presented elsewhere. In doing so, applicants should make the reference specific by using Item and Area designators, for example, see 4.2c.

11. Review each response.

Each response should be reviewed to make certain that it addresses the Item requirements and is consistent with the applicant's key business requirements spelled out in the Business Overview. It is also important to ensure that a response is consistent with information reported in Items that are closely linked.

Reporting Results and Trend Data

1. Results Items require data to demonstrate progress (trend data), achievement (performance levels), and breadth of deployment. Evaluation of achievement is usually based upon two factors: (1) that the performance level has been sustained or is the current result of a favorable trend; and (2) that the performance level can be compared with that of other appropriate organizations.

2. Applicants are required to report trend data to show progress and to show that improvements or outstanding performance levels are sustained. No minimum period of time is specified for trend data. Time periods may span five years or more for some results. Trends may be much shorter in areas where improvement efforts are new. In cases where the trend line is short, the Examiners' evaluation will take into account the demonstrated levels of performance.

3. The spacing between data points on a trend line (annual, monthly, etc.) should reflect a natural measurement/use scheme for such results. That is, how the data are used in process management should determine the spacing between data points. For example, measurement frequency should support timely improvement.

4. In reporting trend data, applicants should be aware that breadth of results is a major factor in the Examiners' evaluation. For this reason, it is important to report data reflecting wide deployment of improvement activities. Use of graphs and tables offers a good means to present many results compactly.

5. Graphs and tables should be integrated into the body of the text, wherever possible.

The following graph illustrates data an applicant might present as part of a response to Item 6.1, Product and Service Quality Results. The applicant has indicated, in the Business Overview and in Item 7.1, on-time delivery as a key customer requirement.

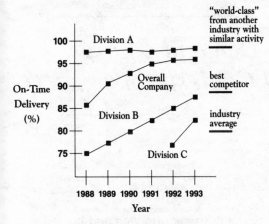

Using the graph, the following characteristics of clear and effective data presentation are illustrated:

- the trend lines report data for a key business requirement
- both axes and units of measure are clearly labeled
- results are presented for several years
- meaningful comparisons are clearly shown
- the company shows, using a single graph, that its three divisions separately track on-time delivery

To help interpret the scoring guidelines (page 34), the following comments on the graphed results would be appropriate:

- the current overall company performance level is excellent. This conclusion is supported by the comparison with competitors and with a "world class" level

- the company exhibits an overall excellent improvement record
- Division A is the current performance leader — showing sustained high performance and a slightly positive trend. Division B shows rapid improvement. Its current performance is near that of the best industry competitor, but trails the "world class" level.
- Division C — a new division — shows rapid progress. Its current performance is not yet at the level of the best industry competitor.

Reviewing the Overall Set of Item Responses

1. It is helpful to review, as a whole, the complete set of 28 Item responses. There are four main considerations in this review:

   a. emphasis on the applicant's most important business requirements. This emphasis should be clear throughout the set of responses, and consistent with the Business Overview.

   b. balance in the use of page limits. Ample page space should be given to results Items which are weighed heavily in the Examiners' evaluation. Items and Areas that address factors particularly important to the applicant's business should receive relatively more emphasis.

   c. overall consistency. Responses should be checked to ensure that responses to related Items are consistent, and that there is appropriate cross-referencing to minimize duplication of information.

   d. final check on deployment information. The overall application should convey widespread and consistent implementation, not merely an outline of approaches. The final review allows an assessment of how well the application as a whole covers all key company requirements, responsibilities, and processes.

APPENDIX B

Why Do Patients Demand a Large Drop in Total Cholesterol?

In explaining the contradiction between the scientific data and how much weight physicians still put on total cholesterol, some physicians comment that "*Patients demand* a significant fall in total cholesterol for the dollar cost and diet restrictions!"

Beyond the early guidelines and the constant messages delivered by the media, like the cartoon in Exhibit 5–1, why do patients demand a large drop in total cholesterol? Probably because they still think that is the best way to reduce risk. An even more important question is "Why don't physicians and medical educators dramatize how important it is to raise HDL by what at first glance seems to be only a 'small' amount?"

The answer may rest in part with the scale used to measure cholesterol and its components. Total cholesterol and HDL cholesterol levels are both measured in milligrams per deciliter. This gives the appearance that the scales and units of each type of cholesterol are comparable. But, when it comes to assessing how changes in levels of different types of cholesterol affect risk, it turns out that a one milligram per deciliter lowering of total cholesterol has only a fraction of the impact that one gets by raising HDL cholesterol by one milligram per deciliter.

To get a rough feel for how much more increasing HDL 5 units reduces risk than lowering TC 5 units, look back at Exhibit 5–2a. The bull's-eye represents a man with a TC level of 300 and a HDL level of 30. This man's TC/HDL ratio is 10 and based on the Framingham data his risk of coronary heart disease is twice the standard risk. There are several ways to improve his TC/HDL ratio to 5, which is just about standard risk (Exhibit A–1).

EXHIBIT A–1

	TC	HDL	% HDL	TC/ HDL	TC – HDL
Start	300	30	10	10	270
Ways to Improve Ratio:					
1. Drop TC	150	30	20	5	120
2. Improve both	225	45	20	5	180
3. Raise HDL	300	60	20	5	240
4. Worsen TC & improve HDL	337.5	67.5	20	5	270

If HDL is unchanged (method 1), the total cholesterol level needs to drop by 150. If TC is unchanged (method 2), HDL needs to increase by 30. In this example, for each point that HDL is raised, the patient needs to lower TC by 5 points to achieve the same level of risk reduction as measured by the TC/HDL ratio in the Framingham risk model. Using method 3, roughly half of the risk reduction is achieved by reducing TC 75 points and half is achieved by raising HDL by 15 points. In milligrams per deciliter, the horizontal scale in Exhibit 5–2 is one fifth the vertical scale. This makes the arrows representing methods 1 and 3, which represent an equal change in the ratio, the same length.

As Dr. Jeffrey E. Harris (cited in Chapter 5, note 7) observed: "Actually, I'm not sure what the experts were thinking when they hung their hats on the total blood cholesterol alone. In any case, they got caught with their pants down." Harris summarizes his extensive review of the literature as follows.

Here's how I look at it: A two point drop in LDL cholesterol is about as potent in preventing heart disease as a one-point rise in

HDL cholesterol. Conversely, the coronary-preventive effect of a two-point drop in LDL would be canceled out by a one-point rise in HDL cholesterol.

Let's switch back from a medical expert focusing on LDL versus HDL to patients who don't understand the relative strength of TC versus HDL. For people in the high-risk zone of Exhibit 5–2 or 5–3, raising HDL 5 or 10 points probably reduces risk more than lowering TC 10 or 20 points does. Yet somehow patients demand the latter and ignore the former because they haven't been told that the scales aren't comparable when it comes to assessing the impact of changes in cholesterol levels on CHD risk.

Building Our Store of Case Examples and Empirical Evidence

While this book contains numerous case examples and powerful empirical evidence, much work is yet to be done to advance the art and science of customer value management. There remain many problems to be solved, questions to be answered, opportunities to be explored, and research studies to be carried out.

Each company needs to develop its own pilot studies and successful case examples. Educators need case examples that are custom designed for teaching the principles of market-perceived quality and customer value management. Consultants and market researchers need to customize the tools and metrics to fit their practices and their customers' needs.

For those who are interested in continuing the process of moving customer satisfaction from a slogan to a science, we are beginning to develop some networks to accelerate the pace:

- A network of companies that grapples with real world application issues and develops interesting case examples.
- A network of executive educators and academics that will develop the ideas further and design better ways to teach them.
- A network of researchers and research programs that will further quantify, calibrate, and clarify the linkages between the components of customer value and the business results

achieved by companies that provide superior customer value. (For an example of part of one research project see questionnaire in Appendix D.)

By building on the base developed by companies that provided the material for this book we can better understand and improve the dynamics of competitive capitalism. If you are interested in learning more about these networks contact:

Market-Driven Quality, Inc.   Fax 508-358-4119

60 Highland Circle

Wayland, MA 01778

USA

Questionnaire to Aid Benchmarking

This questionnaire may be used for benchmarking where you stand relative to the best companies in Stage Three, measuring and improving market-perceived quality and customer value. [1]

To pinpoint how your business or company can develop a world class system for managing customer value, complete the following questions and Exhibit E-3 in the Epilogue.

1. Components of Overall Value or Satisfaction

What do you call the components of overall customer value or customer satisfaction? (Check as many entries as are appropriate to your business.)

__ Customer satisfiers
__ Product or service attributes or features
__ Purchase criteria
__ Quality attributes
__ Selection criteria
__ Other: _____ _____

Which of the following answers in each pair of responses best characterizes your current approach? [Check one on each line.]

a. No components of overall   __ [0]   Several/many components   __ [1]
    value/satisfaction
b. Components overlapping and   __ [0]   Components non-over-   __ [1]
    non-hierarchical   lapping and hierarchical
c. Internal phrases for attributes   __ [0]   Customer phrases   __ [1]
d. Focus: static, current   __ [0]   Dynamic, future   __ [1]
e. Core product/service only   __ [0]   Customer service as well   __ [1]

                                                          Your score
                                                          Best companies   5

2.   Price Metrics

Which of the following answers in each pair of responses best characterizes your current approach? [Check one on each line.]

a. We have no price metrics   __ [0]   We measure price com-   __ [1]
                                                          petitiveness
b. Our price competitiveness only   __ [0]   Our score vs. competitors __ [1]
c. Perceived price vs. competitors: No __ [0]   Yes __ [1]
d. Transactions price vs. comp.: No __ [0]   Yes __ [1]

                                                          Your score
                                                          Best companies   4

If a price profile is relevant for your market add "e"

e. We have no components of price __ [0]   We have components of   __ [1]
                                                          price

3.   Importance of Attributes

Which of the following answers in each pair of responses characterizes your current approach? [Check one on each line.]

a. No importance ratings   __ [0]   Importance scores, by   __ [1]
                                                          component
b. Importance ratings for a non-   __ [0]   Importance ratings for a   __ [1]
    hierarchical attribute list   hierarchically structured
                                                          list

c. List may contain overlap- ping attributes	__ [0]	List of non-overlapping attributes	__ [1]
d. Importance ratings scaled from 1 through 5 or 1 through 10	__ [0]	Importance weights that measure relative impor- tance of attributes [e.g., weights add to a constant sum like 100 percent.]	__ [1]

Your score   __

Best companies   4

4. Sample of Respondents

To what extent does your respondent group reflect the market targeted by you and your competitors?

	Check one:	Bias index*
Clearly biased toward our customers	__	Higher than +30%
Slightly biased toward our customers	__	+10% to +30%
Not biased	__	Between −10% and +10%
Slightly biased toward our competitors' customers	__	−30% to −10%
Clearly biased toward our competitors' customers	__	Lower than −30%

$$*\text{Bias index} = \frac{\% \text{ of your customers in sample} - \text{Your market share}}{\text{Your market share}} \times 100$$

5. Performance Ratings

Which of the following answers in each pair of responses best characterizes your current approach? [Check one on each line.]

a. We conduct ad hoc reviews	__ [0]	We track performance over time	__ [1]
b. We focus on our performance only	__ [0]	We measure performance vs. competitors	__ [1]
c. We do not segment the sam- ple based on whose custo- mer the respondent is	__ [0]	We contrast the responses from our customers with those from competitors'	__ [1]

d. We do not segment the sam-   __ [0]   We contrast the responses   __ [1]
   ple based on customer loyalty   from loyal customers with
                                                those who may switch

                                             Your score   __
                                             Best companies   4

6.   Links to Business Results

Which of the following answers in each pair of responses best characterizes your current approach? [Check one on each line.]

We link our metrics for customer value and satisfaction to:

	No	Yes
a. Employee satisfaction	__ [0]	__ [1]
b. Market share	__ [0]	__ [1]
c. Profits	__ [0]	__ [1]
d. Revenue growth	__ [0]	__ [1]

Your score   __
Best companies   4

7.   Alignment to Market

The alignment of each of the following groups to the voice of our targeted market is:

	Weak	Strong
a. Top management	__ [0]	__ [1]
b. Middle management	__ [0]	__ [1]
c. Front-line associates	__ [0]	__ [1]
d. All other associates	__ [0]	__ [1]

Your score   __
Best companies   4

Use your answers to the preceding questions on seven elements of
your customer value/satisfaction system to plot your current and targeted positions in Exhibit E-3.

Notes

Preface

1. For further information on the Profit Impact of Market Strategy results, see Robert D. Buzzell and Bradley T. Gale, *The PIMS Principles: Linking Strategy to Performance* (New York, Free Press, 1987). [*Italian,* Milano: Sperling & Kupfer, 1988; *Japanese,* Tokyo: Diamond, 1988; *German,* Wiesbaden: Gabler, 1989; *Portuguese,* São Paulo: Livraria Pioneira, 1991.] See also Sidney Schoeffler, Robert D. Buzzell and Donald F. Heany, "Impact of Strategic Planning on Profit Performance," *Harvard Business Review,* March–April, 1974, pp. 137–45. For Schoeffler's earlier work, see *A Diagnostic Study of the Failure of Economics,* Harvard University Press.

Acknowledgments

1. See William M. Carley and Amal Kumar Naj, "End of the Road: Firing of Executive Gives Rare Glimpse of Intrigue Inside GE," *Wall Street Journal,* November 23, 1993, p. A1, 7. As the authors stated, the background documents surrounding the firing of a GE executive "provide a window into the management of the nation's most renowned chief executive." As GE chairman and CEO John F. Welch Jr. noted summarizing a September 1991 strategy review session of GE's industrial diamond business, the executive "didn't get to the heart of the problem, which was De Beers, De Beers' quality, De Beers' yields [of metal-bonding saw diamonds]. . . . He didn't understand the seriousness and the magnitude of the issues we were trying to deal with." Instead of zeroing in on GE's quality and productivity versus De Beers in the high-quality segment of the duopoly market for industrial diamonds, the executive had responded to repeated questions and probes with what Welch described as "50,000 feet, high altitude" answers.

Chapter 1. The Four Steps to Customer Value Management

1. These stages were first described in a guest article, "Making Quality a Strategic Weapon," for Tom Peters' syndicated *On Excellence* column in May 1988, when the Baldrige award was going through its first cycle. A longer version of this article, "The Phases of Making Quality a Strategic Weapon," was published by the Strategic Planning Institute in March 1988.

2. Information for businesses in the PIMS database is typically assembled by a team of managers from the member company, often working with staff members from SPI/PIMS. For information about relative perceived quality, the goal is to input data that reflects how customers in the served market (not just the business's own customers) view the product/service offering of that business versus its key competitors. The managers who input the data draw on knowledge from typical sources (sales force and customer service reports and comments, customer complaints, vendor ratings, personal contact with customers and non-customers, market research reports, etc.). In the PIMS database most of the data represent the management's collective opinion, based on sources like those listed above, of the served *market's* perception of the quality of their products and services *relative* to competitors. In this book we use the phrase "Market-perceived quality" for measures that attempt to capture how buyers in the served market view a business's performance on key product, service, and image attributes relative to the performance of its competitors. We have tried to use the phrase "*relative* perceived quality" when a sample of respondents may be focused on a subset of the served market (your customers *or* your competitor's customers). (See "The War Room Wall" section of Chapter 10.)

3. Three of the first four large-company Baldrige winners had been members of PIMS during the early 1980s.

Chapter 2. Moving "Customer Satisfaction" from a Slogan to a Science

1. For more empirical data on how market-perceived quality and customer value drive business success, see Chapter 12.

2. Always follow this methodology. If you try to calculate the market-perceived quality ratio by dividing the overall customer satisfaction score of Perdue by the overall customer satisfaction score of the average competitor, you will get a slightly different number.

3. Isadore Barmash, "The Quieter Style of the New Generation at Perdue Farms," *New York Times,* July 26, 1992, p. 7.

4. *Consumer Reports,* April 1993, pp. 228, 229.

Chapter 3. How Milliken & Co. Built a Competitive Powerhouse

1. Bradley T. Gale, "Can More Capital Buy Higher Productivity?" *Harvard Business Review,* July–August, 1980, pp. 78–86.

2. See J. Edward Russo and Paul J. H. Schoemaker, *Decision Traps* (New York: Doubleday Currency, 1989), pp. 173–188.

3. Three articles on the nominal group technique were helpful in applying it to relative-perceived quality profiling in the early 1980s: John D. Claxton, J. R. Brent Ritchie, and Judy Zaichkowsky, "The Nominal Group Technique: Its Potential for Consumer Research," *Journal of Consumer Research,* December 1980, pp. 308–313; Louis P. Plebani, Jr. and Hemant K. Jain, "Evaluating Research Proposals with Group Techniques," *Research Management,* November 1981, pp. 34–38; Blair Y. Stephenson and Stephen G. Franklin, "Better Decision-Making for a 'Real World' Environment," *Administrative Management,* July 1981, pp. 24–26, 36, 38.

4. Alyssa A. Lappen, "Can Roger Milliken Emulate William Randolph Hearst?" *Forbes,* May 29, 1989, pp. 52–64.

Chapter 4. *"Customer Value Added" at AT&T: A Competitive Strategy Milestone*

1. William M. Carley, "Head of Steam: GE Locomotive Unit, Long an Also-Ran, Overtakes Rival GM," *Wall Street Journal,* September 3, 1993, pp. A1, 5.

2. Ray E. Kordupleski and West C. Vogel, " 'The Right Choice'—What Does It Mean?" AT&T White Paper, October 24, 1988.

3. The material Kordupleski used is principally in Chapter 6, "Quality Is King," of Robert D. Buzzell and Bradley T. Gale, *The PIMS Principles: Linking Strategy to Performance* (New York: Free Press, 1987), pp. 103–134. PIMS stands for "Profit Impact of Market Strategy," which is what the PIMS database was originally created to measure.

4. Ray E. Kordupleski and West C. Vogel, " 'The Right Choice'—What Does It Mean?" AT&T White Paper, April 17, 1989.

5. "AT&T's Users Shop Around," *Information Week,* July 18, 1988, p. 12.

6. Paul B. Carroll, "AT&T Reports 18% Gain in Net for 2nd Quarter," *New York Times,* July 21, 1989, p. A6.

7. Amanda Bennett, "Brass at AT&T Get New Carrot, but with String," *Wall Street Journal,* March 5, 1992, p. B1. See also cover story by Shawn Tully, "The Real Key to Creating Wealth," *Fortune,* September 20, 1993, pp. 38–50.

Chapter 5. *Communicating the Complex Truth About Cholesterol*

1. "Report of the National Cholesterol Education Program Expert Panel on Detection, Evaluation, and Treatment of High Blood Cholesterol in Adults," *Archives of Internal Medicine* 148 (1988): 36–69.

2. For the Helsinki Heart and Physicians Health studies, see V. Manninen et al., *Journal of the American Medical Association* 260 (1988): 641–651,; V. Manninen et al., *Circulation* 85:37, 1992; Stampfer, Sacks, et al., *New England Journal of Medicine* 325 (1991): 381.

3. See Keaven M. Anderson, Peter W. F. Wilson, Patricia M. Odell, and William B. Kannel, "An Updated Coronary Risk Profile," *Circulation,* January 1991, pp. 356–362.

4. Gerd Assmann and Helmut Schulte, "Triglycerides and Atherosclerosis: Results from the Prospective Muenster Study," *Atherosclerosis Reviews* 22 (1991), pp. 51–57.

5. Neal Santelmann, "The FYI CEO Cholesterol Level Contest," *Forbes FYI,* March 18, 1991, pp. 39, 40; Neal Santelmann, "CEO Cholesterol Contest Furor!" *Forbes FYI,* September 30, 1991, p. 60.

6. Expert Panel on Detection, and Treatment of High Blood Cholesterol in Adults, "Summary of the National Cholesterol Education Program (NCEP) Panel 11 Report," *Journal of the American Medical Association,* June 16, 1993, pp. 3015–3023. For a journalist's summary see Rita Rubin, "Cholesterol, Round 2: The Second Set of Guidelines Adds Recommendations—and Complexity," *U.S. News & World Report,* June 28, 1993, pp. 61–66.

7. Gerd Assmann and Helmut Schulte, "Relation of High-Density Lipoprotein Cholesterol and Triglycerides to Incidence of Atherosclerotic Coronary Artery Disease (the PROCAM Experience)," *The American Journal of Cardiology,* September 15, 1992, pp. 733–737. See also Trudy L. Bush and Denise Riedel, "Screening for Total Cholesterol: Do the National Cholesterol Education Program's Recommendations Detect Individuals at High Risk of Coronary Heart Disease?" *Circulation,* April 1991, pp. 1287–1293. For a journalist's discussion of similar issues, see Betsy A. Lehman, "The Good, the Bad and the Confusion," Health Sense, *The Boston Globe,* March 9, 1992, pp. 27, 29.

   Unlike the PROCAM researchers who chose to examine the impact of the full lipid profile on the risk of coronary heart disease in a single publication, the medical community at large chose to work out two separate consensus statements. The NCEP 2 statement on "detection and treatment of high blood cholesterol" is referenced in the preceding paragraph. A separate consensus development conference statement, "Triglyceride, High Density Lipoprotein, and Coronary Heart Disease," was published by the National Institutes of Health, March 1993. Perhaps someday we will have an integrated consensus statement.

   If you were intrigued by the aspects of this chapter that relate to understanding and controlling your own risk of coronary heart disease you must read Jeffrey E. Harris, *Deadly Choices: Coping With Health Risks in Everyday Life* (New York, Basic Books, 1993), Chapter 5, "The Good Minus the Bad Cholesterol."

Chapter 6. How to Achieve Quality Service

1. Phillip Thompson, Glenn DeSousa, and Bradley T. Gale, "The Strategic Management of Service Quality," *Quality Progress,* June 1985, pp. 20–25, and *PIMSletter* Number 33, the Strategic Planning Institute, 1985.

2. "Baldrige Was Guidebook for Building Universal Card," *Electronic Business,* October 1992, p. 102.
3. Elsa C. Arnett, "Restauranteurs Take on American Express," *Boston Globe,* March 29, 1991, p. 54; Elsa C. Arnett, "American Express in Hub to Cut Losses," *Boston Globe*, April 19, 1991, pp. 69, 70.
4. Michael Quint, "American Express's Big Loss," *New York Times,* October 27, 1992, p. D1.
5. Isadore Barmash, "The 'How' in Home Improvement," *New York Times,* June 14, 1992, p. F5.

Chapter 7. Creating Power Brands

1. See Chapter 1, Note 2.
2. Some of these consumer products are brands and some are not branded products. The PIMS database was not designed to identify which of the products would be classified as brands by the member companies that contributed these business experiences to the database. But the PIMS database does identify which products are consumer durables and which are consumer nondurable products. In this chapter we use the entire consumer products database (807 consumer durable and nondurable products) to study how quality is related to profitability, relative advertising, change in market share, relative price, and market position. To assess the impact of spending on advertising versus promotion, we study 290 consumer nondurable products that met a minimum spending test of at least 0.5 percent of sales for both media advertising *and* sales promotion spending. This excludes businesses that supplied private label or institutional customers and did not spend significant amounts on advertising and/or promotion. For a series of earlier studies, see Bradley T. Gale, "Advertising, Profitability and Growth for Consumer Businesses," *PIMSletter* Number 43, the Strategic Planning Institute, 1989; Bradley T. Gale and Robert D. Buzzell, "Advertising, Sales Promotion, and Profitability, *PIMSletter* Number 44, the Strategic Planning Institute, 1989; Robert D. Buzzell and Bradley T. Gale, "The Role of Advertising vs. Sales Promotion in Building Market Share," *PIMSletter* Number 45, the Strategic Planning Institute, 1989.
3. *Forbes,* 1974.
4. Ken Wells, "Global Ad Campaigns, after Many Missteps, Finally Pay Dividends," *Wall Street Journal,* August 27, 1992, p. 1.
5. Edwin L. Artzt, "Grooming the Next Generation of Marketing Management," address to the Association of National Advertisers, New York, October 28, 1991.
6. In this statistical research, the independent correlation between media advertising increases and market share increases was statistically significant at the level of less than .005. The impact of increases in sales promotion on market share was actually negative. But the correlation coefficient was

.08—outside commonly accepted thresholds of statistical significance. See Ogilvy Center for Research and Development, *Advertising, Sales Promotion, and the Bottom Line,* March 1989, pp. 20–26.

7. Patricia Sellers, "The Dumbest Marketing Ploy," *Fortune,* October 5, 1992, p. 90.

8. Ibid., pp. 5–18.

9. Patricia Sellers, "The Dumbest Marketing Ploy," *Fortune,* October 5, 1992, pp. 88–94.

10. Edwin L. Artzt, "Grooming the Next Generation of Marketing Management," speech delivered at the Association of National Advertisers annual conference, Phoenix, October 28, 1991. See also Edwin L. Artzt, "The Quality Approach," (Washington, DC: Center for Strategic and International Studies), text of executive speech, March 1, 1991; Jonathan R. Laing, "New and Improved—Procter & Gamble Fights To Keep Its Place on the Top," *Barron's,* November 29, 1993. pp. 8, 9, 22, 24, 26.

11. See Gretchen Morgenson, "The Trend Is Not Their Friend," *Forbes,* September 16, 1991, pp. 114–119. *Forbes* was relying on research originally published in *Supermarket Business.*

12. See Subrata N. Chakravarty, "We Had to Change the Playing Field," *Forbes,* February 4, 1991, pp. 82–86, which provides an excellent discussion of Gillette's recovery. See also Lawrence Ingrassia, "The Cutting Edge," *Wall Street Journal,* April 6, 1992, p. R6; Mark Maremont and Paula Dwyer, "How Gillette Is Honing Its Edge," *Business Week,* September 28, 1992, pp. 60, 65; and Lawrence Ingrassia, "Gillette Ties New Toiletries to Hot Razor," *Wall Street Journal,* September 18, 1992, pp. B1, B6.

Chapter 8. Assessing Competing Technologies and
Nurturing a Long-Term Winner

1. Much of this section is based on work I did with Richard Klavans for "Formulating a Quality Improvement Strategy," *The Journal of Business Strategy,* Winter 1985, pp. 21–32. I am indebted to Klavans for helping me understand the tire market.

2. Ibid.

3. David Craig, "Hirsch Makes $59 Million on Options," *USA Today,* March 8, 1993, p. B1.

4. Joseph Schumpeter, *Capitalism Socialism, and Democracy,* New York: Harper, 1942.

5. This section relies heavily on the work of Phillip Thompson, vice president, the Strategic Planning Institute. See his "Strategic Management of Service: The Action Learning Agenda," *Design Management Journal,* Winter 1992, pp. 62–70.

6. Robert Kearns, "Is Everybody Happy?—Here's how one manufacturer measures customer satisfaction," *Business Marketing,* December 1989.

7. Quoted with permission from a letter written by F. Bennett Williams, July 1993.
8. Michael Schrage, "Few Try to Imitate 3M's Successes," *Boston Globe,* October 11, 1992, p. B2.
9. Bradley T. Gale, "Tracking How Competitive Position Drives Shareholder Value," *Global Management 1992* (Brussels: Management Centre Europe, 1992), pp. 367–371. For an earlier study based on PIMS data, see Donald W. Collier, John Monz, and James Conlin, "How Effective Is Technological Innovation?" *Research Management* 27, no. 5 (September–October, 1984).
10. Ralph Gomory, "Leaving the Ladder of Science for the Product Cycle," *Harvard Business Review,* November–December 1989; Kim B. Clark, "Competing on Science: The Agenda for Senior Management," *Harvard Business Review,* November–December 1989.

Chapter 9. The Seven Tools of Customer Value Analysis

1. Arie P. de Geus, "Planning as Learning," *Harvard Business Review,* March–April 1988, pp. 70–74. Emphasis added.
2. Ferdinand Protzman, "Investors Uneasy on Daimler-Benz," *New York Times,* August 5, 1992.
3. Oscar Suris, "Mercedes to Cut Prices as Much as 14.8% on Some Best-Selling Models for 1994," *Wall Street Journal,* September 23, 1993, p. C23.
4. Mercedes advertisement, "To all those who think a sensible Mercedes-Benz is an oxymoron. Introducing the new E-Class," *Wall Street Journal,* September 24, 1993, pp. A6, 7; Mercedes advertisement, "It will send the competition back to our drawing board," *Wall Street Journal,* September 28, 1993, pp. A10, 11; Oscar Suris, "Mercedes-Benz Tries to Compete on Value," *Wall Street Journal,* October 20, 1993, p. B1. For sales in the United States (thousands of cars) by Mercedes, BMW, Acura Legend, Lexus, and Infiniti from 1985 to 1993 see Jerry Flint, "The New Zeitgeist at Daimler-Benz," *Forbes,* December 6, 1993, pp. 44–45.
5. Lawrence A. Bossidy, "Some Thoughts on Strategic Thinking," speech delivered at the Strategic Management Society annual conference, Boston, Massachusetts, October 14, 1987.

Chapter 10. Putting the Power of Your Whole Organization in a Single Room: The War Room Wall and Strategic Navigation

1. For a case discussion of how to make quality process improvements ring the cash register by linking the customer side of quality to internal metrics see "Why Improving Quality Doesn't Improve Quality," by Raymond E.

Kordupleski, Rowland T. Rust and Anthony J. Zahorik in *California Management Review* 35, No. 3 (Spring 1992), pp. 82–95.

2. Winston S. Churchill, *The Gathering Storm* (Cambridge, England: Houghton Mifflin, 1948), pp. 467–468, 730–731.

3. For an excellent case example of how a leading German business unit used a PIMS-based strategic navigation system to improve performance and meet corporate financial requirements, see George Kellinghusen and Klaus Wubbenhorst, "Strategic Control for Improved Performance," *Long Range Planning* 23, No. 3 (1990), pp. 30–40.

   For other articles that stress how to complement financial data with non-financial data see Robert Kaplan and David P. Norton, "The Balanced Scorecard—Measures That Drive Performance," *Harvard Business Review,* January–February 1992, pp. 71–79; Robert G. Eccles, "The Performance Measurement Manifesto," *Harvard Business Review,* January–February 1991, pp. 131–37; and Bradley T. Gale and Ben Branch, "Allocating Capital More Effectively," *Sloan Management Review,* Fall 1987, pp. 21–31.

Chapter 11. Aligning Your Quality Initiatives with the Goal of True Customer Value Management

1. For guidance, see Michael J. Spendolini, *The Benchmarking Book* (New York: AMACOM, 1992).

2. John R. Hauser and Don Clausing, "The House of Quality," *Harvard Business Review,* May–June 1988, pp. 63–88.

3. William D. Vinson and Donald F. Heany, "Is Quality Out of Control?" *Harvard Business Review,* November–December 1977, pp. 114–122.

4. Some powerful new software (Strategic Pointer 2000) is being launched that will help companies move in this direction. Interested persons should see Appendix C.

5. Over time the source of desired attributes has shifted from engineers and executives to the customer, to the targeted market, segments within the targeted market, and mass customization. See B. Joseph Pine II, Bart Victor, and Andrew C. Boynton, "Making Mass Customization Work," *Harvard Business Review,* September–October 1993, pp. 108–119.

6. Talk by James J. Paulsen, general manufacturing manager, Ford Motor Co., to Conference Board Total Quality, 1993 conference, New York.

7. For an executive interview with Chairman Jack Welch describing the evolution of "WorkOut" at General Electric, see John Hillkirk, "Tearing Down Walls Builds GE: CEO Welch Shapes a Culture of Openness, Teamwork," *USA Today,* July 26, 1993, p. 5B.

   Some software (PROMAP) for mapping and improving processes is currently being used at a leading health-care company. Interested persons should see Appendix C for further information.

8. Frederick Reichheld, "Loyalty-based Management," *Harvard Business Review,* March–April 1993, pp. 64–73.
9. Valerie A. Zeithaml, A. Parasuraman, and Leonard A. Berry, *Delivering Service Quality: Balancing Customer Perceptions and Expectations* (New York: Free Press, 1990).

Chapter 12. Here's the Proof: Superior Quality Drives the Bottom Line and Shareholder Value

1. See Chapter 1, Note 2.
2. Some of this research appears with further discussion in Raymond E. Kordupleski and West C. Vogel, Jr., " 'The Right Choice'—What Does It Mean?" distributed by AT&T, April 17, 1989.
3. Previous research on quality and price is summarized in David A. Garvin, *Managing Quality* (New York: Free Press, 1988), pp. 70–74.
4. By contrast, a GAO study of Baldrige applicants that qualified for a site visit had to rely on just the performance of the high-scoring Baldrige applicants with no knowledge or comparison regarding how the low-scoring applicants performed on the same measures. See United States General Accounting Office, *Management Practices—U.S. Companies Improve Performance Through Quality Efforts* (U.S. GAO, May 1991).

   In a similar vein, the *In Search of Excellence* research team screened for companies that were profitable and growing and then described the characteristics of these companies. But the study did not check to see if each of the characteristics identified in growing, profitable companies differed significantly from the characteristics of companies that did not pass the growth and profitability screen. It is possible that some of the characteristics spotted in profitable, growing companies were also present in the companies that were not scrutinized.
5. Bradley T. Gale, "Tracking How Competitive Position Drives Shareholder Value," *Global Management 1992,* Management Centre Europe, July 1992. See also Bradley T. Gale and Donald J. Swire, "Business-Unit Strategies That Create Wealth," *Planning Review,* March/April 1988; Bradley T. Gale and Donald J. Swire, "The Tricky Business of Measuring Wealth," *Planning Review,* March/April 1988.
6. Presentation by David Lowry, entitled "Quality at Travenol Laboratories," at SPI seminar in Minneapolis, November 1986.

Chapter 13. Learning from the Malcolm Baldrige National Quality Award

1. Translated by David J. Lu (Englewood Cliffs, N.J.: Prentice Hall, 1985), pp. 187–189. Originally published in Japanese, 1981.
2. For reasons that are hard for Westerners to understand, the group refers to

itself as "Union of Japanese Scientists and Engineers" in English but then adopts the English acronym "JUSE" rather than UJSE.

3. Gary Spizizen, "The ISO 9000 Standards: Creating a Level Playing Field for International Quality," *National Productivity Review,* Summer 1992, pp. 331–346.

4. Ibid., pp. 331 ff.

5. See Curt W. Reimann, "The Baldrige Award: Leading the Way in Quality Initiatives," *Quality Progress,* July 1989. See also *1994 Award Criteria— Malcolm Baldrige National Quality Award* (Gaithersburg, Md.: National Institute of Standards and Technology, 1993). See also Curt W. Reimann and Harry S. Hertz, "The Malcolm Baldrige National Quality Award and ISO 9000 Registration: Understanding Their Many Important Differences," ASTM Standardization News, November, 1993.

6. The internal results (the size of the gaps between high and low scoring units shared within IBM) would look even stronger if we compared the over-five-hundred scorers with the under-five-hundred scorers.

7. Curt Reimann, "Total Quality: Lessons from Business—Challenges for Education," presentation delivered at Total Quality Forum Five, hosted by Motorola, 1993.

Chapter 14. Comprehensive Alignment: Key to True Competitiveness

1. For a summary of a study of European companies that have made a sustained effort to apply total quality, led by George Binney from the Ashridge management school in the United Kingdom, see Paul Taylor, "Why Customers Must Come First," *Financial Times,* October 26, 1992, p. 8. For the full study, see George Binney, *Making Quality Work—Lessons from Europe's Leading Companies* (London: Economist Intelligence Unit, 1992).

2. Claudia H. Deutsch, "Putting a Practical Spin on Training," *New York Times,* June 23, 1991, p. 25.

3. Bill Weisz, "What Is Six Sigma?" Motorola Inc., June 1987.

Epilogue

1. John J. Keller, "AT&T to End Sales of 'i Plan' Phone Program," *Wall Street Journal,* November 10, 1993, p. A5.

2. Some software exists (ValueWar) that may help your organization quicken its reflexes using competitive role play games. Interested persons should see Appendix C for further information.

3. For a good example of such an article, see Marcia Berss, "Logging off Lexis," *Forbes,* January 4, 1993, p. 46.

Index